Contents

[ ] = nur in Bayern obligatorisch

R *Revision* – Abschnitte, die der Wiederholung und Festigung des Lernstoffes dienen.

Leitfragen für die Bearbeitung, die vorab gelesen werden sollten.

Kurze, zusätzliche Hörverstehenstexte. Die mit einem „L" gekennzeichneten Texte sind nur auf den Cassetten für Lehrer/innen enthalten. Alle anderen befinden sich auch auf der Cassette für Schüler/innen.

[ ] = nur in Bayern obligatorisch

< > = nur in Baden-Württemberg obligatorisch

Arriving in Britain – by air ...

First look at the title and the pictures: What are these two pages about?
Then look at the texts: Find out as much as you can about
- the three young people (their names, where they come from, why they have come to Britain, how they have travelled to Britain).
- London's airports.
- the Channel Tunnel.

Many visitors to Britain arrive at one of London's international airports. Heathrow is the biggest airport in Europe and the busiest international airport in the world. From Heathrow you can get to Central London by underground. Tourists on charter flights often arrive at Gatwick airport. From Gatwick you can take a train to Victoria Station. Stansted is London's most modern airport. From Stansted there is a fast train service to Central London.

I've just arrived at Heathrow airport from Kansas. I'm going to visit my aunt and her family in London. I hope to stay with them for a month. This is my first trip to Britain.
Janet Fisher

I've just flown into London Gatwick from Los Angeles. I'm going to work as an assistant in a holiday centre for five weeks. Then I want to travel and see as much of the country as possible.
Manuel Vargas

… and by sea

I've just arrived at Dover with my parents. We have driven from Ulm and we have crossed the Channel on the hovercraft. My parents are going to take me to a holiday centre in Wales. While I'm there, they want to travel round Britain by car.
Karen Werner

In 1986 Britain and France agreed to build a Channel tunnel. Four years later, on 1st December, 1990, the British and French teams met and shook hands under the sea. Britain was no longer an island. The Channel Tunnel is the longest underwater tunnel in the world. It has two main tunnels 40 metres under the Channel floor. The tunnels are 50 kilometres long, and 38 kilometres are under the sea. Special trains carry cars and their passengers, lorries and their drivers through the tunnel in only half an hour. High speed trains go from city to city.

Project Find out and tell the class: Which is the nearest airport/port to your home town? How long does it take to get there and from there to Britain? What does it cost to fly/drive/go by train or coach?

What do you think is better: to fly to Britain, to drive or to go by train or coach? Why?

HAVE THE TIME OF YOUR LIFE

AT

ST DAVID'S SCHOOL

- *Something for everybody.*
- *Choose from a long list of different activities.*
- *Our instructors can teach you everything from aerobics to volleyball.*
- *Meet lots of other young people.*
- *For our foreign students: English language lessons every morning.*
- *In the evenings – discos, barbecues and games.*

Our activity centre at St David's School offers exciting holidays to all young people.
The centre is in South Wales, only three miles from the sea and a short distance from the mountains.
We have a sports hall, four tennis courts, a large swimming-pool, a lake, sports fields, a computer room, an arts and crafts room and a drama room. Visitors stay in three-bed or four-bed rooms in the main building.

For more information, please phone or write to St David's School. Address and phone number on page 2.

WHAT CAN YOU DO?

You decide what you want to do!
At the beginning of your holiday you can choose a different activity for each morning and each afternoon.
Everybody must choose one specialist activity. (These have an 'S' in the list.) You have one lesson every day in your specialist activity.
To make sure that you are in the right group, write 1 (beginner), 2 (quite good) or 3 (very good) next to your activities and send the list back to us.

Remember:
Don't be shy – try everything!

Abseiling
Aerobics
American football
Archery
Arts and crafts (S)
Badminton
Basketball
BMX and mountain bikes
Canoeing
Computers
Cookery
Creative writing (S)
Cricket
Desk-top publishing (S)
Disco dancing
Drama (S)
Football (S)
Golf
Grass-skiing
Gymnastics (S)
Hockey
Judo (S)
Orienteering
Pony-trekking
Pottery
Rock-climbing

Sailing
Squash (S)
Sub-aqua (S)
Swimming (S)
Table-tennis
Tennis (S)
Trampolining (S)
Video film-making
Volleyball
Water-skiing
Windsurfing

WHAT SHOULD YOU BRING?

Visitors needn't bring special equipment for the different activities, but you should bring some warm clothes. And don't forget to pack the following:

- walking shoes ❑ Wanderschuhe · chaussures de marche
- pullover and anorak ❑ Pullover und Anorak · pullover et anorak
- jeans, trousers ❑ Jeans, Hosen · jeans, pantalons
- T-shirts and shorts ❑ T-shirts und Shorts · tee-shirts et shorts
- swimming costume ❑ Badebekleidung · maillot de bain
- towels, soap, shampoo ❑ Handtücher, Seife, Shampoo · serviettes, savon, shampooing
- toothbrush and toothpaste ❑ Zahnbürste und Zahnpasta · brosse à dents et dentifrice
- comb or brush ❑ Kamm oder Bürste · peigne ou brosse
- pyjamas ❑ Schlafanzug · pyjama

☞ Look at the illustration and the texts on the two pages.
Find out …
where in Britain St David's is,
what the centre offers to visitors,
how visitors can organize their day,
what visitors have to bring to the centre.

– On this page there is part of a list of clothes and toilet articles. What other things do you think a visitor could bring?
– Imagine you want to go to St David's with a friend. Write a letter to the centre and ask them for more details about a holiday there. (For example: How can you get to the centre from Heathrow? Is it possible to stay in the same room as your friend?)

R Focus on GRAMMAR Simple past: positive statements

For many young people it is not easy to make friends when they arrive at the centre. So on the first evening the instructors organize a party with lots of games. This way it becomes easier to break the ice. Here are the rules of one game.

Right or Wrong?
FACTS ABOUT THE PAST

RULES

You need two teams and a quizmaster. The quizmaster has got all the cards and reads a sentence to one team. The people in the team say if it is **right** or **wrong** (the answers are on the back of the cards). Then the quizmaster reads a sentence to the other team.
A team gets a point for each correct answer. Players lose one point for a wrong answer.
The first team with 20 points wins the game.

- Marilyn Monroe was a famous filmstar.
- Pelé played football for Mexico.
- Robin Hood lived in Sherwood Forest.

- Charlie Chaplin was an American filmstar.
- Steffi Graf won Wimbledon in 1990.
- The queen got angry when she saw Snow White.

- The Beatles came from Liverpool.
- Joe Louis and Max Schmeling were tennis players in the 1930s.
- Mark Twain wrote "Robinson Crusoe".

- Elvis Presley had his first big hit in 1956.
- The modern Summer Olympics started in 1796.
- Merlin helped Arthur to become king.

→ Exercise 1

a Look again at the rules of the game and the sentences on the cards. As you can see, the verb forms in the rules are different from the verb forms in the sentences on the cards. Can you say why? (Try to remember what you learned last year. When do you use the simple present and when do you use the simple past?)

b Write down the infinitive of each verb in the rules and in the sentences on the cards.
Write the simple past form next to it. (The list of irregular verbs on p. 230-231 can help you.)
Then put the verbs from your list in two groups: <u>regular verbs</u> (their past forms end in '-ed') and <u>irregular verbs</u>.

infinitives	simple past forms
need	needed
have	had
…	…

c Now look at the group of regular verbs. When do you add '-ed' and when do you add '-d' to the infinitive to make the simple past?
What must you add to each of the following regular verbs to make the simple past form?
answer – bark – collect – describe – fetch – happen – hope – love – need – push – stay – wait

d Compare the simple past forms of these two regular verbs: *play – played; cry – cried.*
When must you change 'y' at the end of an infinitive into 'i' in the simple past form?
(Try to remember what you learned last year about the plural of nouns and about the 's' in the 3rd person singular of the simple present.)
How do you spell the simple past forms of the following verbs?
carry – enjoy (mögen, gern tun) *– stay – try – worry*

e Look at the pronunciation of these regular simple past forms:

[-d]	[-t]	[-ɪd]
called	laughed	added
remembered	barked	hated
…	…	…

Put the following verbs in the right column.
ask – hire – need – open – organize – phone – repair – shout – talk – thank – turn – want – wait

→ Grammar 1: 1, 2a (p.145-146) → Exercises 2, 3

Phone calls from London and Kansas (Questions)

Janet Fisher was at St David's, too. While she was there, she had phone calls from her aunt and uncle in London and from her parents in Kansas. They all asked her a lot of questions:

Is the centre nice?
Do you like the food?
Does Helen really speak with a Scottish accent?
Where does Manuel come from?

Was it warm yesterday?
Did you like the train journey to Wales?
Did you speak to a lot of people at the party?
When did you come back from the lake?

a As you can see, there is one group of questions in the simple present and one in the simple past. Compare the verb form in each simple present question with the verb form in the simple past question next to it.
Make a table and show what is the same and what is different in simple present and simple past questions.
Try to say how you make simple past questions with 'be' and with regular and with irregular verbs.

simple present	simple past
Is the centre nice?	**Was** it ...?
Do you **like** ...?	**Did** ...?
...	...

b Compare the verb forms in these sentences and then translate the sentences into German.

Who helps in the kitchen? – **Who helped** in the kitchen after the party?
Who does Manuel **help**? – **Who did** Manuel **help** yesterday afternoon?

What are the German words for 'who' in these sentences?
Try to remember what you learned about questions with 'who' last year. Then say when you make 'who'-questions without 'do/does/did' and when you need 'do/does/did' in 'who'-questions.

Ex *Now try to make questions in the simple past.*

1. Helen knows about our plan. – Oh, when (you / tell) her about it? 2. I can play tennis with Manuel. – Really? When (you / ask) him? 3. I played a new computer game last night. – How (you / get) in the computer room? It is always so full. 4. I went sailing yesterday. – (Karen / be) in the same boat as you? 5. The journey to Wales took five hours. – (you / have) a meal on the train? 6. First Janet pushed Dominic into the lake, and then Latif pushed Jessica into the lake. – Who (push) Dominic and who (Latif / push)?

→ Grammar 1: 2b (p.146) → Exercises 4, 5

Turbo brain Negative statements

You now know that questions in the simple past are very similar to questions in the simple present. Simple past negative sentences are similar to simple present negative sentences, too. Look at these sentences:

I **don't like** computer games. – I **didn't like** the disco last night.
They **don't have** darts as an activity here. – We **didn't have** a sailing lesson yesterday.

Ex *Now you shouldn't find it difficult to do this exercise.*

1. Janet, did you take my shorts? – Of course I (not take) them. 2. Dominic, you forgot to help with the dishes. – Yes, that's right, I (not help). But I (not forget) to help. 3. Manuel wasn't here today. We had a new instructor, but we (not like) him. 4. You (not come) with us yesterday. – I (not want) to sit in the coach so long. 5. I'm sure the trip was boring. – No, it (not be). We (not have) one boring minute.

→ Grammar 1: 2c (p.146) → Exercises 6, 7

* Diese Struktur ist für Schülerinnen und Schüler in einigen Bundesländern Wiederholung.

Helen MacDonald chose creative writing as her specialist activity. One of her tasks was to write an article, *Why did you choose St David's?,* for the centre magazine. Before she wrote it, she interviewed different young people. First she spoke to Jessica Robins. Jessica was sitting next to the lake with a friend. They were watching Manuel, the American instructor. He was teaching windsurfing. They were laughing because so many people were falling into the water.

– Excuse me. I'm writing an article for the centre magazine. Can I interview you for it?

– Sure.

– Where are you from, Jessica?

– From Totnes in Devon.

– Why did you choose to come to St David's?

– I wanted to have a holiday with other young people and not with my parents.

– What do you enjoy about this activity centre?

– I'm not very good at a lot of sports and I feel uncomfortable when I'm with a group and everybody can do windsurfing or skiing. Here I can learn a lot of new sports.

– What's your favourite activity?

– Sub-aqua. I really enjoy that.

Work with a partner. Use the notes to write Helen's interview with Karen and Latif. Be careful – Helen doesn't always ask the same questions.

Karen Werner, 14, Ulm, Germany

St David's – learn English – meet English teenagers / enjoy the centre – really good time / English lessons – morning – sports and activities – afternoon / favourite activity – windsurfing

Latif Khan, 15, Halifax, North of England

usually spend holidays – parents / this year my parents – at home / a bit nervous – when – arrive / first time – away from home / soon – a lot of friends – really great time / tennis and computers

- Have you been on a holiday with other young people? Where did you go, when did you go there and what was it like compared to St David's?
- Have you done sports or activities like those at St David's? Where? When? And how did you like them?
- What did you do in your summer holidays? Did you meet new friends?

L

→ Exercise 8

Focus on WORDS Talking about people 1 A

This is what Jessica Robins told her parents about the people at St David's on the phone one evening.

"I +share a room with three other girls. They're really nice. Helen is from Scotland. She is quite tall and she's got red +hair. And she's so funny. Karen is German – but her English is really good. And she's got +wonderful clothes. The other girl is American. She is very active and really good at sports. We have a great time together.
We have an American instructor, Manuel. He's – well, you can't imagine. He's got dark hair and beautiful eyes. He looks like a filmstar. He teaches us windsurfing and sub-aqua. …"

1 Collecting words

Collect more words and phrases for each of the following four groups. You can start with the words from the box on the right.

a What can somebody be?

a child, a teenager, a woman, …
an instructor, a filmstar, a doctor, …
somebody's girlfriend/boyfriend, a +stranger, …
English, German, +Irish, …
+rich, famous, …

b What can people look like?

They can be tall, +short, +fat, +thin, …
They can have red hair, …
They can look nice, strange, …

c What +qualities can people have?

They can be
– nice, friendly, polite, +tolerant, fair, clever, …
– unfriendly, unfair, silly, lazy, …

d How can people feel or be?

They can feel/be
– healthy, fine, glad, excited, happy, …
– +bored, unhappy, worried, tired, hungry, …

> an +adult – a boy –
> a neighbour –
> a +relative –
> French – +poor –
> big – small –
> brown hair – blue eyes –
> long legs –
> a +round face –
> funny – beautiful –
> boring – noisy –
> quiet – exciting –
> terrible – careful –
> stupid – +well –
> nervous – +lonely –
> disappointed –
> surprised – +annoyed –
> +alive – dead – …

2 +Arranging words

a Find pairs like these: child – adult, short – tall.

b Think of a famous person or somebody in your class. Write down her/his name and arrange words and phrases round the name to describe this person. The example on the right can help you.

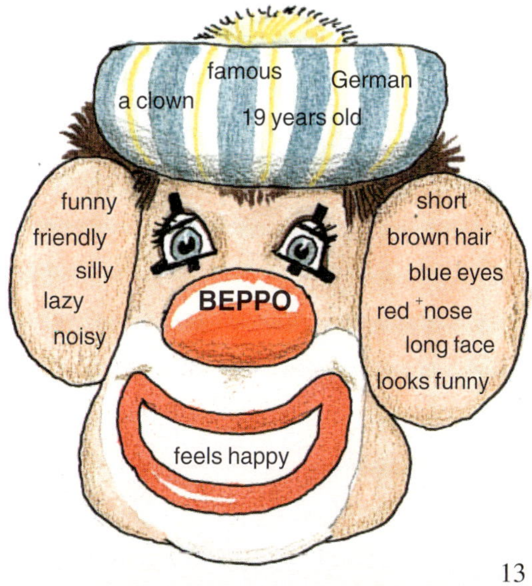

3 Words in +use A game

Take the person from 2b or another person and describe her/him in a short text. Read what you have written. The others must find out who it is.

+ = new words

1 Exercises

1 Facts about the past

Make cards for the game on page 10. Different people can make statements for different topics. You can choose other topics, too, like history, science or geography. But be fair – don't make your statements too difficult!

2 How quick are you? *Practise simple past forms and their infinitives.*

a *Game:* One person says the infinitive of an irregular verb, another person says the simple past form.

b *Look at these four "sentences":*

1. Yesterday Alan … school.
2. Some time ago I … London.
3. Last Sunday … our garden.
4. Last July … Tom.

Try to see how many different sentences you can make. Example: Yesterday Alan *ran to* school. – Yesterday Alan *walked to* school. – Yesterday Alan*'s parents were at* school. – …

3 What is your story?

On the evening of the party at St David's, one girl told the others a story.
Look at the two pictures. The first picture tells you how the story started. The second picture tells you how it ended.

Now you write the story.
You can start like this:
One day I was in our garden with my dog Toby. …

Read different stories to the class. Who has the most interesting story? Who has the funniest or strangest story?

4 Make your own exercise!

Make your own exercise for simple past questions.
First write ten positive statements in the simple present.
Then exchange your sentences with other pupils. They must ask simple past questions about your sentences.
Start with a 'yes/no-question' and then ask a 'wh-question'.

1. I usually play football on Saturdays.
2. I always do my homework in the evening.
3. I often go to the cinema at the weekend.
4. I sing in the school rock band on Mondays.
5. …

Examples:

1. That's interesting. *Did you play* football last Saturday, too?
   Where did you play last Saturday?
2. Always? *Did you do* it yesterday evening?
   Why didn't you watch the film last night?

5 *"Woggle."* – "What did you say?"

a

You:	*Your partner:*	*You:*
1. I *went* (go) to ***woggle*** last summer.	– Where *did you go*?	– To Dresden.
2. My ***woggle*** (go) with me.	– Who … with you?	– My sister.
3. We (visit) our ***woggle***.	– Who …?	– Our aunt and uncle.
4. We (get) there by ***woggle***.	– How … there?	– By train.
5. And we (stay) in Dresden for ***woggle***.	– How long …?	– For two weeks.
6. Our aunt (show) us the ***woggle***.	– What …?	– The Zwinger.
7. And she (tell) us about its ***woggle***.	– What … about?	– Its history.
8. We also (see) ***woggle*** football matches.	– How many …?	– Two.
9. My ***woggle*** (take) us to the matches.	– Who …?	– My aunt.

b *Now write a short text from* ***a****. You can begin like this:* Last summer my sister and I went to …

6 I didn't do it! *Practise simple past negative statements.*

a

Look at this picture. Look at what the two children are saying. Then make some more short dialogues with the words in the boxes.

Here is some help for the dialogues:

eat all the ice-cream/ cake/chocolate/…	– Me? No. …
take my …	– Why me? …
drink my …	– No, …
throw away my …	– Don't be silly. …
use my …	
tell Susan about my new boyfriend/girlfriend …	

b *Work with a partner and make one dialogue a little longer. Then read it to the class.*

7 In English, please – A letter to an English pen-friend

Liebe Jenny,
vielen Dank für Deinen langen Brief. Ich muß Dir erzählen, was Conny und ich letzten Sonntag gemacht haben. Wir sind mit der Bahn nach Bonn ins "Museum König" gefahren. Vielleicht erinnerst Du Dich noch. Wir haben es letzten Sommer zusammen besucht. Weißt Du, was wir dort gesehen haben? Eine Dinosaurier-Ausstellung[1] aus London. Es war toll. Im ersten Raum – er war voller Leute – sahen wir zuerst nicht viel, weil es so dunkel war. Aber dann sahen wir fünf große Dinosaurier. Sie bewegten sich[2] wie richtige Tiere. Mit Computern ist das kein Problem.
Neben einem der Tiere lagen einige Dinosauriereier, und ein paar Baby-Dinosaurier waren auch da. Sie waren etwa so groß wie ein Hähnchen. In einem anderen Raum des Museums sahen wir uns einen Videofilm über Dinosaurier an. Es hat wirklich Spaß gemacht.
Viele Grüße Deine Freundin Gabi

a *Read the letter and try to remember as much as possible. Then say in your own words – in English of course – just a few sentences about what you remember. Don't look at the letter again.*

b *Now look at the letter again and translate it in your exercise-book.*

[1] dinosaur exhibition ['daɪnəsɔːr_eksɪˌbɪʃn] [2] moved [muːvd]

8 A letter from Dominic to his friend Tony (Past progressive)

I'm sitting here in my room – the others are sailing on the lake. The lake! I must tell you what happened yesterday: I was sitting next to the lake with a very nice girl from Devon. Her name is Jessica – I can tell you more about her at home. We were watching the boats and the windsurfers. Everybody was laughing because so many people were falling into the water. I wasn't thinking of a "surprise". But then it happened: I heard some footsteps, felt two hands, they pushed me and the next second I was sitting in the water. A moment later Jessica

– As you can see, there are two present progressive forms in the first sentence. Try to remember what you learned about the present progressive last year. Then say why Dominic uses these verb forms. There are also some past progressive forms in the letter. They are similar to present progressive forms. Try to say what is the same and what is different.

– Look at the letter again and at this diagram. It should be no problem for you to say when you use past progressive forms.

I **was sitting** … We **were watching** … Everybody **was laughing** … … people **were falling** into the water … I **wasn't thinking** of a "surprise" …	I heard footsteps …	I felt two hands …	… they pushed me …	I **was sitting** …

→ Grammar 1: 3 (p.147)

a In the computer room

Example: When the instructor came into the computer room, one girl was … .
Two boys were … . *Go on.*

b Between two lessons

You know that pupils are always very busy in the time between two lessons. What were you and the other pupils in your class doing between the last two lessons? What were the pupils doing outside your classroom in the corridor?

Cornelsen

Hinweise für Eltern und Lehrkräfte

Mit dem Recorder und dem Computer lernen

Textcassetten

Britische und amerikanische Sprecher/-innen geben Aussprachemodelle für den aktiven Gebrauch des Englischen. Um die wichtige Fertigkeit des Hörverstehens auch weiterhin regelmäßig zu schulen, sind für das zweite Englischlernjahr wahlweise folgende Cassetten lieferbar.

(Fortsetzung nächste Seite)

Bestellkarte

Hiermit bestelle ich zur Lieferung durch Nachnahme. Preis zuzüglich Porto (ca. 3,50 DM), Nachnahmegebühr (ca. 5,— DM), Zustellgebühr (ca. 3,— DM).

☐ **English G, Ausgabe C, Band 2**
3 Compact-Cassetten (Vollfassung)
Laufzeit ca. 250 Min. Bestellnummer 71 316 ◇ 49,80 DM

☐ **1 Compact-Cassette (Kurzfassung)**
Laufzeit ca. 88 Min. Bestellnummer 52 605 ◇ 37,90 DM

Disketten: English Coach
Je 1 Diskette; Preis ◇ 98,— DM

☐ PC 3,5" Bestellnr. 919 412
☐ PC 5,25" Bestellnr. 919 420
☐ Amiga: 88,— DM Bestellnr. 919 439

Gewünschtes bitte in dem entsprechenden Kästchen deutlich ankreuzen. Alle Titel können auch durch den Buchhandel zum Ladenpreis ohne die Postgebühren bezogen werden.
Preisstand 1.1.1994. Änderungen vorbehalten. ◇ = Unverbindliche Preisempfehlung.

1 Cassette zum Schülerbuch (Kurzfassung)

Die Cassette umfaßt alle Lieder und die meisten Haupttexte sowie 15 kurze Hörverstehenstexte, die im Schülerbuch gekennzeichnet sind, sowie weitere Abschnitte aus dem A-Teil. Der Cassette ist ein Übungsheft zu den Hörverstehenstexten beigefügt.

3 Cassetten zum Schülerbuch (Vollfassung)

Dieser umfangreichere Cassettensatz enthält alle Haupttexte, Lieder, die Hörverstehenstexte am Ende der Units, alle kurzen Hörverstehenstexte sowie einige Texte aus dem A-Teil der Units. Das Übungsheft ist ebenfalls beigefügt.

Diskette zum Schülerbuch

English Coach ist ein Computerprogramm, mit dem sich Vokabeln abwechslungsreich üben lassen. So kann man den Wortschatz nach Lektionen, nach Wortarten, nach Schwierigkeitsgrad, für einen oder mehrere Lerner wiederholen. Das Programm „merkt sich" gewußte und nicht gewußte Vokabeln und führt durch ein ausgeklügeltes Verfahren zur Beherrschung des bearbeiteten Wortschatzes.
Sofort abrufbare Informationen zum Arbeitsstand, ein Testmodus und ausdruckbare Vokabellisten runden das Programm ab. Es ist sowohl für PC als auch für den Amiga lieferbar.

Bitte in Druckschrift ausfüllen

Name / Vorname

Straße / Hausnummer

Postleitzahl / Ort

Ort / Datum

Unterschrift der / des Erziehungsberechtigten

Bitte freimachen

Antwortkarte

Cornelsen

Verlagskontor

33598 Bielefeld

a *Complete the words in these three word fields with the missing letters a, e, i, o, u.*

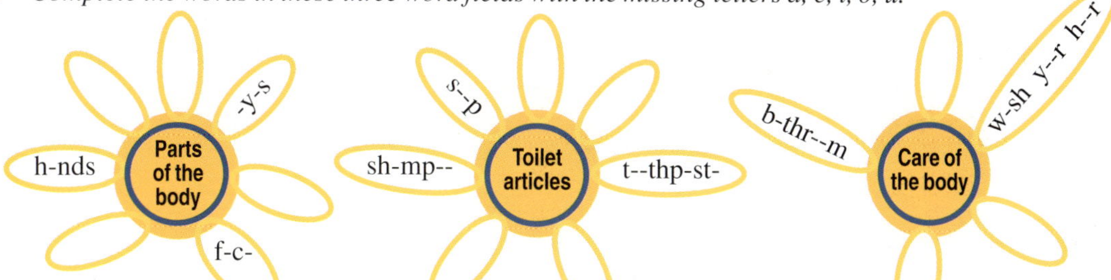

Now complete the words and phrases in the box. Which word field do they belong to?

m--th	-rms	c-mb	t-w-l
h--rbr-sh	--rs	t--thbr-sh	l-gs
w-sh y--r d-rty h-nds		-s- s--p -nd h-t w-t-r	

Here are some new words and phrases. Do you know what they are in German? (The dictionary on pages 210-227 can help you.) Add them to the right field.

head – comb your hair – neck – tooth/teeth – brush your teeth – finger – thumb [θʌm] – foot/feet

b **Looking for friends**

Which words from A and B often go together? Some verbs from group A have got more than one "friend".

A	B
1. (to) have	a) an anorak
2. (to) make	b) a room
3. (to) stay	c) friends
4. (to) wear	d) a foreign language
5. (to) learn	e) cars and passengers
6. (to) meet	f) for more information
7. (to) spend	g) different people
8. (to) share	h) a race
9. (to) speak	i) in a hotel
10. (to) listen	j) into the water
11. (to) carry	k) to a radio programme
12. (to) fall	l) a good time
13. (to) write	m) your holidays at home
14. (to) win	n) windsurfing

c **Trouble spot** Prepositions

Choose the right preposition for each sentence.

about after against along at

1. How many people were … your party?
2. We talked … Manuel all evening.
3. We played … Latif's team.
4. Walk … this road and turn left at the end.
5. What is this story …?
6. On Fridays I usually stay … a friend's house.
7. Janet is very good … tennis.
8. Are you worried … your exams?
9. Don't phone me … 9 o'clock, please. It's too late.
10. Don't put your bike … the shop window.
11. Sorry, I'm busy … the moment.
12. Manuel didn't like the idea and was … it.

d **Trouble spot** Plurals

Find the correct plural forms.

child – ?	foot – ?	knife – ?	life – ?
man – ?	mouse[1] – mice	potato – ?	tomato – ?
tooth – ?	wife[2] – wives	woman – ?	

1. I bought two new kitchen … today. 2. The Khans have got two …, a boy and a girl. 3. I like books about the … of famous … and … . 4. Yesterday our cat caught two … . 5. Mr Stubbs and Mr Shaw have bought some souvenirs for their … . 6. Karen's baby sister has already got lots of … . 7. Can you buy two kilos of … and two kilos of … at the market, please? 8. I can't walk home. My … are hurting.

[1] Maus [2] Ehefrau

1 Text

I think this place is great!

While Jessica Robins was staying at St David's, she wrote about her holiday in her diary. Look at the illustrations. What do they tell you about her week at the centre?

Saturday

I arrived at 4 o'clock in the afternoon and went to my room to unpack.
During the year St David's is a private school and in the summer the school organizes activity holidays. I share a room with three other girls, Helen, Karen and Janet. Helen is from Scotland. Karen is German and Janet is American. Helen and Karen are 14 like me. Janet is a year older. I felt a bit nervous when I met them, but they were very friendly. I had to laugh when Janet said, "I love your English accents." Helen cried, "What English accents? I'm Scottish. Don't forget that."
For tea we had roast beef with potatoes and vegetables. It was good. Later we all walked round the centre and met some of the others. I also met Janet's cousin Dominic. One boy, Stephen, was very noisy and not very nice. He seemed to be a bit wild. I hope there aren't too many here like Stephen. In the evening we had a party and played games.

Sunday

We got up at 6.30 and went to the lake to swim. It was great, but the water was very cold. Some people stayed in bed.
For breakfast we had sausages, eggs, beans, tomatoes and toast. Stephen ate enough for three people. Later he was sick. I've chosen sub-aqua as my specialist activity. In the morning I also tried pony-trekking. We wore special hats and rode slowly over the fields. It was very boring. Stephen shouted, "Let's play cowboys and Indians. We can have a race." But the instructor said, "Be quiet."
In the afternoon we went rock-climbing. That was much more interesting. I was nervous at first, but I soon enjoyed it. Stephen shouted, "I am Tarzan." And he wanted to jump from the rocks. The instructor was very angry and sent Stephen back to his room. In the evening there were activities like video film-making, but we were too tired.

Monday

When we got up, everything hurt: our arms, legs, feet, everything.
Breakfast was sausages, eggs, tomatoes, beans and toast again. Then we went to the archery field. That was fun. In the afternoon we had BMX races. We also had a slow race. Stephen didn't understand the rules and when he rode over the finish line, he shouted, "I've won." "Oh no, you haven't," said another boy. "It was a slow race." And everybody laughed.
In the evening we got tents and went camping. Before we went to bed, we went to the river with our towels. But there was mud everywhere, so we ran back fast. Janet's towel fell in the mud. I lost my toothbrush. It was dark in the tent when we put on our pyjamas. Karen and I tried to put on the same pyjamas.
During the night some of the boys walked round the tent while we were sleeping and shouted, "We are the ghosts of St David's!"
We said, "Go away." Then the tent fell on us.

Tuesday

In the morning we went windsurfing on the lake. Brilliant. And the weather was great, too. A really nice day.

Helen, Janet and I all fell into the water. Janet fell in about five times because she really likes Manuel the instructor. He had to pull her out each time. Tea was fish and chips. After tea we played some games with the other groups.

Wednesday

It rained today. And we went sailing. Helen didn't go because she didn't want to get wet again. It was a good idea because Stephen and his friends played pirates. In the afternoon we went grass-skiing. I really enjoyed that. We wore funny skis with wheels. I watched Karen in her group. She was really good. After the evening meal we had a Welsh evening with Welsh songs. I had to explain to Janet that Wales, like Scotland, is not in England and the Welsh are not English. She couldn't believe the Welsh have their own language and a lot of people still speak it today. Now she wants to learn it. I saw Dominic again. We want to do the same activities tomorrow.

Thursday

Janet found a Welsh programme on the radio. She couldn't understand a word, but we all had to listen to it. In the morning we went orienteering. The instructor drives out of the centre with you and leaves you in a field. You have got a map and you must find your way back to the centre. Latif Khan from Halifax was the leader in our group. We walked across fields and climbed over walls. We waited behind one wall and pushed some boys in the river. Everybody was dirty and wet. It was brilliant. In the evening we made a camp fire. Then we sang songs with our instructor Manuel. I talked to Dominic. He's going to visit me in Devon.

Friday

Today was the best day of all. We went canoeing on the river and we played Indians. Everybody fell in the river, even Manuel. Then we went to the sports room and had a lot of fun on the trampoline. I must go home tomorrow. It's a pity. I think this place is great. I've learned a lot of sports and made some great friends.

Working with the text

a 1. Work in groups and collect what Jessica says about Janet, Helen, Karen, Stephen and Dominic. Then present to the class what you have found out. 2. Which activities did Jessica like? Which activities didn't she like? 3. Why do you think Jessica wrote "this place is great" in her diary?

b What does the text say? And what do you think this means? Use "Well, the text says … . That means/Perhaps that means …" to answer the following questions:

1. What did Janet think when she heard Jessica's and Helen's accents? 2. What did the rock-climbing instructor think of Stephen? 3. How did Jessica like their night in the tent? 4. Helen didn't go sailing on Wednesday. Why was that "a good idea"? 5. What does Janet think of the Welsh language? 6. What does Jessica think of Dominic?

c After a week at St David's Janet wrote to her friend Kimberley in Kansas. Write Janet's letter.

Listen to the telephone conversation on the cassette between Stephen and his parents.

→ Spotlight on history (p.140-141)

Unit 2 London

After their holiday, Janet and her cousin Dominic went back to London. As soon as they arrived home, Dominic's mother had some questions about their trip.

Mrs Foster: What do you think of Britain now, Janet? Did you meet any new friends?

Janet: It's beautiful, and we met some very nice people. In the States, I learned that Britain is very small, but there is so much to see. And London is huge. I can't believe how big it is. It has taken over an hour to get here from Paddington Station. And there are so many people on the train and underground. It's worse than New York. What's it like to live here?

Dominic: I enjoy living in London. There is so much to do. You can watch some of the country's best football teams. There are concerts and theatres in the West End, cinemas, discos. But one problem is that I have to travel to everything. There isn't anything here where I live. That means I have to use the buses and the underground a lot. But I don't mind too much. I've got a travelcard.

Janet: And at night?

Dominic: I never travel alone late at night. London can be very dangerous.

L

- What do you get to know about the Fosters from the photo and illustrations on this page?
- What is Janet's impression of London?
- Why does Dominic like living in London?

→ Exercise 7

A letter from Janet to her parents

… Dominic's house is very different from most houses in Kansas. His parents have what they call a +terraced house. In the States we call them town houses. There isn't a +detached house in the street. They don't have a garage, so they have to leave their car in the street.
Inside, the house is very big, with six bedrooms and two bathrooms. They have a beautiful living-room downstairs. My room is upstairs next to Dominic's. Outside, they have a small +yard. …

A typical house in Kansas

1 Collecting words

Look at the four groups of words, then collect more words for each group. The photo and the words in the box can help you.

a What kinds of homes do people live in?

A terraced house/town house, a flat, …

b The main parts of a house

+Roof, +chimney, +stairs, balcony, …

c Rooms

Bedroom, kitchen, +cellar, …

d +Furniture and other things in a house

Shelves, +cooker, +fridge, +washing machine, …

Inside the Fosters' house

> back door, bed, block of flats, bungalow, +ceiling, chair, +cupboard, dining-room, floor, +front door, hall, +lamp, letter box, living-room, semi-detached house, sofa, table, +wardrobe

2 Arranging words

After you have collected the words, arrange them so that you can remember them better. You can choose a "key word", for example, and add more words and phrases.

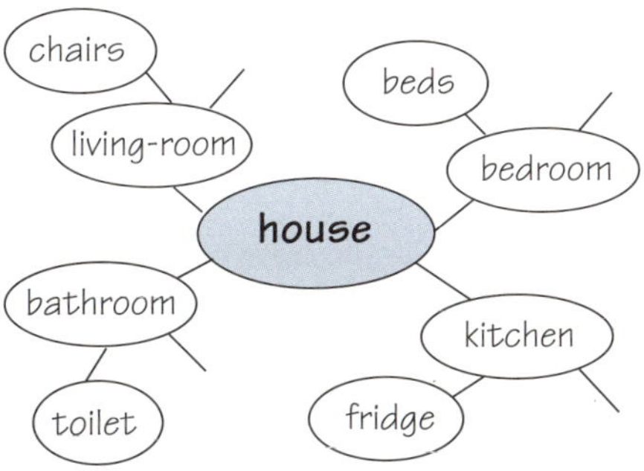

3 Words in use

a Work with a partner: Give your partner the name of a room or a piece of furniture. Your partner says what you can do in it/with it. *Examples:*
<u>kitchen</u> – You wash the dishes in the kitchen, you cook a meal in the kitchen, …
<u>cupboard</u> – You can keep cups, plates and glasses in a cupboard, you … .

b When people hear the word "home", they often think of "safe", "warm", "parents", etc. Which words do you think of? Write them down.

c Imagine you could build your own dream house. Describe it. (Perhaps you'd like to draw it, too.)

A tour of London

London is one of the most famous cities in the world. Millions of tourists go there every year to visit the sights. Janet wanted to see them, too, so she went with her aunt and Dominic on a bus tour. "I'm sure you've seen pictures of Big Ben before," said Mrs Foster. "Well, there it is." "It's wonderful," said Janet.

On your left you can see the Tower of London. The Tower is over 900 years old. It's one of the most famous castles in Britain. It was once a royal palace where England's kings and queens lived. Later it was a prison and a place for many executions. Some people say there are still ghosts in the Tower. Today it's a museum and over two million people visit it every year to see the Crown Jewels and the Beefeaters.

St Paul's is the third largest church in the world. From the top of St Paul's to the ground it is 365 feet – one foot for every day of the year. The architect was Christopher Wren. He designed St Paul's and many other buildings in the capital after the Great Fire of London in 1666.

After the tour, Mrs Foster took the two teenagers to Covent Garden. "This is one of my favourite places," she said. "It was once a real market, but today you can listen to street musicians, sit in the cafés, and have a wonderful time." They went to one of the cafés. "Well, Janet," asked Dominic, "How did you enjoy the tour?"

☞ What do the photos tell you about the tour of London? Use the map to describe the bus route.

☞ What do you know about the sights and places on the two pages?

- What does the guide tell the tourists?
- What do you think was Janet's answer to Dominic's question?
- Make up a dialogue between Janet and Dominic about the tour.

→ Listening comprehension, p.33

Focus on GRAMMAR Relative clauses (I)

Let me tell you a story about a **tourist who** went on this tour last week.

Look at the beautiful **church which** is on your left now; that's Westminster Abbey.

Big Ben isn't the name of the tower; it's the name of the **bell which** is in the tower.

Does anybody remember the name of the **woman who** was Prime Minister in the 1980s?

The **man who** designed St Paul's and over 50 other London churches was Christopher Wren.

Those of **you who** want to visit St Paul's can leave the bus here.

Those who don't want to wait for another bus can go by boat from the Tower to Westminster Bridge.

And this is the **bridge that** most people know from films about London.

Most of the theatres are in a **part of London that** is very popular with tourists.

People that want to fly to Paris or Brussels can now use London City Airport.

Look at what the guide said. In each of the sentences you can see a <u>relative pronoun</u>: **who**, **which** or **that**. Relative pronouns come at the beginning of relative clauses.

Now look at the first two sentences again:

main clause	relative clause
Let me tell you a story about a tourist	→ **who** went on this tour last week.
Look at the beautiful church	→ **which** is on your left now.

The grammatical term for these relative clauses is <u>defining relative clauses</u>. Try to say why they are called "defining" relative clauses. Why are relative clauses necessary in these sentences?
Look at the other sentences at the top of the page. Say which part in each sentence is the relative clause, and also what the relative clause defines in each sentence.

Now make a table with three columns – one for each relative pronoun. Fill in the nouns or pronouns that are before the relative pronouns. Then try to say when you use **who**, **that** or **which**.

who	that	which
tourist	…	church
…	…	…

We use **who** after …
We can use **that** …
We use **which** …

Ex *Can you say which relative pronouns can go in each of these sentences?*

1. Most tourists … come to London want to see the Houses of Parliament.
2. Everybody … wants to become a London taxi driver has to do a very difficult exam.
3. Mum knows a guide … can tell you all about Jack the Ripper.
4. I don't think we should go on the tour … starts at 4.05 pm. It's much too late.
5. The building … is over there on your left now is St Paul's Cathedral.
6. Have any of you heard about the large black birds … live in the Tower of London?

→ Grammar 2: 1a (p.148) → Exercise 1

The Fosters at work

Dominic's father, Simon Foster, is an accountant for a large company. He works in Broadgate, a modern business centre in London. He leaves the house at seven o'clock every morning. First he takes the train and then the underground to Liverpool Street.

"The trains and underground are always very crowded in the morning and in the afternoon. It's often seven o'clock before I get home in the evening. I sometimes get really fed up. I would like to move to a small town in the country. But the salaries are much higher in London, and the best jobs are in the capital. So we stay here."

Dominic's mother works at home. She is an American and writes articles about Britain for American magazines.

"I like my office at home. I have a computer, a printer, a fax, a telephone. I prefer to work at home. I'm more independent that way. Unlike Simon, I don't have to travel into the city in the morning, so I don't have his problems with London. I can always travel when it's quieter. I can go to a museum when I want and I still have time for Dominic when he comes home from school."

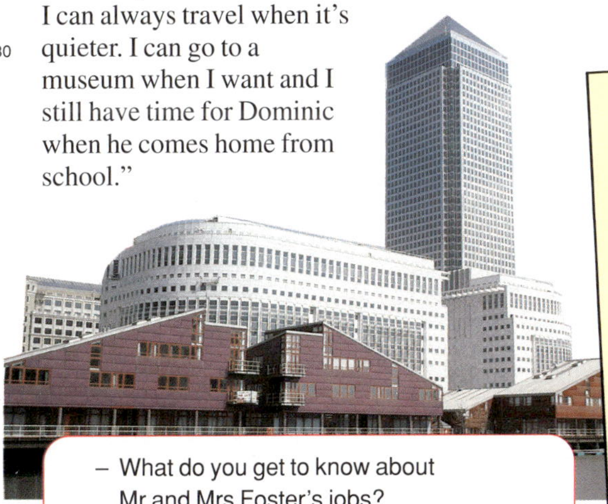

- What do you get to know about Mr and Mrs Foster's jobs?
- What does Mrs Foster tell her American readers about Docklands?
- Who do you think has got the "better" job, Mr or Mrs Foster? Why?

Docklands – 21st century London

by Laura Foster

Once an area of great poverty, London's docks have become the site of a huge redevelopment program. This is the London of the future, the architects say. But the modern office buildings give you the impression that you are in Chicago, not London.

One tower block is the tallest in Britain and you can see it from every part of the city. There are plans for new houses, a "shopping village", new roads, schools, restaurants, cafés, open areas for sports. Docklands is a city in a city – with its own airport. The development is huge, but the risk is, too. The developers need lots of people who want to live and work here. Without them the project could be a huge disaster. There are also other large developments, like Broadgate, for example. This is also very modern and much nearer to the center of the city.

Focus on GRAMMAR Relative clauses (II)

A fax from the USA (Contact clauses)

Dear Mrs Foster,
Thank you for the article which you sent us last week.
The information which you got about Docklands from the architects is very interesting. But the comments from all the other people who you interviewed are interesting, too. ...

"Mum, there's a fax about the **article you sent** to America last week. The **information you got** from the architects and from all the other **people you interviewed** seems to be interesting for American readers. ..."

Look at the following table and try to explain how
- the first relative clause is different from the second relative clause.
- the second relative clause is different from the third relative clause.

main clause	relative clause			
		subject		
Where is the newspaper article		**which**	was	on my desk?
Thank you for the article	which	**you**	sent	us last week.
There's a fax about the article		**you**	sent	to America last week.

Now try to say why you can leave out the relative pronoun in some relative clauses, but not in others.

Relative clauses without a relative pronoun are called contact clauses. Can you explain that name? Find another example of a relative clause with a relative pronoun and an example of a contact clause in the texts at the top of the page.

Ex *Make contact clauses with the words in brackets to make the sentences precise.*

1. The underground ... is always very full. (Mr Foster / take) 2. He knows some of the people ... . (he / meet on the underground) 3. The guide answered all the questions ... . (Mrs Foster / ask) 4. The fax ... makes life much easier for her. (Mrs Foster / buy) 5. One of the museums ... is the Museum of London. (she / like very much) 6. The salaries ... are higher than in other cities. (accountants / get / London)

→ Grammar 2: 1b (p.148-149) → Exercise 2, 3

Contact clauses with prepositions

The guide	who	you **wrote about**	is very nice.
The guide		you **wrote about**	is very nice.
The museum	which	you **took** me **to**	doesn't open on Mondays.
The museum		you **took** me **to**	doesn't open on Mondays.

Translate the sentences into German and then compare the place of the preposition in the English clause and the German *Relativsatz*.

Ex *Use contact clauses to make sentences.*

1. The Londoners ... were very friendly. (I / speak to) 2. Here is the book ... . (I / get this information from) 3. Some parts of Docklands ... are like Chicago. (I / take a photo of) 4. One of the nicest places ... was Covent Garden. (I / go to) 5. The shop owners ... were all very happy. (Mrs Foster / talk to) 6. In England you can't buy the American magazines ... . (Mrs Foster / write for)

→ Grammar 2: 1c (p.149) → Exercises 4, 5

1 Puzzle it out! *Practise relative clauses.*

a *Look at the following pictures. Then complete the sentences with the right relative pronoun and tell the class what you think each picture shows.*
You can start like this: I think the first picture shows a woman *who* is wearing a hat with flowers.

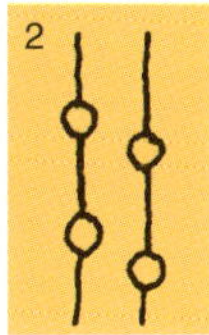

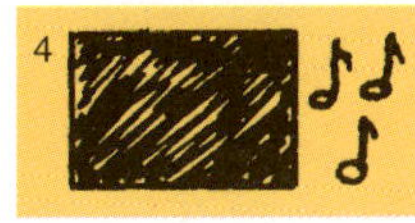

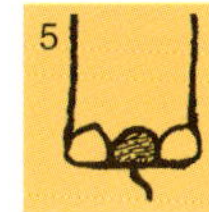

… a woman … is wearing a hat with flowers.
… a cat … is climbing up a tree.
… a child … is reading a comic.
… four people … are walking up a hill.
… a mouse … is standing in front of an elephant.
… a big man … is sleeping on the floor.
… a car … is driving past a window.
… somebody … is singing in the middle of the night.

b *Perhaps you can make up some more pictures like these and ask the class what they are.*

2 Homeless in London

a *Read the text. What does it tell you about the situation of young homeless people in London?*

Claire is sixteen. She is a homeless teenager who lives on the streets of London. She has run away from a home for difficult children which she hated all the time she was there.
She says, "When I came to London, I was very worried. But now I see that there are lots of teenagers who are homeless. And many of them are people who are very friendly. They are people who can give you advice and who help you when you need their help. My parents never really talked to me."
Organizations which help homeless people say that teenagers like Claire are in an impossible situation. They have no job and so they haven't got the money which they need to pay for a room. They also have no family or friends who want them.

b *Go through the text, find all the relative clauses and say if you need a relative pronoun or not.*

3 London Docklands

First read all the main clauses and all the relative clauses. Then decide which of them go together. Put in a relative pronoun where necessary.

main clauses

1. *Some years ago, Docklands was an area …* → h)
2. Today it is a part of London …
3. On some tours you can listen to guides …
4. Some of the places there have a history …
5. But Docklands is not only for tourists …
6. It is also important for business people …
7. Docklands is now a business centre …
8. In Docklands you can now find the offices of many newspapers …

relative clauses

a) … you can even reach by plane.
b) … would like to see modern London.
c) … you could see in London's famous Fleet Street a few years ago.
d) … goes back to Roman times.
e) … are planning for the future.
f) … every visitor to the capital should see.
g) … know about all the places in Docklands.
h) … *most visitors avoided.*

4 From different conversations Janet had with her Uncle Simon

Make a main clause and a contact clause out of the two main clauses.

Example: Our guide told us some jokes. (I just couldn't laugh about them.)
Our guide told us some jokes I just couldn't laugh about.

1. The bus wasn't full. (We waited for it.) 2. I really liked that little café in Covent Garden. (Aunt Laura took us to it.) 3. Some of the people were from America. (We sat next to them in the café.) 4. The musicians in Covent Garden were quite young. (We listened to them.) 5. Some of the clothes were very expensive. (We looked at them in the Covent Garden shops.) 6. The most interesting sight was Big Ben. (I took a photo of it.) 7. The Beefeaters were very friendly. (We talked to them in the Tower.)

5 In English, please – Ein Brief aus Deutschland

In this exercise you have to use the relative pronouns 'who', 'that' and 'which' and the relative pronoun 'whose' (German: deren, dessen).

Lieber Andy,

ich habe jetzt die CD, deren Titel Du nicht wußtest. Nicole, ein Mädchen, das mir manchmal hilft, Deine Briefe zu übersetzen, und deren Vater in einem Schallplattengeschäft[1] arbeitet, hat sie für mich gekauft. Der Name der Gruppe, die das Lied spielt, ist "Toxoplasma". "Toxo" ist der Name, den die Fans der Gruppe benutzen. Ich weiß das von einem Nachbarn, dessen Tochter Hannah bei einem ihrer Konzerte war. Hannah möchte auch Rockmusikerin werden. Ich glaube, das ist ein Traum, den viele Jungen und Mädchen einige Zeit träumen.

Viele Grüße von Deiner Tante Gisela

[1]record shop ['rekɔːd ʃɒp]

R 6 Mixed tenses: An interview for the school magazine

a *Read Dominic's interview with Diana and then complete it with the correct verb forms.*

Where (you / go) in your last holidays, Diana?	To Germany.
(be) that your first holiday there?	Yes, it … .
Where (you / go) in Germany?	To Düsseldorf. That (be) a city on the Rhine.
And how (you / get) there?	By plane. I (fly) from Gatwick to Düsseldorf.
(you / stay) with a family?	Yes, I (have) a friend in Düsseldorf.
What (be) her name?	Tina. Tina Meier. She (be) very nice. And she (have) two younger sisters. We (have) a great time together.
(Tina / want) to come to England?	Yes, she (want) to come in her Easter holidays. I (bring) her to school for some lessons.
Thank you very much, Diana.	That (be) all right.

b *Now write Dominic's report for the school magazine:* "In her last holidays Diana Jackson went …"

7 Dangerous places (*some/any* and their compounds*)

– I'd like to see **some** of these really dangerous places, Dominic. Can you take me to **any** of them at night?

– Are you crazy? I'm not going to take you to **any** dangerous places.

– Perhaps you know **somebody** …

– No, Janet, I don't know **anybody**! … But I could take you on a Jack the Ripper walk through the East End of London. Do you know **anything** about Jack the Ripper?

– Well, I've heard the name, but I don't know **anything** about him.

– Well, then I think the walk will be **something** for you. …

Make a table with three columns and put 'some', 'somebody', 'something' and 'any', 'anybody', 'anything' in the right places. What German words can you use for these six English words? Now try to make up a rule: In what sentences do you use 'some' and its compounds and in what sentences 'any' and its compounds?

positive statements	negative statements	questions
some	…	…
…	…	…

→ Grammar 2: 2 (p. 149)

a "some" or "any"?

1. Katrin, please go and fetch … chalk, there isn't … in the cupboard. 2. Let's look at … of the pictures on page 23. 3. Give me … of your exercise-books, please. 4. Sorry, Mrs Haß, I couldn't do … of these exercises, they were too difficult. Are … of the other exercises easier? 5. There aren't … empty disks in the computer room. We must ask Mrs Klug to buy … . 6. Why don't you have … pictures in your classroom? I can bring … posters tomorrow. 7. We must ask Mr König for … new chairs. … of these here are terrible. 8. We haven't got … books on modern music in the library.

b In English, please

1. Ich brauche keine Filzstifte. 2. Hat jemand meinen Füller gesehen? 3. Jemand muß mir bei dieser Übung helfen. 4. Entschuldigung, aber ich kann nichts sehen. 5. Ich kann niemanden im Büro finden. 6. Ich glaube, einige Schülerinnen sind noch im Klassenzimmer. 7. Laßt uns alle etwas für die Schülerzeitung schreiben. 8. Hast du nichts für die letzte Schülerzeitung geschrieben?

8 Text production: A thank-you letter to somebody you know quite well

A few days after Janet got home, she wrote to her aunt, her uncle and Dominic.

How you can write a thank-you letter:
- Say thank you and what you are saying thank you for.
- Say how you like the present/enjoyed the visit/…
- Say what you like most of all/remember best.
- Ask how everybody is.

Now write Janet's letter. Here are some phrases to help you:
enjoyed everything, but most of all … (tour/tea at Covent Garden/…) – often think of … (week at St David's/Jack the Ripper walk/…) – perhaps Dominic … (come to visit/write a letter/…) – …

* Dies ist für Schülerinnen und Schüler in einigen Bundesländern Wiederholung.

Words Words Words

a **A game** *Guess my word*

One pupil chooses a thing from the green box and says what you can do with it. The verbs in the yellow box can help. The other pupils try to guess the word. The pupil who has guessed it gets a point and goes on with the game.

door bus shirt test milk car cake
magazine bike hat key letter
apple housework bag window book
sandwich lemonade homework coffee

wear write buy make do
eat lose clean send open
carry drive read drink

Example:
Pupil 1: My word is something that you can wear. – Pupil 2: You can wear a shirt. Is it a shirt?
Pupil 1: No, it isn't. – Pupil 3: You can wear a hat, too. Is it a hat?
Pupil 1: Yes, it is. You go on. – Pupil 3: My word is something that you …

b **Trouble spot** One word in German = two words in English

Find the right place for these words:

bag/pocket card/map card/ticket clock/watch hour/lesson lake/sea story/history

1. We went swimming in a wonderful … in Austria last year, but I still prefer the coast and the … . 2. The station … says it's 10.30, so my … must be wrong. 3. Sandra sent me a … with her address, but I can't find the street she lives in on the … . 4. Sorry, I can't play …s this evening, I've got a … for the theatre. 5. I'm sure I put the money in my trouser … and not in my school … . 6. When does your English … start? – In an … . 7. Karen is reading a … about a girl in the 17th century. She is very interested in 17th century … .

c **Word builder's corner** Nouns and verbs with the same form

Examples:

answer – Antwort
(to) answer – (be)antworten

call – Anruf
(to) call – (an)rufen

dream – Traum
(to) dream – träumen

help – Hilfe
(to) help – helfen

Here are more words of this kind. Write them down in your exercise-book and translate them. You can use a dictionary for help.

change cook cost cry end fight
hope list love plan play race rain repair
sail sleep sound start test visit

Now complete the sentences 1 to 10 with the words from the box.

change cook help list
plan race sail
sleep sound test

1. I'm so tired because I didn't get enough … last night.
2. I'd like to get a job as a … in a famous restaurant.
3. The maths homework was too difficult for me, so I asked my sister for … .
4. We usually … our summer holiday early in the year.
5. Can you … all the words that end in "-y", please?
6. My old job was so boring that I needed a … of job.
7. There was a … of ten different shampoos in yesterday's paper.
8. Did Tina win the 10,000 metre … last weekend?
9. … doesn't travel as fast as light.
10. We could get a boat and … along the coast.

Song: Streets of London

Have you seen the old man in the closed down market,
Kicking up the paper with his worn-out shoes?
In his eyes you see no pride, hands held loosely at his side,
Yesterday's paper telling yesterday's news.

Chorus:
So how can you tell me you're lonely,
And say for you that the sun don't shine?
Let me take you by the hand
And lead you through the streets of London.
I'll show you something to make you change your mind.

– What do you think of when you listen to or read the words of the song and look at the picture?
– What do you think the story is about?

What happened to Mrs Middleton?

Dominic and Janet were in Brixton, a part of London near Herne Hill. They were walking along the busy main street when an old woman who was carrying two big shopping bags stopped them outside a supermarket.

"You're strong young people," she said. "Can you carry these bags for me, please?"

Dominic and Janet were so surprised they didn't know what they should do, but the old woman didn't give them time to think.

"I live just two or three streets from here," she said. "In Rainbow Street. It isn't far. But these bags are so heavy."

Janet laughed. "Sure."

So together they carried the old woman's shopping bags. She was very slow and she talked all the time. When they reached her house in Rainbow Street, she opened her bag and gave Dominic the key for the door. "Well, open it," she said.

Janet laughed again. "She's nice. Let's go in and talk to her."

"OK," said Dominic and the two cousins went into the small house.

The woman's name was Mrs Middleton.

"Have you always lived here, Mrs Middleton?" asked Janet.

"I was born in this house 79 years ago," she said. "Can you imagine that? I can even remember a time when there were trams in London."

"Real trams?" said Janet. "I've only seen those in history books."

"Oh yes," said Mrs Middleton. "London was very different when I was a girl. I've got some old photos you can look at. Would you like a cup of tea while you're here?" she asked.

Janet looked at Dominic. Mrs Middleton doesn't get many visitors, they thought.

"Yes, please," said Dominic. "But we can't stay long."

"Have you got any children or relatives who live near you?" asked Janet.

"No. My husband is dead and my daughter lives in Australia. I haven't got any other relatives."

"Wouldn't you like to leave this old house?" asked Janet.

"Oh, no. I was born here and I'm going to stay here till they carry me away in a box. This is my home. And I like it here. The streets are always full of young people. When you're as old as I am, you need a lot of people round you. Before my daughter moved to Australia, I went to her house in the winter when it was cold. But now I can't. It isn't nice when you're old and alone."

"Do your neighbours help you?" Janet asked her.

"Sometimes, but they've got their own families. Who's interested in an old woman?"

* * *

Janet and Dominic decided to visit Mrs Middleton again. Janet found the old woman so interesting and she wanted to listen to more of her stories and look at her photos of old London before she flew back to Kansas.

They went back the following day. Mrs Middleton was happy to see them and they had a wonderful time. While they were talking, they also helped her with the housework. When they left, they promised to come again at the weekend.

On the following Saturday morning Dominic and Janet rang the bell at number 50 Rainbow Street, but Mrs Middleton did not open the door.

"I don't think she's at home," said Dominic.

"She knows we're coming," said Janet. "We said Saturday morning."

"Perhaps she has gone to the shops. We can come back later."

* * *

They came back later that afternoon. Although they rang the bell several times, Mrs Middleton did not open the door. Janet looked through the window, but she could not see anything.

"Let's look through the back window," she said.

"Do you suppose she has had an accident?" asked Dominic. "Perhaps she has fallen over and can't get up again."

Dominic and Janet ran round the house and climbed over the wall into her small garden. They ran to the back door, but they couldn't open it. And then a man who was working in the next garden shouted, "What are you doing there? I'm going to call the police, so stay where you are."

"No, don't, please," said Janet. "We want to visit Mrs Middleton."

"Why don't you use the front door, like other people? What are you doing here where nobody can see you?"

"She didn't open the door when we rang the bell. We think she has had an accident."

The man climbed over the wall. He looked through the kitchen window, but nobody was there. Then Dominic saw her through the living-room window. "She's on the floor! Mrs Middleton," he shouted. "It's Dominic and Janet!"

Mrs Middleton was lying on the floor. She opened her eyes and tried to lift an arm, but she was too weak.

The man broke the window and they climbed into the room.

"Mrs Middleton," he said. "What happened?"

What do you think happened?

Working with the text

1 Right – hard to say – wrong?

a Explain why some of these statements are right/wrong, or why it is hard to say if they are right or wrong.

1. Mrs Middleton's house is in one of the poorer parts of London.
2. Mrs Middleton seems to like young people.
3. Dominic and Janet aren't really interested in the old woman.
4. Mrs Middleton doesn't want to live with her daughter in Australia.
5. Mrs Middleton's neighbours don't know much about her.
6. Mrs Middleton had an accident on the day when the children wanted to visit her.
7. She didn't hear the children when they rang the bell.
8. A neighbour fetched the police.
9. They got into the house through a window.

These phrases can help you:

I think that's right/wrong → because ← It's hard to say if that's right or wrong

because → she/he/the text says …

because → she/he/the text doesn't say …

b Perhaps you can think of more sentences about the text. The other pupils in your class can say why they are right/wrong, or why it is hard to say if they are right or wrong.

2 Say it in English

a Read these sentences. Then go through the text and find out how the people say these things.

- Könnt ihr mir bitte diese Taschen tragen?
- Könnt ihr euch das vorstellen?
- Ich kenne die nur aus Geschichtsbüchern.
- Hättet ihr gern einen Tee? – Gern.
- Würden Sie gern aus diesem alten Haus ausziehen?
- Wer interessiert sich schon für eine alte Frau?
- Ich glaube, sie ist nicht zu Hause.
- Meinst du, sie hat einen Unfall gehabt?
- Nein, bitte nicht.
- Warum benutzt ihr nicht die Eingangstür?
- Dominic und Janet sind hier.

b Look at the following situations. For each situation you can choose one or two of the sentences you found in **2a**. Change them a bit and then use them in these situations.

Example: Your brother can't do his homework because it is so difficult.
He could say: "Can you help me with my homework, please?"
or: "I don't think I can do this. Can you help me …?"

1. One of your friends is going to the swimming-pool. He asks you: "Would …?" 2. The doorbell has just rung and Susan's mother has opened the door for Susan's friends Jenny and Ann. – "Susan, …" 3. Your friend has got two tickets for a football match. She knows that one of the teams is your favourite team and says, "…" 4. Tony has just heard about a friend's visit to a model of a Viking village. – "…" 5. Your mother has just had a letter. She has won a trip to the USA. – "…" 6. Your father says that the car parks are always full when he goes to town. – "…" 7. Alan is walking with Sarah. It is very hot, and Sarah hasn't got anything to drink, but he has. – "…"

Listening comprehension Hector the raven

raven A large black bird, about 60 cm long with a big beak and a strange cry. It eats small animals, living or dead, and different kinds of fruit. It lives in large colonies.

- Work with a partner: Though you don't know anything about Hector, try to imagine what he could have to do with the Tower. Write down your ideas in a few sentences. Then present your ideas to the class.
- Listen to the text on the tape and find out if some of your ideas were right.
- Listen again and then say what the following words have to do with the story of Hector:

the end of Britain – a coin – London Zoo – Americans – human souls

Project
- Perhaps you know a strange animal story. Tell it to the class.
- Choose your story or the story of Hector and write an article for the front page of a sensational newspaper. Write the article in columns on a computer or a typewriter.
  Now make the "real" front page with the help of a pair of scissors and some glue. Make up a big headline, choose an illustration, find a name for your newspaper and choose a date.

1

The easiest way to travel in London is by underground. (Londoners also call it "the tube".) Here is the central part of the London underground plan.

a Imagine you and your English friend are at Victoria Station and you would now like to visit some of the sights.

Your English friend:	*You:*
Let's go to Madame Tussaud's.	OK. But where …?
In … .	How … get there? By underground?
Yes, we must take the … Line.	Do we have to change?
Yes, we must get off at … and take the … Line to … .	And how far must we walk?
About … ./ I'm not sure.	Do you think … enough time to …?
Well, it's open from …, and it's … o'clock now.	OK. Let's go. We haven't got much time./We've got lots of time.

British Museum
Great Russell Street
Open Mon–Sat
10.00 –17.00
Sun 14.30 –17.00
10 minutes from
Tottenham Court Road

Science Museum
Exhibition Road
Open Mon–Sat
10.00 – 18.00
Sun 11.00 – 18.00
5 minutes from
South Kensington

Madame Tussaud's
Marylebone Road
Open 10.00 – 18.00
Baker Street

Tower of London
Tower Hill
Open Mon–Sat
10.00 – 17.00
Sun 14.00 – 17.00
Tower Hill

b Now write and act similar dialogues for one of the other places.

2 Mrs Foster had to go to Oxford for a meeting, so she phoned British Rail to get some train times.

Mrs Foster: Good morning. I'd like to go to Oxford tomorrow morning.
Assistant: What time would you like to travel?
Mrs Foster: About nine o'clock.
Assistant: There's a train at 8.20 from Paddington. It arrives in Oxford at 9.28.
Mrs Foster: That's a bit early. Is there a later train?
Assistant: The next train leaves at 9.20. It arrives at 10.15.
Mrs Foster: That's fine. Thank you.

Mrs Foster also asked about the return journey. Here is what she wrote down. Work with a partner and make up the dialogue.

British Rail

dep. Oxford	arr. London
14.24	15.55
15.24	16.35
16.31	17.43

Info box In London trains for different parts of Britain leave from different stations. Altogether there are sixteen main railway stations in Central London. The map shows the seven biggest stations. People who arrive at one station and want to leave from another must travel across London by tube, bus or taxi.

3 Imagine you have arrived at Victoria Station from the Continent (that is what the British call the rest of Europe) and you want to travel by train to one of these towns: Nottingham, Glasgow, Edinburgh, Bournemouth, Manchester, Cardiff or Norwich. Which station do you leave from?
Say how you can get from Victoria to King's Cross, Liverpool Street or Paddington by tube.

4 A popular way to travel in Britain is by coach. Coaches have the advantage that they sometimes travel to places where there is no direct train connection.
Imagine you want to get from Cardiff to Heathrow airport. Look at the timetables and compare these connections and guess why it is so popular to travel by coach.

Which is the quickest way to travel from Cardiff to London? Why is the coach more convenient to the airport?

NATIONAL EXPRESS

Cardiff	09.15	10.45	12.15
Newport	09.40	11.10	12.40
Heathrow	12.00	13.30	14.55
London (Victoria Coach Station)	12.40	14.10	15.35

Fare: £19

British Rail

Cardiff	09.25	10.25	11.25
Reading	10.40	11.50	12.51
Reading (bus)	11.15	12.15	13.15
Heathrow	12.00	13.00	14.00
London Paddington	11.14	12.27	13.27

Fare: £63

Unit 3 A visit to a British school

Focus on WORDS Talking about school

What do pupils think of when they talk about school?

Some of my teachers are very nice and I like them. Others are much too +strict. We've got a nice +headteacher at our school and I really like my drama teacher. *Carol, 14*

My favourite subjects are +physics and +biology. I think some of my other subjects are quite boring, so I don't +pay much attention. *Richard, 13*

I always seem to be in +trouble. Last week I wrote my own +note after I was +absent for a day and the teacher sent me +straight to the headteacher. *Amy, 14*

I hate reports. My parents are happy when they see the good +grades like A and B, but they're disappointed when they see the other grades. They don't like a C or a D and they are quite angry when I get an E. *Alex, 13*

I'm always nervous when we have a test. Once my French teacher +caught me while I was +copying from a +classmate, so I +failed. I felt terrible. Next year I've got my +GCSE exams. I am going to work hard because I want to +pass. *Jessica, 14*

1 Collecting and arranging words

Use "school" as the main key word and other key words like "teachers", "subjects", "reports", "tests", etc. and make two networks with "school words" in your exercise-book. One network can show what you like about school, the other can show what you don't like. Here is an example:

What I like about school:

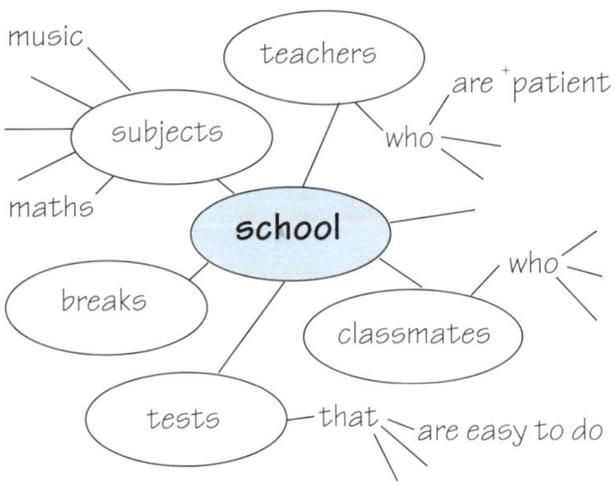

What I don't like about school:

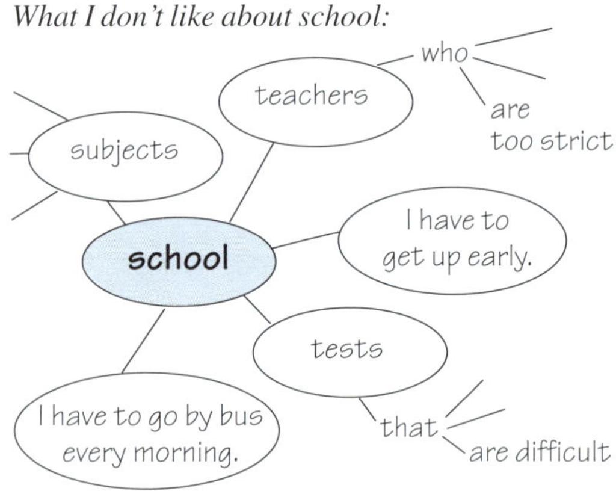

2 Words in use

a Last year you learned some things about British schools. What do you remember?

b Make a timetable that you would like to have.

c Choose two subjects and write down what you do in the lessons, what you like about the subjects or what you don't like about them.

d Write a short text about "The school of my dreams". (Perhaps you'd like to draw a picture.)

Life at a British school

Jessica Robins lives in Totnes, a town in Devon. She is a pupil at King Edward VI Comprehensive School. With over 1500 pupils it is a very large school.
"During the week school takes a lot of my time. Lessons finish at four o'clock but it's often five o'clock before I get home. Then I have tea, so it can be six, sometimes seven o'clock before I start my homework. After that it's usually too late to go out. I watch TV, read or listen to some music and then go to bed."

Look at the text and the pictures. What's a typical day like for Jessica? Compare it with your day.

The British school system

	Age	Year	
Secondary school			**A-level exam → leave school** (work/university/college)
Secondary school	16-18	13, 12	
Secondary school			**GCSE exam → leave school**
Secondary school	14-16	11, 10	
Secondary school	11-14	9, 8, 7	
Primary school	7-11	6, 5, 4, 3	
Primary school	5-7	2, 1	

Info box

- Over 90% of secondary schools in Britain are comprehensive schools.
- British pupils go straight from one year to the next. Nobody has to repeat a year as in Germany.
- Pupils are often in sets for each subject: a high set for those who are good at a subject, a low set for those who are not so good.
- To check the development of pupils, there are special tests when they are 7, 11, 14 and 16.

Use the table and the info box to describe the British school system:
Children in Britain start school …
The first kind of school they go to …
When they are 7 years old, they have the first …

- Make a similar table which shows what the school system is like in your part of Germany.
- Explain your system to a British or an American friend or visitor.

→ Listening comprehension, p.48

R Preparations for an exchange

Jessica's school has an exchange with Bad Essen in Germany. The teacher who organizes it is Mrs Dillon. Last autumn she went to Bad Essen with a group of pupils. While she was there, she invited the Germans to visit Totnes the following March.
Today Mrs Dillon is talking to her headteacher, Mrs Price, about the preparations:

"Last weekend I **phoned** Frau Michelbach and we **spoke** about the exchange.
I'm happy to say that we**'ve finished** all the preparations. Mr Buxton **has** now **found** homes for all the German pupils. Here's the list. I think he **has spoken** to all the parents and he **has given** them our programme, too. **I've arranged** some interesting trips, as you can see from the plan. Some pupils **have helped** me."

Look at what Mrs Dillon is telling her headteacher.
Why does Mrs Dillon use simple past forms when she talks about the phone call to Frau Michelbach? (Look at the adverbial of time in Mrs Dillon's first sentence and try to remember what you learned about the simple past in Unit 1.)
Now look at Mrs Dillon's other sentences: It is not important when these things happened, perhaps Mrs Dillon doesn't even remember the details. It is only important that they have happened and you can see the results. The tense she must use in this situation is the present perfect.
Look at the six present perfect forms and then say how you form the present perfect. (What does the *'ve* stand for? How is the third person singular different from the other forms? Why do only some of the past participles have *-ed* at the end?)

Ex *Now try to say what different people have done.*

1. Mr Buxton – visit all the parents 2. he and Mrs Dillon – make a programme for the week 3. the pupils – think of different activities 4. one group – organize a disco 5. some pupils – make a German-English phrasebook for the German visitors 6. Mrs Dillon – send some information about Totnes to the German teachers 7. the English pupils – write to their German partners

→ Grammar 3: 1a, b (p.150) → Exercise 1 → List of irregular verbs (p. 230-231)

The present perfect with adverbs of indefinite time*

Look at the adverbs in bold print in this dialogue between Mrs Price and Mrs Dillon. Then make up a rule: Where can you put *always, ever* (je, jemals), *just, never*? Where can you put *so far* (bis jetzt)? Where must you put *not … yet* (noch nicht)?

I'm sorry that I have**n't** talked to the pupils **yet**. I've **always** wanted to talk to them, but I've **never** had the time to do it **so far**. Have they **ever** asked to speak to me?

No, **so far** they've been too busy. But I think now they would very much like to talk to you about their plans. They've **just** finished all their work.

Ex *Now put the adverbs in the right places.*

1. Have you been to Berlin? (ever) 2. I've wanted to go to Berlin, but I haven't been there. (always / yet) 3. How many of the German pupils have visited an English school? (never) 4. I don't know, but I believe most of them haven't been to England. (so far) 5. We've learned some things about the southwest of England. (just) 6. Has Holger watched English television? (ever) 7. He has been so busy that he hasn't watched any TV. (yet)

→ Grammar 3: 1c (p.151) → Exercise 2

* Diese Struktur ist für Schülerinnen und Schüler in einigen Bundesländern Wiederholung.

20th German Exchange Totnes – Bad Essen

16th – 29th March

What have the pupils done so far during the exchange?

At the youth club disco

A geography lesson in English

Making new friends

Seeing the sights together

Wednesday, 21 March
Morning in school: Lessons 1 + 2: pottery, drama. Lessons 3 + 4: German students go to lessons with partners. Lunch at school with partners.
Afternoon: Visit to Totnes Museum.
Evening: (7.30 - 9.45 pm) Disco for exchange students at Totnes Youth Club.

Thursday, 22 March
Day trip for German students and English partners to Longleat Safari Park. Please bring packed lunch. Return at 8 pm. Parents should collect their son/daughter and partner.

Friday, 23 March
Day trip to Dartmouth and the coast. Visit to Dartmouth town and castle. Lunch on the beach at Slapton Sands. Please bring packed lunch and swimming things.
Evening: Youth club.

Weekend with families

What are they going to do during the rest of the visit?

What would you like to know about life in Britain or in a British school? Perhaps you can write to a British school class and ask them.

Some opinions about Britain and Germany

At the end of the visit to Totnes the teachers talked to both groups of pupils about the exchange. Mrs Dillon said, "Some of you from Totnes went to Germany on the exchange last year. Today we'd like to ask you all what you think is different about the two countries."

School

The German opinions about Britain

The school day is longer than ours. Pupils leave the house at 8 o'clock in the morning and sometimes don't come home till 5 o'clock.

Marion Ostermann

School plays a big part in pupils' lives. They belong to a "house", and the houses have sports competitions. There are often clubs and activities after school.

Holger Neumann

The British opinions about Germany

I didn't like starting school so early in Germany, but I enjoyed finishing school at 1 pm. You can do homework in the afternoon and have the evening free.
They have a really nice bell at the end of lessons – our bell is much louder than theirs!

Jessica Robins

The school building is better than ours and has better equipment. There are no rules about school clothes or uniforms, German pupils wear what they like.
I think that's good. At 8 o'clock they go straight to their first lesson. There's no assembly.

Maxine Clark

Free time

After they've had their evening meal and done their homework, most pupils stay at home and watch TV. After TV, they go to bed. They might go out during the week to the youth club or a friend's house. Friday and Saturday are the big nights – they go to a disco or a party.

Sabine Meyer

A lot of pupils have jobs to get more pocket-money. They deliver newspapers early in the morning before they go to school, or they work in a supermarket.

Corinna Kuhn

A lot of Germans are members of a sports club. In Britain we go to a leisure centre to swim or to play tennis or badminton.

Scott Thompson

I was surprised to see that it was so easy for young people to drink alcohol. In Britain you can't drink in a pub till you are 18.

Sarah Parnell

Other things

Everything is much more relaxed in Britain. Nobody gets annoyed or complains when something goes wrong.

Uwe Klein

The food was brilliant. I enjoyed all the meals. The buses are good, clean and tidy – and the trains are on time!

Simon Shelley

- Choose one or two comments which you didn't expect. Why were they surprising for you?
- What do you prefer about life in Britain/Germany? Why?
- Imagine one of your friends could go on an exchange, but she/he isn't sure about it. – Tell her/him what you think of exchanges. Perhaps you have been on an exchange. Tell her/him about it.
- Perhaps your town or a town in your area has a partner town in another country. Find out what kinds of exchanges there are. (Who started them? How did they start? Who helps to organize them?)

→ Exercise 7

Focus on GRAMMAR *since* and *for* with the present perfect

A lesson with Mr Buxton: "The United Kingdom – four in one"

"... many pupils from foreign countries think that 'England' is another name for 'Britain' or 'United Kingdom'. Britain is the name of this large island. You can see that there are three countries in Britain. The other island is Ireland with the Republic of Ireland and Northern Ireland. Together, Northern Ireland and the three countries in Britain are the 'United Kingdom' or the 'UK'.
Wales and England **have had** one parliament **for about 500 years**. But Wales **hasn't** really **been** independent **since 1282**. Scotland and England **have had** the same parliament **for almost 300 years, since 1707**. The smallest part of the UK is Northern Ireland. The Republic of Ireland is not a part of the UK. It **has been** an independent country **since 1921**. ..."

a Look at what Mr Buxton told the German pupils and at the 'time diagram' on the right.
Translate the phrases in the diagram.
Compare what comes after 'since' and after 'for'.
Why do you think 'since' and 'for' are problem words for German pupils?

Now try to say which of the following expressions of time go with 'since' and which go with 'for':
three weeks – ten minutes – 3 o'clock – Friday – almost two days – last July – last night

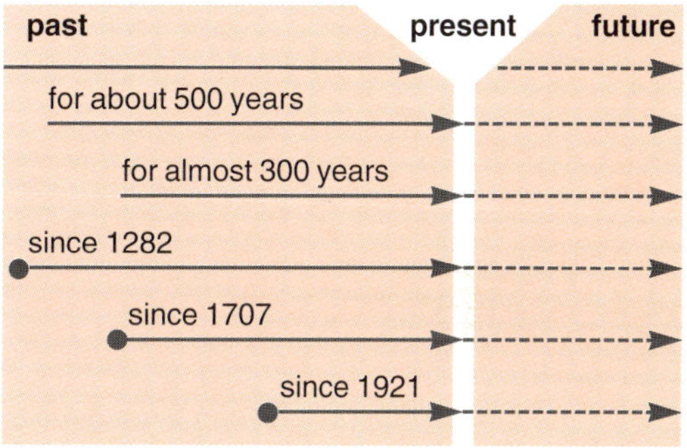

b Look at the following sentence from the text at the top of the page:

Wales **hasn't been** independent **since 1282**.

What does this sentence tell you about the time before 1282? What does it tell you about today? What does it tell you about the span of time from 1282 to today? Here is some help: Before 1282 Wales was ... and today it ... . That means it hasn't ... from ... to ... .

Now see if you can do the same for the other present perfect sentences in the text.
Then try to say what you can express with the present perfect + 'since/for'.

c Look again at the text at the top of the page and translate those sentences that have present perfect forms. Compare the verb forms in the German sentences with those in the English sentences. Then try to say why you think the present perfect is difficult for German pupils. → Grammar 3: 1d (p.151) → Exercises 3-5

Turbo brain Present perfect progressive

Twenty minutes ago Mr Buxton gave the pupils a piece of paper with questions about the United Kingdom. The pupils **have been working** in pairs since that time. They **have been talking** about the questions and they **have been writing** down the answers to many of the questions. Nobody has finished so far. They are all writing and trying to finish before the bell goes.

From this short text you can see that there is also a progressive form of the present perfect. Look at the forms in bold print and say how you make positive statements. Then try to say how you make negative statements and questions.
Draw a time diagram: Show when the activities in the text (*work, talk, write)* started and where they lead to.
The verb forms in the first and in the last sentence can help you.
Now say in your own words what the forms of the present perfect progressive tell you about the activities.

→ Grammar 3: 1e (p.151) → Exercise 6

3 Exercises

R 1 From a conversation between Mrs Price and Mrs Dillon

Make questions and negative statements in the present perfect.

a I'm very sorry, Mrs Dillon, that I have to ask you again, but I've forgotten some of the things you've told me. *Have* you *made* …?

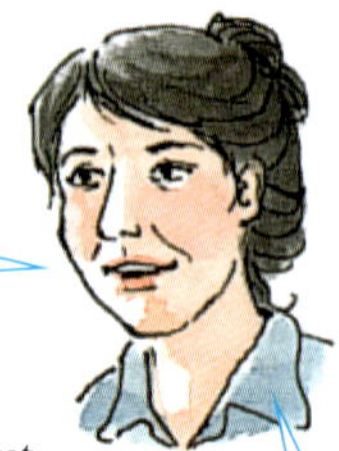

1. you – make a plan for the week 2. you – organize a disco 3. all the pupils – write to their partners 4. Mr Buxton – send them the information about Devon 5. he – practise German conversation with our pupils 6. he – inform all the parents 7. any of the parents – make suggestions for the programme 8. you – check my letter to the parents 9. I – remember to say all the important things

b I'm very happy that everything is going OK. But I must tell you that I *haven't done* all the things I must do. And I know that Mr Flour *hasn't organized* anything for our sports day. …

1. I – not inform all the other teachers 2. I – not practise any German 3. I – not make a timetable for them 4. Mr Flour – not speak to the other sports teachers 5. he – not find enough players for the football team 6. we – not arrange all the outings 7. Mr Buxton – not find a home for the German bus driver 8. my husband – not finished the preparations for the party

2 Some mini-dialogues

Work with a partner and make a dialogue from the prompts in the first box. Be careful and look at all the prompts first because you have to use all kinds of tenses.
Then practise the dialogue with a partner.

1. A: What – you – do – so far, Marion?
   B: Oh, – I – be – to some lessons and – we – have – a disco.
   A: you – be – to Dartmouth yet?
   B: No, I – not be – there yet, but one of the teachers – take – us there tomorrow.

Here are some prompts for two more dialogues:

2. A: I – just – see – a very funny film on TV.
   B: you – see – the film on BBC1 last night, too?
   A: No, we – not watch – TV last night. you – like – English television?
   B: Very much, I – see – lots of good programmes so far.

3. A: you – like – Indian food, Jutta?
   B: Well, I – not know. I – not eat – any Indian food yet.
   A: you – really never have – an Indian meal?
   B: No, there – not be – many Indian restaurants in Germany. …

Try to make dialogue 3 a little bit longer.

3 Some British history

a *Read through the exercise first. Then close your books and see which facts about British history you can remember.*

1. England (have) kings and queens … about 1200 years. But they (not have) much power … the end of the 17th century. Parliament (be) more important than kings or queens … that time.
2. There (be) a kind of parliament in England … about 700 years. And … the 13th century Parliament (become) more and more important. At first there were a lot of problems, but there (not be) any great problems … a long time.
3. England (only have) a few queens and women (only be) in Parliament … the 1930s. Only one woman (become) Prime Minister … that time.

b *Now complete the texts with the right present perfect forms and with 'since' or 'for'.*

4 Puzzle it out – one verb form in German, three in English

Look at the three groups of German sentences. In each group you can find one verb form three times ("spielt", "sehe", "feiern"). The English infinitives for these are "play", "watch" and "have a party". Translate the German sentences, but be careful: You need three different English verb forms in each group.

Susan kann jetzt nicht ans Telefon kommen, sie spielt Tennis.

Sie spielt jeden Donnerstag Tennis.

Ich glaube, sie spielt seit mehr als 10 Jahren Tennis.

Ich sehe mir seit Februar jede Sendung mit Joan Evans an.

Ich sehe mir jeden Dienstag die Sendung mit Joan Evans an.

Kannst du bitte später anrufen, ich sehe mir gerade die Sendung mit Joan Evans an.

Können die Müllers nicht kommen, weil sie auch gerade eine Party feiern?

Feiern sie wirklich seit 20 Jahren jedes Jahr eine Weihnachtsparty?

Feiern sie häufig Partys?

5 School trips

Two pupils have met on holiday. Read what they are talking about. Then decide if you need a present perfect or a simple past form.

(you / ever / have) a holiday without your parents before?

No, never. I mean I (be) on school trips without my parents, of course.

Oh, (you / be) on more than one school trip?

Yes. Two years ago we (stay) in York for a week. And last year we (go) on a school trip to Germany. That (be) super.

To Germany? I (never / be) to Germany. Everybody says it's a nice country.

I (like) it very much there. Our German teacher (take) us to some very interesting places. I think I (never / enjoy) a holiday more.

You're lucky. We (go) to Cornwall last year with our English teacher. It (be) so boring.

Why (be) that?

Oh, she (not take) us anywhere. We (only / sit) in our room and (play) games.

That really is a pity. But I (hear) things like that about some of our teachers before, too.

6 So many questions

Practise the present perfect progressive with 'since' and 'for'.

1. Are the German pupils still talking about British history with Mr Buxton? – No, they (talk) about other things with him … a long time. 2. Does Mrs Price want to come with us to Dartmouth? – I don't know. I (try) to reach her … 9 o'clock this morning, but she's never in her office. 3. Where is Mr Buxton? – On the tennis courts. He (help) Mr Flour with the preparations for our sports day … early this morning. 4. Why is it so noisy in the music room? – Oh, it's the school band. They (practise) every day … two weeks now. 5. Where are Holger and Corinna? – In the car park. They (wait) there for you … twenty minutes. 6. Why do you look so fed up? – I (try) to phone home … lunchtime, but nobody is answering the phone. 7. Where is Marion? Is she ill? – Yes, she (not feel) well … last night. 8. Do you have to listen to that song all the time? – What's wrong with it. I (only / listen) to it … two hours.

7 Possessive adjectives and possessive pronouns

All pronouns are useful because they can help to make sentences shorter. Look at the following examples:

I've forgotten to do **my** homework, can I copy **yours**?
Have you forgotten **your** sandwiches? You can have some of **mine**.

possessive adjectives	possessive pronouns
my	mine
your	yours
her, his, its	hers, his, its
our	ours
your	yours
their	theirs

What do the possessive pronouns 'mine' and 'yours' stand for in these two sentences?
Why do you think we don't need a noun after possessive pronouns? → Grammar 3: 2 (p.152)

a *Now look at these two short dialogues from the time before the "invention" of possessive pronouns. Put in possessive pronouns for the underlined words.*

1. I've lost my pen. Can I have your pen?
   – I'm sorry, I can't give you my pen. Why don't you ask Sue. Perhaps she can give you one of her pens.
   Good idea. I've often given her one of my pens.
2. Oh, no, our overhead projector doesn't work. I don't know why our OHP never works.
   – The class in room 301 broke it. Perhaps we can have their OHP.
   OK, please ask if we can have their OHP.

b **In English, please**

1. Wir haben nicht genügend Stühle. Können wir einige von euren haben? 2. Ich brauche das Buch heute nicht. Du kannst meins haben. 3. Ich habe Jenny mein Lineal gegeben. Sie hat ihres vergessen. 4. Die Klasse in Raum 300 hat so viele Pflanzen[1] in ihrem Klassenzimmer. Vielleicht können sie uns ein paar von ihren geben. 5. Wir haben keinen Schwamm. – Kein Problem, ihr könnt unseren haben. 6. Alan hat einen besseren Computer. Ich kann vielleicht seinen benutzen. 7. Ann und Sue haben viele CDs. Sie geben mir ein paar von ihren für meine Party. 8. Mein Fahrrad hat einen Platten. Kann ich eines von euren haben?

[1] plants

8 Text production: A postcard to somebody you know quite well

Imagine you are one of the German exchange pupils in Totnes and you have promised your grandparents to write them a postcard, in English – just for fun.

How you can write your postcard:

date

Dear …,

- write an introductory sentence
- describe the place
- say something about the weather
- say what you have done so far
- say how you feel
- talk about your plans

Love, …

Here are some words and phrases you can choose from:
place: popular/not far from …/interesting/…; **weather:** wonderful/rain all day/…; **activities:** swimming/dancing/…; **feelings:** have a great time/tired/proud of my English/…; **plans:** visit castle/go shopping/…

a *Find the missing word.*

1.	cupboard	– furniture	5.	woman	– wife	9.	find	– found
	guitar	– ?		man	– ?		leave	– ?
2.	March	– month	6.	car	– drive	10.	hair	– comb
	autumn	– ?		bike	– ?		teeth	– ?
3.	organize	– organization	7.	plane	– airport	11.	sausage	– butcher's
	dream	– ?		boat	– ?		newspaper	– ?
4.	hot	– cooker	8.	boat	– sea	12.	pen	– pencil-case
	cold	– ?		lorry	– ?		car	– ?

b *All the words in the box have got something to do with "up" or "down". Put them in two groups.*

carpet ceiling cellar climb downstairs drop fall fly ground high hill lift lose low rain sit top tower win write

c Trouble spot Words that you mustn't mix up

Put in the correct form of "bring" or "take":

1. Please … me your exercise-book. 2. Can you … these letters to the post office for me, please? 3. I'm late. Can you … me to the station, please? 4. Did you remember to … me the Sunday newspaper? 5. We had to … Grandad to hospital last week. 6. Our neighbours … us some sweets every day. 7. You can … my CDs home with you, but please don't forget to … them back tomorrow. 8. Don't forget to … your books back to the library, Mark.

Put in the correct form of "do" or "make":

1. Can I … a suggestion? Why don't we … the housework together? 2. I can only … half of the sentences. 3. Jane … all her own clothes. 4. Try not to … too many mistakes in the test. 5. Look what you've …! There's mud all over the place. 6. Excuse me, I must … a phone call. 7. Fiona doesn't want to … Latin next year. She thinks it's too difficult. 8. What are your clothes … on the floor? 9. Who is going to … the beds, and who is going to … the shopping?

d Word builder's corner Adjectives that you can make from verbs

You can add **-able** [-əbl] to a verb like **drink** to make an adjective: **drink<u>able</u>** ['drɪŋkəbl].
You can put **un-** in front of this adjective and you have got its opposite: **<u>un</u>drinkable** = not drinkable.

Here are some more adjectives. Write them down in your exercise-book together with their verbs.

enjoyable lovable readable understandable washable
unanswerable unavoidable unbeatable unbelievable unbreakable unforgettable
unimaginable unthinkable

Now complete the following sentences with the right verb and adjective:

1. Don't … that dirty water from the river. It's quite … . 2. How could I ever … that wonderful holiday? It was really … . 3. I didn't … the book very much. But you might find it more … than I did. 4. I find it very difficult to … these silly text questions. I think some of them are quite … . 5. Careful! Don't … those glasses. They're not …, you know. 6. I … how you feel. It's … that you don't want to go. 7. Is this shirt … ? – Yes, but you mustn't … it with other clothes. 8. What a … little cat! – I don't understand how anybody can … cats. I can't stand them. 9. Our TV prices are …! No other shop can … our prices. 10. I tried to … an argument with Stephen, but it was … – Stephen is so difficult.

3 Text

Imagine the young people in this picture have just arrived at a youth club disco. Nobody has invited them. What do you think they are going to do? How do you think the people at the disco are going to react? What is going to happen?

There were five of them. They walked towards the open door of the youth club. From inside they could hear the loud music from the disco.
They walked into the club. In the hall two girls were sitting behind a small table. They had a box full of money. The girls saw the five youths and shut the box.
"I see you've organized another big disco," said Jimmy.
"Yes," said Natalie. "But you can't come in. It's for the German exchange pupils who are visiting our school."
"Who is going to stop us?" asked Jimmy. "You?"
"It costs a pound to come in," said the second girl.
"We might pay later," said Jimmy, and the youths walked past the two girls and into the disco.
Mike Walls, the club's new leader, heard the last words and came out of the kitchen where he was talking to the German exchange teachers, Frau Michelbach and Herr Wolff. "Who were they?" he asked.
"I'm sorry," said Natalie, "I couldn't stop them."
Just then, Brett came towards them with two of his friends. He seemed to be quite nervous.
"Who invited Jimmy Leech and his gang?" he asked.
"Don't get worked up," said Mike. "They haven't done anything yet. Calm down."
"Is there anything we can do?" asked Frau Michelbach.
"Let's hope we don't have to do anything," said Mike. "So far everything is fine. Let's hope it stays like that."
"Should I go and talk to him?" asked Natalie.
"Yes, please," said Mike. "Tell him he can stay but we don't want any trouble. He might listen to you."
"Jimmy Leech doesn't listen to anybody," said Brett.
"I said, I don't want any trouble, so don't provoke them," said Mike. "Remember that, please."
"All right," said Brett, and the teenagers walked back into the disco.
"Do you have many problems with gangs in a country area like this?" asked Frau Michelbach.
"Oh yes," said Mike. "It's not as bad as in some of the big cities like London where I worked before I came here, but it is a problem, and very often at weekends."
"I suppose we should go into the disco," said Herr Wolff. "I can tell our students they must be careful that they don't say anything stupid."
Jimmy and his friends stood near the stairs. It was dark at that end of the room. "Can you get anything to drink here?" he asked one of the girls.
"Yes, there's a snack bar at the other end of the room," she said. "All drinks are 50p tonight."
Jimmy Leech and his four friends walked across

the room and most people had to stop dancing. Nobody said anything.
Jessica Robins was working behind the bar. Jimmy asked for five drinks and paid her. Jessica gave Jimmy the drinks and his change.
"I gave you ten pounds," Jimmy said.
"I'm sorry," she said. "You only gave me a five pound note."
"I gave you ten pounds," he said. "Are you going to give me the right change back or have I got to take it?"
Everybody stopped dancing.
"Wait a minute, Jessica," said Natalie. "I'm going to fetch Mr Walls. You can try to take the money from him, Jimmy. He does karate."
She wanted to run across the room, but Mike was already there.
"Where's the problem?" he asked.
"I gave this girl ten pounds," said Jimmy.
"He only gave me five pounds, Mr Walls," said Jessica. "Never mind, Jessica. Nobody is blaming you for anything," said Mike. "Give me ten pounds."
Jimmy smiled. "That's better," he said, and looked at Jessica. "You know, you should be nicer to your customers."
Jessica gave Mike a ten pound note, but he gave it back to her.
"Give me two fives," he said. Then he looked straight at Jimmy Leech. "It costs a pound to come in. That's five pounds."
He gave Natalie one of the five pound notes. He gave Jimmy the second five pound note. Then, so that only Jimmy could hear him, he said, "Here, your drinks are free. Now you can leave. You can walk out or your friends can carry you out. Is that clear?"
Nobody spoke. Jimmy looked at Mike. He looked at Herr Wolff and the other teenagers. Then he put the money in his pocket.
"This is a lousy disco," he said. "Lousy music, lousy drinks. Let's go."
Jimmy and his friends walked across the room and left the disco.
The music started again and soon everybody began to laugh and dance.
"Natalie," said Mike. "Can I talk to you?"
"I'm sorry about that, Mr Walls," she said.
"Natalie, please don't say things like that again."
"All right, Mr Walls. But you see, my boyfriend Tony does karate and Jimmy is afraid of him, so I thought, well ... do you do karate?"
Mike smiled. "Yes, I do," he said. "But I don't do it to throw people out of youth clubs. I think we should find a better way to solve this kind of problem in the future."

Working with the text

1 A closer look at the text

a Read the following questions. They can help you when you talk about the story.
1. Who are the young people in the picture? 2. Why do you think they came to the disco? 3. How did they try to provoke the others? 4. How did the people solve the problem? 5. Who do you think is the "hero" of the evening? Why?

b The story could have a different ending: Natalie could say something different (p.47, ll.13-15), for example, and this could change what happens.
Work with a partner and make up another possible ending. What is similar/different in your ending? What kind of ending do you prefer?

2 Beyond the text

a Something to remember when you are in another country: In the story (p.46, ll.45-58) Mike is worried that the German pupils might provoke the gang, or that the gang might provoke them. – Why might there be problems, although nobody really wants trouble?

b Some more things to talk about: Why do you think some young people become members of gangs? Do you think there is a difference if you become a member of a sports club or a gang? Why/Why not?

3 Say it in English

a Look at the short German sentences in the box. Then go through the text on pages 46 and 47 and find out what they are in English. It is important to look at the context because the sentences are not word for word translations.
Make a list of the English sentences in your vocabulary book and write the German sentences next to them. (The sentences in the box are in the same order as in the text.)

> *page 46:* Reg dich nicht auf! – Beruhige dich! – Können wir irgendwie helfen? – Provoziert sie nicht! – Sie sollen vorsichtig sein und nichts Freches sagen.
>
> *page 47:* Moment mal. – Was ist los? – Laß mal! – Kann ich bitte mal mit dir sprechen? – Es tut mir leid.

b Work with a partner: Read the following sentences and imagine a situation in which you could hear them. Then choose one of the sentences you have found in the text to react and add another sentence. – There is more than just one "right" reaction, of course.

Example: I was late, Joan. You told me the wrong time.
Reaction 1: *I'm sorry about that.* Didn't the film start at half past seven?
Reaction 2: *Calm down.* I'm sure you've made a mistake before, too.

1. I'm so angry with Tony. He promised to help me and now he says he can't.
2. I don't know how I can get out of this silly situation.
3. I've had enough. I'm leaving.
4. This is too much for me. I'm going to call the police.
5. I've decided to tell these bullies that they should stop hurting other children.
6. Mr Miller, could you come here for a moment and talk to John, please?
7. Nick has taken my pencil-case.
8. I've been asking you for weeks to give back that CD. Why don't you do it?

L 9 Listening comprehension **A radio broadcast on private and state schools in Britain**

- What do you think of when you hear "private schools"?
- Imagine you could choose: Would you prefer to go to a private or a state school?

Now listen to the radio programme twice:

- Don't make any notes while you are listening for the first time, just try to remember as much as possible.
- After you have listened for the first time, write down what you remember and compare your notes in class.
- Then look at the key words in the box and listen to the programme a second time. Make notes.
- Use your notes and give a short talk to the class about private or state schools in Britain. (Remember that most of the information about one kind of school is indirectly also information about the other kind of school.)
- Look at the first two questions again: Which kind of school would you prefer now, a private or a state school?

> 1. reasons for a private education: …
> 2. 7%: …
> 3. Oxford University and Cambridge University: …
> 4. tradition: …
> 5. after 1945: …
> 6. from 1975 on: …
> 7. pupils at a state school: …
> 8. pupils at a private school: …
> 9. about 50%: …
> 10. price: …

Great Britain and the sea

Journeys to unknown places

Henry VIII (1491-1547)

As king of an island nation, Henry knew how important ships were. He built the biggest navy in the world.

Elizabeth I (1533-1603)

Elizabeth was the daughter of Henry VIII. While she was Queen, English ships ruled the seas. English explorers discovered new parts of the world and traded with other countries. English ships also attacked Spain's and Portugal's colonies in America.

Sir Francis Drake (1540?-1596)

was the first Englishman who sailed round the world. He explored the west coast of America as far as Canada. He brought gold back to the Queen. When the King of Spain tried to invade England, Drake helped to defeat the Spanish Armada.

Sir Walter Raleigh (1554-1618)

tried to start an English colony, "Virginia", in North America, but it wasn't successful. He looked for Eldorado, a city of gold, but he never found it. He introduced the potato and tobacco into England.

Captain James Cook (1728-1779)

made three famous trips to the Pacific Ocean to find out more about the geography of the world. He explored New Zealand and the southeast coast of Australia. He was the first captain who gave his sailors healthy food to make sure they did not become ill.

Project Find out some more about famous sailors, not just from Britain. Make a poster to show where they went, when they went there, how long it took them, etc.

Two counties which people think of when they talk about the sea are Devon and Cornwall. Explorers like Drake and Raleigh came from Devon and often sailed from Plymouth. The Pilgrims, a small group of people who started one of the first colonies in America, sailed from Dartmouth in Devon in 1620. In the 17th and 18th centuries smugglers used the coast along southwest England to bring things like tobacco and wine from France to Britain.

The cruel sea

The coast of Cornwall is famous for other reasons. The "foot" of Cornwall, round Land's End from the Channel into the Atlantic Ocean, has some of the worst winter storms. In bad weather the strong winds can push a ship onto the rocks under the sea. Round this part of Cornwall's coast there are over 300 shipwrecks, more than 15 for every mile of the coast.

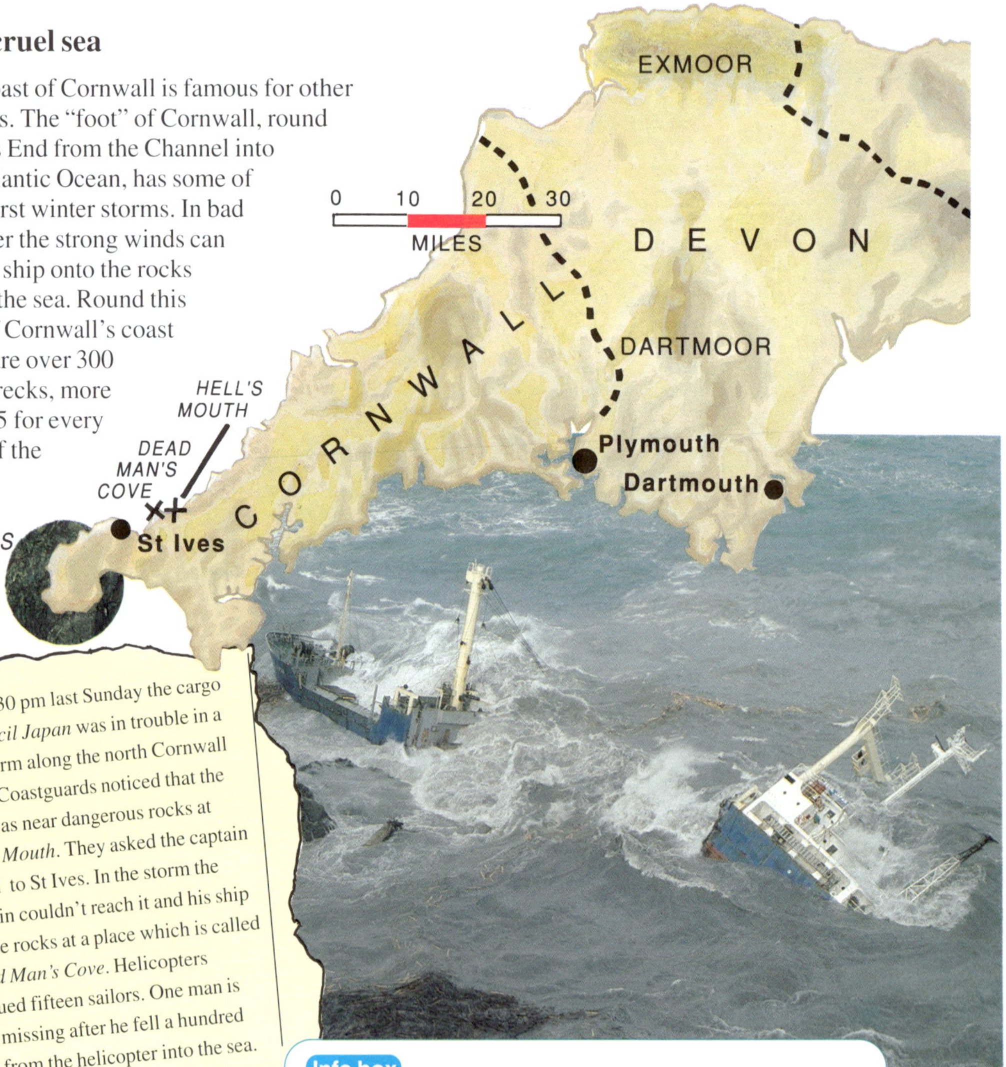

At 9.30 pm last Sunday the cargo ship *Secil Japan* was in trouble in a bad storm along the north Cornwall coast. Coastguards noticed that the ship was near dangerous rocks at *Hell's Mouth*. They asked the captain to sail to St Ives. In the storm the captain couldn't reach it and his ship hit the rocks at a place which is called *Dead Man's Cove*. Helicopters rescued fifteen sailors. One man is still missing after he fell a hundred feet from the helicopter into the sea.

From: *The Cornishman*, 16th March 1989

Look at a map of the world. Why do you think Devon and Cornwall have always been so important for Britain's link with the world?

Info box

- The British coast is over 6,000 miles long.
- Great Britain has got more than 300 ports.
- No place in Britain is more than 75 miles from the sea.
- Most British families go to the coast for their holidays.
- Fish and other sea food are very popular in Britain.
- An important form of energy comes from under the sea: North Sea Oil.
- The English Channel is only 22 miles wide between Dover and Calais, but it has the most sea traffic in the world.

L

Unit 4 The North of England

Latif Khan

A family from Halifax

I was born in Halifax, but my parents come from Pakistan. My father is a doctor. He has a surgery in town. My mother doesn't go to work.
For a long time we lived in a flat in an area where only Asian people live. Last year we moved into a new semi-detached house on the outskirts of Halifax. Now we're the only Asian family in the street.
Although our new house is much bigger and much nicer than the flat, my mother says she was happier where we lived before. She feels some neighbours avoid us.

At home we speak Urdu because my mother has never really learned English.
I've got a sister, Bina. She's 17. My parents are very strict with her. She can't go out alone and she can't do all the things I can do.
Sometimes, when she comes home late or when she and her friend Tahira want to go out with boys, my mother gets very angry. Bina doesn't think this is fair. She says her English girlfriends can all do much more.

Bina Khan

☞ Collect in the form of a network what Latif says about his family.
- Who in the family seems to have the most difficulties? Why?
- What do you know about the situation of immigrants in Germany?

Info box There are lots of Asian families in Britain. Many came in the 1950s and 1960s when Britain needed more workers for its factories. The British government promised the immigrants jobs and houses. Many came to the North of England because there were a lot of factories, and houses were much cheaper than in the south. At the same time Britain's hospitals needed doctors. So, many Asian doctors came to work in the National Health Service. A lot of immigrants who came to Britain hoped to find the "promised land". Many have become successful, but others have had a lot of difficulties.

4 A

A region of contrasts

- Look at the photos on these two pages. What contrasts do they show? Find some details in the pictures which show these contrasts.
- Read the poem on p. 53. Try to say how the poem helps to understand the pictures better.

The beautiful north

There are ten National Parks in England and Wales. Four of them are in the North of England. The Lake District is the biggest and the most famous.

L

The industrial north

With a quarter of Britain's population, the North of England is one of the largest industrial areas in the country. In the past the region produced much of the nation's coal, iron, steel, cloth and machines. Today Britain is no longer the "workshop of the world" and a lot of the old industries have closed. Modern industries have grown in their place. But in some areas the old factory buildings still stand empty, like forgotten ruins.

"King Coal"

Britain was the first and most important industrial country in the world. For most of the 19th century there were more factories and machines in Britain than in other countries in Europe. And many of these were in the North of England, an area that was especially rich in coal. Towns grew round the factories and the mines when people came to look for work.

My song is of that
city which
Has men too poor and
men too rich;
Where some have beds
to warm their bones,
While others sleep on
hard cold stones;
Where some people
dress in fur and silk
And fine rich women
wash in milk,
While starving mothers
have no food
To make them fit
in flesh and blood;
Where one man does
the work of four
And dies worn out
before his hour.

W. H. DAVIES

The pay queue, Wigan, 1894

Life was not easy for the people who lived and worked here. The towns were dirty. Smoke from the factories polluted the air and the countryside. At work there were few laws which protected the people. The wages they earned were often so low that families couldn't buy enough food to live. It is not surprising that the lives of working people were short.

The mine owners and the factory owners, however, were very rich and had comfortable homes. They owned huge areas of land, the coal under the land and also the houses their workers lived in.

Find out from the texts on pages 52 and 53
- what the north is like today.
- what it was famous for in the past.
- what life was like for most people in the north.

Why do you think
- towns in the north grew so quickly? (Where did all the people come from?)
- the lives of working people were so short?
- parents sometimes could not find work, but their children could?

→ Listening comprehension, p.63

bone *Knochen* · dress *sich kleiden* · fur [fɜː] *Pelz* · silk *Seide* · starving ['stɑːvɪŋ] *hungernd* · flesh and blood [blʌd] *Fleisch und Blut* · die *sterben* · worn out [ˌwɔːn_'aʊt] *erschöpft*

Focus on GRAMMAR Ways to talk about the future

In English you can use different verb forms to talk about the future.
When you are looking at the following two pages, decide which of these "labels" is for which verb form:

for future arrangements

for plans about the future

for travel programmes and timetables

for predictions about the future

predictions [prɪ'dɪkʃnz] *Voraussagen, Vorhersagen*

R **1** **New land for old**

Two hundred years of industrial activity have left Britain with large areas of derelict land, especially in the North of England.

Latif and Bina have decided that they would like to work in a new forest which an organization called *Groundwork* wants to develop.
Latif: "Our biology teacher, Mrs Smith, is planning a trip to a new forest. She **is going to take** 20 pupils for a weekend. Bina and I **are going to help**, too. We **are going to stay** in a camp and plant trees."

Look at what Latif said.
Try to remember from last year what the verb form in these sentences is called and how you make positive statements, negative statements and questions. Can you also remember when you use this form? (The box at the top of the page and the verb in Latif's first sentence can give you a clue.)

Ex *Now use this future form to complete the following sentences.*

1. The European Community (give) the British government money. But the government (not do) the work. 2. Local groups (ask) the government for money. These groups (plant) millions of trees. 3. What kind of trees (they / plant)? 4. Schools (collect) money, too. 5. (our school / collect) money, Bina? 6. Some pupils from Bina's class (not help) the group. → Grammar 4: 1 (p.152) → Exercise 1

2 **A changing countryside***

With the help of the European Community, Britain ***will redevelop*** *derelict land and create new forests, four of them in the North of England.*

Look at a map of Britain and you **will not find** many forests. A long time ago there were lots of forests, but for hundreds of years people cut them down.
The new forests **will recreate** some of the atmosphere of the lost forests and they **will bring** derelict land back to life. But there **won't**[1] only be forests. Only up to 50% of the land **will be** for trees, the rest **will be** for lakes, rivers, farms and open areas for sport and free-time activities. As you can imagine all this **won't happen** overnight.

[1]won't [wəʊnt] = will not

* Die hier behandelte Struktur ist für Schülerinnen und Schüler in einigen Bundesländern Wiederholung.

You already know what you can use the *going to*-future for. The text about the changing countryside at the bottom of page 54 shows you another verb form to talk about the future. The grammatical term for this form is *will*-future.
Look at the top of page 54 again and find the right label for the *will*-future. Make up a rule: What do you use the *will*-future for?
From the text you can see that positive and negative statements are the same as statements with 'can', 'must' and 'should'. There is only one form for all "grammatical persons".
Questions in the *will*-future are also the same as questions with 'can', 'must' and 'should'. Try to say how you make 'yes/no-questions' and 'wh-questions' in the *will*-future.

When people talk about the future and use expressions like *I'm sure …, I hope …, I suppose …, perhaps …* or *probably …*, they often use the *will*-future. Why do you think this future form often comes after these expressions?

Ex Parents' advice

Decide if you need a positive or a negative will-future form to complete each sentence.

1. Go to bed early, then you (feel) tired in the morning. 2. Don't forget your warm sleeping-bag or you (be) cold in the night. 3. Take something to drink, then you (get) thirsty. 4. Take these tablets, or you (be) sick on the coach. 5. Take the early bus to the station, then you (miss) your train. 6. Ask Susan to help you, then you (get) everything into your rucksack. 7. Write down everything you need, then you (forget) anything. 8. Don't forget to write a postcard to all your friends or they (talk) to you in the future.

"God knows what we're going to show you today, but you'll watch everything."

→ Grammar 4: 2, 3 (p.152-153) → Exercises 2, 3

3 The trip

Are you **coming** with us at the weekend?
– Yes, my parents **are driving** me. We are taking Sue and Tricia with us.
…

On the last day of school Mrs Smith informed the pupils:
"Our bus **leaves** at 8.00 on Saturday morning. It **arrives** at the camp at about 11.00. …"

From these two short texts you can see that in some situations you can also use the present progressive and the simple present to talk about the future. Look at the top of page 54 again and find the right label for each of the two forms. Then say when you use the present progressive and when you use the simple present to talk about the future.

Ex *Complete this short dialogue with the present progressive:*

… Bina and I (go) with Mrs Smith's group. We (take) the school minibus. Why (you / not come) on the bus?
– My parents (go) on holiday to Scotland, so they can just take me there.

Complete this short text with the simple present:

"… I've already told you about the programme for Sunday: Breakfast (be) at 9.00, and work (start) at 10.00. There (be) a break for tea in the morning and in the afternoon. We (stop) for lunch at 12.00. We (start) again at 1 o'clock. All work in the camp (stop) at 6 o'clock."

→ Grammar 4: 4 (p.153) → Exercises 4, [8], [9]

Focus on WORDS Describing places

1 Collecting words

Look at the four groups of words, then collect more words and phrases for each group. The box on the right can help you to start the exercise.

a Words for places:

a small town, a +seaside resort, a skiing resort, an island, a region, a +district, …

b Where can a place be?

in the north of Germany, in the middle of England, north of Frankfurt, between Bremen and Osnabrück, about … kilometres from London, on the coast, …

c How can you get to a place?

You can walk/go by car/go by +ferry/…
There's a good road/motorway/… to …

d Why can a place be famous, interesting or popular?

Because of its interesting sights/…
Because it has got interesting museums/+sandy beaches …
Because you can go walking/…

country – capital –
village –
near Cardiff –
miles away –
not far from the sea –
in the mountains –
take the bus –
fly – sail–
cheap hotels –
beautiful countryside –
+lovely weather –
+fresh air –
clean lakes –
+woods –
castle – ruins –
do sports –
go swimming –
have picnics

2 Arranging words

Arrange the words and phrases that you have collected in different ways. Here are three suggestions:

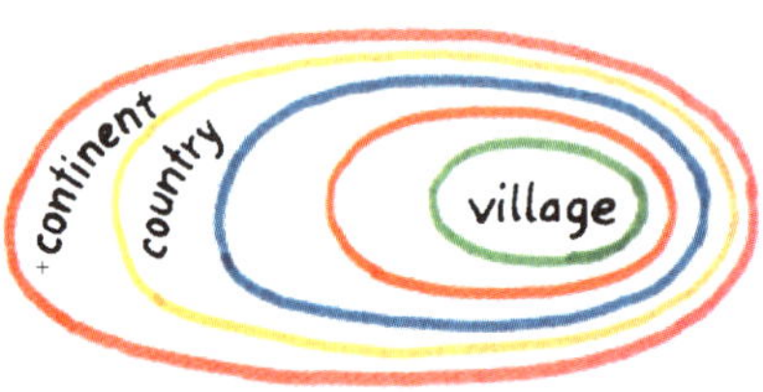

3 Words in use

a Totnes is a small town in Devon. What are Rostock, Garmisch-Partenkirchen, Paris, Cornwall, California, Mexico?

b Hamburg is a big city in the north of Germany. It is on the Elbe. Where are London, Hatfield, Cardiff, Cornwall?

c Say how you can get from Frankfurt to London, from Aberdeen to Cardiff, from Calais to Dover, from Leipzig to Berlin, from London to New York.

d Say why the following places are famous or popular and what you can do there: the Lüneburger Heide, Munich (München), Cologne (Köln), Dresden, Heidelberg, London, Cornwall.

e Choose a nice place that you know very well and tell the other pupils in your class why they should go there. You can also describe a place of your dreams.

1 "You've won!"

Practise the going to-future.

Decide what you are going to do and then write a letter to the firm and tell them about your plans.
– But remember: You only have 48 hours.

Dear ...,
You have won our "FREE-TIME COMPETITION": Two days to do what you want with all the money you need. Please write and tell us the dates you have chosen and also what you are going to do on those days so that we can arrange everything for you. ...

2 Make up your own future.

Practise the will-future.

You have met the world-famous fortune-teller Madame Zora. People say that she is always right.

Make up what Madame Zora told you about your future and write it down in about 6-8 sentences. You can write about what will happen in the next few days or in several years. Here is how you could begin:

3 A week in London The *will*-future

Anette and Felix from Kaltenengers have two cousins, an aunt and an uncle in London. They are going to fly to London in their holidays. Here are some sentences from a phone call their mother had with her brother in England a few days ago. *Translate the sentences. Be careful: In some of the sub-clauses you don't need the will-future.*

1. Felix hofft, daß ihr alle am Flughafen seid, wenn sie ankommen. 2. Ich glaube, er wird sehr froh sein, wenn er euch sieht. 3. Wenn wir zu Hause sind, ruft Anette dich an. 4. Ich kann mir vorstellen, daß Anette und Felix nicht viel schlafen, wenn sie hier sind. 5. Ich bin sicher, eure Kinder haben unseren viel zu erzählen. 6. Wahrscheinlich reden sie bis spät in die Nacht. 7. Mary und ich gehen einen Tag nicht zur Arbeit. Wir fahren dann vielleicht zusammen nach Brighton. 8. Ich glaube nicht, daß eure Kinder viel an euch denken werden während ihrer Woche hier in London. 9. Ich hoffe, sie vergessen nicht, an alle Verwandten Postkarten zu schreiben.

4 One-upmanship

'One-upmanship' is the word the English use to describe people who always want to be better than others. Here are two examples:

1. I'm going to fly to Peru next year. – Oh, I'm flying there tomorrow.
2. I'd love to meet the Queen. – Haven't I told you yet? I'm meeting her on Sunday.

Now try to make some more short dialogues like these.

5 Liverpool – a city in the north

Read this short text about Liverpool and try to understand as much as possible. Tell the other pupils in your class what you have understood. When you know what the text is about, read it again and complete it with the missing words.

When people … another country hear the name "Liverpool", they usually think … "The Beatles", perhaps the world's most famous group, and … the famous Liverpool football teams. … the middle of the 19th century Liverpool was an important and rich city. It had one … the largest ports in the world. … this port thousands … English and Irish people went … the USA.
Eighty years later, … 1930, the city had a population … more … 800,000. … 1990 however, it had less … half a million. …1960 and 1990 it lost … 300,000 people because lots of firms and factories closed. … these years Liverpool became one … the poorest cities … Britain.
Only … the middle of the 1970s the government started to help the city. When you walk … some parts of the city today, you can see that things have got better, but there are still areas where nothing has changed.

6 Text production: The English countryside

Read the beginning of the text and the prompts. Then write the text.

Not only the North, the South of England also has very few forests. Look at Dartmoor in the southwest of England, for example. …
only – very small area – where – find – trees / once – Dartmoor – large forest / 12th century – forests – cover – almost one third – England / where – all the forests – go?
for a long time – people – use – wood – build – houses – make fires / shipbuilders – use – wood, too / in the 16th century – they – need – 2,000 trees – one royal ship / 17th century – people – begin to see – bad for the countryside / man – whose name – John Evelyn – suggest – people should plant new trees / people – start – do this / but – not very successful / however, since – 1920s – people – look after England's forests – bit better.

7 Muddled sentences

Put the parts of each sentences in the right order and you will get a short text about a problem of the past which is still a problem today.

1. coal mines / more and more / in the second half of / became / the 18th century / important
2. lots and lots of coal / the new iron industry / needed / from that time on / in England
3. moved / today / to the big cities / from the country / as in developing countries / people
4. in the mines / believed / they / that / earn / could / they / more money / than on a farm
5. like today / many problems / there / caused / not enough houses / were / because / this
6. the life of / in the end / was / worse / these people / than / in the cities / in the country

[8] Let's walk into the future. (Future progressive)

Some time ago Bina's English teacher came into the class and said: "Let's walk into the future." At the same time he held up an advertisement by a large computer firm which looked like this:

Here are some of the pupils' reactions to the advertisement.

Look at the first two and then try to complete the third:

Silly question. **I'll be celebrating** the New Year at home, of course.

Who knows? Perhaps some of us **will be dancing** and **singing** on the moon on New Year's Day in 2025.

People (fly) round the earth in a spacehotel. Perhaps we (visit) some people on another planet.

You have not seen the verb forms in bold print so far. They are called <u>future progressive forms</u>. What tells you that they are future forms? And what tells you that they are progressive forms? (Think of how you form the present and the past progressive, then this won't be difficult to answer.)
Remember when you use the present progressive and the past progressive, then try to say what you can use the future progressive for.
Draw a time diagram and try to show what the difference is between the simple 'will-future' and the 'will-future progressive'. Explain your diagram to the class. → Grammar 4: 5 (p.153)

Choose one of the following birthdays and say what you will be doing on that day: Your 18th, 20th, 40th, 50th, or 60th birthday. – Your answers needn't be too serious.

[9] Turbo brain More perfect? (Future perfect)

Here is what another pupil said:

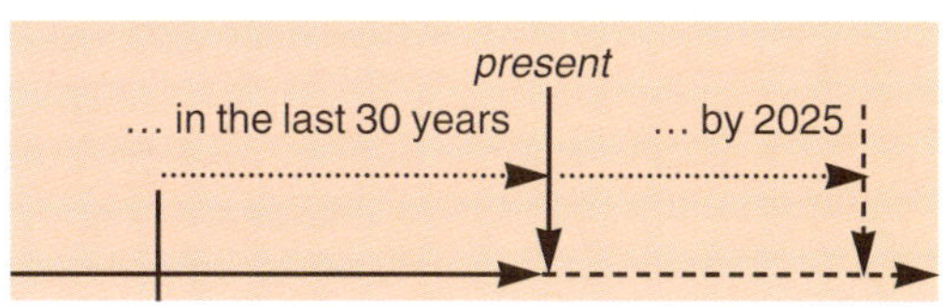

"I can't say where I will be celebrating in 2025. So much **has changed**, people **have created** so many new things in the last 30 years.
By the year 2025 the world **will have changed** more. Who knows what people **will have created** by then? I can't imagine that the world will be more perfect in the year 2025."

The new verb form in this text is the <u>future perfect</u>. You can often find it with *by* + point of time *(by 2025, by tomorrow).*
Compare the form of the future perfect with that of the present perfect.
Then look at the time diagram and try to explain what the present perfect and the future perfect have in common.
Now try to make up a rule: What can you express with the future perfect? → Grammar 4: 6 (p.154)

What do you think? Write down a few things which will or won't have changed by 2025.

Words Words Words

a **Word stress** *Read the words in the box aloud and put them in the right group.*

address already although argument balcony company concert energy expensive fifteen fifty hospital hotel important interesting machine mistake nervous notice police programme project region relative republic shampoo subject toilet

group 1: ['--]	*group 2:* [-'-]	*group 3:* ['---]	*group 4:* [-'--]
concert	address	argument	already
…	…	…	…

b **"Say" or "tell"?** *Complete the sentences with the right verb in the right tense.*

1. What did the police … about the accident? 2. Can you … me the time, please? 3. Jessica … us about her father's new job last night. 4."I'm hungry," Latif … when he came home. 5. Only the driver can … us what happened. 6. Sorry, what did you …? – I …, "You're late". 7. The story Sharon … us yesterday can't be correct. 8. Dominic … only a few words and left the room.

c **Trouble spot** Prepositions after verbs

1. I don't always agree … my friends. 2. Not many people believe … ghosts. 3. I think I'll take this shampoo. They haven't tested it … animals. 4. We must get … the train at the next station. 5. Why are you looking … me like that? 6. A neighbour looks … my hamster when we're on holiday. 7. I can't find my pen. Can you help me to look … it? 8. I don't think you've paid … your drink yet. 9. Have you ever fallen … a bike? 10. What did you enjoy most … your stay at St David's?

d **Word builder's corner** Adjectives from nouns

1. *Look at these pictures and see how you can make adjectives from nouns.*

rain + y = **rainy**

wind + y = **?**

snow + y = **?**

ice + y = **icy**

sun + y = **sunny**

fog + y = **foggy**

Now find the missing adjectives or nouns in these examples:

nouns:	storm	fun	-?-	-?-	-?-	-?-	hunger	-?-	thirst
adjectives:	stormy	-?-	rocky	dirty	noisy	juicy	hungry	sandy	-?-

2. *Use the nouns on the right to make combinations like* a rainy evening, a hungry animal, *etc. Then use your combinations in sentences, e.g.* The accident happened one rainy evening.

animal beach children day evening house night office orange path people sea shoes story weather

3. *In English, please:* hungrig, durstig, saftig, salzig, sonnig, neblig, regnerisch, windig, sandig, stürmisch, verschneit, vereist, lustig, felsig, schmutzig

A difficult daughter

What do you think is a difficult daughter?

"I'm going to a birthday party on Saturday afternoon," said Tahira.
"How nice," said Mrs Malik. She always spoke to her daughter in Urdu. "Whose party is it?"
"Nasneen's. She's a new girl at school."
"And her parents? Do I know them?"
"No. They live on the other side of town. They only came here a few weeks ago."
"Have you thought of a nice birthday present?"
"Don't worry, Mum. I've still got some money that I've saved. I'll get something for her."
Mrs Malik prepared the evening meal. She was lucky to have a daughter who did not ask for money for a present. She would like to do more for her two children, give them more than they had, but she got so little money from her job with Mr Awan.
On Saturday Mrs Malik suggested that Tahira should wear her best *shalwar kameez*. She was going to another Asian house and the people should think that Tahira came from a good home. Tahira agreed. For her mother it was so important to wear the correct clothes and make the right impression.
Before she left the house, Tahira put her jeans and a T-shirt into a bag.
Downstairs Tahira kissed her mother.
"You are leaving early," said Mrs Malik. "It is only 12 o'clock."
"I'm going to Bina's house first, then we're going into town to look for presents together."
Mrs Malik gave her daughter five pounds.
Tahira was surprised. "This is for the bus and to buy a nice birthday card and some nice paper for your present."
"Mum, I've got enough. Really."
"Take it," said Mrs Malik.
"Mum, you shouldn't."
Mrs Malik watched through the window as her daughter left the house. Some minutes later the phone rang. It was Mr Awan. She listened, then she said to her younger daughter, "I must go to work this afternoon. Mr Awan needs me. Can you stay next door with your cousin Anwar till I come back? I will only be away for two or three hours."

* * *

Tahira got off the bus and walked to her friend's house. Bina was waiting for her.
"Any problems?" she asked.
"No," said Tahira. "I just hate the stories I have to make up all the time. I'd love to say, 'Look, Mum. Bina and I have met these two boys. One is called Jamie and the other is Tom. We're going to meet them in town. We might go out with them and have a good time.' " She sighed. "It's so much easier for English girls."
"You can say that again," said Bina. "Mum and dad are out. You can get changed here."
Tahira took off her Asian clothes. Bina was already wearing jeans and a pullover. Tahira put her *shalwar kameez* in the bag and the two girls left the house.
"You know, she gave me five pounds," said Tahira.
"What for?"
"For a birthday present! I didn't want to take it, but what could I say? I feel terrible."
"Tell her you found a nice present and you had just enough money."

* * *

Tahira and Bina took the bus into town. They went into a department store and looked at different clothes. They went to a record shop and listened to some music. Later they went to a café.
Jamie and Tom were already waiting for them. They were sitting at a table with a group of other young people, some Asian, some English.
Tahira and Bina sat down at the table. Jamie put his arm round Tahira's shoulder.
"Where have you been?"

"Listen," said Tom. "I've got my brother's car. I can borrow it for the afternoon."

Tahira looked through the window. An old sports car was standing outside. Four seats, no roof, and it was a summer day. "Can you drive?" she asked.

"Of course I can. I'm 17. I passed my test three months ago."

The four teenagers got up from the table. They said goodbye to the others and ran out of the café and jumped into the car. Tahira and Bina climbed in and waved at the group still inside the café.

* * *

Mrs Malik left Mr Awan's "factory" at 5 o'clock. You couldn't really call it a factory. It was a dark unhealthy room where she and several other Asian women worked to make clothes for large department stores. It was not the best kind of work, but it was a job and Mrs Malik had to be grateful for that. She did not speak good English and so she had little chance to get a job with an English firm.

When the bus arrived, Mrs Malik climbed in. She found a seat near the window and looked at the scene outside. At the traffic lights the bus stopped. While the driver was waiting for the green light, an open sports car stopped next to the bus. The music from the car's radio was so loud that Mrs Malik could hear it in the bus. The driver of the sports car was singing to the music and laughing. Two girls were sitting on the back seat. They had long black hair.

The lights turned green and the bus moved forward. At that moment one of the girls in the car threw her head back as she laughed, and Mrs Malik saw that she was Asian. For a second and no more the girl's eyes and Mrs Malik's eyes met. The girl turned away at once. She spoke to the driver and the car drove away.

"It was my mother," screamed Tahira.

"Are you sure?" asked Bina.

"Yes, it was her. I'm sure it was."

"Do you think she saw you?" asked Bina.

"I don't know."

"Where's the problem?" asked Jamie. "It's not two o'clock in the morning."

* * *

That evening Mrs Malik prepared to go to the mosque. Just before she left, Tahira arrived home. She greeted her mother. Mrs Malik noticed that Tahira was wearing her *shalwar kameez*.

"Did you have a good time?" she asked.

"Yes, I enjoyed it," said Tahira. She gave her mother the five pounds. "I had enough money for a present. Thanks." And she went upstairs to her room.

Later Mrs Malik was in the mosque with her younger daughter. Tahira no longer came with her. Mrs Malik felt disappointed. The rules of Mrs Malik's culture meant nothing in this country and nothing, she now realized, to her daughter. Tahira, it seemed, did not want to learn how a girl should behave. And Mrs Malik did not have a husband any more who could help and support her, who could talk to Tahira. Other families seemed to have no problems with their children. They came to the mosque. They knew how they should behave. Why should she have a difficult daughter?

Mrs Malik looked at Tahira's younger sister. How much longer, she wondered, before she was alone in the mosque.

Working with the text

1 Some questions about the text

a Who is "difficult", Tahira or Mrs Malik? Write a short text. (Try not to look at the text when you talk about this question, but think of the answers you gave to the pre-question on p. 61.)

b Now look at the text again and try to see the situation from both sides, from Mrs Malik's and from Tahira's side. Take the following questions about the mother and the daughter into consideration while you are talking about the story:

Mrs Malik
Why does she think her daughter is difficult?
How does she feel about Tahira's behaviour?
What or who is responsible for this situation?
How do you imagine Mrs Malik? What kind of person do you think she is?

Tahira
Why does Tahira find the situation difficult?
Where exactly does this show in the text?
How does she imagine her life in Britain?
How do you imagine Tahira? What kind of person do you think she is?

c Look again at the text you have written for **1a**. Do you still agree with everything you have written? – Why is it difficult to take sides with one of the two people?

2 Say it in English: Explaining how you feel about something

Imagine Tahira wants to talk to her mother about what happened, but she thinks it is better to write her a letter to explain how she feels. She wants to tell her mother that she would like to live like other British teenagers. Now *you* write Tahira's letter. You can start like this:

> Dear Mum,
>
> I feel terrible. I don't know if you saw me in the sports car, but I must tell you the truth about this afternoon. …

Here are some words and expressions from the text that you could use:

Don't worry, Mum. – I hate the stories I have to make up. – I'd love to say … – You think I should behave like … – I enjoyed/didn't enjoy … – We had a good time. – I can imagine that you feel … – Perhaps you think other families have no problems with their children. – I'm sure …

Listening comprehension The miner's story

1. Before you listen to the tape, look again at the picture of the pay queue on page 53. How do you think the people in the photo felt? Why do you think they felt like this? What do you think their day was like compared to a day in the life of a working person today?
2. When you have talked about all this, listen to the tape just once. It tells you about the life of miners, about a particular event which took place in Wigan in 1893 and about the effects it had. Make notes about what you could understand and compare your notes with those of the other pupils in class.
3. Listen a second and perhaps a third time to understand as much as possible. Make notes while you are listening and finally write down in a few sentences what happened.

Project Find out from a history book what the life of miners was like in Germany at that time.

At the doctor's

Dr Khan is a GP. Every day he treats people for different reasons.

I've got a pain in my chest, Doctor.
back
leg

I've got a bad headache.
earache.
(a) stomach ache.
a sore throat.

My head aches.
stomach aches.
arms and legs ache.

I've hurt my arm.
knee.
foot.

I've got a cold.
the flu.
a (high) temperature.

There's something wrong with my right eye.

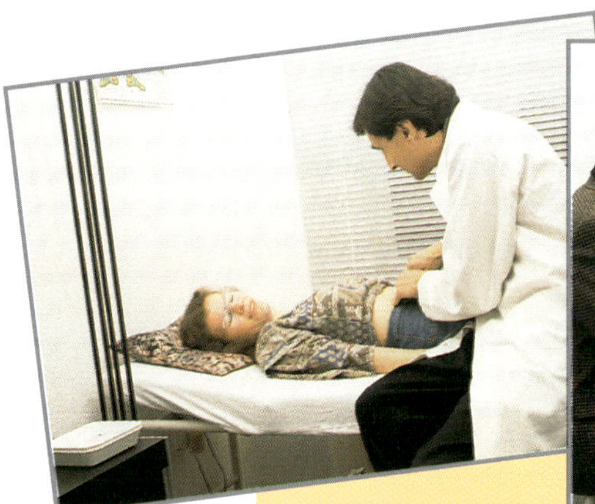

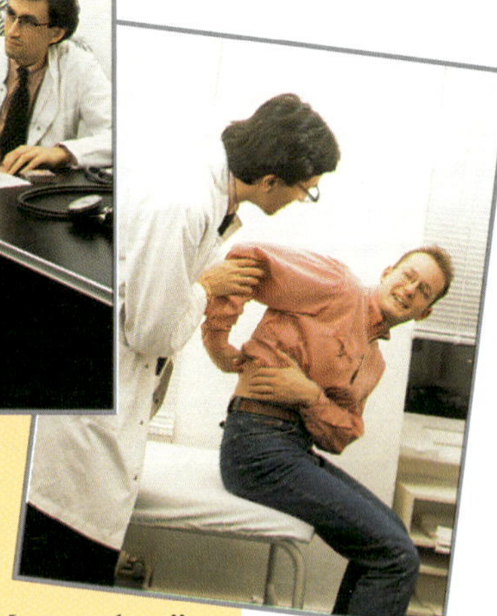

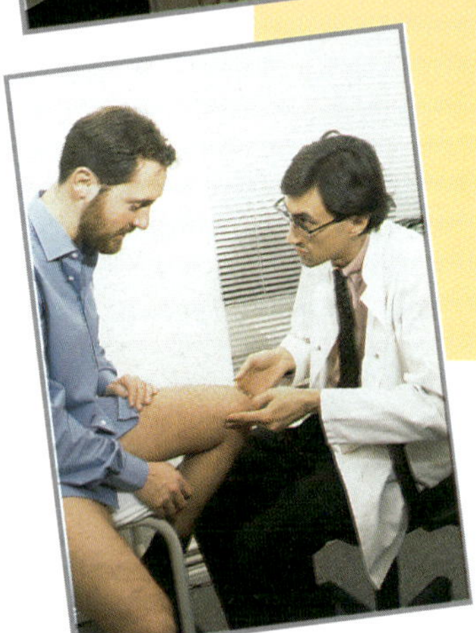

What did these people say when Dr Khan examined them?

"I've got a terrible …, Doctor."
"I don't feel very well, Doctor. My … aches."
"…"

Just for fun
Just for fun

Imagine something is wrong with you. See if your friends can guess what it is.

At the surgery

Jennifer is at Dr Khan's surgery. She doesn't feel very well. Her mother has phoned the surgery and made an appointment with Dr Khan.

Dr Khan: Hallo, Jennifer, what's wrong with you today?

Jennifer: I don't feel very well. I've got a bad headache and an upset stomach.

Dr Khan: Have you taken your temperature?

Jennifer: Yes. It was normal this morning. But I feel sick.

Dr Khan: OK, I'll examine you now and we'll try to find out what it is.

Dr Khan examines Jennifer.

Dr Khan: Yes, I think you've got a virus. Take this prescription to the chemist's. Go straight to bed, take the medicine three times a day and stay in bed for the rest of the week. You should feel better in a couple of days.

Jennifer: Thank you, Doctor. Goodbye.

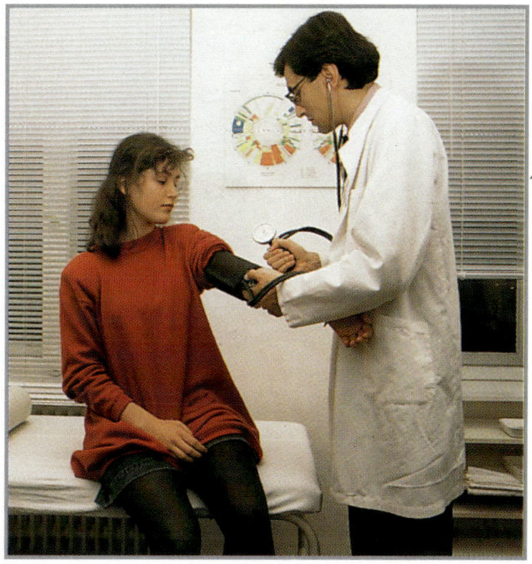

Role play

Work with a partner and try to make dialogues for the following situations. One of you is the patient, the other is Dr Khan.

a You feel very ill. Your arms and legs ache. You feel cold all the time. It could be the flu. Dr Khan examines you and gives you a prescription. You should go straight to bed and keep warm.

b You fell and hurt your leg during a tennis match. Your foot aches, but you can still move it. Dr Khan checks it. He doesn't think it's broken, but he wants to be sure, so he sends you to the hospital for an X-ray.

Info box In Britain people have to go to their GP first when they feel ill. The GP examines them and decides if it is possible to treat them or if the patient should go to the hospital and see a specialist. People can go to a chemist to buy cough medicine or tablets for a headache. However, chemists in Britain also sell a lot of the things you usually find in a German "Drogerie", for example shampoo or toothpaste.

Unit 5 Scotland

Helen MacDonald and Karen Werner have become pen-friends. In one of her letters Helen invited Karen to visit her in Scotland. Karen's parents have agreed that Karen can spend three weeks in Aberdeen during the summer holidays and they have invited Helen to return to Germany with Karen for three weeks.

Dear Karen,

I'm glad that you can come to Aberdeen in August. And thanks for the invitation to Germany. I'm sure you'll like it here in Scotland. I'm sending you some information with my letter. When you read through it, you'll see that we can do a lot of things while you're here.

As you noticed at St David's, I have a Scottish accent. But my accent isn't really so strong (and I tried to speak "proper" English to you). Just wait till you come here. A lot of people have really strong accents, and I've got a surprise for you: we also have our own Scottish language. It's called Gaelic. Like Welsh, it's very old and very difficult. I can't speak it. In fact, only about 80,000 people still speak it, and they live mostly on the islands and in the northwest of Scotland. English has taken one very important word from Gaelic: "whisky"! It comes from the Gaelic words "uisge beathe" and means "water of life".

Yes, I can tell you a bit more about Aberdeen, but you'll find a lot in the information. It's the third largest city in Scotland (after Edinburgh and Glasgow). It's famous as an oil town because there are a lot of oil rigs in the North Sea. As you know, my mother has been working for Britoil since my parents got divorced, so she can tell you about the oil industry.

We've now moved into our new house. It's near the sea, but don't worry, the beaches are clean. You won't be covered with oil when you come out of the water. My sister says that you can have her room. She will sleep in my room while you are staying with us. She's quite nice, really (when she's sleeping, ha, ha!). Of course, you can also share my room with me, but we can discuss all that when you're here.

Well, I'm looking forward to seeing you again and hope you'll have a nice time in Scotland. Don't forget to say hallo to your parents for me.

Love,
Helen

Now imagine you are Helen's pen-friend. Answer Helen's letter and say what you can do together in your region when she visits you.

English and German accents

Read what Helen told Karen in some of her letters and find out what she says about their new German assistant and about German and English accents.

... We have a new German assistant. His name is Gerald Funke and he's from Dresden. He's **quiet** and he also speaks **quietly**. So it's sometimes difficult to hear what he says. ...

... I know that you have **different** accents in Germany but I've never heard anybody with Gerald's accent. It's very **different** from yours. He pronounces many words **differently** from the way you pronounce them. ...

... Perhaps you know that a **proper** German 'ü' or 'ch' is difficult for English people. It isn't for Scottish people. It was a great surprise for Gerald that Scottish people can say words like 'ich' and 'kühl' **properly**. ...

In Helen's sentences you can find three adjectives in bold print: 'quiet', 'different' and 'proper'. The following sentences show you what adjectives can refer to.

Gerald Funke is **quiet**. / He is a **quiet** person. His favourite music is **quiet**. / He likes **quiet** music.

Now look again at the second and third short text. What do 'different' and 'proper' refer to?
There are some more adjectives in the texts. Find them and say what they refer to.

The other three words in bold print in Helen's letters are adverbs of manner**.** The following sentence shows you what adverbs of manner often refer to.

He **speaks quietly**.

Look at Helen's letters and find out what the adverbs 'differently' and 'properly' refer to.
Now compare the form of the adverbs of manner with the adjectives in the text. It should not be difficult for you to find a rule for the formation of regular adverbs of manner.
Look again at the texts and try to make up a rule about the position of adverbs of manner ...
a) when there is no object in a sentence,
b) when there is an object in a sentence.

Ex Three tricky tasks:

Task 1: *The following six adjectives form their adverbs regularly with '-ly', but one adverb in each pair has a tricky spelling. Which do you think it is? How do you spell it?*

strange – true   easy – shy   beautiful – full

Task 2: *Find out what the six words in bold print refer to and say if they are adjectives or adverbs. What can you say about the adverbs of 'good', 'hard' and 'fast'?*

... I think it is **good** to listen to cassettes in our German lessons although not everybody understands the people **well**. When they speak **fast**, it is **hard** work for me to understand them. But usually we all work **hard** and so we even find out what the **fast** speakers are saying.

Task 3: *The following short text shows you six adjectives in bold print. Why do three of them seem to be "wrong"? – What does this tell you about the verbs 'sound' and 'seem'?*

... Last week I listened to a BBC programme on German dialects. Some German people talked very strangely. There were some very **strange** accents. But I suppose my English sounds **strange** to you, too. – Perhaps it is **strange**. ...
... After one year of German I'm certain that it isn't an **easy** language. I hoped I could learn German easily. You are lucky. English seems so **easy** for German people. – Do you think it is **easy**? ...

→ Grammar 5: 1a-d (p.154-155) → Exercises 1-4

* Dies ist für Schülerinnen und Schüler in einigen Bundesländern Wiederholung.

5 A

The top country

Project While you are doing the unit, develop a wall display about Scotland. Perhaps you can get some old wallpaper and glue some pieces together. Make the top stronger with some cardboard and then put the paper on a wall in your classroom.
To start your display, make a network with the information you get from the title, the illustrations and the texts on these two pages.

Scotland covers about one third of Britain. The loneliest and wildest parts are in the Highlands of Scotland, an area about the size of Baden-Württemberg, but with a population of only 368,000.

For over 400 years Britain was a part of the Roman Empire, but the Romans never conquered Scotland. In fact, the Scots attacked back. The Roman Emperor Hadrian built a wall from the west coast to the east coast to form the northern frontier of the Empire, and the Romans made sure the Scots stayed on the other side.

In the thirteenth and fourteenth centuries three English kings tried to conquer Scotland, but without success. In the seventeenth century a Scottish king, James Stuart, also became King James I of England. A hundred years later in 1707 Scotland and England united and became one country: Great Britain.

Today the Scottish Highlands is one of the last untouched areas in Europe. Every year people visit the region to go walking, climbing, sailing or fishing.

A large number regularly go to Loch Ness, the longest lake in Britain. It is 24 miles long and almost a thousand feet deep. And somewhere down there is Nessie, the Loch Ness Monster. People have sat with cameras in the hope that they might see Nessie; divers have gone down to look for her, but the water is so dark that they cannot see anything when they go down. So far nobody has found Nessie, but that is what makes her so interesting.

No visit to Scotland is complete without an evening of Scottish music. *The Skye Boat Song* is one of the most popular Scottish songs. Listen to the song and read the words at the same time. Try to get an idea of what the song is about. The illustration can help you.

1. ***Speed bonnie boat***
   like a bird on the wing.
   "Onward," the sailors cry,
   "Carry the lad that's
   born to be king,
   Over the sea to Skye."

   Loud the winds howl,
   loud the waves roar.
   Thunderclaps fill the air.
   Baffled our foes
   stand by the shore.
   Follow they will not dare.

2. ***Many's the lad***
   fought on that day,
   Well the claymore
   could wield,
   When the night came,
   silently lay
   Dead on Culloden's field.

   Loud the winds howl …

Info box In the past some Scots, especially in the Highlands, believed that a member of the Scottish royal family should be king of England and Scotland.
In 1745 the Scottish prince Charles Edward Stuart – or Bonnie Prince Charlie as he is often called – led an army of Highlanders against the English king. In the end the English army defeated the Highlanders at Culloden, near Inverness, in 1746. After the battle, the English army tried to find the prince, but he escaped. With the help of Flora Macdonald he sailed to the island of Skye. The English army looked everywhere for the prince. They even offered £30,000 for information where Charlie was, but nobody said a word. From Skye he later sailed to France. He never came back to Scotland again.
Today Bonnie Prince Charlie is still a popular hero in Scotland. And some Scots still think of Culloden as the place where they lost their independence.

- Read the info box to find out what exactly the song is about.
- Why do you think *The Skye Boat Song* is still so popular?

L

→ Listening comprehension, p. 78

speed bonnie boat *fahr zu, prächtiges Boot* · lad *Junge* · waves *Wellen* · Baffled our foes stand by the shore. Follow they will not dare. *Verwirrt stehen unsere Feinde am Ufer. Zu folgen wagen sie nicht.* · many's the lad fought on that day, well the claymore could wield *etwa: viele junge Männer kämpften an diesem Tag und schwangen kräftig das Highlander-Schwert*

Focus on WORDS Describing buildings and places in a town

Aberdeen has many interesting +historical sights, for example the beautiful cathedral and the famous university buildings. It also has +attractive parks and +public gardens with pleasant restaurants. One day Karen, Helen and Mrs MacDonald visited the +harbour because Karen wanted to know more about the oil industry. They looked at the +supply ships and then they drove to the +heliport on the outskirts of the city. Karen knew from Helen's letters that it was the biggest helicopter airport in the world.

1 Collecting words

Look at the five groups of words, then collect more words and phrases. The words on the right can help you.

a Places where you can buy things or eat and drink:

- supermarket, the butcher's, the +baker's, …
- restaurant, pub, cafeteria, …

b Sights, public buildings and places that you can find in a town:

castle, +town hall, park, theatre, football +stadium, +guest house, …

c Where can a place in town be?

in Smith Street, in the centre, in the suburbs, on the outskirts, opposite the post office, …

police station – library – museum – zoo – bookshop – café – next to the park – in Trafalgar Square – a ten-minute +ride by bus from the centre – dirty – large – expensive – closed at lunch time – open 24 hours – hospital

d What can a place in town be like?

big, old, +well-known, busy, crowded, …

e Information about opening times:

open on weekdays from 9 am to 5 pm, closed on Sundays, open daily, …

2 Arranging words

It can be fun to arrange words and phrases in different ways – and it can help you to remember them, too. Here are three suggestions, but perhaps you have got other ideas:

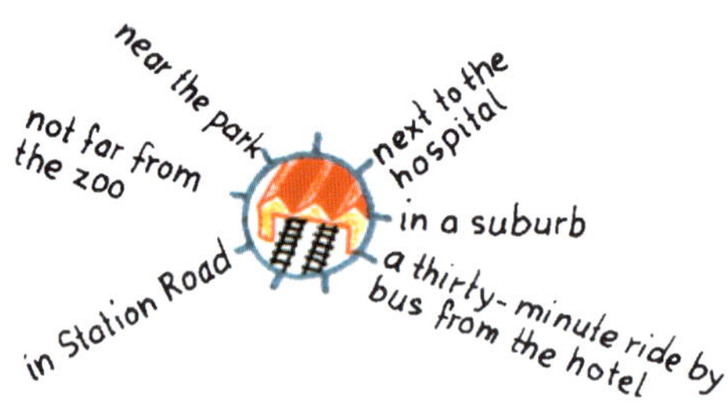

3 Words in use

a Where do you go when you want to …

- see a film?
- go swimming?
- take your dog for a walk?
- have a really good meal?
- buy bread?
- buy stamps?

b A game: Hot or cold?

Example: I'm thinking of a building in Heidelberg. Can you guess what it is?
Is it in the centre? – No, you're cold.
Is it a historical building? – Yes, you're warm.
Do many tourists visit it? – Yes, you're hot.
Is it a ruin? – Yes, you're very hot.
Is it Heidelberg Castle? – Yes, you're right.

Aberdeen – city of flowers

Aberdeen's parks and gardens flower **beautifully** all year. However, in the summer they flower **more beautifully than** in all other towns in Britain. During these months you can see **better than** at other times why Aberdeen has won the *Britain in Bloom* competition so often.
Duthie Park with its *Mountain of Roses* is the place where you can enjoy Aberdeen's roses **best**. The park offers its visitors many places to relax at the end of a busy day: While some people like to relax in the world-famous *Winter Gardens*, others relax **more easily** in the pleasant restaurant. Only one thing is certain: Children relax **most easily** in the park's many play areas.

a Look at the words in bold print.
They show you how you form the comparative and superlative of adverbs which end in '-ly'. Try to make up a rule for the comparison of adverbs from these examples.
You can also find two forms which you already know, the comparative 'better' and the superlative 'best'. Check what 'better' and 'best' refer to in the text. What word class must they be?

b Puzzle it out:

ABERDEENSMILESBETTER

This is an advertisement for Aberdeen. Can you find out what it means?
Here is some help: You can read this slogan in two ways. Once 'better' is an adjective, and once it is an adverb. In one of the sentences you must add an apostrophe.

→ Grammar 5: 2 (p.155) → Exercise 6

Aberdeen – centre of new technologies

When Karen was in Aberdeen, Mrs MacDonald and the two girls went on a tour of the city.
"Before the discovery of oil under the North Sea this was a very poor region of Britain, wasn't it?" said Helen. "Yes," said Mrs MacDonald. "Aberdeen was just a quiet university city. The oil industry has brought a lot of changes. First they had to make the harbour bigger for all the supply ships. And the airport was too small for the number of people who came here to work on the rigs."
"They made it bigger, didn't they?" said Helen, "and they had to build a heliport for the helicopters that fly over the sea to the rigs."

"The money from the oil industry has helped in other ways," said Helen's mother. "It has brought life back to the region. Scotland is now an important centre for what we call 'sunrise technologies'. It's hard to believe but here among the mountains and lakes is one of the biggest centres of the electronics industry in Western Europe."

What does the text tell you about …
… Aberdeen and the Aberdeen region before the discovery of oil?
… the changes that came with the discovery?
… the effects the discovery has had on the Scottish economy?

→ Exercises 7, 8

* Dies ist für Schülerinnen und Schüler in einigen Bundesländern Wiederholung.

5 Exercises

1 Looking for adverbs

How can you do these things?

politely – excitedly – coldly – quickly – hungrily – impatiently – dangerously – carefully – fairly – unfairly – nervously – noisily – quietly – shyly – patiently – safely …

1. ride a bike
2. eat breakfast
3. watch a football match on TV
4. speak to your girlfriend/boyfriend
5. speak about somebody you don't like so much
6. wait for a bus
7. play a game
8. talk about your next holiday

Here is how you can start: 1. You can ride a bike *dangerously* or *safely*. You can also ride a bike *nervously*/… . 2. You can eat breakfast …

2 But how did they behave …?

It is easy to say a person is calm, pleasant, impatient, polite or excited. It is a bit more difficult to say how this person might behave in a certain situation. *Here is an example:*

It is easy to say "Tom Ripley was *calm*." But what exactly does this mean?
Perhaps it means: He sat down *slowly* and spoke *calmly* to the police officer. He described the situation *precisely*. Then he listened *patiently* to the police officer.

Work with a partner and write three or four more sentences in which you say how you imagine each of the following people behaved. Of course it is possible to imagine different situations.

1. It was 8.20 and Sue was *impatient*. She walked up and down …
2. All I can say is that at school Lisa was *good* at music. She …
3. At the age of 80 my grandfather was still as *fit* as a fiddle. He could …
4. After the match everybody was *excited*. Some people … . Others … . A boy …

3 You decide: adjective or adverb?

a *Here is what eight young Germans said about their life as pupils. Complete their sentences.*

1. For me it's difficult to understand people who have a … accent. ← strange
2. The worst situation for me is when people don't speak … . ← clear
3. I'm always very … when people speak too … . ← impatient / slow
4. I can never remember … when I must use the present perfect. ← precise
5. I feel … and make … mistakes when a teacher says she wants to know something … . ← nervous / terrible / urgent
6. I don't like tapes with … speakers who have … voices. ← different / similar
7. When I don't understand something …, I just can't sit … on my chair. ← exact / patient
8. When I've had problems at home or with a friend I can't listen … in a lesson. ← proper

b *What about you? What situations are difficult, uncomfortable for you?*

4 In English, please – Banff and Buchan

Die Gegend nördlich von Aberdeen heißt *Banff and Buchan*. Man kann sie mit dem Auto oder dem Bus von Aberdeen aus ziemlich schnell erreichen. Für Besucher bietet sie wirklich viele interessante Dinge: Leute, die ihren Urlaub ruhig verbringen möchten, können sich dort gut entspannen. An der Küste von *Banff and Buchan* und auf dem Land gibt es Dörfer und Städtchen mit kleinen Hotels, in denen man seine Ferien behaglich verbringen kann. Das Essen ist nicht zu teuer, und es schmeckt gut.
In einigen der kleinen Dörfer gibt es ein Heimatmuseum[1]. In Aden, zum Beispiel, gibt es ein Heimatmuseum, in dem man sehen kann, wie hart die schottischen Bauern dieser Gegend in der Vergangenheit arbeiten mußten. Ein anderer interessanter Ort ist *Slains Castle*, nicht weit von Aberdeen. Manche Leute sagen, daß der Schriftsteller Bram Stoker es in seiner Horrorgeschichte „Dracula" (1897) als Modell für Draculas Schloß benutzte.
Für Touristen, die aktiv sein möchten, gibt es viele Orte, an denen sie leicht alle Arten von Sport treiben können. Von über 50 Golfplätzen[2], die Touristen in der Gegend um Aberdeen benutzen können, sind zehn in *Banff and Buchan*.

[1] local museum [2] golf courses

R 5 Victoria's Britain *Muddled sentences with adverbials*

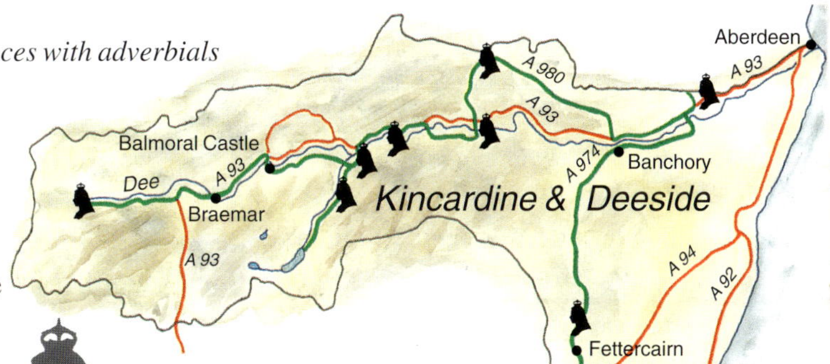

Balmoral [bæl'mɒrəl] · Kincardine [kɪn'kɑːdɪn] · Deeside ['diːsaɪd] · Fettercairn ['fetəkeən] · Banchory ['bæŋkərɪ] · Braemar [ˌbreɪ'mɑː]

1. in the Scottish Highlands – Queen Victoria – at Balmoral Castle – the happiest days of her life – spent
2. very much – from her letters – she – the Kincardine and Deeside area – we know that – loved
3. on the new *Victorian Heritage Trail* – today – the things Victoria liked so much – you can see

4. with her husband, Prince Albert – in 1861 – you can see – in Fettercairn – the places which Victoria visited
5. is – one little town on the trail – Banchory / since Victorian times – which hasn't changed – it has a High Street
6. people – on the first Saturday – come – each year – in September for the famous *Braemar Gathering* – from all over the world – to the village of Braemar / this festival – visit – often – members of the Royal Family

6 Silly competitions *Practise the comparison of adverbs.*

Another Celtic country, Wales, is famous for its singers and choirs. Every year there is a festival with a competition for the best singer and the best choir. But there is also a "silly" competition: In this competition the person or the choir who sings worst is the winner.

Make up some "silly" competitions and explain what people should do in your competitions. Here is an example:

"In my competition people should ride a bike very slowly and not fall off.
The winner is the person who can ride most slowly.
or the person who can ride more slowly than the others."

Perhaps these prompts can help you: sit patiently on a chair; behave most pleasantly; …

7 Question tags*

In German and in English you can use tags to ask if somebody agrees with what you have said.
In German we use for example *ne?* or *gell?* in more informal situations, and *nicht wahr?* or *nicht?* in more formal situations. From the following example sentences you can see how you can express this in English:

The English can't really understand the Scots, can they?
The Scots have got the same school system as the English, haven't they?
The religious life in Scotland is different, isn't it?
The Scottish National Party wants complete independence, doesn't it?
London doesn't want to give Scotland complete independence, does it?
In 1992 about a third of all Scots wanted independence, didn't they?

Look at the main clauses and the tags. Then complete the table in the box and make up a rule: How do you make tags in English?

main clause	tag
the English can't understand	can they
the Scots have got	...
the religious life is	...
...	...

→ Grammar 5: 3 (p.155)

Here are some more sentences. Complete them with the right tag.

1. Scone was the Scottish capital before 1300, ...? 2. There is a "Stone of Scone" in Westminster Abbey, ...? 3. In 1296 the English King Edward I stole this stone in Scotland, ...? 4. When this stone is back in Scotland, the country will be independent again, ...? 5. After the discovery of oil, the voices for Scottish independence became stronger, ...? 6. Perhaps the British government will give Scotland some more independence, ...? 7. It doesn't want to give Scotland complete independence, ...? 8. The Scots hope that they will get more independence through the European Community, ...?

8 The electronics industry in Scotland (Verbs with two objects)

When Mrs MacDonald and the girls got home, Mrs MacDonald **showed Karen a brochure** about the electronics industry in Scotland. She saw that Karen was interested and said, "I can also **show you a map**. It gives you all the important centres of the industry. – But let's have a cup of tea first, then I'll **show it to you**."
Later Mrs MacDonald said, "You can get this brochure from the Scottish Development Agency. Then you can **show it to your English teacher in Germany**. I'm sure he doesn't know that Scotland has attracted firms from all over Europe, the USA and Japan."

As in German, several English verbs can have two objects: a direct object (normally a 'thing') and an indirect object (normally a person).
Look at the four examples in bold print. Then try to say how the first two examples are different from the other two examples.

→ Grammar 5: 4 (p.156)

Now use the objects correctly in the following sentences.
1. The SDA offers (land / electronics firms from all over the world). 2. And so far the SDA has sold (them / lots of land). 3. These companies are now offering (40,000 jobs / the people of Scotland). 4. Eight Scottish universities teach (their students / Computer Science and Physics). 5. They have realized how important it is to teach (these subjects / them).

* Dies ist für Schülerinnen und Schüler in einigen Bundesländern Wiederholung.

a Trouble spot Same letters – different pronunciation: '-ea-' [iː], [e], [eɪ], [ɜː], [ɪə], [eə]

area	clear	early	healthy	heavy	mean	ready	theatre	wear
bread	dead	great	hear	idea	please	steak	unbreakable	weather
clean	ear	head	heard	learn	read	teacher	weak	year

Put the words from the box in six groups:

1. [iː] … 2. [e] … 3. [eɪ] … 4. [ɜː] … 5. [ɪə] … 6. [eə] …

b Trouble spot Adverbs: two forms – two different meanings

There is a small number of adjectives with two adverbs. One adverb has the same form as the adjective, the other has '-ly'. *Look at the following example sentences and translate them:*

adj: They paid a **high** price for the picture.

adv: The plane is flying **high** over the sea.
adv: *The Police* were a **highly** popular rock group in the 1980s.

Here are five such adjectives and adverbs:

adj/adv:	**high**	**late**	**near**	**hard**	**most**
	hoch	(zu) spät	nahe	schwer, hart	meiste(n); am meisten
adv:	**highly**	**lately**	**nearly**	**hardly**	**mostly**
	höchst, sehr	in letzter Zeit	fast, beinahe	kaum	meistens, größtenteils

Now look at the following sentences and then complete them with an adverb from the box.

1. I've … finished the book. I've only got ten more pages to read and then you can have it.
2. The train arrived … again. It got to London at 10 o'clock and not at 9.30.
3. Helen's house is in the next street, so she lives very … .
4. The group has worked very … . They have planted over 200 trees.
5. I … know Jamie. I've only spoken to him once. I don't know what he is really like.
6. Has anybody seen Joanne …? – No, she doesn't live here any more. Her family has moved.
7. How … can you jump? – Oh, I jumped 1 metre 50 during the last sports competition.
8. What did you enjoy … at St David's? – Canoeing. That was wonderful.
9. People who speak Scots Gaelic live … in the northwest of Scotland.
10. There's a … interesting article in the newspaper about London's Docklands.

c Word builder's corner Nouns that end in '-er'

A lot of nouns that end in '-er' describe people and the things they do. Here are three examples:

dreamer	= dream	+ -er	A dreamer is a person who dreams.
runner	= run	+ -er	A runner is a person who runs races, for example.
loser	= lose	+ -er	A loser is a person who often loses or who has lost, e.g. a game.

Now say what the following nouns mean, or use them in a sentence.

watchmaker writer beginner listener
reader climber traveller landowner interviewer
learner worker rider storyteller winner

Example: A *watchmaker* is somebody who makes and repairs clocks and watches.
My watch is broken, I must take it to a *watchmaker*.

5 Text

The price of oil

Look at the title and the illustration.
What do you think the text will be about?

The sea was calm that evening. There were no winds and no clouds in the sky. From the oil rig where he was working, Tony Watson looked across the quiet sea. It was eight o'clock, not yet dark, although the night was not far away. He could already see the lights on other rigs. A helicopter was flying from one rig to the Scottish coast, about an hour away. Next to Tony's rig, a supply ship waited to take some equipment back to Aberdeen.

A hundred miles away the lights in his own home were probably on. This was his seventh day on the rig. He had seven more days and then he could go home for two weeks. And then back again for two more weeks on the rig, twelve hours a day, seven days a week. He didn't really like the work. But he enjoyed the fourteen days at home with his wife and young child. Ben was one year old and Tony missed him every minute he was away.

Tony finished his job – he had to check a small problem with one of the gas turbines – and walked back to his cabin. The rig was huge. Over 200 men lived and worked on it. The platform stood 100 feet over the sea, higher than the highest waves, stronger than the strongest winds. And there were strong winds in the North Sea.

Waves were often over 40 feet high. The men trained regularly for accidents so they knew how they should react. They knew where they should go and how they should leave the rig quickly. Each lifeboat carried 60 men and each man on the rig had a number for a place in one of the lifeboats. They all had survival suits in their cabins and there were survival suits at different places on the rig. Tony went to his cabin to take off his working clothes. He shared the cabin with three other men. As they all worked twelve hours each day, two men slept, while the other two worked.

Tony took off his working clothes, washed and went to the dining-room. He asked for a steak and took a cup of milk and a piece of fresh apple pie. He sat down next to Steve Ryan, an Australian oil worker. They talked about their work for a few minutes. Then Steve said, "How's your boy?"

Tony smiled. "Great. I really miss him."

"When are you going home again?"

"Next week. I'd like to stay at home. I've had enough of this routine, but there's no money in any other job."

Steve agreed. "It's a hard life, but you always come back. Boy, we really pay a price for our oil." He finished his drink. "I'm going to the recreation room. Would you like a game of pool?"

"I think I'll watch TV. There's a film I want to see."

The two men finished their meals and started to walk out of the cafeteria towards the recreation room.

Then it happened.

There was a terrible explosion. And then sirens. Tony's first reaction was to run to his cabin to get his survival suit. But seconds later smoke and fire were everywhere. A voice shouted, "Get out. Get out as fast as you can."

Tony ran through the smoke and felt another explosion. He was filled with fear and panic. He ran outside onto the rig's platform. Huge flames burned in the night and smoke filled the air. He felt the heat against his body. He could hear sirens everywhere. Then one side of the rig sank towards the sea.

Some men fell over, others jumped. Tony fell towards the side. He saw Steve. He was climbing

up the side of the rig to save another worker. Tony felt he had to help him. He tried to follow the big Australian but flames and smoke came across the rig and the heat sent him back. When he looked again, he couldn't see Steve.
Tony hung to the side of the rig. Everybody knew the training routine, but there was no time to get to the lifeboats, no time to get a survival suit, no time to do anything. He had only one choice: jump or burn. He jumped.
Hands over his nose and mouth, his body straight, he fell 70 feet towards the sea. He felt only panic as he fell along the side of the rig. Then he hit the water. The shock filled him with more panic. He swam to the top and pushed his head out of the water. Tony was a good swimmer, but without a survival suit he knew he couldn't live longer than a few minutes in the North Sea. He looked for a piece of wood, something he could hold. A short distance away he saw a lifeboat but the men inside couldn't possibly help him. The boats were sealed. He looked round. Over his head the sirens screamed in the night. The fire from the rig was so hot that he had to go under the water to keep his head cool.
When he came up, a light suddenly shone on him. The supply ship was looking for men in the water. Other men in inflatable boats were pulling workers out of the water. Tony shouted as loudly as he could and tried to swim towards one of the boats. But now the sea was burning. He saw a hand. He felt fingers, he felt the side of the boat, but they couldn't pull him into the boat. The heat was terrible. A wave came and he fell back into the water. The boat was suddenly going away from him. The sea was carrying it away. The men couldn't leave him there! They couldn't! He swam to the boat, but he couldn't reach it. He sank under the water. As he went down, he felt a hand in his hair.

Tony opened his eyes. He was in a hospital bed. His wife Jenny was sitting next to him. Other workers from the rig were in other beds. He noticed that Jenny was holding his hand. "How many died?" he asked.
"A lot," she said. "So far it's 122."
Tony closed his eyes. "Steve Ryan. Is he all right? What about Pierre, Rolf and Alan, my room-mates?"
"Nobody knows yet," she said. "They're still looking for them in the sea and on the rig."
He hoped Steve was alive. He hoped as many as possible were alive, but he knew many weren't. As he lay there he remembered Steve's words, "We really pay a price for our oil."

Working with the text

1 Talking about the text

a
1. First compare what you expected with what the story is really about. Then say what happened in a few sentences only and without any details.
2. Now have a closer look at the first part of the story (up to l. 63, p. 76) and talk about it. The following questions could help you:
   What does this part of the story tell you about an oil worker's life on a rig? What does it tell you about Tony Watson and about Steve Ryan? How do they feel about their job? How old do you think they are? What do you think they look like?
3. Look at the rest of the story and talk about it. Here are some questions to help you:
   What do both Tony and Steve do in this situation? What does Steve's and Tony's behaviour tell you about these two people? How do you think they felt?

b
1. Imagine you are Steve or Tony. Write down what went through your head when you heard the explosion *or* when you were outside on the platform *or* when you were fighting for your life.
2. What do you think went through Jenny's head when she heard the news about the accident? What do you think she did then?

c A point for discussion: "Accidents happen" is a well-known expression. Again and again we see how true this is. What do you think: Is the price we pay for some of our modern technology worth paying?

2 Say it in English: Avoiding one-word answers in a conversation

One-word answers often make a conversation difficult. In some situations they even sound impolite. Look at the following mini-dialogue from the text.

Steve: How is your boy?
Tony: Great. I really miss him.
Steve: When are you going home again?
…

Tony doesn't answer with just one word, he adds a short sentence, "I really miss him." This tells Steve that Tony would like to continue with the conversation. It also makes it easier for Steve to say something. Here is another situation.

Speaker A: When are you going to London?
Speaker B: On Sunday.
Speaker A: Are you going by train?
Speaker B: Yes.

Speaker B's answers show that she/he is not really interested in a conversation.
Find possible sentences which you could add to Speaker B's answers to make them more polite and to show that she/he is interested in a conversation.

Now work with a partner. Choose one of the following questions and develop it into a dialogue.

1. When does your train leave? 2. Did you phone Susan? 3. Where is Bill? 4. Are you going by car or by train? 5. How was school? 6. Can I help you?

L 9 Listening comprehension The legend of Dunvegan Castle

Look at the pictures. What do you think happened at the castle?

Look at the pictures again while you are listening to the tape.
Before you listen a second time read the following questions. They will help you to find out more about the legend. Where is Dunvegan Castle? Who lives there? Who are the people in the second picture? Who is the baby? What is happening in the fourth picture? Why are the people celebrating? What happened while the guests were celebrating? What was special about the flag? How did the flag help the McLeods?

Clothes

1 What is in the shop window? There is/there are: a … / some … / a pair of … / two pairs of … / a few … / a lot of …

Look at the picture again and say what Helen is wearing. What is Karen wearing? What is your partner wearing today?

2 Karen would like to buy some clothes while she is in Britain. She is with Helen in a department store in Aberdeen.

Karen: I like this black jacket.
Helen: Yes, it's nice. What size do you take?
Karen: In Germany I take size 36.
Helen: You're the same size as I am and I take size 10. Try this on. Does it fit?
Karen: Yes, it fits very well. But does it suit me?
Helen: It suits you really well, and it matches your trousers.
Karen: I like it very much. It's a bit expensive, but I think I'll buy it.
Helen: We can try somewhere else. We might find something cheaper.

Practise similar dialogues with a partner for some jeans, a T-shirt, …

L Listen to the cassette. You will hear different people who will describe what kind of clothes they have just bought in a shop. Make notes and then say what you can remember.

blouse [blaʊz] · coat [kəʊt] · dress [dres] · glove [glʌv] · jacket ['dʒækɪt] · scarf, *pl.* scarves [skɑ:f, skɑ:vz] · skirt [skɜ:t] · sock [sɒk]

3 When Karen was back at Helen's house, she tried on her clothes and found that there was something wrong with the jacket. Helen suggested that they should take it back the next day.

Karen: Excuse me. I bought this jacket from you yesterday.
Assistant: Yes, I remember. Is there something wrong with it?
Karen: It's got a hole in it.
Assistant: Can I see it, please?
Helen: She didn't do it. It was like that when we took it out of the bag.
Assistant: Didn't you notice it when you were here in the shop?
Karen: I only noticed it when I got home.
Assistant: Would you like to exchange it for another?
I think we still have one or two in your size.
Karen: Yes, I'd love to. Is that possible?
Assistant: Have you got your receipt?
Karen: Yes, it's here.
Assistant: See if you can find something you like. I'm sorry about this.
Helen: Thanks.
Assistant: You're welcome.

4 **Make similar dialogues.**

Imagine you have bought a T-shirt, a pair of shoes or a pair of jeans and you have to take it/them back to the shop where you bought it/them because …

– it doesn't/they don't fit.
– there's something wrong with … .
– you've changed your mind because you don't like it/the colour/style/… .
– you bought it/them as a present, but … .
– you'd like to change it/them for … .
– it was/they were damaged.

Remember to be polite. Use phrases like:

Excuse me … . Is it possible to …?
Do you mind if I …?
I'm not happy with … . May I exchange …?

And as an answer:

Certainly, …/Of course, …/See if you can find another … .
I'm afraid we've run out of … ./I'm afraid I have to ask the manager first./…

5 **Just looking!**

How often have you been in a shop and you just want to look at something, but the assistant won't leave you alone. Act the scene with a partner and try to find polite excuses to get out again. The assistant can use phrases like:

It really suits you. – It looks a dream on you. – It makes you look wonderful.
You look fantastic, believe me. – Shall I put it in a bag?

6 **Choices:** Do you prefer to buy cheap clothes in a supermarket or expensive clothes in a fashion shop? Which are your favourite shops/stores? Do you buy clothes there regularly?

7 **Packing for a week's holiday**: What might you pack in your suitcase or travel bag for a skiing holiday, a holiday in Spain, an activity centre like St David's, or a trip to London?

8 **Fashion and dreams:** What are your favourite clothes at the moment? How do you imagine your favourite person/your dream boyfriend or girlfriend? What do you think she/he could wear? Or are clothes not important?

Unit 6 Roman Britain

One day Dominic Foster went with his class to St Albans to do a history project. Their teacher, Mrs Bailey, took them to a large park next to the river Ver. There were lakes, paths and tall trees. Some people were walking on the grass; others were enjoying the sunny afternoon. Some boys were playing cricket. Half a mile away, on a hill on the other side of the river, they could see St Albans Cathedral and the first roofs of the town. It was all very quiet. "Here under our feet," said Mrs Bailey, "is the site of one of the most important Roman towns in Britain and possibly in the western part of the Roman Empire: the city of Verulamium."

Mrs Bailey led the pupils to the remains of the old city walls. Behind them was a narrow path that led between the trees and across fields. "This path," she continued, "was once a Roman road. In front of us was once a busy Roman city and here was the main gate into the city. Where we are now, Roman soldiers once stood long ago. Today it has all gone. But on the other side of the river you can see the town of St Albans. That is still there. Today we are going to find out about the history of these two towns, where the name St Albans comes from and what happened here almost two thousand years ago." Mrs Bailey took some worksheets out of her bag. She divided the class into groups and said, "Right, we've done group work many times before. You all know what to do."

L

How does Mrs Bailey try to make Verulamium interesting for her pupils?

→ Exercises 1, 2

Focus on GRAMMAR The passive

In the following text there are seven verb forms which you have not seen in the book so far. But because you know the context, it should be no problem to understand the text.

Preparations for group work

Mrs Bailey divided the class into three groups: a 'museum group', a 'cathedral group' and a 'Roman remains group'. She gave worksheets to one pupil in each group and said, "Please read the tasks carefully. You will see that it doesn't matter in which order the tasks **are done**." The pupils all sat down on the grass and started their work.

Worksheets **were handed** to each pupil.

Each task on the group's worksheet **was discussed**.

Smaller groups **were formed** in each group to do certain tasks.

Leaders **were chosen** for each group.

The name of each member of the group **was written** on the group's worksheet.

Before the pupils went away, Mrs Bailey said, "Please remember, your answers should **be written** clearly so that I can read them."

Look at the verb forms in bold print. They are passive forms. The first form is an example of the simple present, the following five forms show you the simple past, and the last example is a passive infinitive. As you can see, passive forms have two parts. Try to find a rule: How is the passive formed in English? Translate the passive sentences into German and compare the German passive forms with the English passive forms. What is the same, what is different?

Ex *Look at the seven sentences and the seven forms of 'be' in the box. Then try to find out from the context and the adverbials which form of 'be' is correct for which sentence.*

1. The path along the River Ver … used for over 2000 years.
2. Parts of the Roman town wall can … seen today.
3. When Tessa Wheeler worked in Verulamium, many remains … found.
4. Since then lots of Roman coins, pottery and other things … discovered.
5. Nobody can say how many buildings and streets … found in the future.
6. Most of these things … kept in the Verulamium museum.
7. Verulamium museum … opened in 1939.

be
are
was
were
has been
have been
will be

→ Grammar 6: 2a (p.157) → Exercise 4

When are passive forms used?

Look at pictures one and two and the sentences under the pictures. Why do you think the speaker of the first sentence used the passive and the speaker of the second sentence didn't. (Here is a tip: Compare the subjects of the sentences.) Now look at the third picture and sentence. Why do you think the speaker used the passive?

1

This vase **was found** in 1840.

2

Dominic **found** this piece of glass. He thinks it is Roman.

3

This vase **was found by** Tessa Wheeler in 1936.

→ Grammar 6: 2b (p.157) → Exercises 5, 6

1 At St Albans Cathedral (The passive with verbs that can have two objects)

The 'cathedral group' had to find out about St Alban. In the cathedral **different brochures were given** to the leader of the group. And before the pupils started their work, **the leader was given** a historical map of the cathedral.
Then **they were shown** some windows with scenes from the life of St Alban. **The pupils were** also **told** the story of St Alban: Alban was a Roman citizen who became a Christian. He was executed by the Romans on a hill outside the town of Verulamium. Later a church was built on the hill. The cathedral was built by the Normans. They used stones from the old city of Verulamium to build the cathedral.
Later that day **the pupils were shown** the site where Alban died.

Look at the first two sentences that have a verb in bold print.
Translate the first sentence and compare the subject and object of the English and the German sentence. Then translate the second sentence and again compare the subject and object of the English and the German sentence. – What happens to the subject *(the leader)* and the object *(a historical map)* of the English sentence when you translate the sentence into German?
Now translate the other sentences that have a subject and verb in bold print. How many "good" translations can you find? (A tip: In German we often use subjects like *man* or *jemand* to avoid the passive.)

Ex Braintwisters *Here are some sentences without subjects, but with two objects. Make two passive sentences from each sentence.*

Example: xxx offered the pupils *a tour* of the cathedral.
a) The pupils were offered … .   b) *A tour* was offered to … .

1. xxx tells all the groups the most important things about the cathedral. 2. xxx tells all visitors exactly the same things. 3. xxx will give us some information about the museum. 4. xxx won't give the group a tour of the museum. 5. xxx has shown me Susan's photos of St Albans. 6. xxx haven't shown the class all the photos yet.

→ Grammar 6: 2c (p.158) → Exercise 7

2 Back at school (The passive of verbs like 'speak about' *sprechen über*, 'look up' *nachschlagen*, 'agree on' *vereinbaren*, 'put up' *aufhängen*)

The next day Mrs Bailey went to the library with her class. There the pupils prepared a wall display about the Romans in Britain. First all the tasks **were spoken about**. Exact dates **were looked up**. A date **was agreed on** when the display should **be put up**. – A few days later the display **was put up** …

In English there are a number of verbs which have two or more parts (e.g. *agree on*). The passive of these verbs is formed quite regularly. From the example sentences it is easy to see where words like 'about', 'up' and 'on' go in passive sentences. Translate the first two sentences with verbs in bold print into German. Compare the verbs in the German and the English sentences. Then try to say why it is often difficult for German pupils to use these verbs in the passive.

Ex *Try to translate the following sentences.*

1. Die Bilder für die Ausstellung wurden von den Gruppen zusammengestellt *(put together)*.
2. Verschiedene Poster und Texte wurden an den Wänden ihres Klassenraumes aufgehängt *(put up)*.
3. Über die Ausstellung wurde in der Schule mehrere Tage gesprochen *(talk about)*.
4. Nach einer Woche wurden die Poster und Texte wieder abgehängt *(take down)*.

→ Grammar 6: 2d (p.158) → Exercise 8

Find out from the two pages:
- when and in what way Britain was invaded by the Romans
- how Britain was ruled before the Romans came
- who Boudicca was and what she is known for
- what Hadrian's Wall is and why it was built
- how long the Romans stayed in Britain
- why Verulamium was an important Roman town and what it was like
- what Watling Street is.

VERULAMIUM

A wall display by Class 10B

① The Romans under the Emperor Claudius invaded Britain in July, AD 43. At the time the island was divided into hundreds of small tribes. Each tribe had its own king. The Romans captured the capital of southeast Britain, Camulodunum, or Colchester as we call it today. They also captured eleven kings from different British tribes. They claimed the land as a province and called it Britannia. Verulamium was the name they gave to a British settlement that they captured next to the river Ver.

Sarah Bond

② The conquest of England was not easy. In AD 61 the Romans plundered Queen Boudicca's kingdom after the death of her husband and killed many of her people. Queen Boudicca attacked the Romans with a large army. She rode through southeast England and destroyed the Roman colonies at Camulodunum, Londinium and Verulamium, where she burned many of the buildings. 70,000 Romans died. From there she travelled north to meet the Romans for the final battle. The Roman army had fewer men, but they were better organized and so they defeated Boudicca's army.

Dominic Foster

⑥ Roman visitors to Verulamium often went to the public baths first, especially after a long journey. Then, clean and fresh, they went into the town. Verulamium was a large town with busy shops and busy streets. It had a forum, the only Roman theatre in Britain. The city also had large villas with glass windows and central heating.

Mark Wallace

⑤ Verulamium was 30 miles from Londinium, the capital of the province. Visitors came along the famous Watling Street, a Roman road that led from London to Chester. They came into the city through London Gate. Today Watling Street is still a busy road from London to St Albans.

James Fisher

③ In Scotland the Romans had to fight even harder. In AD 122 the Roman Emperor Hadrian visited Britain. As the Romans couldn't defeat the Scots, he decided to build a wall 80 miles long from the west coast to the east coast to hold back the "barbarians" and protect the Roman province in the south.

Ruth Walker

④ During the four hundred years that they were in England, the Romans built many towns and over 6,000 miles of roads. During this time Verulamium became an important Roman centre of administration, a "municipium", a name that was given to no other Roman town in Britain.

Laura Bishop

→ Spotlight on history (p.142-143)

Roman soldiers built thousands of miles of roads across the Roman Empire. They were so well planned and built that some of today's modern roads still follow the Roman routes.
The Romans built these roads so that their armies could move quickly to all parts of the Empire. But they also used the roads to +transport food and +goods from the countryside to the towns or from one part of the Empire to another.
Sometimes it was necessary to transport armies or goods across the sea and on rivers. The places where the ships +landed often became towns and important ports.
Today we have many more ways to transport people and goods. We have motorways and we have air routes, we use lorries and trains, planes and even +spaceships. However, we have problems the Romans didn't have. Our roads and air routes are very crowded and the air is polluted by the +engines in the many +vehicles which we use.

1 ◆Collecting words

Find all "travel words and phrases" in the text and put them in one of the following three groups. Then collect more for each group. (Try to do it without the help of the picture first.)

a Vehicles for travelling and transport

car, moped, +motorbike, +ambulance, …

b How and why do people travel?

– They go by car, take a taxi, …
– They use public transport, e.g. buses/…
– They go on holiday, …

c "A mixed bag"

airport, station, underground, road, +crossroads, traffic lights, +traffic jam, +pedestrian crossing, +pavement, +petrol station, fare, route, speed, mph, …

2 ◆Arranging words

Arrange the words and phrases you have collected in different ways. You can make several small networks, for example.

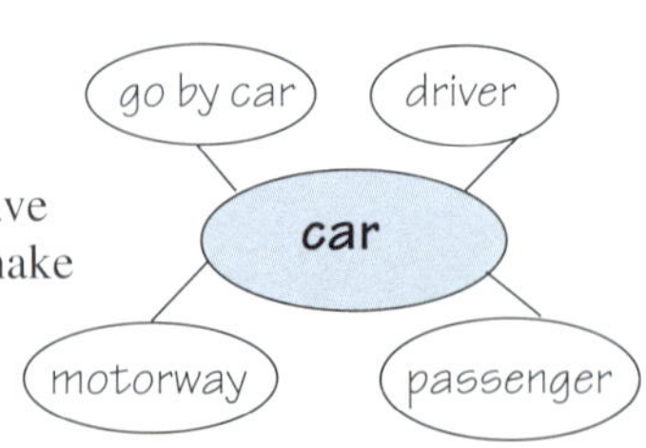

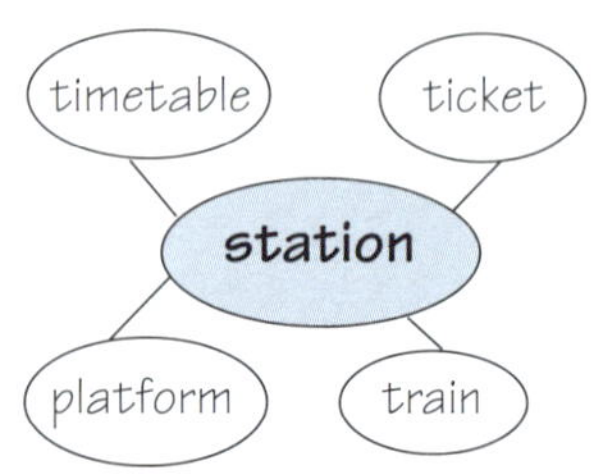

3 ◆Words in use

What is your idea of the perfect car?
How do you think goods will be transported and people will travel in the future?

A Roman time-traveller in Verulamium today

R **1 First impressions: comments and questions** A mixed bag of tenses

1. When I (live) here almost 2,000 years ago, there (not be) any buildings on that hill over there.
2. Later this afternoon I think I (walk) to that big building on the hill. I (try) to find out what it (be). I (remember) that a man with very strange ideas (die) there when I (be) a soldier here.
3. How long (they / have) these funny machines on their roads? We only (have) horses. And their roads (be) different, too.
4. That light in the street (just / change) from red to green. What (that / mean)?
5. Look at all the people in the street. Why (they / wear) these strange clothes? I (not see) one person yet who (wear) the same clothes as me.
6. I (not understand) the world any more. Why (all the people / look) at me? (be) anything wrong with me?

2 Lost in modern Britain ('how', 'what', 'where', etc. + *to*-infinitive)

When Gaius Optimus arrived at the place that was once the Roman town of Verulamium, he felt lost. The place was so different 2,000 years ago. He felt strange because he didn't know **what he should do** and he didn't know **how he should behave**.

→ Grammar 6: 1 (p.156)

a *Imagine you have just met Gaius and would like to help him. What would you tell/show/teach him?*

Here are some prompts to help you:

to stay – to find out about modern Britain – to use a telephone – to learn English – to have a bath – to buy food – to find the theatre …

Find some more things to tell/show/teach your Roman friend.

"Well, I would tell him **where to stay**. I would show him **how to find out about modern Britain**. I would teach him **how to** …

b *What do you think Gaius asked people? What did he find out about life today? What did he learn?*

3 Text production: The diary of Gaius Optimus

Because Gaius was such a strange "sight" in the streets of St Albans, the police took him to the police station. There he spent the first night of his new life. While he was lying on his bed, he started a diary:

Dear Diary,

I don't really know how and why this has happened, but I've started a new life in a place and among people that I don't know. Well, that's not quite true, I know that I've been here before, it must be almost 2,000 years ago, but everything has changed. Let me start at the beginning …

Now you go on with Gaius's diary.

4 Some questions Different tenses in the passive

Make the questions and then try to find answers to them.
Remember: All you need for the passive is the right form of 'be' and the past participle of the verb.

The Olympic Games

1. Where / first Olympic Games / hold?
2. Where / Olympic Games / hold / in the year 2000?
3. How many modern Olympic Games / hold / so far?
4. How often / Olympic Games / hold?

Languages

1. Where / Gaelic / speak?
2. How many languages / teach / schools / in the year 2020?
3. For how long / English / teach / German schools?
4. What languages / speak / North America / before the white people came?

Fruit and vegetables

1. What new kinds of fruit and vegetables / eat / Europe / in 50 years from now?
2. When / potatoes / first bring / to Europe?
3. How long / tomatoes / know / in Europe?
4. What fruit / sell / in hands?

5 Do you remember St David's? The passive with 'by'

Have a look at the three boxes. Then choose one prompt from each box to say what you remember about St David's.

Example: Karen was taken to St David's by her parents. Dominic and Jessica were …

Karen	organize	Latif Khan from Halifax.
Dominic and Jessica	speak	Janet and Latif.
A party	send back to his room	*her parents.*
Stephen	lead	Manuel Vargas.
Janet	invite to Devon	the instructors on the first day.
Dominic	*take to St David's*	more people than today.
The orienteering group	push into the lake	the rock-climbing instructor.
In the past, Welsh	pull out of the lake	Jessica.

6 Immigration to Britain Simple past active and passive

In the 1950s and 1960s lots of workers … in Britain.	need
In those years the British government … immigrants jobs and houses in Britain.	promise
Many immigrants … to the north because lots of jobs … in the factories there.	move / offer
At that time doctors … in Britain, too. So, many Asian doctors … to Britain.	need / come
Later the immigration laws for non-European citizens … by the government.	change

Just for fun

bullying power maniacs ['bʊlɪɪŋ 'paʊə ˌmeɪnɪæks] *etwa: machtbesessene Tyrannen*

7 "Things that have happened to me" – From the life of a cathedral guide

Decide if you need the passive in the simple past or in the present perfect.

1. *I've been given* lots of presents by visitors.
2. offer – a holiday in 1988
3. show – photos of homes and people from all over the world
4. tell – the strangest stories

5. teach – twenty Chinese words last year
6. send – postcards from people in the most far-away places
7. give – a ticket to a concert several years ago

8 In English, please – Germany and the Germans (based on Tacitus, *Germania*, AD 98)

Translate the following comments on Germany and the Germans. Here is how you should begin:
1. So far only few ships from our world have been heard of that …

1. … Bis jetzt hat man nur von wenigen Schiffen aus unserer Welt gehört, die Germanien besucht haben. Wer möchte gern Asien[1], Afrika[2] oder Italien verlassen, um Germanien zu besuchen, mit seinem schlechten Wetter und seiner langweiligen Landschaft? …
2. … Die Germanen lieben Geschenke. Wenn Gäste weggehen, gibt man ihnen die Geschenke, die sie gern haben möchten. …
3. … Jeder Gast wird mit einer guten Mahlzeit vom Gastgeber[3] willkommen geheißen. Niemand macht sich Sorgen, wie die Mahlzeit bezahlt wird. Wenn alles gegessen ist, wird der Gast zu einer anderen Familie geschickt. Der Gastgeber geht mit ihm zum nächsten Haus. …

4. … Wenn es keine Kämpfe gibt, schlafen und essen die Männer den ganzen Tag. Das Haus und die Felder werden von den Frauen, Kindern und alten Männern versorgt. …

[1] Asia ['eɪʃə, 'eɪʒə] [2] Africa ['æfrɪkə] [3] host [həʊst]

9 A mixed bag

Look at each sentence and decide what you need to complete it. In some sentences there is more than one possible answer.

1. Have you … your pencil-case, Mike? – Yes, it was under … desk here.
2. Can you spell … words, Susan? – I … so. I practised for half … hour yesterday.
3. Wales is famous for its countryside, coal and sheep, but it is even … for its singers and choirs.
4. I haven't been to London … last January.
5. I had a … headache yesterday and my throat ached … . I couldn't speak … because it hurt so … .

Just for fun

Tracy, John, Helen, Sue, Stuart and Elaine all left London and went on holiday this summer. Their friend Tom got postcards from the USA, from Australia, from Spain, from Blackpool, from Greece and from Iceland. Not one of the postcards had a name on it.
Can you say which of his friends went where?
Here are some clues:
Tracy and Elaine didn't have a holiday in a European country. – Only Helen had to pack warm clothes. – Tracy crossed the equator. – Sue only took a train to go on holiday. – Stuart flew to Athens airport.

equator [ɪ'kweɪtə] Äquator

Words Words Words

a Looking for bigger friends

Here are some "little friends" who are looking for "bigger friends". Choose the "bigger friends" from the second list and write them next to the "little friends" in your exercise-book.

Little friends

bag	cold	hurt	smile	teenager
big	country	important	snack	village
bungalow	girl	lake	speak	walk
café	group	nice	stone	warm
car	hill	road	story	windy

Bigger friends

ADULT BEAUTIFUL BUS CONTINENT HOT HOUSE HUGE
ICY KILL LAUGH LEGEND MEAL MOTORWAY MOUNTAIN
ORGANIZATION RESTAURANT ROCK RUN SEA SHOUT
STORMY SUITCASE TOWN URGENT WOMAN

b Trouble spot   of mine, of yours, of his, of hers, of ours, of theirs

Compare: Jeff is **my friend**. = I've got a friend. His name is Jeff.

Jeff is **one of my friends**.
Or: Jeff is **a friend of mine**. (⚠ *not:* ~~of me~~) = I've got several friends. Jeff is one of them.

Use 'of mine', 'of yours', etc. to change the following sentences.

1. One of my cousins has been to Kansas. 2. When Helen needed help, she called one of her friends. 3. Jessica's brother is going to meet some of his friends tonight. 4. Is Mrs Bailey one of your teachers? 5. I want to meet two of my classmates. 6. Does Dominic know Mrs Black? – Yes, she's one of his relatives. 7. We haven't been to the United States. But some of our friends were there on an exchange visit last year. 8. John doesn't know much about computers. But one of his friends is a computer expert.

c Word builder's corner   Words with prefixes and suffixes

Prefixes		Stems				Suffixes		
dis-	inter-	advantage	formal	nation	read	-able	-ful	-ly
im-	un-	arrive	friend	organize	sun	-al	-ing	-ment
in-		begin	home	polite	tidy	-ation	-ity	-ness
		develop	invite	possible	use	-er	-less	-y

1. *Add a prefix or a suffix (or both) to the stems. How many words can you make? You should only make words you have read or heard. You can use a dictionary to check your answers.*

   Example: **nation** – nation**al** < nation**al**ity / **inter**national

   Remember to make the necessary spelling changes with words such as 'arrive' or 'begin'.

2. When you add a suffix to a stem to make a new word, the new word belongs to a different word class: When you add *-ity* to the adjective *national*, you get the noun *nationality*. That's why syllables like *-ity* are called noun suffixes.
   Now look at the words you have made and put the suffixes into groups of noun suffixes, adjective suffixes and adverb suffixes.

The story of St Alban

Think of what you have learned in your history lessons about the Roman Empire.
- What do you think of when you hear the name "Emperor Constantine" and the date "315 AD"?
- How did this date change life for a lot of people in the Roman Empire?
- What do you know about St Alban, from this unit of the book or from other books?

During the first and second centuries neither the Romans nor the British were Christians. In Verulamium, for example, the Romans and the British each worshipped their own gods. And in other parts of the Empire, the Romans accepted all the different religions. But with Christianity it was different. The Romans persecuted all the men and women who followed this religion, not only in Rome, but all over their Empire. Roman soldiers were ordered to find Christians, kill them and burn their churches.

One day in the year 209, a Welsh priest arrived in Verulamium along Watling Street, the Roman road from London to Chester. His name was Amphibalus. He was a Christian and he was hiding from Roman soldiers. While he was in Verulamium, he met a young man called Alban. Alban was British. He was not a Christian, but he knew about Christ and the new religion that priests were trying to bring to people. Alban was a kind man and he decided to give the Welsh priest food and a bed in his house.
Although Amphibalus was always in great danger, the priest loved God so much that every day and night he prayed and sang. Alban was so interested in this new religion that he wanted to learn more about it. Night after night they sat in Alban's house and Amphibalus taught Alban about Christianity. Finally Alban decided to become a Christian.
Amphibalus lived with Alban for some time but soon stories reached the Romans that a Christian priest was hiding in Alban's house, and some soldiers were sent to look for him. They came down the narrow streets towards Alban's house. As soon as Alban noticed that Roman soldiers were outside his house, he knew that Amphibalus was in great danger. Alban decided to save the priest's life.
"Give me your cloak quickly," he said. "And do everything that I tell you. After I have left the house, wait for a moment and then when you think it is safe, leave Verulamium."
"What are you going to do?" asked the priest. But Alban didn't answer. He put on the priest's cloak, opened the door and ran out of the house along the dark streets. The soldiers ran after him at once. They followed him until they caught him. The real priest, Amphibalus, could escape.

The soldiers took Alban to a Roman judge. The judge was worshipping his gods when Alban was brought to him. The judge soon realized that this was the wrong person who was standing before him. He became very angry and ordered Alban to worship the Roman gods or he must accept Amphibalus's punishment. Alban refused and said, "I am a Christian." Then the judge looked at Alban and asked him his name. Alban said, "I am Alban. I worship the true God who created all things." Again the judge ordered Alban to give up his Christian religion. But Alban refused. He ordered Alban to kill an animal and offer it to the Roman gods, but still he refused. So the Roman soldiers were ordered to take him away and execute him.

It was the custom in those days that Christians were killed by gladiators or wild animals. But this was not possible with Alban. He was rich and what was more important: although he was British, he was also a Roman citizen.
On June 22nd in the year 209 Roman soldiers took Alban out of Verulamium to a hill half a mile from the city walls. The hill was on the other side of the river Ver, and to get there Alban and the soldiers had to cross a bridge. Stories say that so many people followed Alban from the town that they could not all cross the bridge over the river. Alban stopped, looked up to the sky and prayed that a way could be made across the water. Suddenly, the river went dry, and they could all cross to the other side. When the executioner saw this, he was so frightened that he threw his sword on the ground. He wanted to die instead of Alban or with him. The sword lay on the ground for a long time before one of the soldiers picked it up.
From the river Alban walked to the top of the hill. It was a beautiful day in early summer and the ground was covered with flowers of many different colours. Alban asked God for some water and a fountain suddenly came up from the ground.
Then Alban was executed, together with the soldier who threw his sword on the ground. And so Alban became the first Christian martyr who died for his religion in Britain. But the man who executed him was punished. As Alban's head fell off, the executioner's eyes fell from his head and onto the grass.
When the judge saw what happened, he was so surprised that he stopped persecuting Christians. In fact, after Alban's death the Romans never persecuted Christians in Britain again, and the site of Alban's execution became a place that Christians remembered. First they built a small wooden church. Today the cathedral stands on that hill.

In the year 410 the Roman army left Britain to fight in other parts of the Empire. After 350 years the British were suddenly alone. And they could not defend their island against the Angles and Saxons who started to invade the country along the east and southeast coasts.
The Saxons did not live in the Roman towns and over the years these slowly fell into ruin. But when the Saxons became Christians, they, too, remembered Alban. They built a new larger church on the site where Alban died. And while Verulamium stood empty, a new town grew round the hill where St Alban was once executed. The name of that town became St Albans.

Working with the text

1 Retelling the story

Try to retell the story of St Alban in two parts with the help of the following notes. If possible, don't look at the text. You can start like this: Alban was British, but he was also a Roman citizen. One day in the year 209 …

1. met Amphibalus / Amphibalus – Christian / Alban – interested in – new religion – became Christian / helped Amphibalus – escape – Roman soldiers / caught – taken to – Roman judge
2. Alban – refused – give up – Christian religion – executed / on the way – place of the execution – had to cross – river / Alban – prayed – river – dry / top of the hill / executed / executioner's eyes / judge – stopped persecuting / wooden church / later – cathedral

2 Beyond the text

a Perhaps you have heard about other legends, not just Christian legends. If you haven't, try to find out about some. Retell some legends in a few sentences and compare them with the legend of St Alban. How are they similar?

b Try to tell the history of the St Albans area from the information you get in this unit. Talk about the time before AD 43, the time up to AD 410, the time after AD 410 and the present.

3 Writing an article for a newspaper

a You may know that our modern newspapers really only started in the 19th century. But let's forget about that and imagine that about 1800 years ago you were writing for **THE VERULAMIUM TIMES**. It is your job, perhaps in group work, to write an article about the execution of St Alban for the newspaper of June 23rd, 209.
Perhaps you can even use a computer to produce the first page of your newspaper.

Here is some help for you:

- Find a title and a sub-title for your article.
- Write an introductory sentence with the following prompts: yesterday afternoon – young man – Alban – execute – Roman soldiers – hill outside Verulamium
- Report in more detail what happened on the way to the place of the execution and what happened to the executioner.
- You could also have a picture of one scene of the event as part of your article.

b A suggestion for a second article: Perhaps some of you could write an article in which you express your opinion on the event. You could, for example, support what the Romans did, or you could say that they did something wrong. But please don't forget to give reasons for your opinion. (You can also write a *Letter to the Newspaper* in which you express how you feel about Alban and what happened to him.)

Listening comprehension **Aquae Sulis**

"Before the Romans came to Britain, the Celts knew a place in the south of the country near a large river which for them was very mysterious. The land round this place was wet, smoke came up from the ground, and in the coldest times of the year the water that came from the ground was hot. ..."

The text on the tape tells you more about this place. But before you listen to the tape, have a look at the following pictures and try to say what the text might be about.

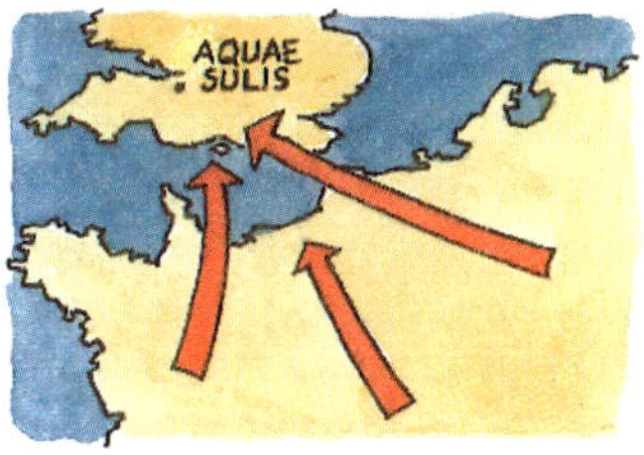

- Now listen to the tape and find out what exactly the six pictures show.
- Then listen a second or third time and make notes about other information which you get about "Aquae Sulis".
- Compare notes with other pupils and then say in a few sentences what you know about the place.

February 14th, Valentine's Day

I love you!

February 14th is Valentine's Day. On this day people send cards, little presents or flowers to somebody they love. They do not write their names on the cards, so the person has to guess who sent them. Sometimes the cards have funny rhymes.

> Make a Valentine card for somebody you like very much – and send it!

April Fool!

April 1st is April Fool's Day. People play tricks on their friends on this day. Even the newspapers and television have their April Fool's joke. It can be great fun to find the article or programme that looks serious – but isn't!
But in Britain you must not play tricks on people after 12 o'clock.

> What happens in Germany on April 1st?
> Have you ever played an April Fool's trick on anybody? What was it?
> Can you think of a good trick? Tell the class about it.

April 1st, April Fool's Day

October 31st, Halloween

Ghosts and witches

October 31st is Halloween. But it is not a Christian festival. It goes back to Celtic times, when the end of summer and the beginning of winter was celebrated. People believed that on this night dead people came back to the places where they once lived. In the evening young people have Halloween parties. The girls put on witches' clothes and the boys come as ghosts or monsters. In many places young people go to a house and ask 'Trick or treat?'. You can choose to give them a 'treat' (sweets or money) and they will go away, or you can choose to give them nothing – and they will play a trick on you. They might, for example, make a lot of noise outside your house.

Penny for the guy

November 5th is Guy Fawkes Night. All over the country people make bonfires and burn a figure of Guy Fawkes. This custom goes back to a historical event. On this day in 1605 a man who was called Guy Fawkes tried to blow up the King of England in the Houses of Parliament. But he was caught and later executed in the Tower of London. About a week before Guy Fawkes Night, children make their 'guy' from old clothes and newspapers. Then they carry their guy through the town and ask people for a "penny for the guy". They collect the money for fireworks. Fireworks are an important part of Guy Fawkes Night.

November 5th, Guy Fawkes Night

December 25th, Christmas Day

Merry Christmas ...

Christmas time starts early in Britain. In the weeks before Christmas, people send cards to everybody they know, and when they get cards, they hang them on all the walls. British people put up their Christmas trees many days before the real holiday, Christmas Day.
Father Christmas, or Santa Claus, brings his presents late on Christmas Eve. He usually comes down the chimney and the children find their presents in the morning. Christmas dinner with turkey and Christmas pudding is the main meal of the holiday.

... and a Happy New Year!

There are no fireworks on New Year's Eve, but Christmas and especially New Year are a time for parties. In Scotland, New Year's Eve is called Hogmanay. It is the most important holiday in the year for many Scots. In Scotland and parts of northern England, a tall man with dark hair must be the first person who comes into the house after midnight on New Year's Eve. He must carry a piece of coal in his hands. Then the people in the house will be lucky all year.

December 31st, New Year's Eve

How is Christmas different in Germany?
What happens in your family on New Year's Eve?

Work in groups and describe a custom in your part of Germany. Perhaps these words will help you:
Umzug – procession [prə'seʃn] · *Maske* – mask · *Kostüm* – costume ['kɒstju:m] · *Kirmes, Rummel* – fair · *Wein-, Bierfest* – wine/beer festival · *(Musik-)Kapelle* – band

So far you have learned quite a lot about Britain, British teenagers and their way of life. In the following units you will get to know something about the USA and about some teenagers from two places in the USA – where they live, their way of life, the kinds of schools they go to and how they spend their free time.

- What do you think of when you hear the word "America" – the American flag (the "Stars and Stripes"), the Statue of Liberty, …?
- Choose two or three famous Americans or places in the USA and tell the class what you know about them. Write down a few notes first.

Project Make a collage with pictures that in your opinion are typically American.
Explain your collage to the class.

→ Spotlight on history (p.144)

British English and American English

American English is quite different from British English, although they are two varieties of the same language. What you will notice first when you listen to Americans is their accent because it is different from a British accent.
When Janet Fisher was in Wales, she noticed that there are many different British accents. It's similar in the United States. A person from New York has an "American" accent, of course, but he or she also has a different accent from a person from California.

Listen to the cassette and try to say who you think is American and who is British.

American English pronunciation

Americans pronounce a lot of English words differently. Here are some examples of differences between AE and BE.

BE		AE
[t]	city, better	[d]
[ɑː]	ask, dance, last	[æ]
[juː]	new, Tuesday, stupid	[uː]
[ɒ]	bottle, hot, everybody	[ɑː]
[ɪə], [ɔː], [ɜː], [ɑː]	here, more, shirt, farm	[ɪər], [ɔːr], [ɜːr], [ɑːr]

American English spelling

Here are some words you already know, but they are spelled the American way.

favorite	color	traveled	center	catalog	neighbor	mom
theater	dialog	traveler	harbor	kilometer	pajamas	humor

What is the British English spelling? Write the words down in your vocabulary book and arrange them like this:

AE: '-or'	BE: '-our'	AE: '-er'	BE: '-re'	others: AE	BE
...	...	...	...	...	...

American English vocabulary

What can be confusing is that Americans have different words for a number of things. The British talk of 'petrol', while Americans say 'gas'. Instead of a 'caravan' Americans talk of a 'trailer'. The British have 'autumn' after summer and the Americans have 'fall'. Read these sentences and find out from the context what the BE words are for the underlined AE words.

1. Tom and Alice have a very nice apartment in New York.
2. I saw a great movie on TV last night.
3. Several students in Kenny's class are learning German.
4. I'd like to have French fries with my hamburger.
5. Take the subway to Times Square. It's quicker than a taxi.
6. We all went to Florida for our summer vacation. Disney World was great.

film
pupils
holidays
flat
chips
underground

In the vocabulary (p. 195) you will find short lists of words that are different in AE and BE. It is a tradition in German schools to teach BE. That's why we have used BE so far. However, in authentic American texts and when Americans write or speak in this book, AE vocabulary and spelling are used. And the speakers on the cassette speak, of course, with their own American accent.

Unit 7 Golden Kansas

- What impression of Kansas do you get from the two photos, the map and the statistics?
- What other information does the text give you?

Kansas – size: c 212,000 sq km
– population: 2.5 million
Germany – size: c 357,000 sq km
– population: 79 million

Kansas is often called the "wheat state" or the "breadbasket of the nation". Much of the land is flat and covered with wheatfields and cornfields. From the middle of June to the middle of July it looks like a huge sea of gold. However, the state has little water – something that was a problem for the early farmers. Most of the lakes today are man-made.

The state takes its name from the *Kansa* or *Kaw* Indians who once lived in this region. The word 'Kansas' means *people of the south wind.*

Western Kansas is part of the Great Plains, where the buffalo lived and where the Indians hunted them.

Settlers who wanted to move west to California came through Kansas and from there they continued their long journeys along one of the famous wagon trails such as the Santa Fe Trail.

One of the most famous cities in Kansas is Dodge City, the "Cowboy City of the World". During the days of the "Wild West" it was the largest cattle market in the world. Today this old cowboy town is popular with tourists. Other cow towns in Kansas are Abilene and Wichita.

What else do you know about the settlers who moved west, about Indians and about cowboys?

"Hi, welcome to Kansas …"

Janet's parents own a farm about 30 minutes from the small town of Tonganoxie. They grow mostly wheat and corn on their farm. The really huge farms are further west. There all you can see are wheatfields for miles and miles and miles. Your nearest neighbour can be over ten miles away.

Janet and her brother Tommy go to high school in Tonganoxie. School starts at 8 o'clock, so they **must get up** early every morning. Sometimes they **must help** their parents with the animals before they have breakfast.

"Then we **have to wait** for the school bus. The bus drives around most of the small towns and farms and picks up all the students. We're lucky. We **don't have to travel** far. Some of the kids are on the bus for almost an hour each way. …

"… Of course, as soon as I got on the bus after my vacation in Britain **I had to tell** everybody about my trip. I **had to describe** every place I visited."

You know from last year what the modal auxiliary 'must' and the full verb 'have to' are in German.
Look at the sentences with 'have to':
They show you how you form positive statements in the simple present and the simple past. They also show you how you form negative statements in the simple present.
Try to say how you form negative statements in the simple past and how you form questions in the simple present and the simple past.
There are also two sentences with 'must'. Can you remember what you learned about 'must' last year? What can't you do with 'must'? What is *nicht müssen/brauchen* in English? What is 'mustn't' in German?

Ex 1 *Which tense of 'have to': simple present, simple past, present perfect or will-future?*

1. I … get up at 6 o'clock every day from Monday to Friday. 2. On Saturdays and Sundays I … (not) get up so early. 3. I … get up at 6 o'clock since my 15th birthday. 4. I … get up early for the rest of my life on the farm. 5. Before I was 15, I … (not) get up so early. 6. Sometimes Tommy is really fed up because he … get up at 6 o'clock.

Ex 2 *'have to' plus active infinitive ('pick up') or passive infinitive ('be picked up')?*

1. Some students have to … from school by their parents. There is no bus to their farm. 2. Not many parents have to … their kids. 3. Scott didn't have to … by his parents yesterday. 4. Don't forget, Mom, you'll have to … Tommy and me tomorrow. 5. I didn't feel well. I had to … from school yesterday.

Ex 3 *Here are some sentences that only give or ask for facts. Now you want to say what is/was/will be necessary.*

Example: Our animals *are fed* twice a day. → Our animals *have to be fed* twice a day.

1. This morning Tommy *fed* them, and I'*ll feed* them tonight. 2. I *got* a job at the Pizza Palace last year. 3. *Did* you *get* a part-time job when you were a pupil? 4. My parents *work* twelve or more hours a day and we *help* them. 5. On most small farms everything *is done* by the family members.

→ Grammar 7: 1, 2 (p.158-159) → Exercise 1

Scenes from an American teenager's life

While you are reading the text and looking at the pictures on these two pages, make notes about
- an average day for Janet
- Tonganoxie High School
- the role of sports in American high schools.

Info box Janet, her brother and most of her friends go to Tonganoxie High School. An American high school is similar to a German *Gesamtschule*. Most students usually go to the same high school in the neighbourhood.

MONDAY
Pizza Palace (4 p.m. - 7 p.m.)
Visit Jody on the way home

TUESDAY
Drama Club (3 p.m. - 5 p.m.)
Meet Jerry, Tom and Kenny in Dino's Ice-Cream Parlor

WEDNESDAY
Cheerleader practice (3 p.m. - 4:30 p.m.)
Meet Scott (5 p.m. in the Ice-Cream Parlor)

THURSDAY
Pizza Palace (4 p.m. - 7 p.m.)

FRIDAY
Cheerleader practice (5 p.m. - 6 p.m.)
School basketball game (6:30 p.m.)

SATURDAY
Tennis with Scott (10 a.m.)
Pizza Palace (4 p.m. - 7 p.m.)
Miranda's party (8 p.m.)

SUNDAY
Church

"My school day starts at eight o'clock in the morning and finishes at three. During the week I often stay at school for an hour or two after classes. At most American high schools there is a huge choice of sports, clubs and activities such as music or drama. We also have regular school dances and parties.

"In Kansas a lot of students drive to school as you can get a driver's license when you are 16. It's not unusual to see students arrive at school in their own cars. There are sometimes more students' cars in the parking lot than teachers'.

...

"... On three days a week I work at a restaurant in town. Nearly all my friends have part-time jobs. After that I sometimes meet some of my friends, so it can be late before I finally get home to do my homework."

"Sports are very important in American schools, especially football and basketball. The students who are chosen for the school teams are very popular. Games between two schools are big events. There's usually one every Friday night. Everybody comes to watch them: students, teachers, parents – even people from the town. Reports about the games and star players – girls and boys – appear in the local newspapers. The school band plays fight songs and the cheerleaders make sure there's a really good atmosphere. The people have a great time and really enjoy themselves.

"My brother Tommy is a basketball player. I myself am one of the cheerleaders. Cheerleaders are a group of students. They wear uniforms with the school colors. At Tonganoxie High they are black and white. Cheerleaders appear before every game. It is their job to make sure the crowd is excited and cheering wildly. But first, before the game starts, everybody stands and sings the national anthem. Then the cheerleaders dance and lead the cheering during the game.

"When I have some free time – that is after school, after clubs, after sports and work – I visit my friends at their houses. We often meet in "Dino's Ice-Cream Parlor" in town, where we sit and talk, or we go for a ride in somebody's car. A lot of my friends have their own cars. (That's why they all have jobs – to pay for them!) We go cruising. That means we don't drive anywhere special."

Use your notes to make a network in which you combine the three aspects from the box at the top of p.100. Compare your life to Janet's. Would you like to change places with her?

→ Exercises 2, 3 → Listening comprehension, p.109

Focus on GRAMMAR Modal auxiliaries II

As with German *können*, it is possible to use the modal auxiliary 'can' to express different things:

- to ask for permission[1], give permission or to say that somebody has or doesn't have permission to do something.
- to say that somebody has or doesn't have the ability[2] to do something.

Look at the following two short dialogues and decide how 'can' is used in each sentence.

[1] permission [pə'mɪʃn] *Erlaubnis*
[2] ability [ə'bɪlətɪ] *Fähigkeit*

"Mom, **can** I go to the ice-cream parlor tonight and tomorrow night?"

"Sorry, Janet, you **can't** go out tonight. I **can't** feed the animals for you because I'm going to Aunt Susan's. Tomorrow evening is no problem. You **can** go out with Scott tomorrow."

"How is your knee, Tommy? **Can** you walk properly again or does it still hurt?"

"I **can** walk without any problems, but I **can't** play this week. I'd like to see the game, however."

"No problem. Mom is taking me in her car. You **can** come with us."

You already know that it is not possible to make all the tenses with modal auxiliaries. There are, however, other verbs to talk about 'permission' or 'ability'. It is possible to use these for all the tenses.
The following sentences show you two of these verbs. Read all the sentences and then

- decide which of the sentences express 'permission' and which of them express 'ability'?
- find out the infinitive of the verb that is used for 'permission' and the infinitive of the verb that is used for 'ability'.

My sister didn't need her walkman, so I **was allowed to** use it.
Because I had her walkman, I **was able to** listen to some tapes on the trip to New York.

Tony has had an argument with his parents. Do you think he**'ll be allowed to** come to my party?
I've got to babysit tonight, so I **won't be able to** come to your party.
Let me look at your English homework. Perhaps I**'ll be able to** help you.

I never have enough time. I **haven't been able to** talk to Scott for weeks.
Tom always gets what he wants. He **has been allowed to** leave school early.
My parents don't like discos. That's why I**'ve** never **been allowed to** go to a disco.

Ex **"A lucky teenager"**

"Make up" a teenager who is allowed to do things which most teenagers aren't allowed to do. Write a short text about her/him. Say what "your" teenager is allowed to do, how long she/he has been allowed to do these things and what she/he will be allowed to do in the future.

"Superman or Superwoman"

Write a text about a "superperson". Say what "your super-person" is able to do, how long she/he has been able to do these things and what you think she/he will be able to do one day.

L

→ Grammar 7: 3 (p.159) → Exercises 4-6

1 Jobs – as children, as teenagers or as adults *Practise 'have to'.*

a *What jobs did you have to do when you were a child? What jobs do you have to do now as a teenager? What jobs do you think you will have to do in the future?*

When I was … years old, I had to … . Now I have to … .
I suppose soon I'll have to …

fetch the newspaper –
dry the dishes –
help in the garden –
…

b *And here is something for all those who have brothers or sisters.*

I always have to …
… never has to …

Yesterday I had to …
… didn't have to …

… will have to …
I'm sure … will never have to …

c *Write a dialogue with your mother or father in which you complain about your brother or sister. – But don't be too hard on them, please.*

2 Who is to blame? (The *-self* pronoun)

The Tonganoxie High School football team usually wins its games. But when they lost some time ago this is what you could hear …

You shouldn't blame one person. You should all blame **yourselves**.

Why should I blame **myself**? I played as well as I could. Nobody can blame me.

Why should we blame **ourselves**? The better team won. We shouldn't blame anybody.

myself
yourself
himself
herself
itself
ourselves
yourselves
themselves

Look at the six sentences with 'blame'. Decide which of the two diagrams might belong to which of the sentences.

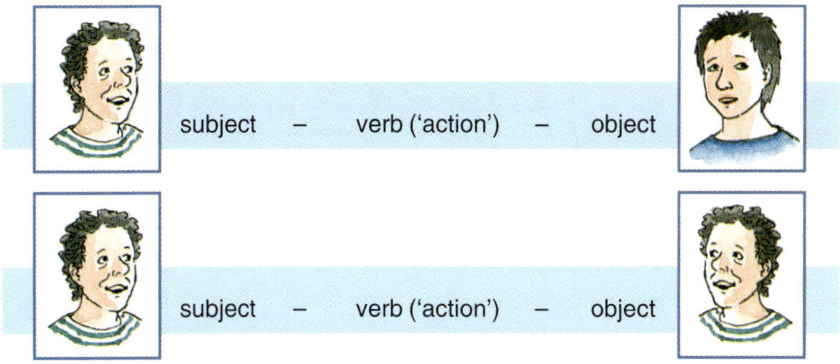

→ Grammar 7: 4a (p.160)

Collect verbs and then see if you can use them with a reflexive pronoun.

Here are some examples: cut – write – eat – look after – give – cook – run – …

I suppose you can cut bread, and you can also cut yourself. – You can write letters to other people. Why shouldn't I write a letter to myself? – *What about 'eat'? …*

Now use the right reflexive pronoun in these sentences:

1. Be careful, or you will cut … . 2. I'm so angry with … . 3. Let's put the camera on a wall and take a photo of … . 4. They fetched some pizza for … . 5. Tom has hurt … . 6. Our cat cleaned … in the bathroom.

3 Cheerleaders (More about the *-self* pronoun)

1. When I saw **myself** on the video of our cheerleader practice, I had to laugh. I don't know why everybody likes it so much. I **myself** don't think we were so good on that day.

2. Janet asked me to make a copy of the video for Scott. Why can't he make a copy for **himself**? He has two VCRs **himself**.

You already know that the *-self* pronoun can be used as an object.
Look at the two short texts and find out which of the *-self* pronouns is used as an object.
What about the other pronouns in bold print? Read the sentences aloud and try to find out what the function of the *-self* pronouns is in these sentences.
Now translate the four sentences with *-self* pronouns. What are they in German? → Grammar 7: 4b (p.160)

Now do these short dialogues with a partner.

Example: Who wrote that article for you? – Nobody, I wrote it myself.

1. Who gave you my new CD? – You … gave it to me. 2. Who bought you two those ice-creams? – Nobody, we bought them … . 3. Did Janet's mother make those trousers for Janet? – No, Janet … . 4. Why didn't you feed the animals for Tommy? – He … . 5. Did you make the pizzas for the basketball team? – No, they … . 6. Can you ask Tommy to take me to the dance? – Why don't you … ? 7. Scott is waiting for a phone call from Janet. – How silly! Why doesn't he … . 8. Mr Weizel is going to pick Sue up. – Oh, but I … .

4 It's unfair.

Practise 'be allowed to' in different tenses.

I think it's unfair. I'm 17, three years older than my sister Becky. My brother Ryan is one year younger than me. When I was 14, I … (not) go out all the time in the evening. Becky is 14 now, and she … go out when she wants – Ryan, too.
Of course I … go out now, but there is a problem: I can't often go out alone. Becky and Ryan always want to go with me.
I really think younger brothers and sisters are lucky. They … (often) do things that an older sister … (not) do when she was younger.
Sometimes I have a terrible dream: In a year or two Becky and Ryan … do things that I … (not) do although I'm older.

5 Upside down

Practise 'have to' and 'be allowed to'.

a Imagine a school in which everything is upside down. Pupils **are allowed to** or even **have to** do all the things that pupils **aren't allowed to** do in a normal school.
Write a letter to a friend in which you tell her/him what this school is like.

b You could, of course, also have an upside down family. What do you think life is like for parents and children in such a family?

6 In English, please. Questions with 'have to', 'be allowed to' and 'be able to'

In some of the questions you will be able to use more than one of these verbs.

1. Wann dürfen junge Amerikaner und Amerikanerinnen ihren Führerschein machen? 2. Wie schnell darf man in Amerika fahren? 3. Wie viele Stunden pro Tag müssen amerikanische Schüler und Schülerinnen in der Schule bleiben? 4. Warum mußten die Landwirte in Kansas Seen anlegen? 5. Warum konnten die meisten Siedler nicht alleine nach Westen ziehen? 6. Warum durften die Indianer ihr Land nicht behalten? 7. Wie lange kannst du schon Auto fahren? 8. Seit wann hast du auf der Farm deiner Eltern schon helfen müssen? 9. In welche Schule mußt du nächstes Jahr gehen? 10. Welche Spieler können nächstes Jahr noch in eurer Basketballmannschaft spielen?

R **7 The USA – a country of people's dreams** Comparisons of adjectives and adverbs

Amerika, Du hast es besser
Als unser Kontinent, der alte …

I really don't think Goethe was right. But today some people still believe that Americans have a *better* life *than* people in the rest of the world. What's your opinion?

a I think/I don't think …

1. … Americans make … cars in the world. (large) 2. … American cars are … German cars. (comfortable) 3. … roads in Germany are … in the USA. (bad) 4. … Americans drive … Germans. (slowly) 5. … American food tastes … German food. (good) 6. … Americans go on holiday … other people. (often) 7. … Americans are … sports … Germans. (interested in)

b *What other ideas do people have when they compare the USA with Germany?*

8 Germany and America

a The name "America" *Read the text and then complete it with the right tenses.*

Martin Waldseemüller (be) a German who (live) from about 1470 to 1520. He (be) a teacher, but he also (make) maps. In 1507 he (use) the name of a famous Italian, Amerigo Vespucci, and (make) up the name "America". – Vespucci (go) on three trips to the New World about 1500. – Waldseemüller (write) the name "America" on one of his maps for what (be) today South America. Later "America" (become) the name for the "New World".

b Text production: The first Germans in America

Look at these prompts and then write a text about the first group of Germans in America.

Franz Daniel Pastorius – 1651-1720 / at that time – many people – hard life – Germany – and – not really free / 1683 – he able to take the first group of Germans – America / sail – thirteen families – come from – Krefeld area / after 75 days – America / now – allowed to be free – New World / name of their new home – Germantown / there – one thing – not like – in America / there – people – have slaves / people of Germantown – one of the first groups – speak against slave-owners

Words Words Words

a Trouble spot One word in German – two words in English

German: **"nächster"** English: 1. **nearest** = nächst(gelegener) *(fast nur örtlich)*
2. **next** = nächst(folgender) *(örtlich und zeitlich)*

Example: The *nearest* bank is in the *next* street on the left.

1. Who would like to do the … sentence? 2. Do we have to change at the … bus stop? 3. Excuse me, where's the … post office? 4. When's the … train to Dover, please? 5. This is a very lonely place. Our … neighbours live a mile away. 5. Take the … road, it's the … to the station. 7. After the accident the girl was taken to the … hospital. 8. Where will you be during the … few weeks?

German: **"letzter"** English: 1. **latest** = letzter/neuester
2. **last** = a) (aller)letzter; b) voriger

Example: I like Donna Winter's *latest* CD very much. I hope it won't be her *last*.

1. 'Z' is the … letter of the alphabet. 2. How do you like Steven Spielberg's … film? – It's much better than his … film. 3. You must work harder. This is the … time that I'm going to tell you. 4. Is that your … word? 5. My friend has got the … music video by UFO. 6. Have you heard the … news about the accident? 7. When did you see Jane the … time? 8. This computer is the … model we've got.

German: **"weiter"** English: 1. **farther/further** = weiter (entfernt)
2. **further** = weiter, zusätzlich, noch

Examples: I'm so tired. I can't walk much *farther/further*. Have you got any *further* questions?

1. Let's hope there'll be no … problems. 2. I think there's a cinema … down the street. 3. For … information please write to our tourist centre. 4. Are you sure you won't need any … help? 5. Aberdeen is … away from London than Edinburgh. 6. We haven't walked far today. We walked much … yesterday. 7. It was … than we thought. 8. I have nothing … to say.

b Word builder's corner Abstract nouns that end in '-ness'

You can often add **-ness** to an adjective to make an abstract noun.

	English: **-ness**	German **-heit**	**-keit**	**others**
Examples:	ill + **-ness** = ill**ness**	Krank**heit**		
	lonely + **-ness** = loneli**ness**		Einsam**keit**	
	nervous + **-ness** = nervous**ness**			Nervosität

1. *Here are some more adjectives like these. Add them to the list.*

clever fit friendly happy
polite sick silly impolite weak
tidy unfair unfriendly

2. *Now change the adjectives in the following sentences into "-ness nouns". Remember that you will also have to change other parts of the sentence or even the word order.*

Example: How do you explain the fact that he was so *silly*?
How do you explain his *silliness*?

1. Kate is seriously *ill*. 2. I can understand that he is *bitter*. 3. It always helps to be *polite*. 4. It makes me very angry that he is so *lazy*. 5. You can't see when it's *dark*. 6. I don't know the reason why he is so *tired*.

The star player

- What do you think of when you hear the word "star"?
- Why do you think some people admire stars and others dislike them strongly?
- Where do you see the problems of young people who have become stars?
- Read the text to find out what happened to Tommy Fisher, the star player of the Tonganoxie Tigers.

"We, we will succeed!
We've got the power, the power we need!"
"We, we will succeed!
We've got the power, the power we need!"

It was Friday night and the crowd in the Tonganoxie High School gym was shouting and cheering wildly for their basketball team, the Tigers. Janet and her team of cheerleaders were dancing and leading the cheering, while the band was playing as loudly as it could. The atmosphere was really exciting. "Come on, Tigers," shouted Mr Fisher. "Just one more basket, pl-e-e-ease."

The Tigers *had* to win this game against St John's High School. There were only a few more seconds and the score was Tigers 91 : St John's 92 – and the Tigers had the ball. One more basket, and the game was theirs! As the Tigers players ran across the floor, Janet's eyes never left her brother Tommy. Tommy was the star player in the Tonganoxie team. He always made the most baskets.

The ball came to Tommy. He caught it, but at once there were St John's players round him. "Here, Tommy, here!" shouted Steve Hitchcock from a good position near the St John's basket. Tommy wasn't able to shoot, but he didn't pass the ball to Steve. Instead, he jumped high into the air and threw the ball. It hit the side of the basket and was caught by a St John's player. Two more seconds and the game was finished. The Tigers lost again, for the fourth time.

As soon as Sid Lawrence, the team coach, saw Tommy after the game he shouted at him, "How many times do I have to tell you, Tommy? The plan was that you should draw the St John's players away from the basket and then pass the ball to Eddie or Steve so that they could score. But you don't listen! You think only of yourself, never of the team." Tommy usually had a lot of respect for Mr Lawrence, but today he wasn't able to control himself.

"What are you talking about? I *am* this team! Without me this team would be nothing."

"Shut your big mouth, Tommy," said Steve, Tommy's greatest rival. "Why didn't you pass the ball?"

"Steve is right, Tommy," said Rick. "It's your fault that we lost today."

"Look, you guys, I took a chance. It was our only chance to make that basket. Don't you see that?"

"That's where you're wrong, Tommy," said Mr Lawrence. "Steve was in a much better position. Why didn't you pass the ball to him? You didn't even look at him – your eyes were only on the basket. Basketball is a team game, Tommy. When are you going to learn that?"

Tommy took his things and walked to the door. "OK," he said. "You all know better – I'm quitting. You're playing against Weston next week. Let's see how good you are without me. I'll be there when you lose." The door shut behind him.

The next day everybody knew that Tommy Fisher was no longer in the school basketball team.

Tommy was glad that the students and teachers were talking about him. He felt important. And he liked that.

"Who do these guys think they are?" he said one afternoon as he drove through Tonganoxie with Janet. "I can't wait till they play Weston. They have no chance."

"Don't be too sure," said Janet. "You're not the only player on the team."

"I'm the best," he said. "They won't be able to win without me."

They drove along the main street and Tommy parked outside the ice-cream parlor. Inside their friends were sitting at different tables, where they were laughing and talking about school.

"Hi," said Tommy, and everybody turned round as he came through the door. He sat down with Janet at an empty table. "You don't seriously think this team will get better without me? Weston will walk all over them. Just wait. They'll soon ask me to come back. They'll be on their knees after the second game."

Janet smiled at some of her friends. "Open your ears, Tommy. A lot of the kids are saying the same thing. You think the other players are only there to make sure you get the ball. Some even think Steve will make a much better captain. They say that with him as captain, it'll be a team and not a one-man show."

Tommy looked at her angrily. "Whose side are you on?"

"I'm not on anybody's side," she said. "The truth sometimes hurts."

"Come on, finish your drink. I'm going home. Mom wants the car back."

"Maybe I don't want to go," she said.

"Okay, then stay here."

He got up and started to leave but a girl at the next table said, "Hi, Tommy. Are you going to be at the dance tomorrow night?"

"Sure, Marcia," he said. "Who are you going with?"

"Oh, there are a couple of guys I could go with," she said. "I haven't decided."

"Why don't I help you to decide. You can go with me." Tommy took a chair and sat down next to her. Soon he was laughing and talking. Janet got up and went to another table where some friends from her class were sitting together.

It seemed at first that Tommy was right. The basketball team lost against Weston, and in the game after that they lost again. But the third game finished with the score Tonganoxie Tigers 74 : Benjamin Franklin High School 63. The Tigers won the fourth game, too. Steve Hitchcock, the new captain, was doing his job well. The whole team was now playing better with him as captain. Suddenly people were not talking about Tommy Fisher any more. He was once one of the most popular students at school. He had lots of girlfriends. He usually went to all the parties, but now the students were laughing and talking about parties he knew nothing about. Tommy no longer felt so confident. He also missed basketball – the game was more important to Tommy than everything else.

Everybody in Tonganoxie was happy that the basketball team appeared to be back in form again. Everybody except Tommy Fisher.

Then the team played – and won – again. This time the students decided to organize a dance to celebrate.

What should Tommy do now? He couldn't just go and celebrate with the others, and nobody offered to invite him. In the end he decided to ask Marcia. She always wanted to go out with him when he was captain. The next day, when all the other students went for lunch, he had a chance to talk to her. "Are you going to the dance at the weekend?" he asked.

"Sure," she said.

"We could go together." He smiled, the same old confident Tommy Fisher.

She looked up at him, thought for a second and said,

"I'm sorry, Tommy. I'd love to, but I've agreed to go with somebody." And she walked away.

Try to say in a few sentences what happened after the game against St John's and in the following weeks.

1 Working with the text

Why …? Try to answer these questions on the text. The phrases on the right can help you.

1. … is everybody so excited on the night of the game against St John's?
2. … doesn't Tommy pass the ball to Steve or Eddie?
3. … is Mr Lawrence so angry after the game?
4. … do Tommy and Janet sit down at an *empty* table in the ice-cream parlor?
5. … does Tommy want to leave the ice-cream parlor alone?
6. … does Tommy want to go to the dance with Marcia at the end of the story?

The text says …
Perhaps that means …
There are several reasons why …
Firstly, …; secondly …
The text doesn't say so directly, but …
I think it's hard to say why/what …

2 Say it in English: Some suggestions for role-plays

Look again at lines 33 to 64 on p.107. Then work in groups of four and role-play the situation. It is best to make cards on which each person writes what she/he has to say. When you have practised the situation several times, try to do the role-play without the cards.

Here are three more situations which you can develop as role-plays:
- How do you think the conversation between Sid Lawrence, Steve and Rick continued after the game?
- Imagine a situation at home at the Fishers' house. Both Mrs and Mr Fisher are trying to talk to Tommy over lunch about what happened and how he should behave.
- Because Tommy didn't have anybody to go to the dance with, he talked to his sister and asked her for advice.

Listening comprehension **Ridin' along in my automobile …**

Before you listen to the tape:
1. In Germany many young people, especially those who live in the country, buy their own car at the age of 18. Why do you think these young people buy a car? What do they use their car for?
2. Terry, a visitor to Tonganoxie, has only just arrived there. He is in a car with some friends. Why do you think they are all together in the car? – Write down your ideas with a partner.

Now look at the pictures, listen to the tape and find out …
1. who the people in the conversation are. 2. what they are doing. 3. what exactly "cruising" is.
4. what time of year it seems to be. 5. what a car means to Americans, young and old.

Some points to talk about:
1. What do you think of cars? 2. What do you think should be done to solve the problems caused by cars? 3. Many states in the USA have a 65 mph speed limit. Do you think it would be a good idea to have such a law in Germany, too?

At the post office

– Look at these pictures. Which do you think show an American post office, which a British post office?
– What is similar/different to a German post office?

Role play At a post office in Britain

Read this dialogue and then make up a similar dialogue for the situation at the bottom of the page.

Assistant: Can I help you?
Helen: Yes, please. I'd like to send a letter to Germany and one to the United States.
Assistant: Can you put them on the scales, please? Your letter to Germany is under 20 grams, so that's 24p. Do you want to send your letter to the United States by airmail?
Helen: Yes, please.
Assistant: That will cost 57p.
Helen: I'd also like a 24p stamp for this letter to London, please, and can you give me six 20p stamps for these postcards?
Assistant: That makes £ 2.25 altogether.
Helen: Thank you.

When Karen was at St David's, she wanted to send several postcards to her friends and relatives in Germany. At the post office she found out that postcards cost 20p.

Imagine you are Karen. Act the dialogue in the post office. You can also send a postcard to a pen-friend in the United States. L

Info box
- Letters in Britain can be sent first or second class. First class means they arrive the following day. Second class letters take longer.
- You can use your German *Postsparbuch* to get British money at some British post offices.
- Many smaller post offices in Britain sell cards, writing paper, newspapers and even food.

Making a phone call

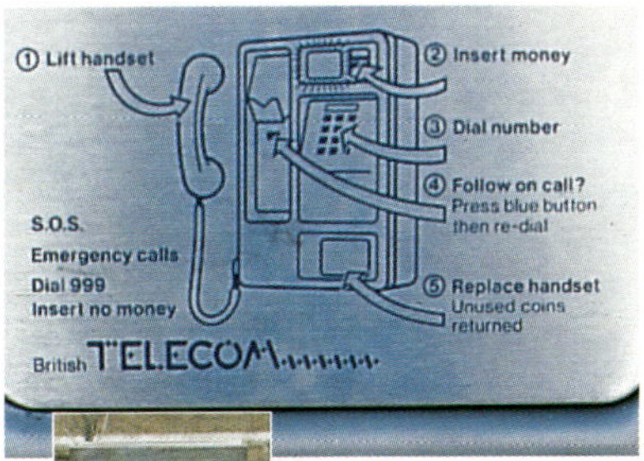

- Which of these things do you think are American and which are British?
- How do you make a call from the different telephones?
- Collect as many "telephone" words and expressions as you can and arrange them in a network.

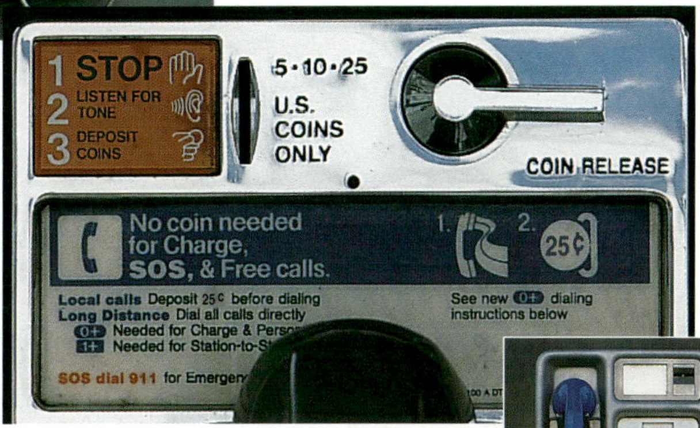

Info box

- In Britain you can buy a phonecard for a few pounds at a newsagent's, a post office or at a shop that has a phonecard sign, so you can phone easily without coins.
- In the USA you cannot make phone calls from post offices. You have to use a public phone. You'll need lots of coins, so make sure you have enough.

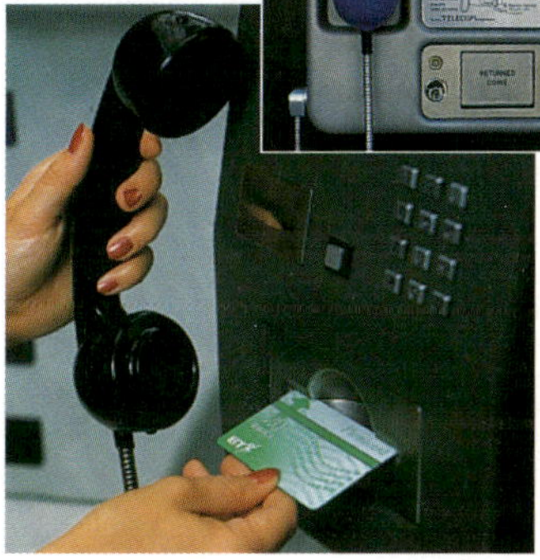

Terry is living in the United States for a year as an exchange student. He is staying with the Walden family and their son Joey.

Terry: Excuse me, Mrs Walden. May I use your phone to call my parents?

Mrs Walden: Sure, Terry. You know where it is.

Terry: Thanks. How will I know what the call costs?

Joey: You can call the operator and ask, or you can look at your watch and write down how many minutes you've used.

Mrs Walden: He doesn't need to do that. We get an itemized phone bill with the number and cost of each call.

Joey: Take my advice, keep an eye on your watch, or mom and dad will keep your pocket-money to pay for the phone bill.

Mr Walden: Do you know the dialing code for Britain?

Mrs Walden: It's 01144. And don't forget to drop the first zero from the number of your town.

Mr Walden: And don't listen to what Joey says.

Role play

Imagine you are staying with a family in Britain and you want to call your parents from their home.

You want to phone somebody in the USA. Find out the code for the United States and the city of your choice. Find out what the time difference is and the best time to phone.

Unit 8 San Francisco, CA

What do the photos tell you about San Francisco and California?
Read the texts on these two pages and find out what other information they give you about the pictures and California.
Would you like to live in San Francisco? Why/ Why not?

California's beautiful climate attracts a lot of people. The winter in some places can be as warm as a German summer. More than one in ten Americans (about 27 million) already live in California and it is the dream of many others to go and live there. One of the most interesting and most beautiful cities is San Francisco. It symbolizes the "Good Life". But the city, like the state, is not without its problems. L

California is sometimes called "earthquake country". In 1906 San Francisco was almost completely destroyed by the worst earthquake in its history and the fires that followed it. Almost 700 people died and over 300,000 lost their homes. There have been other earthquakes since then, and scientists believe another very bad earthquake could come soon, perhaps worse than the earthquake of 1906. Surprisingly, most San Franciscans are happy to live there. Children have "earthquake practice" at school and buildings have to be built in such a way that they can survive an earthquake.

→ Listening comprehension, p.124

San Francisco grew during the gold rush in 1848/49. A year earlier, in 1847, the population of San Francisco was exactly 479. Then a workman called James Marshall found a piece of gold in a river in the hills not far from San Francisco. His words "Something is shining" changed the history of the whole state. Seven years later San Francisco's population was 34,000 – and it has never stopped growing.

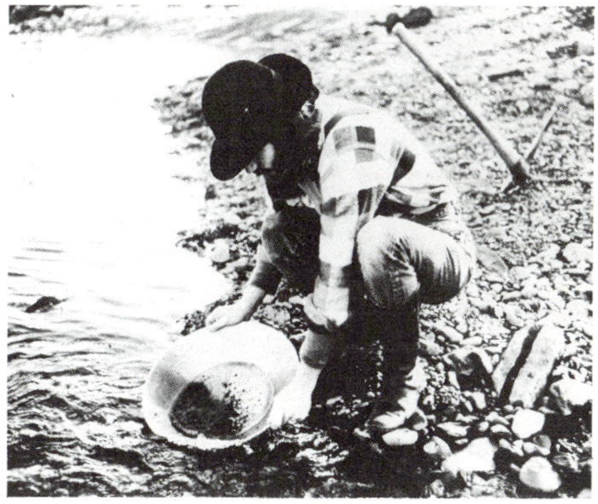

The Spanish were the first Europeans who settled in what is now California. That is why many towns have Spanish names today. Between 1769 and 1823 Spanish priests built a chain of 21 missions along the Pacific coast to educate and convert the Indians. One such mission was Mission San Francisco de Asis, or – as it was popularly known – Mission Dolores. Today the mission area in San Francisco is where the majority of Hispanics in that city live and work.

Project Try to find some more information about California and tell the class what you have found out.

Focus on GRAMMAR Conditional sentences I

1 A new life in California (*if* and *when*)

Naomi Welch lives in New York, but she doesn't like it there. She'll probably leave New York and move to San Francisco next year.

If you find the right job in San Francisco, you'll have a wonderful time.

When I get an apartment, I'll send you my address. You can come and visit me then.

But remember, **if** somebody wants to sell you an apartment very cheaply or very quickly, don't buy it.

Don't worry. I won't forget to ask you for advice **when** I get an offer.

Look again at this short dialogue between Naomi and a friend of hers.
First try to find one German word for the English words in bold print.
Then find two different German words which show that *if* and *when* have different meanings.

Now look at the following short dialogues. One of them must be completed with *if*, the other with *when*. Which is the right conjunction for each sentence? Try to explain your decision.

1. I might fly to San Francisco in March or April. – I'll come with you … you go in April.
2. I'm going to San Francisco in October. – Then you'll be there … it is warmest in the city.

→ Grammar 8: 1 (p.161) → Exercise 1

2 Different people – different opinions (Conditional sentences I)

Here are some things different people have recently said to Naomi:

"Perhaps you**'ll have** a better life if you **move** to California next year."
"San Francisco **won't be** the right place for you if you **like** hot summers."
"You **should start** to learn Spanish if you **are** serious about your plans."
"You **might** also **feel** unhappy in San Francisco if you **don't feel** happy in New York."

As you can easily see, the four main clauses of these sentences refer to the future.
Try to find out what time the speaker refers to in each *if*-clause: the past, the present or the future.
Example: … if you move to California next year. – *Question:* When? – *Answer:* …

Now look at the verb forms in bold print. Make a table and write down the verb forms in the main clauses and the *if*-clauses.
Then try to make up a rule for these conditional sentences:
What time do the main clauses refer to? What verb forms can be used in the main clause? What time can the *if*-clause refer to? What verb form is used in the *if*-clause?

	main clause:	*if*-clause:
1.	'll have	move
2.	won't be	…
3.	…	…
4.	…	…

Ex *Now work with a partner and try to find more than one ending for each sentence.*

1. If the scientists are right, … 2. You'll have to do earthquake practice if … 3. Lots of people will die if … 4. You'll be able to buy an open car if … 5. If more and more people move to California, …

→ Grammar 8: 2 (p.161) → Exercises 2-3

A Californian family

Start a network with the names of the Vargas family. Add the information you get in the text to each name. With the help of the network try to sum up what Manuel says about his family.

"*Buenos días. ¿Cómo estas?* Or should I say 'Hi, how're you doing?' I live with my parents, my younger brother Paul and my sister Cristina in the mission area of San Francisco. Dad is an architect, and mom is an accountant with an export company. At home we speak Spanish all the time. Where we live, the people in the stores speak Spanish, there are Spanish-language newspapers, movie theaters and, of course, we watch the Spanish-language TV station ESPN. When I'm with my friends at school, I speak Spanish or English.

"I'm going to start college after the summer vacation. I'd like to become a sports instructor. My brother Paul goes to Mission High School. My sister Cristina goes to a private Catholic school. The teachers are all nuns. She complains because Paul and I can go where we want and do what we want. She says she's only allowed to go to school dances because dad knows that the nuns will keep an eye on the girls.

"After school I help in the boys' club. It's organized by the local church. There's a gym, and the kids can play football, basketball and other sports. Paul goes there, too, sometimes. We also have a library and a game room. The idea of the boys' club is to keep the kids off the streets while their parents are at work. The barrio – that's what we call the neighborhood – has gotten rough in the past few years. Street gangs of Mexicans, Cubans and Filipinos often fight. If the kids come to the boys' club, they might not get into trouble so easily.

"At home our parents keep a lot of the Mexican traditions and customs alive. My mother usually cooks Mexican food, and when we have parties, mom and dad prepare it the Mexican way.

"We go to Mass on Sunday and celebrate the main Mexican holidays like *Independencia de México* – that's on September 16th – and the *Cinco de Mayo* on May 5th."

Info box Spanish-speaking people are often called Hispanics. That means their families once came from one of the Spanish-speaking countries like Mexico, Nicaragua, Costa Rica, Cuba or El Salvador. Today there are 4.5 million Hispanics in California and they are one of the fastest-growing ethnic groups. By the year 2010 over half the population of California will be Hispanic, black or Asian.

Focus on WORDS Food and drink

Both Mr and Mrs Vargas are good cooks and their children love the meals they make, especially the Mexican +ones: tacos, burritos, chili and fresh salads. The barrio where they live has very good stores where people can buy fresh meat, fish, vegetables and fruit.
The Vargas family also likes American food: hamburgers and French fries, +grilled steak and chicken, corn and butter.
Both Paul and Cristina have part-time jobs in +fast-food restaurants. Cristina +serves customers in a +drive-in pizza place and Paul works in an ice-cream parlor.
Mr and Mrs Vargas usually eat dinner together with their children in the evening. During the week Manuel, Paul and Cristina have lunch in the school cafeteria. Mr and Mrs Vargas sometimes have a +light meal or a snack in a +diner during their lunch hour, or they buy a salad from a store.

1 Collecting words Collect more words and phrases for each of the following groups.

a Different +types of food and meals:
– bread, +rolls, meat, fish, fruit, …
– cornflakes, toast, sandwiches, …

b Types of drinks:
– tea, coffee, …
– fruit juice, …
– beer, …

c Things you eat with or from:
– knife, …; plate, +bowl, +tin/can, …
– +mug, cup, +saucer, …

d Mixed bag:
– +menu, +waiter/waitress, …
– +book a table, +order a meal, +pass the salt, …

2 Arranging words Arrange the words you have collected in different ways, for example:

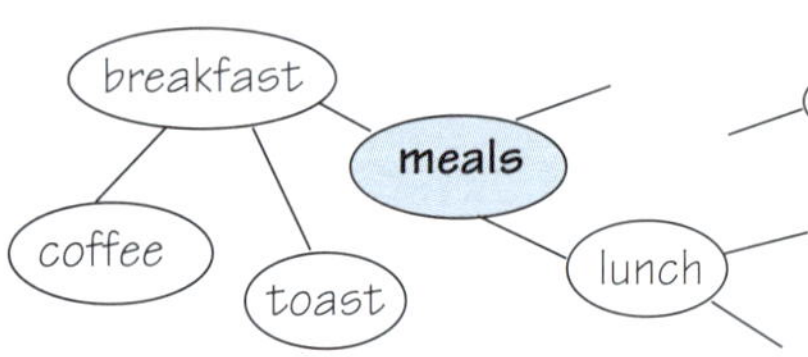

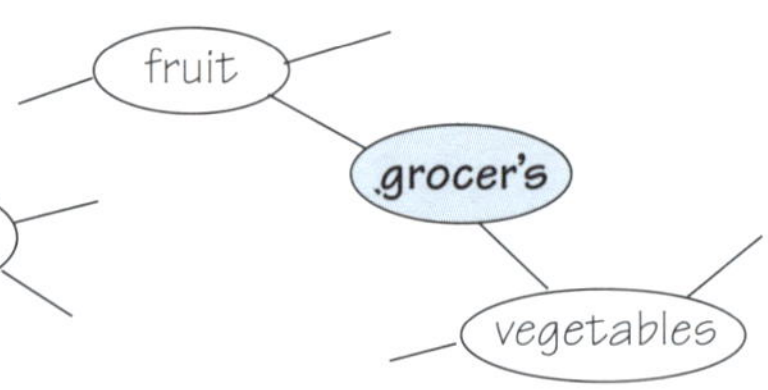

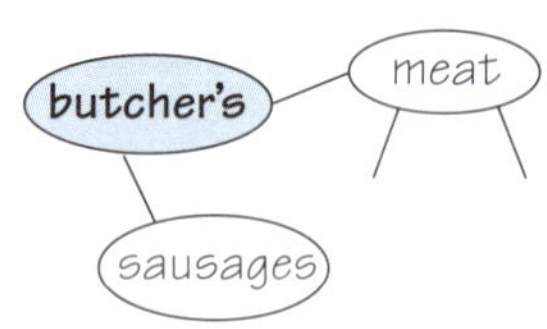

3 Words in use

a Imagine you want to have a party for some friends. What kinds of food and drink would you like to offer?

b Make a shopping list for your family for the weekend. What will you buy?

c Make two tables and write down what kinds of food you think are healthy and what kinds are not. What do you prefer to eat if you are at home or if you are in a café/restaurant?

Speculations – unlikely to come true

The Vargases have been living in California for 15 years. However, Mr and Mrs Vargas have never forgotten Mexico, the country where they lived when they were young.

1. If the economic situation **was** better now, we **would** probably **go** back to Mexico.
2. I **would move** back tomorrow if the situation **was** better in Mexico.
3. It's true. We **might go** back if they **offered** better wages.
4. If we **moved** back, we **couldn't give** the children such a good education.
5. Even if we both **found** jobs, we **wouldn't be able** to send them to a good school.
6. But **I'd feel** very unhappy if we **had to** give up our Mexican traditions here.

First look at the context again and then ask yourself for each sentence (main clause and *if*-clause) what time the speaker refers to in these sentences. *Example*:

main clause: … we would probably go back to Mexico.
Question: When? *Answer:* In the future. The speaker refers to the future.
if-clause: If the economic situation was better now, …
Question: When? *Answer:* …

Then make a list (as on p.114) of the verb forms in the main clauses and the *if*-clauses.
Now try to make a rule for the conditional sentences II on this page:
What time do all the main clauses refer to? What verb forms are used in the main clauses?
What time can the *if*-clauses refer to? What verb forms are used in all the *if*-clauses?
Finally translate the first, the fourth and the sixth sentence. What do you notice about the verb forms in the *if*-clause and the German *Nebensatz*?

Ex If all the world was apple pie, and all the sea was ink, … – what then?

Make at least five or six statements that are very unlikely to come true.

Examples: If, from tomorrow on, all parents had to go to school and all children had to go to work, …
If the government closed all schools, … If, very suddenly, we no longer had cars, …

→ Grammar 8: 3a (p.162) → Exercise 4

Conditional sentences I and II: a comparison

Naomi: I'll move to San Francisco if I find a job.

Mrs Vargas: I would go back to Mexico if I found a job there.

What time are *both* speakers talking about?
Look again at the contexts on pages 114 and 117. Then decide who, Naomi or Mrs Vargas, believes that her ideas will probably/will probably not become reality?

Now answer these questions and complete the tables:
What time do all the main clauses of the conditional sentences I and II on pages 114 and 117 refer to?
What time can the *if*-clauses refer to?
What does the speaker of a conditional sentence I/II believe about his/her ideas?
What verb forms are used in the main clause/the *if*-clause of the conditional sentences I on page 114?
What verb forms are used in the main clause/the *if*-clause of a conditional sentence II?

cond. sentences I
– *main clause:* future *if-clause:* …
– will probably come true
– *verb forms* *in main clause:* … *in if-clause:* …

cond. sentences II
– *main clause:* … *if-clause:* …
– …
– *verb forms* *in main clause:* … *in if clause:* …

→ Grammar 8: 3b (p.162) → Exercise 5

8 Exercises

1 ***If* or *when*?**

a *Here are five main clauses and two sub-clauses for each of them. Decide which sub-clause needs 'if' and which of them needs 'when'.*

1. I'll study at the University of California for a year { … I'm twenty-one. / … they accept me.
2. I'll have to earn some money { … I'm in the USA next year. / … the university is expensive.
3. I won't fly back to Germany at once { … I don't have to. / … I've finished my year in the USA.
4. I'll fly to New York for a week { … it isn't too expensive. / … I know the country a bit better.
5. I'm going to get a ticket for a Broadway musical { … the prices aren't too high. / … I'm in New York.

b *Here are three more main clauses. Complete each of them with a sub-clause that begins with 'if' and a sub-clause that begins with 'when'.*

1. Perhaps my parents or one of my friends will visit me …
2. I might not want to go back to Germany …
3. But I think I'll be quite happy …

2 **Some more things about San Francisco** *Practise conditional sentences I.*

Read all the sentences and then decide what to do with the verbs in brackets. In some of the sentences more than one verb form is possible.

1. If you *look* at a map, you (see) that there is water on three sides of the city.
2. If you *read* about the history of the cable car, you (find out) that a man from Scotland put the first cable car on the streets of San Francisco.
3. If tourists (visit) the prison on the island of Alcatraz, they (see) that today it is only a tourist attraction.
4. If tourists (ask) a guide, she or he (show) the group where Al Capone was kept in Alcatraz.
5. Tourists might be asked in their hotel to save water if they (visit) the city in the summer.
6. We (go) on one of the tours through Chinatown if we (get a ticket).

7. Your friend (have to) visit the Christmas Store if she (want) to have Christmas in the summer.
8. About 100,000 cars (drive) past you if you (stand) on the Golden Gate Bridge for one day.

Just for fun
Just for fun

What will you get if you cross … 1. … a cow and a tiger? 2. … a dictionary and a tin of soup? 3. … a fast runner and a car? 4. … an elephant and a mouse?

1. An animal that's too dangerous to milk *(melken)*. 2. Alphabet soup. 3. A sports car. 4. An animal that makes big holes in the wall.

3 Not certain, but … *Practise conditional sentences I.*

a *Example:* I think I'll stay at home tonight. — Well, if you stay at home, I'll go out.

or: If you stay at home, I can go out.

Try to make up one or two reactions to the following statements. Perhaps you can think of some funny reactions, too.

1. I think I'll watch football tonight.
2. Sue will probably go to a disco tonight.
3. We'll work in the garden this afternoon.
4. I believe Tony will pick Ann up at the station.
5. There won't be any petrol for private cars one day.
6. Perhaps nobody will go to work tomorrow.
7. One day mice might not work for scientists any more.
8. I think children should do the jobs of politicians.

b **A game** *Choose one of the statements from* ***a*** *and make an 'if-chain'. Work with a partner and see how many conditional sentences (type I) you can make.*

Example: I think I'll stay at home tonight. → Well, if you stay at home, I'll probably go out. → If you go out, I'll invite Pete. → you (invite Pete) – I (ask his brother to come with me) → his brother (go out with you) – you (probably stay out late) → we (stay out late) – … *Can you continue this 'if-chain'?*

Now choose another statement from ***a*** *and make your own chain.*

<4> If I had a time-machine … *Practise conditional sentences II.*

Imagine you have a time-machine and you are allowed to have three stops in time. You can have stops in the past and you can have stops in the future. – Where would you stop? What would you do there? Who would you meet?

Example: If I had a time-machine, I would first fly back to the year 1492. I would land on Columbus's Santa Maria if it was possible to find it in the middle of the Atlantic Ocean. Then I would tell Christopher Columbus to stop his trip to "India". The "Indians" in America would have a better life if he listened to me. …

Now decide which years you would like to fly to.

<5> In English, please

Test yourself and see how many of these conditional sentences I and II you can get right.

1. Wenn das Wetter morgen gut ist, können wir zum Strand gehen. 2. Ich könnte mit dir kommen, wenn du um sechs Uhr fahren würdest. 3. Wenn du dich beeilst[1], kannst du den Bus noch bekommen. 4. Ich käme immer zu spät, wenn unsere erste Stunde um 8.00 Uhr beginnen würde. 5. Ich würde dir sagen, wie spät es ist, wenn ich eine Uhr hätte. 6. Wenn ich die Zeit habe, schreibe ich dir jeden Tag eine Karte aus Spanien. 7. Wenn du noch nicht zu müde bist, können wir einen Spaziergang machen. 8. Wir wären viel zu früh in New York, wenn deine Uhr richtig ginge[2].

[1] (to) hurry up [2] (to) be right

6 The rock concert (Prop-word *one/ones*)*

Look at this dialogue between Manuel and his friend Steve.

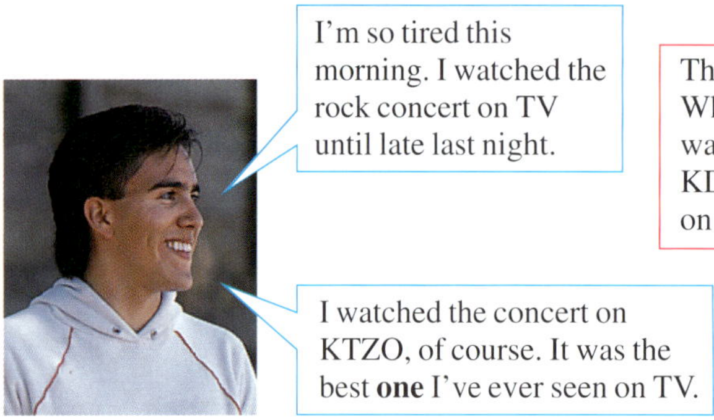

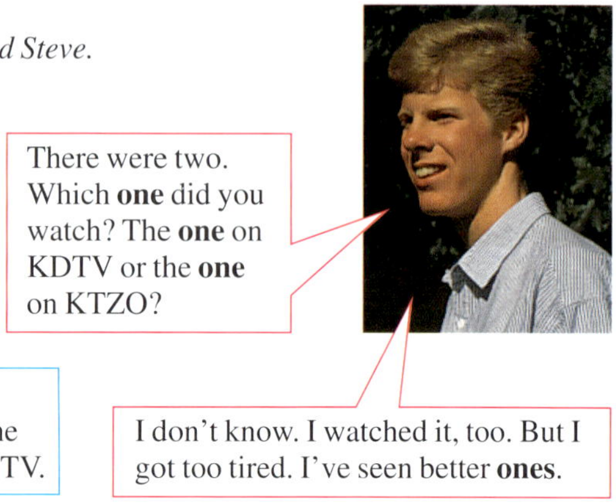

Look at the dialogue again and find out which other word could be used instead of *one/ones* in the dialogue. Why do you think the speakers use *one/ones*?
Translate the sentences with *one/ones* and compare the English and the German sentences. Then try to say why German speakers of English often have problems with the prop-word *one/ones*.

→ Grammar 8: 4 (p.162)

See if you can do these in English.

1. Which of these spoons are from your grandmother? – (Die großen in dem Schrank dort drüben.) 2. Why are there only five saucers for six cups on the table? – (Ich konnte die für deine Tasse nicht finden.) 3. Can you pass me that plate, please? – (Welchen? Den kleinen oder den großen?) 4. Do you like rolls? – (Ja. Die, die meine Mutter macht. Gekaufte esse ich nicht so gern. Die schmecken nicht so gut.) 5. We've broken almost all our glasses. (Ich muß ein paar neue kaufen. – Ich habe ein paar sehr schöne in einem kleinen Laden in der Stadt gesehen.)

7 Across the Rio Grande to the USA

Many Mexicans would like to live in the USA. Although they know that life isn't easy there, especially for illegal immigrants, they believe it is better than in Mexico. That's why lots of Mexicans try, again and again, to cross the Rio Grande into the USA. Some people have made a lot of money out of this situation.

Read the following prompts and then write a text for a magazine about Carlos Carrera. You could write it as a report or as an interview.

Name: Carlos Carrera
Home country: Mexico
Age: 23
Job: "coyote" (person who takes Mexicans across the US border illegally); several thousand Mexicans in four years
"Wages": in last four years more than most Mexicans in their whole lives

Price of a "trip across the border": across the river only $2; reason: illegal immigrants often caught and sent back by border police; to New York about $2000; reason: "safer" for illegal immigrants (Carlos: "Everything has its price.")

* Dies ist für Schülerinnen und Schüler in einigen Bundesländern Wiederholung.

a Personal nouns in English

In English only a small group of personal nouns clearly refer to male or female persons, e.g. *girl – boy, wife – husband, mother – father.*

Find the "partner" for the personal nouns on the right and write them down as pairs in your exercise-book.

uncle – king – madam – son – mum – Mrs/Ms – sister

German personal nouns often have the suffix *-in* to refer to a female person. In English, personal nouns like *friend, pupil, teacher, doctor, nurse, manager, politician, Indian, cousin* can refer to male or female persons, so you must always look carefully at the context:

My *cousin* Linda goes to Birmingham University. *(Cousine)*
My favourite *cousin* lives in Bristol. He's called Dave. *(Cousin)*

Sometimes, of course, it may be necessary to say clearly if a noun refers to a male or female person. There are two ways to do this in English:

1. You can add *male* or *female* to make the meaning clear.
   Example:
   Most *female readers* found that article quite enjoyable, but most *male readers* didn't.
2. When you read texts, you might see words like *actress (Schauspielerin)* or *manageress (Geschäftsführerin).* The suffix *-ess* refers to a woman or girl. Today, however, most speakers of English try to avoid personal nouns that end in *-ess*, and many women do not like them.

Translate the following sentences into English. Use 'male/female' only where they are needed.

1. Tina Turner ist eine sehr berühmte Rocksängerin. 2. Es gibt mehr Studentinnen als Studenten an unserer Universität. 3. Janes Mutter ist Richterin, aber Jane möchte Tänzerin werden. 4. In unserem Krankenhaus arbeiten 14 Krankenpfleger und 38 Krankenschwestern. 5. Unser Nachbar ist Inder. Er arbeitet als Krankenpfleger in unserem Krankenhaus. 6. Obwohl es heute mehr Politikerinnen gibt als vor zwanzig Jahren, werden viele Entscheidungen nur von Männern getroffen.

b Word builder's corner   Phrases with '(to) get'

(to) get	+	hungry thirsty dark ill well better worse fat strong weak older tired warm interested angry popular cold wet nervous famous rich dirty married ready sick

Use as many phrases with 'get' as you can in your answers to questions 1-10.

Example: What might happen if you stay out in the rain? – You might *get wet.*/You might *get ill.*

What might happen if …

1. … you eat too many sweets?
2. … you do lots of sports?
3. … you take your medicine regularly?
4. … you don't take anything to drink with you?
5. … you can't find your keys?
6. … you don't put on warm clothes?
7. … you save all your pocket-money?
8. … you don't have lunch?
9. … you sing in a pop group?
10. … you can't answer the questions in a test?

8 Text

The big brother

- Who do you think the people in the pictures are?
- Read the text to find out exactly what situations the pictures show.

Paul knew when there was danger. He could feel it. In an area where gangs often fought, he had a special instinct that warned him to be careful. That's the way it was today.

On his way to school, he saw a group of Cubans out of the corner of his eye. He felt that they were going to come towards him. He walked more quickly, but a voice said, "Hey, Vargas." Paul walked on.

"Hey, why don't you stop when I want to talk to you?" Paul stopped. The leader of the gang was Carlos Duran. Most of the kids in the barrio were frightened of him. Paul hoped it was just money they wanted, but he kept his hands from his pockets, so that they didn't think he had a knife there.

"What do you want?" asked Paul.

"I want to talk to you," said the Cuban. "You go to the boys' club a lot?"

Paul looked nervously at the big, athletic Cuban. "Most afternoons. Why?"

"I hear a gang of Filipinos robbed you two days ago."

Paul nodded. "They took my money." Carlos Duran took some notes out of his pocket and offered them to Paul. "I got them back for you. If they ever give you trouble again, just tell me." And he walked away.

Paul couldn't believe it. It was a trick. It had to be. All morning Paul wondered what was happening. Was it real or was it some trick that he couldn't understand?

During the break, he saw the Filipinos. But when they saw him, they walked away and left him alone. It wasn't possible. Later, while he was playing basketball with some friends, Carlos Duran came past and shouted. "Hi, Paul. Everything OK?" Paul was too surprised to answer.

After school he met Carlos again. This time the Cuban was in his car and he shouted. "Get in, man. I'll drive you home."

This is it, thought Paul. If I get in, he'll drive away and take me to the others. But why me, he thought. Why me?

"It's all right," said Paul. "I'll walk."

"Get in, man. I'm going your way." Paul got in.

When they drove into 21st Street and stopped outside Paul's house, Carlos took an envelope out of his pocket. He seemed nervous. "Give this to your sister." Paul took the envelope and looked at it. There was no address on it, nothing. He nodded and got out of the car.

"And don't open it," shouted Carlos before he drove away.

Paul walked up the steps to the front door. Cristina was standing at the living-room window and she was waiting for him near the stairs as he came through the door.

"I got this for you," said Paul. She took it from him and ran to her room before he could ask what was inside.

For the rest of the week Carlos was more than friendly. "If the kids give you trouble, just tell me," he said.

"Sure," said Paul. But nobody gave him any trouble. It seemed as if the whole barrio knew that Paul was protected. And by Carlos Duran. He found out why at the weekend.

"Paul," said Cristina on Friday. "There's a dance this evening. Would you like to go?"

"I'm not interested," said Paul.

"Oh, come on. You know what dad's like. If he knows we're going together, he won't cause any problems." She worked on him for 15 minutes until he agreed to talk to their father when he came home from work. Mr Vargas nodded and said, "OK, but be sure to come home early." And Paul, of course, had to keep an eye on his sister.

When they walked into the club that evening, Paul went first, the "big brother" although he was two years younger. They were hardly inside when Carlos Duran came towards them. He didn't even see Paul. "Hi, Cristina," he said. "Glad you came." Then he turned to Paul. "Hi, Paul. How are you keeping?"
Paul couldn't think of anything to say, while Cristina started to laugh and talk happily.
"Come on," said Carlos, "Let's have a drink."
Carlos and Cristina danced together all evening while Paul sat at the table and drank his soda. When Cristina came to the table to rest, Paul said, "Do you know who he is?"
"He's nice," said Cristina.
"There are a lot of people who feel differently about that. Dad will go crazy if he finds out."
"Well, it's obvious that he won't find out."
"He will," said Paul. "I'll tell him."
At ten o'clock Paul said, "I think we ought to go home, Cristina. Dad will be angry if it gets too late."
"I'll drive you home," said Carlos.
But what Carlos didn't say was that he wanted to take them on a trip across San Francisco first. They finally stopped at the beach. It was warm and they could hear the sounds of the sea outside.
"Let's go for a walk," said Carlos. Paul sighed and opened the door. He felt like one of the nuns at Cristina's school. But Carlos was only thinking of a walk with Cristina. "You can stay in the car," he said. "I've got some great tapes. The best."
"I'm coming with you," said Paul.
"Stay here," said Cristina.
But Paul wasn't staying. So Cristina and Carlos walked along the beach while Paul stayed five metres behind them like a dog without a home.

When they finally arrived home, it was after midnight and their parents were angry. "Where have you been?" their father shouted. "Do you kids know what time it is?"
Cristina looked at Paul – and he understood.
"Sorry, Dad," he said. "But the dance was so good we forgot what time it was."
"Well, … . OK," he said as he calmed down.
"Now go to bed. It's late."
"Oh, Dad," said Cristina as they started to leave the room, and Paul's heart sank. "There's another dance next week. You won't mind if we go, I hope."

Working with the text

1 A closer look at the text

a First explain what situations the two pictures show and who the people in the pictures are. – What did you think of these people before you read the text, what do you think now?

b Now look at the text again.

1. What impression of Carlos does one get from p.122, ll.1-22? What impression does one get from the rest of the story? – How do you explain the different impressions?
2. You know a little bit about Cristina's and Paul's roles in the family from p.115. Find places in the text where their roles are completely different. – Why do you think this is possible?
3. Imagine you are Paul, Cristina or Carlos. Tell a friend what happened on that Friday evening. (Remember to add how you felt and what you thought of the other two.) – Compare the different texts and explain why each person might feel differently about what happened.

2 Say it in English

Look at the following short German sentences. Then find out from the text what they are in English. Write the English sentences into your vocabulary book.
All the sentences have useful phrases which you can also use in other situations.

Ich fahre dich nach Hause. (p.122, l.43)
Ich gehe zu Fuß. (p.122, l.47)
Ich sag's ihm. (p.123, l.19)

Er schien nervös zu sein. (p.122, l.51)
Das ganze Barrio schien es zu wissen. (p.122, l.68)

Er war mehr als freundlich. (p.122, l.64/65)
Wenn dir die Kids Ärger machen, sag's mir. (p.122, l.65/66)
Sie bearbeitete ihn eine Viertelstunde lang. (p.122, l.76)
Er mußte auf seine Schwester aufpassen. (p.122, l.80)

Komm, wir trinken etwas. (p.123, l.10)
Wir haben vergessen, wie spät es war. (p.123, l.46)
Es macht dir doch nichts aus, wenn wir dort hingehen. (p.123, l.51/52)

Now look at the following situations and use one or two of the phrases to react to each of them.

1. Why didn't you invite Tony to the party? – (Er schien mehr als beschäftigt zu sein.) 2. Has Susan finished her letter? – (Ich weiß es nicht, aber ich frage sie.) 3. I'm bored. – (Komm, wir gehen ins Kino.) 4. Can you come to my party? – (Ich sag's dir später. Ich muß meine Eltern noch bearbeiten.) 5. Did your parents say anything about your problems at school? – (Ich hab's ihnen noch nicht gesagt. Aber sie scheinen schon etwas zu wissen.) 6. We won't be at home this weekend. – (In Ordnung. Ich passe auf euer Haus auf.) 7. Can we all go to your house this afternoon? – (Natürlich. Meinen Eltern macht es nichts aus, wenn ich Freunde mitbringe.)

L 9 Listening comprehension The good life

The text you are going to hear is about earthquakes in California. It also tells you about some people's attitudes to the danger of earthquakes and about a place called Parkfield.
Before you listen to the text, talk about what you know about earthquakes. How do you think Californians feel about earthquakes?
Then make a table in which you can write the information while you are listening.

Now listen to the tape twice and find out
- what the San Andreas Fault is
- what some Californians think about the danger of earthquakes
- what is special about Parkfield.

San Andreas Fault	attitudes to danger	Parkfield
...	...	...
...	...	...

Compare with a partner what you understood and then present the information to the class.

Beyond the text

1. You have now heard several people and how they feel. What do you think of their attitudes?
2. What do you think about the Parkfield experiment and about the way Parkfield advertises itself?
3. "Enjoy life today. Tomorrow the roof of your house might fall on you." What do you think of this idea?

Holidays in the USA

When British immigrants went to America, they took many customs with them. Today, Americans still celebrate Valentine's Day, April Fool's Day and Halloween, for example. People from other nations introduced their own special customs, too. But of course Americans also have a number of holidays that you can find only in the USA. On these days they celebrate the birthdays of great Americans or important historical events. Together these holidays tell us something about the history of the country.

Martin Luther King Day
(Third Monday in January)

Martin Luther King was the most important black leader of his time. He fought hard to win full civil rights for blacks in the USA. On April 4th, 1968, a gunman shot him dead in Memphis, Tennessee. Almost 20 years later, in 1986, the American government made the birthday of Martin Luther King (January 15th) a national holiday.

George Washington's Birthday
(Third Monday in February)

On this day Americans celebrate the birthday of the first president of the United States of America, George Washington (February 22nd). He led the American soldiers against the English army during the War of Independence (1775-1783).

George Washington (1732-1799)

The Washington Monument in Washington, D.C.

Memorial Day
(Last Monday in May)

On Memorial Day Americans remember relatives or friends who have died in wars. This custom goes back to the American Civil War (1861-1865). People chose this day to put flags or flowers on soldiers' graves.
Memorial Day Weekend is also the beginning of the summer season. Americans look forward to the first picnics of the year. They go to the beaches or they go to the swimming-pools, as these usually open on this day.

Info box Most federal holidays in the USA fall on a Monday – although the event which they celebrate often took place on another day. This means that Americans can enjoy a long weekend. This is very useful, as most Americans only have about 12 days vacation a year.
On federal holidays banks, offices and schools are usually closed. Most shops, however, stay open.

Firework display in San Francisco

Independence Day

(July 4th)

On Independence Day Americans celebrate the birthday of their country as a free and independent nation. Before the War of Independence the Americans lived in colonies that belonged to Britain. With the Declaration of Independence on July 4th, 1776 and the war that followed, the American colonies broke away from Britain and a new nation was born: the United States of America.
Every year Americans all over the country celebrate the Fourth of July with fireworks. However, they do not usually buy their own fireworks. They go into parks, where they have a picnic and watch the public fireworks in the evening.

Columbus Day

(Second Monday in October)

On this day Americans remember that Christopher Columbus reached America on October 12th, 1492. For Italian-Americans this is a very special holiday. Columbus sailed for the Spanish king and queen, but he was in fact an Italian. The biggest celebrations are in New York City, with huge parades through the streets.

Parade in New York

Family celebrations

Thanksgiving Day

(Fourth Thursday in November)

On Thanksgiving Americans remember the first English families, the Pilgrims, who came to America almost 400 years ago. During the first terrible winter many settlers died, but those who survived learned from the Native Americans how to plant and grow food. The following autumn the Pilgrims celebrated their harvest with a meal of wild turkey with the friendly Native Americans.
Today Thanksgiving Day is still a very special day in the USA. Families always try to be together on this day, even if they live hundreds of miles away. As a lot of people do not work on the following Friday either, families can enjoy a long weekend together. People often call Thanksgiving "Turkey Day" because dinner with a huge turkey is the main event of the day.

Collect as much information as you can about these and other American holidays and make a wall display. Perhaps you know some Americans you can ask? Then organize these events in the correct historical order.

Unit 9 The National Park Service

– When Americans talk about a national park, a German might easily misunderstand them. Look at the photos and the information at the bottom of the page to find out what the National Park Service looks after.
– Look at the map at the end of the book. Find out the names of other national parks and say where they are.

Grand Canyon National Park, Arizona

"The best idea America ever had"

Mission San José, San Antonio, Texas

Statue of Liberty, New York, New York

NATIONAL PARKS AND MONUMENTS

Name and state	*Other information*
Yellowstone National Park (Wyoming)	World's first national park (1872); famous for its spectacular scenery, hot springs, beautiful waterfalls and wildlife; home of the last bison in the United States.
Grand Canyon National Park (Arizona)	One of the world's natural wonders; 1 mile deep, 4-18 miles wide and 217 miles long; world's most well-known example of the power of erosion.
Boston National Historical Park (Massachusetts)	The National Park Service preserves buildings from the time of the War of Independence in one of the oldest cities in the United States.
San Antonio Missions National Historical Park (Texas)	The Park Service preserves the missions from America's Spanish colonial days.
Statue of Liberty (New York)	The Park Service looks after this world-famous monument in New York Harbor.

9 A

Yosemite National Park

– Find out from the texts what exactly the photos on these two pages show.
– What would *you* like to see in Yosemite? Tell each other why.

When Americans want to camp, go climbing, cycling, fishing or just have a barbecue with their family, they usually drive to one of their national parks. They stay in the park for as long as they like: a day, a weekend or even for a whole vacation, as the larger national parks have campgrounds, hotels, restaurants and picnic areas. However, they often have to pay an entrance fee.

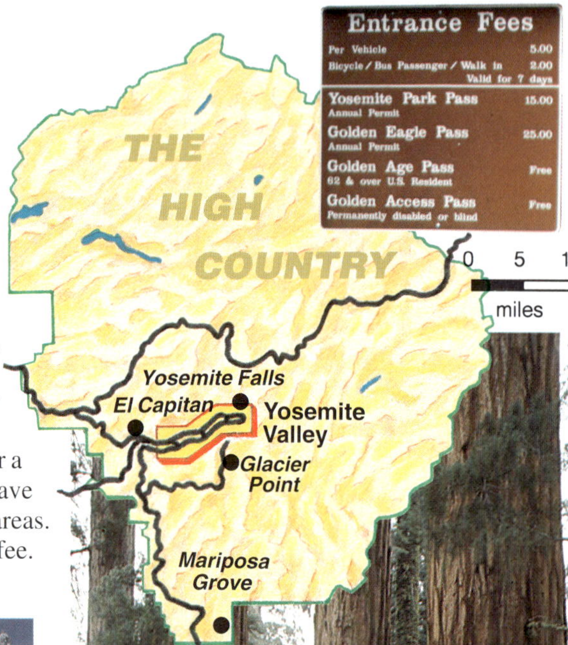

One of the most popular national parks in the United States is Yosemite National Park in California. The name itself possibly comes from the Indian word *uzumati*. It means grizzly bear. Yosemite is an area of great natural beauty. Among its famous attractions are Yosemite Falls. These are the highest waterfalls in the United States. Altogether the water falls 2,425 feet (739 metres).

The Big Trees in Yosemite are the tallest trees in the world and among the oldest living things on earth. The Grizzly Giant, for example, is 2,700 years old.

→ Exercise 1

Although millions of Americans visit Yosemite every year, few of them go walking in the wilderness. The High Country in Yosemite is one of the few areas in the USA where a lot of the land is completely untouched and unspoiled. There are over 800 miles of trails here. However, if you want to stay for more than a day, camp or make a fire, you must get a permit from a ranger's office.
Yosemite National Park is the home of lots of wild animals, even bears. In Yosemite, most of the bears now live in the High Country, but they sometimes go into campgrounds at night. Bears love food, so visitors have to be very careful where they leave things to eat.

From the valley floor to the top of El Capitan it is 3,564 feet (1,086 metres) – that is as high as a 300-storey building. Climbers need four to six days to get to the top. It is only something for the experienced. → Exercise [2]

Project Find out about an area of natural beauty near you. Work in groups and make a brochure for visitors from English-speaking countries.

Focus on GRAMMAR [Past perfect]

A visit to Yosemite during Memorial Day weekend

Last May, in the week before Memorial Day weekend, the Smiths from Denver flew to San Francisco. While they were there, …

… they read some brochures about Yosemite.

They decided to drive to Yosemite.

They hired a car.

They packed the car.

They left San Francisco.

They ran into the first traffic jam after about an hour.

Look at the verb forms in these six sentences. You know, of course, what tense is used in them. Can you also still remember when exactly you use this tense?
As in German, you can combine the six sentences in the following way:

> After they **had read** some brochures about Yosemite, they decided to drive there.
> After they **had decided** to drive there, they … .
> After they **had** …

The verb forms in bold print are past perfect forms. How are they formed? How do you think negative statements and questions are made in the past perfect?
Look at the actions in the sub-clauses and in the main clauses and decide which happened first. Then try to say what you can use the past perfect for.

Ex *Simple past or past perfect? Decide what happened first, then put the infinitives in the correct tense.*

1. We (drive) into the park after we (pay) the entrance fee. 2. After we (park) our car, we (go) to the ranger's office. 3. When we were in Yosemite, we (meet) some visitors who (climb) El Capitan three times. 4. After we (buy) a camping permit from the ranger's office, we (leave) the valley. 5. We (feel) happy when we (leave) because we (have) such a nice time.

→ Grammar 9: 1 (p.163) → Exercise 3

Turbo brain [Past perfect progressive]

On the Tuesday after Memorial Day the rangers finished work at six o'clock in the evening. They had started work at eight o'clock in the morning and **had been working** all day with hardly any break. Some **had been picking up** rubbish, others **had been repairing** picnic tables. …

As you can see from this short text, there is also a past perfect progressive.
Look at the verb forms and say how you make positive statements. Then try to say how you make negative statements and questions.
Look again at the text and the time diagram:
When did the activities *(work, pick up, repair)* start?
What time did they lead to?
Now try to say in your own words: What can you express with the past perfect progressive?

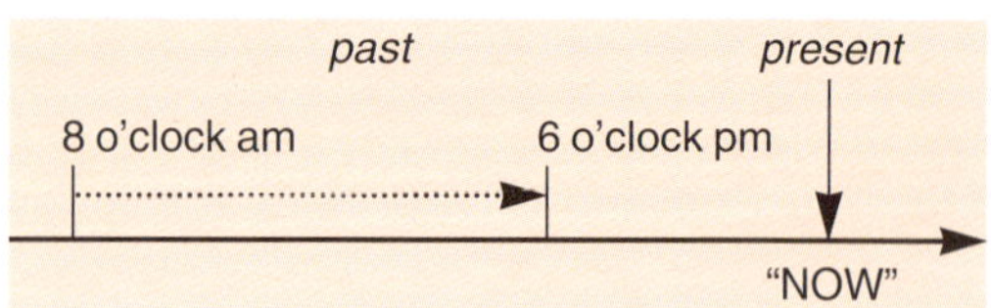

How is the past perfect progressive similar to the present perfect progressive and the future progressive?

Ex **Why?** *Make past perfect progressive sentences with the words in brackets.*

Example: In the evening of Memorial Day there was rubbish on the campgrounds everywhere.
(visitors / throw away / all day) → Visitors **had been throwing away** rubbish all day.

1. On Friday evening the Smiths were very tired. (drive / all day) 2. On the evening of their first day in the park their feet were hurting. (walk / all day) 3. When they looked out of their tent the next morning, the ground was very wet. (rain / all night)

→ Grammar 9: 2 (p.163)

The national parks have some of the most spectacular scenery in the United States. They +include North America's highest mountains +as well as natural wonders like the Grand Canyon. The parks protect wild rivers, huge canyons, +deserts and untouched wildernesses, so that visitors can see what North America looked like when the first Europeans came.
But the national park system does more than +conserve the nation's natural wonders. In a world where many +plants and animals could die out, the national parks also offer a last hope for some to survive. The last +panthers in the United States are now protected in the Everglades in Florida. Most have been killed by hunters. The last bison live in Yellowstone. Trees that are thousands of years old are protected in Yosemite so that +timber companies cannot cut them down.

1 **Collecting words** Collect all the words and phrases that have something to do with nature in this text and on pages 127-129 and put them in one of the three groups. Find more words from memory and from the picture. If you want to know more, use a dictionary or ask your teacher.

a **Words which describe a +landscape**

– fields, rivers, …
– flat land, … mountains, … lakes, …
– sandy beaches, rocky coast, …

b **"Weather" words**

– sky, clouds, …
– +sunshine, rain, …
– dry, cold, icy, …
– (to) shine, (to) rain, +(to) melt, …

c **Words for animals and plants**

– dog, sheep, +monkey, …
– +bushes, grass, …
– wheat, corn, carrots, …
– The fruit is still green, +ripe, juicy, +sour, …; it smells good, tastes sweet/bitter, …

2 **Arranging words** Arrange the words and phrases you have collected in your own way. Here is how you could start a network, for example.

3 **Words in use**

a Cut out a picture of a landscape from a magazine or draw your own picture of a place where you would feel happy. Describe the place in a letter or a postcard to a pen-friend. You can begin like this:
Dear …, At the moment I'm sitting …

b Which season of the year do you like best? Give your reasons.

c If you can, write a poem with the words from your network.

Blue is the sea

Blue is the sea,
Green is the grass,
White are the clouds,
As they slowly pass.
Black are the crows,
Brown are the trees,
Red are the sails
Of a ship in the breeze. (Anon.)

pass *vorüberziehen* · crow [krəʊ] *Krähe* · breeze [bri:z] *Brise*

Focus on GRAMMAR [Reported speech: statements]

→ Revision: Grammar 9: 3 (p.164)

One side of a ranger's job

Rangers in national parks often have to look after visitors who get into trouble. Every year people get injured, some even die, because they don't listen when the rangers warn them of the dangers.
Mary Benally and Bobby Mattos, rangers in Yosemite National Park, recently had to go to the High Country to look for two people who were camping there and had lost their way.
The rangers had given them advice, but the visitors had not listened and had got into trouble. Bobby and Mary were quite angry when they finally found them. *Here is what they said to them:*

1. Mary **told** you on Friday that very few people **were camping** up here. I remember it quite clearly.
2. We **told** you that many people **had lost** their way in the High Country before. We even **told** you that a tourist **had had** a very bad accident a few weeks ago.
3. We **said** that the weather **would** probably **change** soon and that it **was going to get** colder at the weekend. Why didn't you listen?
4. I **said** then that it **was** dangerous and that careless campers often **got** into trouble. As you can see, I was right.

a In these sentences Mary and Bobby are repeating what they originally told the visitors. What do you think they said on the Friday before the visitors went to the High Country? Here is some help:
"At the moment very few people are … ." "Many people have … . A few weeks ago … ." "The weather … . It … ."

When you talk about what somebody else or you yourself said before, you often use <u>reported speech</u>. In texts with reported speech there is a <u>reporting verb</u> and one or more <u>reported clauses</u>.
Look again at the four bubbles and find out: What are the reporting verbs? What are the reported clauses? What verb form is used for all the reporting verbs?

b Now find out more about the reported clauses. Look at the following time diagram:

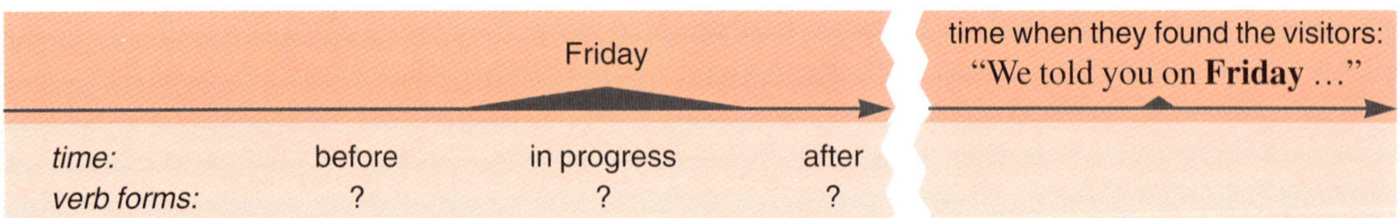

As you can see there are three question marks. Try to find out which verb forms in the first three bubbles go with which question mark. But first, here is a tip: It is easier if you ask yourself questions like the following:

"What does 'were camping' refer to,
- the time **before** Friday?"
- something **in progress** on Friday?"
- the time **after** Friday?"

Answer: "Well, I think 'were camping' refers to … because …"

Finally try to explain why the forms *was* and *got* in the fourth bubble don't refer to any special time.

Ex *To show if you understand what the following reported statements mean, say what they were in direct speech. Be careful, in some of the sentences you have to change the pronouns.*

1. We said we were going to visit a friend. 2. I told you yesterday I had seen Susan a few days ago. 3. Susan said she was helping her parents. 4. They told us they usually went to Spain in the summer. 5. Tony said his parents were working in the garden. 6. I repeated that I didn't want to go to the cinema. 7. You said you had never forgotten your homework and you would never forget it.

→ Grammar 9: 4a (p.164-165) → Exercises 4, 5, 6

Focus on GRAMMAR [Reported speech: questions; orders and requests]

Visitors' questions (Reported questions)

One evening the rangers met and told each other what different visitors had asked them.

1. Not long ago a young couple **wanted to know why we had had** so many forest fires this summer. And one visitor **asked** me **whose idea it had been** to have national parks.

2. Yesterday a tourist **asked** us **if a lot of people were camping** in the park at the moment.

3. Last Sunday somebody **asked** me **how many visitors we had** each year. I **was** also **asked if many people climbed** El Capitan and **if there were** many accidents in the park.

4. A student **wanted to know how long it would take** to get to the High Country. Some people who had heard about an accident in the High Country **asked if we were going to use** a helicopter to get there quickly.

As you can see, the verb forms in reported questions are the same as in reported statements.
Try to say what you think the visitors actually asked the rangers. Here is some help:
"Why have you had …? And whose idea was …?" "Are a lot of people …?" "How many …? Do …?" …

Then compare the following two reported questions with the two direct questions (a 'wh-question' and a 'yes/no-question'):

They wanted to know	**why**		**we**	**had**	**had**	so many forest fires this summer.
	Why	**have**	**you**		**had**	so many forest fires this summer?
Some people asked	**if**		**we**	**were going to use**		one of our helicopters.
		Are	**you**		**going to use**	one of your helicopters?

Finally try to answer these questions:
What do 'wh-questions' start with in reported speech and in direct speech? What do 'yes/no-questions' start with in reported speech?
What is the word order in reported questions? How is it different from the word order in direct questions?
What do you notice about the pronouns in these two pairs of questions?
What do you notice about the punctuation in reported questions in English and in German?

Ex **Oh, no, not again. You asked me yesterday …**

1. Did you help Susan to do the dishes? – Oh, no, not again. You asked me yesterday if I … . 2. Are you still reading that book about national parks? – Oh, no, not again. … . 3. Has your brother ever been to America? – … 4. When did they see that film about Yosemite? – … 5. Why is Alan not at school? – … 6. What can we do next weekend? – … 7. Where are they going to buy a house? – …

→ Grammar 9: 4b (p.165) → Exercises 7, 8

Heard from visitors to Yosemite (Reported requests/orders)

1. They **asked me to park** in one of the car parks. And they **asked me not to leave** the keys in the car.

2. One ranger **told me to stay away** from the bears. And she **told me not to feed** them.

Which of these statements do you think reports an order, which a request?
What do you think the original sentences were? Here is some help:
"Please park … . And don't …" "Please … . And …"
Try to say how you can report orders and requests in positive statements and in negative statements.

→ Grammar 9: 4c, d (p.165)

9 Exercises

1 Back from a trip to the USA ('each other')

Christine and Norbert Wolter have just been to the USA – she to Arizona, he to Kansas.

1. Last night they **met** for the first time after four weeks.
2. They told **each other** about their holiday.
3. They both bought souvenirs – for **each other** and for **themselves**.
4. Christine bought **herself** an Indian dress and Norbert a ring.
5. Norbert bought **himself** a cowboy hat and Christine a purse.
6. He **doesn't remember** exactly how much it cost.

Translate these six sentences into German. Compare the translations of the words in bold print and you will see that one German word appears in all six sentences.
What does the comparison tell you about some German reflexive verbs and their English translations?
What must you do in the translation of sentences 2 and 3 to make it perfectly clear what the English sentences mean?
Look at the English sentences again and try to say why the one German word can cause a lot of problems to German learners of English.

→ Vocabulary (p. 207)

See if you can take the right decision. *Fill in 'each other' or a '-self' pronoun wherever possible. If you think both are possible, explain why.*

1. Norbert often asks … why he is afraid to fly. 2. Christine and Norbert wrote … several letters in their holidays. 3. In different places they both relaxed … in the sun. 4. Verena and Jörg, their children, looked after … while their parents were away. 5. They cooked for … and they helped … with their homework. 6. One night they were frightened, so they hid … under their beds. 7. The children and their grandmother spoke to … on the phone every day. 8. All their neighbours said that the children behaved … very well while their parents were away.

[2] Changes in society (Adjectives and participles used as nouns)

Fifty years ago you hardly ever saw **a handicapped person** in a place like Yosemite. Today it is quite normal to see **handicapped people** in the park.
Like other minorities in society, **the handicapped** have had to fight for their rights and they still have to fight for some of them. But in many places one can see that they have achieved something. **The good** that has generally come from their fight can be seen in Yosemite and other national parks. There is, for example, a special access for **handicapped people** to the Visitor Center, to the restrooms and to the campgrounds. The guide-book to national parks which you can get from the National Park Service shows you if a park is suitable for **handicapped people** or not.
The good thing about these particular changes in society is that **handicapped women, children** and **men** can live a more 'normal' life than they could in the past.

NATIONAL PARK SYSTEM	
California: Yosemite National Park:	
Handicap Access/Campgrounds	✔
Handicap Access/Restrooms	✔
Handicap Access/Visitor Center	✔
Picnic area	✔
Hunting	X
Swimming	✔
California: Redwood National Park:	
Handicap Access/Campgrounds	X
Handicap Access/Restrooms	✔

Very often you can express things in English in a much shorter way than in German. However, this short text shows you that sometimes it is the other way round.
Look at the sentences that have words in bold print. Then translate the words in bold print into German.
In which of the examples can you make the translation shorter than the English original?
Then try to say what is possible in German with participles like 'handicapped' and adjectives like 'good', but not in English.

→ Vocabulary (p. 208)

How quickly can you translate these into English?

1. ein Blinder, eine Blinde, einige Blinde, die Blinden 2. die Obdachlosen, eine Obdachlose, obdachlose Menschen, ein Obdachloser 3. ein schwacher Mensch, die Schwachen in unserer Gesellschaft, schwache Menschen, ein schwacher Mann 4. die Alten und die Jungen, die Kranken und die Gesunden, das Bekannte und das Unbekannte, die Armen und die Reichen

1. Die meisten Leute ziehen das Neue dem Alten vor. 2. Die Bremsen *(brakes)* sind das Neue an diesem Fahrrad. 3. Das Gute an diesem Programm ist, daß wir früh weggehen können. 4. Hast du schon einmal einen Film gesehen, in dem das Gute nicht siegt? 5. Du hast mir noch nicht erklärt, was das Schöne an deinem Urlaub war. 6. Sag mir, was das Unmögliche an dieser Aufgabe war.

[3] Changes in the countryside. *Practise the past perfect.*

Imagine you are showing a friend some pictures: "This is where my family comes from. …"

1930

"… As you can see from this picture, my grandmother lived in the country when she was little. There were fields with … ."

1960

"… When my mother was little, all the fields … (go), people … (cut down) all the trees. Well, not all the trees, they … (leave) one. …" *Go on.*

[4] Reporting verbs

Here are some verbs. Try to replace 'said' in the following sentence with each of them to find out which ones can be used as reporting verbs.

He said that his parents had been to Yosemite without him.

act – add – admit – agree – answer – arrive – collect – complain – deny – explain – give – go – hope – inform sb. – need – promise – remind sb. – repeat – reply – run – save – shout – think – win – write

[5] What did Andrew say?

James has had a phone call from his friend Andrew who is on holiday in Yosemite. His wife has asked him what Andrew said.

Andrew said *it was raining* just now and *it had taken* him a long time to get there. …

Now you go on:
run into a lot of traffic jams on the way to Yosemite / car park – full / but – find a place to park after half an hour / already put up their tent / hope – have a good time for the rest of the week / weather – fine tomorrow

[6] But didn't you say ...? *Complete the reactions to sentences 1 to 7.*

I'm going to stay at home in the holidays.

But you said you were going to fly to Spain for three weeks.

1. Our new neighbours are terrible. – Oh, I thought you said they (be) nice people.
2. Susan loves working in the garden. – But she told me she (not like) working in the garden.
3. Tony went to the theatre last weekend. – But didn't you say he (go) to the cinema?
4. We'll probably buy a new car. – I thought you said you (not buy) a new one.
5. I built a cupboard last weekend. – Yesterday you said you (not do) anything.
6. I'm reading *Tom Sawyer* at the moment. – A minute ago you told John you (read) *Huckleberry Finn*.
7. We often go to expensive restaurants. – Susan told me you (not go) out for meals very often.

[7] What did they want to know? Questions in reported speech

Don Carter has just come back from a year's exchange visit to Germany. He is telling his parents what questions his German friends asked him about the States and his family: *They asked me where I lived in the States. And they wanted to know if we had always lived here in New York. ...*

a *Here are the questions he was asked:*
1. Where do you live in the States? 2. Have you always lived in New York? 3. What kind of school do you go to? 4. How long do you still have to go to school? 5. When exactly are you going to leave school? 6. How long are you going to stay in Germany? 7. Who are you staying with? 8. Why did you decide to come to Germany?

b *Some people asked some silly questions:*
1. Do all Americans wear cowboy hats? 2. Who made the first hamburger? 3. Are all Americans rich? 4. Are cowboys and Indians still fighting in the Wild West? 5. Does American ice-cream taste better than German ice-cream?

Can you think of other silly questions which people might ask an American visitor?

[8] In English, please

One weekend the school Don visited in Germany was broken into. Two police officers talked to the pupils in Don's class. Here are some of the things they wrote down.

Wir fragten Daniel Seifert, wo er am Samstag, dem 29.2.1992, gewesen sei. Er sagte, daß er Gitarre spiele und nach der Schule mit seiner Rockgruppe geprobt habe. Dann sei er zu seinen Großeltern gegangen und habe ihnen im Garten geholfen. Er fügte hinzu, daß ein amerikanischer Austauschschüler, Don Carter, auch dagewesen sei, als die Gruppe probte. Daniel Seiferts Großmutter erklärte, daß Daniel ihr seit zwei Jahren jeden Samstag nachmittag helfe. Daniels Eltern hätten nicht viel Zeit für ihren Sohn, da sie beide arbeiteten. Sie sagte, daß Daniel sie deshalb oft besuche. Sie fügte hinzu, daß Daniel sie gefragt habe, ob er das nächste Mal einen amerikanischen Austauschschüler mitbringen könne. ...

When the police officers wanted to ask Don a few questions, they first had to tell him in English what they had been told by Daniel.

Translate what they had written down.

A prophet in the wilderness

"Everybody needs beauty."

One day in 1868 a tall young man arrived in San Francisco. His name was John Muir – a Scot who had come with his parents to the USA in 1849 when he was eleven years old. He had often traveled through the mountains, forests and canyons of the United States. It was his hobby to make notes about plants, animals and the geography of an area. He was not a city man, and the growing city of San Francisco with its population of 149,000 was not a place where he wanted to stay long. After five days John Muir left the city for Yosemite Valley. He had read a lot about it and now he wanted to visit it himself.

In those days Yosemite was already quite well-known. In 1851 a group of soldiers who were following Indian trails had found this wonderful valley with its fantastic scenery. Four years later, the first groups of tourists had started to visit the valley. In 1864, during the Civil War, President Lincoln made Yosemite Valley a state park so that farmers could not use it, and settlers could not build homes or put up fences and walls. People should be able to enjoy Yosemite, unspoiled, for all time. But in those days in a country as big as the United States a law could soon be forgotten in an area so far away from Washington.

The journey to Yosemite was not easy. John Muir did not have enough money for a horse, so he and a friend walked for weeks through the Californian valleys, knee-deep in flowers. When they saw Yosemite Valley for the first time, John Muir, like others before him, was fascinated by the landscape: the straight walls of El Capitan, the tree-covered floor of the valley, the silver line of water from Yosemite Falls. During the following years he went back again and again. "I love Yosemite like a mother loves a child," he once wrote. But as the years passed, his eyes saw something else: not only hotels and campgrounds, but also thousands of sheep; and he saw lots of workers who were cutting down trees, even the famous Big Trees. On a visit in 1889, instead of open fields, he saw fences and cows. John Muir was horrified. But while he looked at the scene, his great idea was born – a system of national parks where the land could be conserved and kept in its original state. "Everybody needs beauty," he once wrote, "as well as bread." Over the years, John Muir became well-known as a conservationist. Through his work and influence Yosemite National Park was established in 1890.

In 1903 John Muir got a letter from "an important man in Washington" who wanted to make a trip to the Yosemite Valley with him. That important man was the President of the United States, Theodore Roosevelt. He and Muir camped alone in Mariposa Grove among the Big Trees, where they talked together round a camp fire. "I've had the best time of my life," said the President the next day. "Just think where I was last night. Up there." And he pointed to the cliffs and the trees in the high rocks. As a result of those few days President Roosevelt decided that over a million acres of beautiful countryside in the United States should become national parks. It was a great success for John Muir, but not the end of his long fight as a conservationist.

"There are people good enough and bad enough for anything."

Hetch Hetchy Valley as John Muir saw it

In 1905 the city of San Francisco wanted to put a dam across Hetch Hetchy Valley. As the valley was inside Yosemite National Park, the city needed permission from the federal government in Washington. John Muir loved Hetch Hetchy. For him it was one of the most beautiful valleys that he knew. "It is sad to say," he wrote in his diary, "that they want to turn Hetch Hetchy into a reservoir to supply San Francisco with water and electricity. They are going to flood it from wall to wall and bury its gardens two hundred feet deep. I can't sleep any more. This fight promises to be the worst ever."

John Muir realized that for all those people who were interested in conservation, there were so many who did not care. For Muir the battle for Hetch Hetchy became part of the universal battle between right and wrong. "That anybody should destroy this is unbelievable. But sad experience shows that there are people good enough and bad enough for anything."

On October 9th, 1909 – John Muir was 71 years old – he had the chance to be alone with President Taft on a tour of Yosemite. Muir talked to him about conservation. The President listened carefully, but soon became tired. "But don't you think," said the President, "that as these valleys are so far from the centers of population, they might just as well be used commercially?" And as a joke the President pointed to the narrowest part of the canyon. "Now that would be a fine place for a dam." John Muir became very angry. "A dam! Dam Hetch Hetchy? Why not dam a cathedral or a church?" The President became serious, listened more carefully – and decided to stop the project. But four years later, in 1913, the United States had a new president, Woodrow Wilson, and the battle for Hetch Hetchy started again. John Muir wrote: "This is the twenty-third year of my battle to protect Yosemite National Park." Then in December: "The battle for Hetch Hetchy is not yet lost. I still hope we will win." Two days later the federal government gave San Francisco permission to build the dam. Muir felt bitter. "I have done my best," he wrote. "It is a huge mistake … a huge crime." But even then he hoped that people would see that the government was wrong. His great dream was that people would come together and stop similar plans. But he didn't live long enough to see that dream come true.

John Muir was tired, old, ill and alone. His wife and best friends were all now dead.

Friends and relatives tried to help him out of his loneliness and bitterness, but without success. He died on the morning of December 24th, 1914, one year after the decision to build the dam in Hetch Hetchy Valley. The dam was finally finished in 1924.

(Based on *John Muir in Yosemite* by Shirley Sargent)

Working with the text

1 Check what you have understood

a Pages 137 and 138 have three titles. First try to explain what you think the main title means. Then explain what the other two titles might mean.

b Say which of the following statements are right or wrong; explain your opinion. The phrases on the right will help you.

1. John Muir became interested in nature when he first went to Yosemite Valley.
2. Many Americans knew about the valley before John Muir's first visit in 1868.
3. The idea of a system of national parks came to John Muir when he saw the beauty of the valley.
4. Over the years Yosemite Valley changed, and Muir liked this.
5. Only very few people knew about Muir's work as a conservationist in the 1880s.
6. President Roosevelt wasn't interested in Muir's work.
7. During the fight for Hetch Hetchy Muir realized that not enough people were interested in conservation.
8. President Taft was interested in Muir's work from the first moment on.
9. The fight for Hetch Hetchy ended after more than 20 years.
10. Muir was sad and disappointed about Woodrow Wilson's decision.

I think that's right: If you look at the text, line … says … . (That means …)

or:

I don't think that's right. In line(s) … the text says … . (That means …)

2 Go through the text and collect all the dates and facts …
– about John Muir's life
– about the "history" of Yosemite.
Then make one time line for John Muir's life and one time line for Yosemite. – Some of the dates will appear on both time lines. This is how you could start:

John Muir's life		
1838	1849	…
born in Scotland	came to …	…

the history of Yosemite		
1851	1855	…
group of …	…	…

Finally write a "John Muir biography" or a "History of Yosemite".

3 Say it in English: Making an interview

Imagine it is the year 1909 and you are a reporter for a newspaper. Another pupil can take the role of somebody who supports the dam in Hetch Hetchy Valley, and a third pupil can take the role of somebody who is against the dam.
Each member of your group can make a role-card for his/her role. Then role-play an interview between the reporter and the supporter of the dam and the person who is against the dam.
If possible, record your interview with a cassette-recorder and play it to the class.
When you have made the interview, write it down as an interview for a magazine.

Spotlight on history The Celts*

While Janet was at St David's she met Megan, a girl from Wales. Megan wrote to Janet in London.

11 Gower Road
Swansea
Wales
SA99 1AB
August 2nd

Annwyl Janet,

Rydw i'n hapus chi wedi cael amser ardderchog yn Saint David. Fe ges i amser da iawn hefyd. Roeddech chi'n o hyd ddiddordeb mawr yn ein iaith Cymraeg pan yn ystod eich wyliau, felli rydw i wedi penderfynu i dechrau fy llythr i chi yng Nghymraeg.

I'm sure you didn't understand a word of that, so here it is again in English: Dear Janet, I am very happy you had a wonderful time at St David's. I had a very good time, too. You were always very interested in our Welsh language during your holiday, so I decided to start my letter to you in Welsh.

You asked me to tell you more about Wales and our language. Do you remember? Well, about half a million people in Wales (one fifth of the population) speak Welsh. Most of them live in villages and small towns in the north and the west. Here in South Wales only the older people still speak Welsh. We all learn Welsh at school, but I'm afraid my Welsh isn't very good. Mum is from Cardiff, so she also doesn't speak much Welsh. Dad speaks the language very well. (He helped me with the beginning of the letter!) When we visit my grandparents in Aberystwyth, he speaks Welsh all the time.

It's a pity that I can't understand more Welsh, because there are Welsh programmes on the radio and on TV. And of course lots of writers and poets write in Welsh. I really must work hard on my Welsh next year!

Love, Megan

Celtic jewellery

Welsh is a Celtic language. It comes from the language of the Britons[1]. This Celtic tribe[2] gave the island its name – Britain. As you can see from Megan's letter, it is not like English or German. (People from Brittany in France can understand Welsh, by the way[3], because they speak a similar Celtic language – Breton[4].)
Celtic tribes came to Britain from Europe over two thousand years ago. The different tribes often fought against each other[5] and they made strong swords[6] and other weapons[7]. But they also loved music and made beautiful jewels[8] and fine[9] clothes. The Celts wrote no books and they left no buildings.

* You can find a translation of the most important new words in the *Spotlights on history* at the foot of each page.

[1]Briton ['brɪtn] *Brite/Britin* • [2]tribe [traɪb] *Stamm* • [3]by the way *übrigens* • [4]Breton ['bretɒn] *bretonisch* • [5]each other *einander* • [6]sword [sɔːd] *Schwert* • [7]weapon ['wepən] *Waffe* • [8]jewel(s) ['dʒuːəl(z)] *Juwel(en)* • [9]fine [faɪn] *schön*

The Druids

Stonehenge

The most powerful[1] people in the Celtic tribes were the Druids. They were not only priests[2], but also judges[3] and teachers. The head druids gave the king his crown[4] and his power[5]. It was the Druids' job to look into the future and see what could happen to the king.
The Druids had special places in the country where they met and where the king came when he needed advice. One such[6] place is Stonehenge, the oldest Druid ruin in the country.

Invasions

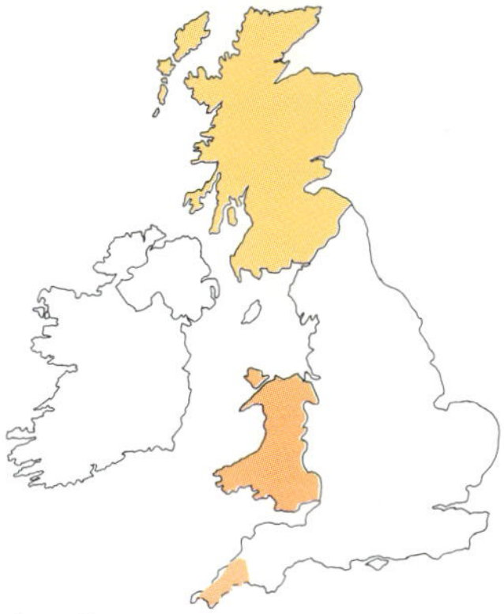

Over the centuries[7] first the Romans, later the Angles and Saxons from Germany and Denmark, and finally[8] the Normans from France invaded[9] Britain. The Romans and Celts lived together peacefully[10]. But the Angles and Saxons attacked the Celts and burned[11] many of their villages. Many Celts left their homes and went to what is now Wales, Scotland and Cornwall. In these places you can still find signs[12] of Britain's Celtic past in the language and culture.

The Welsh today

The Saxons called the Celts in Wales the *wealas*, the 'foreigners'. During the following centuries this name became *Welsh*. The Welsh and the English fought many battles[13] till, in 1282, the English King Edward I defeated[14] the last Welsh prince, Llywelyn. Edward built seventeen large castles in Wales to control[15] the Welsh.
King Edward's son became the Prince of Wales. Today this is still the title for the first son of the British king or queen. Prince Charles is the most famous Prince of Wales. He became Prince of Wales at Caernarfon Castle in 1969.

Caernarfon Castle

[1]powerful ['paʊəfəl] *mächtig* • [2]priest [pri:st] *Priester/in* • [3]judge [dʒʌdʒ] *Richter/in* • [4]crown [kraʊn] *Krone* • [5]power ['paʊə] *Macht* • [6]such [sʌtʃ] *solch* • [7]century ['sentʃərɪ] *Jahrhundert* • [8]finally ['faɪnəlɪ] *schließlich* • [9](to) invade [ɪn'veɪd] *einmarschieren* • [10]peacefully ['pi:sfəlɪ] *friedlich* • [11](to) burn [bɜ:n] *niederbrennen* • [12]sign [saɪn] *Spur* • [13]battle ['bœtl] *Schlacht* • [14](to) defeat [dɪ'fi:t] *schlagen* • [15](to) control [kən'trəʊl] *beherrschen*

The Romans in Britain

The Romans were in Britain for more than 350 years. During that time British life and culture greatly[1] changed. The Romans built cities, towns and roads, developed trade[2] and set up[3] industries. There are many places in Britain today where

Roman coins

you can see Roman remains. Much of Hadrian's Wall, the largest protective[4] wall in the Roman Empire, for example, still exists. You can also visit the baths at Bath or the city walls and gates in Chester or Colchester. These place names come from the Latin word *castra* – 'camp'. The names Manchester, Lancaster, Worcester ['wʊstə] and Gloucester ['glɒstə] have the same origin[5]. Many modern motorways and roads follow the Roman roads like Watling Street or Fosse Way. These roads usually go straight from one former[6] Roman town to the next. It was a long time before certain things that were normal in Roman times became available[7] again. Houses did not have glass windows till the 16th century. People did not have central heating again till after the Second World War!

Hadrian's Wall

The Angles and the Saxons

When, in 410, the Roman army left Britain to fight against Germanic tribes in other parts of the Empire, a period[8] of relative peace[9] and good government came to an end. In the years that followed, the Angles and Saxons came to Britain to settle[10], not just to plunder as they did earlier. The time between the departure of the Romans and the invasion of the Normans in the 11th century is often called the "Dark Ages"[11], partly[12] because we know so little about this time.
As more and more Germanic people settled in Britain, Celtic, the native language[13] of the population, was replaced[14] by Anglo-Saxon. The new invaders divided the land into different kingdoms.

[1]greatly ['greɪtlɪ] *sehr* • [2]trade [treɪd] *Handel* • [3](to) set up [ˌset_'ʌp] – set – set *gründen* • [4]protective [prə'tektɪv] *Schutz-* • [5]origin ['ɒrɪdʒɪn] *Herkunft* • [6]former ['fɔːmə] *ehemalige(r,s)* • [7]available [ə'veɪləbl] *verfügbar* • [8]period ['pɪərɪəd] *Zeit(spanne)* • [9]peace [piːs] *Frieden* • [10](to) settle ['setl] *sich niederlassen* • [11]the Dark Ages *das dunkle Zeitalter* • [12]partly ['pɑːtlɪ] *zum Teil* • [13]native language ['neɪtɪv] *Muttersprache* • [14](to) replace [rɪ'pleɪs] *ersetzen*

Together these kingdoms became known as England and the people who lived there as the English. The name 'English' comes from the Angles, and a part of England today is still called East Anglia. There are many names in England that remind[1] us of its Saxon past. Sussex was once the South Saxon Kingdom – and Essex …, well, what do you think that once was?
Town names that end in '-ton', '-ham' or '-bury' also tell us that they were once Saxon villages. Anglo-Saxon was a Germanic language and that is why many English words today are similar to German words. Examples are: *man, wife, house, father, mother, sister, brother, see, eat, sleep, speak* … .

7th century-3rd century BC: Celtic tribes invaded Britain.

AD 43-400: The Romans were in Britain.

400-600: The Angles and the Saxons invaded Britain and stayed there.

1066: The Normans under William the Conqueror invaded Britain and stayed there.

The Normans

In 1066 England was invaded for the last time. On October 14th Duke[2] William of Normandy defeated the English army at Hastings on the south coast. The battle started early in the morning and lasted all day. In the evening Harold, the last Saxon King of England, was dead. One of the oldest and richest kingdoms in Europe now belonged to the Normans. On Christmas Day, 1066, Duke William – or William the Conqueror as he later became known – was crowned[3] William I, King of England, in Westminster Abbey.
With William the Conqueror the English didn't just get a new king but also a new culture and a new language. French was spoken at court[4] and over the years the Anglo-Saxon language took over many French words.
The Normans ruled England for the next three hundred years. At first the Saxons hated the Normans and they had good reasons for this. King William divided the country among his Norman lords[5] and these lords forced[6] the Saxons to work on the land for them. The forests now also belonged to the Normans and the Saxons were not allowed[7] to hunt[8] animals in them. The men who controlled the forests and the people for the Norman kings were the Sheriffs. They lived in the larger towns in different parts of the country.
Under the Normans, the Saxons had few rights[9]. The only hope for those who broke a law was to leave their villages and hide[10] in the forests where they lived as outlaws[11]. One of the most famous Saxon outlaws was Robin Hood and his home was in Sherwood Forest. His enemy[12] was, of course, the Sheriff of Nottingham.

[1](to) remind of [rɪ'maɪnd] *erinnern an* • [2]duke [dju:k] *Herzog* • [3](to) crown [kraʊn] *krönen zu* • [4]court [kɔ:t] *(königlicher) Hof* • [5]lord [lɔ:d] *Adliger* • [6](to) force [fɔ:s] *zwingen* • [7](to) be allowed to [ə'laʊd] *dürfen* • [8](to) hunt [hʌnt] *jagen* • [9]rights *(pl.)* [raɪts] *Rechte* • [10](to) hide [haɪd] – hid – hidden *(sich) verstecken* • [11]outlaw ['aʊtlɔ:] *Geächtete(r)/Bandit/in* • [12]enemy ['enəmɪ] *Feind/in*

Finding a new home in America

Discovering the New World

Although it is Christopher Columbus who people think of when they talk about the discovery of America, it is almost certain that the Vikings[1] landed in what is today Canada round AD 1000. They called it Vinland – probably because they made wine from the berries[2] they found there. When Columbus landed on an island near the southeast coast of America in 1492, the stories of the Vikings' trips were no longer known. Columbus was really looking for a sea route to Asia. He called the people he met Indians because he thought he was in India.
The early explorers[3] were not looking for new places to settle[4]; they were looking for gold, spices[5] and countries that they could trade with[6].

Columbus on San Salvador, 1492

Settling North America

After Columbus's "discovery" of the New World, the European expansion across the Atlantic began. The first permanent English settlement in North America, Jamestown, was founded[7] in Virginia in 1607. It did not start well. The trip from England was long and dangerous, and many passengers – all men – died. What made things worse was that they chose an unhealthy, marshy[8] place for their settlement.

The reconstructed Jamestown settlement

After they arrived the settlers did not build proper houses or grow[9] their own food. They thought they could make the Indians work for them. At the end of the first year, less than half of the settlers were still alive. The rest survived[10] only because the Indians brought them food and showed them how to grow corn. However, because the settlers began to steal the Indians' corn, the relations[11] between them turned bad.
It was the discovery that tobacco grew well in Virginia that helped the early colonists to survive the "starving[12] times". In 1619 the first African slaves[13] arrived in Jamestown to work on the tobacco farms. By 1624[14] Virginia was exporting 200,000 pounds of tobacco.

The Pilgrims

In 1620, 102 English men, women and children sailed to America on the 'Mayflower'. They settled in Plymouth, Massachusetts. There they hoped to find religious freedom[15]. In England at that time it was dangerous to have different religious ideas. After a stormy nine-week trip, a cold, hard winter lay before them. They did not have enough food and many became ill and died. Again, it was a tribe of Indians who showed the settlers how to find and grow food.

[1]Viking ['vaɪkɪŋ] • [2]berry ['berɪ] *Beere* • [3]explorer [ɪk'splɔːrə] *Entdeckungsreisende(r)* • [4](to) settle ['setl] *(be)siedeln* • [5]spice [spaɪs] *Gewürz* • [6](to) trade (with) [treɪd] *handeln (mit)* • [7](to) found *gründen* • [8]marshy ['mɑːʃɪ] *sumpfig* • [9](to) grow *anbauen* • [10](to) survive [sə'vaɪv] *überleben* • [11]relations [rɪ'leɪʃnz] *Beziehungen* • [12](to) starve [stɑːv] *(ver)hungern* • [13]slave [sleɪv] *Sklave/-in* • [14]by 1624 *im Jahr 1624* • [15]freedom ['friːdəm] *Freiheit*

1 Die einfache Form des Präsens (The simple present)

Every year our visitors **meet** lots of other young people.
Often they **don't find** it easy to make friends at first.
Why **don't you** write to us for more information**?**

Du verwendest das *simple present*, um auszudrücken, daß etwas regelmäßig, oft, üblicherweise, immer, selten oder nie geschieht.

2 Die einfache Form der Vergangenheit (The simple past)

→ Focus on Grammar, p.10

Marilyn Monroe **was** a filmstar.	*Marilyn Monroe war ein Filmstar.*
Pelé **played** football for Brazil in the 1960s.	*Pelé hat in den sechziger Jahren Fußball für Brasilien gespielt./ Pelé spielte in den sechziger Jahren Fußball für Brasilien.*
Steffi Graf **won** Wimbledon in 1991.	*Steffi Graf hat 1991 Wimbledon gewonnen./ Steffi Graf gewann 1991 Wimbledon.*

Du verwendest das *simple past*, um auszudrücken, daß etwas zu einem bestimmten Zeitpunkt (Frage: *wann?*) in der Vergangenheit geschah, z.B. in Erzählungen und Berichten über vergangenes Geschehen.
In *simple past*-Sätzen findest du häufig Zeitbestimmungen wie *yesterday, in 1968, last week/year/ Saturday/..., two minutes/hours/months/... ago.* (Wenn aus dem Zusammenhang klar ist, wann etwas geschah, wird auf solche Zeitbestimmungen oft verzichtet.)
Im Deutschen verwenden wir das Perfekt oder das Präteritum.

a Das *simple past* in bejahten Aussagesätzen (The simple past in positive statements)

→ Focus on Grammar, p.10

(to) be

I **was**	[wəz]	here yesterday.
You **were**	[wə]	
He/She **was**		
We/You/They **were**		

Regelmäßige Verben

I/You	**play**ed a game last night.
He/She	
We/You/They	

Die meisten englischen Verben sind **regelmäßige Verben**. Man bildet *simple past*-Formen, indem man *-ed* an den Infinitiv hängt. Es gibt für alle Personen nur eine Form.

Merke dir bei der Schreibung:	arrive → arriv**ed**, move → mov**ed**	Wegfall des stummen End-*e*
	stop → sto**pped**, prefer [-'-] → prefe**rred**	Verdopplung des Endkonsonanten nach einem als <u>ein</u> Buchstabe geschriebenen, <u>betonten</u> Vokal
	try → tr**ied**, tidy → tid**ied**	*-y* nach Konsonant wird zu *-i-*
Merke dir bei der Aussprache:	lov**ed**, turn**ed**, call**ed**, remember**ed**, play**ed** [-d]	nach stimmhaftem Auslaut (z.B. [-b], [-v], [-n], [-l], [-eɪ])
	look**ed**, help**ed**, laugh**ed**, miss**ed**, watch**ed** [-t]	nach stimmlosem Auslaut (z.B. [-k], [-p], [-f], [-s], [-ʃ], [-tʃ])
	hat**ed**, need**ed**, last**ed**, shout**ed**, test**ed** [-ɪd]	nach [-t] oder [-d]

Grammar 1

Unregelmäßige Verben

I **went** to Wales last year.
(Infinitiv: (to) **go**)
We all **fell** into the water yesterday.
(Infinitiv: (to) **fall**)
Janet **wrote** a letter an hour ago.
(Infinitiv: (to) **write**)

Es gibt im Englischen etwa 100 gebräuchliche **unregelmäßige Verben**. Die unregelmäßigen *simple past*-Formen mußt du auswendig lernen. Es gibt für alle Personen nur eine Form.

Liste der unregelmäßigen Verben: p. 230-231

G

b Das *simple past* in Fragen und Kurzantworten (The simple past in questions and short answers)

→ Focus on Grammar, p. 11

(to) be

Were you here**?** – Yes, I **was**. [wɒz]
Was she in Wales**?** – No, she **wasn't**.

Were they here**?** – Yes, they **were**. [wɜː]
When **were** they in York**?** – Last month.

Regelmäßige und unregelmäßige Verben

Did you **play** a game last night**?** – Yes, I **did**.
When **did** you **play** a game**?** – From 7 to 9.

Did Latif **help** Karen yesterday**?** – No, he **didn't**.
Who **did** Latif **help?** (= Wem ... ?) – Janet.

Wie du weißt, werden Fragen im *simple present* mit dem vorangestellten Hilfsverb *do* gebildet. Im *simple past* bildest du Fragen, indem du *did* voranstellst. Das Vollverb steht dabei im Infinitiv, nicht in der *simple past*-Form.
Diese Regel gilt für regelmäßige und unregelmäßige Verben und für alle Personen.

⚠ **Who did** Latif **help?** – Janet. — *Wem hat Latif geholfen? – Janet.*
Who helped Janet**?** – Latif. — *Wer hat Janet geholfen? – Latif.*

Beachte: Keine Umschreibung mit *did* bei Fragen nach dem Subjekt.

c Das *simple past* in verneinten Aussagesätzen (The simple past in negative statements)

→ Focus on Grammar, p. 11

(to) be

I **wasn't** ['wɒznt]	in Wales.
You **weren't** [wɜːnt]	
He/She **wasn't**	
We/You/They **weren't**	

(Langformen: **was not**, **were not**)

Regelmäßige und unregelmäßige Verben

My parents **played** a game last night.
I **didn't play** a game last night.

Robin Shaw **went** to York last week.
Latif **didn't go** to York last week.

Auch die Verneinung im *simple past* ist einfach, wenn du dich an die Verneinung im *simple present* erinnerst. Du bildest verneinte Sätze im *simple past* mit *didn't* (Langform: *did not*). Das Vollverb nach *didn't* steht im Infinitiv, nicht in der *simple past*-Form.
Auch diese Regel gilt für regelmäßige und unregelmäßige Verben und für alle Personen.

3 Die Verlaufsform der Vergangenheit (The past progressive)

Das *past progressive* wird mit *was/were + -ing form* gebildet.

a What **were** you **doing** at 7 o'clock last night?
– I **was writing** letters from 6 to 8.

Was hast du gestern abend um 7 Uhr gemacht?
– Ich habe von 6 bis 8 Briefe geschrieben./
Ich war von 6 bis 8 dabei, Briefe zu schreiben.

Du verwendest das *past progressive*, um auszudrücken, daß etwas zu einem bestimmten Zeitpunkt oder über einen bestimmten Zeitraum in der Vergangenheit im Gange (englisch: *in progress*) war.
Im Deutschen verwenden wir das Perfekt oder das Präteritum.

Vergleiche:

Police officer: What **were** you **doing** between 2 and 4 yesterday afternoon?

Answer 1: I **was working** in the garden.
(I was working there all afternoon.)

Answer 2: I **worked** in the garden from 2 to 3.30.
(Then I went to see a friend.)

Antwort 1 *(past progressive)* drückt aus, daß die Sprecherin/der Sprecher die fragliche Zeit **und die Zeit darüber hinaus** mit Gartenarbeit verbracht hat. Antwort 2 *(simple past)* bedeutet, daß die Sprecherin/der Sprecher **von genau 14 Uhr bis 15 Uhr 30** im Garten gearbeitet hat.

b The girls **were sitting** in their tent. Helen **was telling** Janet and Karen a story. Jessica **was sleeping**. Nobody **was expecting** a surprise when suddenly it happened: They heard footsteps, the tent fell on them, and the next moment they **were sitting** in the dark.

Die Mädchen saßen in ihrem Zelt. Helen erzählte Janet und Karen gerade eine Geschichte. Jessica schlief. Niemand rechnete mit einer Überraschung, als es plötzlich geschah: Sie hörten Schritte, das Zelt fiel auf sie, und im nächsten Augenblick saßen sie im Dunkeln.

Das *past progressive* verwendet man, um in Berichten und Erzählungen die Situation oder „Szene" zu beschreiben, in der etwas Wichtiges geschah („was gerade vor sich ging, als etwas Wichtiges passierte").

Vergleiche:

1. When Jessica came in, her dog **was barking**.

In Satz 1 *(past progressive)* bellte der Hund bereits, **bevor** Jessica hereinkam.

2. When Jessica came in, her dog **barked**.

In Satz 2 *(simple past)* begann der Hund erst zu bellen, **als** Jessica hereinkam.

Unit 2

1 Bestimmende Relativsätze (Defining relative clauses)

→ Focus on Grammar, p.24

a Is that the man **who/that designed St Paul's**? — *Ist das der Mann, der St. Pauls entworfen hat?*

Look at the church **which/that is on your right**. — *Sehen Sie sich die Kirche an, die rechts von Ihnen zu sehen ist.*

Wir benutzen Relativsätze, um ein Nomen genauer zu bestimmen. Ohne diese Relativsätze wissen wir nicht genau, was die Sprecherin/der Sprecher meint. (Welcher Mann? Welche Kirche?) Diese Relativsätze heißen daher **bestimmende** Relativsätze *(**defining** relative clauses).*

Vergleiche Wortstellung und Zeichensetzung in englischen und deutschen Relativsätzen:

We met a woman	**who**	**knew**	everything about Jack the Ripper.
Wir haben eine Frau getroffen,	**die**		alles über Jack the Ripper **wußte**.
Where is the newspaper article	**which**	**was**	on my desk?
Wo ist der Zeitungsartikel,	**der**		auf meinem Schreibtisch **lag**?

Wie für alle Nebensätze gilt auch für Relativsätze die Wortstellung ***subject – verb***, d.h. das Verb steht an derselben Stelle wie im Hauptsatz.
Bestimmende Relativsätze werden im Englischen nicht durch Komma vom Hauptsatz getrennt.

Die Relativpronomen *who, which* und *that*

- Wir verwenden *who* für Personen und *which* für Dinge. (Merkhilfe: *who* – Pers**o**nen, *which* – D**i**nge)
- Wir können *that* für Personen und Dinge verwenden.

⚠ Nach *all, everything, something* und *nothing* steht das Relativpronomen *that.*
I'd like **something that** is less expensive. Stephen likes **everything that** is sweet.

Das Relativpronomen *whose*

I met a boy **whose mother** works in Hollywood. — *... einen Jungen, dessen Mutter in Hollywood arbeitet.*
This is the flat **whose owners** live in Paris. — *... die Wohnung, deren Besitzer in Paris leben.*

- Wir verwenden *whose (= deren, dessen)* für Personen und Dinge. Auf *whose* folgt immer ein Nomen.

⚠ Verwechsle *whose* nicht mit der Kurzform *who's (= who is).*
The girl **whose** parents are divorced is called Emma.
The girl **who's** waiting at the bus stop is called Emma.

b ***Contact clauses***

→ Focus on Grammar, p.26

	object	*subject*		
The people	**who/that**	**Mrs Foster**	**interviewed** were very nice.	*Die Menschen, die Mrs Foster*
The people		**Mrs Foster**	**interviewed** were very nice.	*interviewte, waren sehr nett.*
The answers	**which/that**	**they**	**gave** were very interesting.	*Die Antworten, die sie gaben,*
The answers		**they**	**gave** were very interesting.	*waren sehr interessant.*

Wenn das Relativpronomen nicht Subjekt des Relativsatzes ist, sondern Objekt, kannst du es weglassen. Relativsätze ohne Relativpronomen heißen *contact clauses.*

Die folgenden Beispiele zeigen dir noch einmal zwei bestimmende Relativsätze, in denen die Relativpronomen unterschiedliche Funktionen im Satz haben. Nur im zweiten Satz kannst du es weglassen. Relativpronomen, die Subjekt sind und daher direkt vor dem Verb stehen, darfst du nie weglassen:

	object	*subject*		
Is that the man		**who/that**	**designed St Paul's**?	*..., der St. Pauls entworfen hat?*
Is that the man	**(who/that)**	**we**	**met last week**?	*..., den wir letzte Woche getroffen haben?*

c *Contact clauses* mit Präpositionen (Contact clauses with prepositions) → Focus on Grammar, p.26

The people **who/that** **we spoke to** were very friendly. *..., **mit** denen wir **sprachen**, ...*
The people **we spoke to** were very friendly.
The tour **which/that** **you wrote an article about** seems interesting. *..., **über** die du einen Artikel **geschrieben hast**, ...*
The tour **you wrote an article about** seems interesting.

Auch in diesen Beispielen sind die Relativpronomen nicht Subjekt und können daher weggelassen werden. Beachte, daß die Präpositionen in den englischen Relativsätzen nicht an der gleichen Stelle wie im Deutschen stehen, sondern an derselben Stelle wie im englischen Hauptsatz. Vergleiche:

Some parts of Docklands **(which/that)** Mrs Foster wrote an article **about** are like Chicago.
Mrs Foster wrote an article **about** some parts of Docklands.

2 *some/any* und ihre Zusammensetzungen (*some/any* and their compounds)

I'd like to go **somewhere** and do **something** interesting with **some** friends. — *Ich würde gern irgendwo hingehen und etwas Interessantes mit ein paar Freunden unternehmen.*
I have**n't** seen **anybody** today. — *Ich habe heute noch niemanden getroffen.*
Is there a disco **anywhere** near here**?** — *Gibt es hier irgendwo in der Nähe eine Disco?*
Do you have **any** other suggestions**?** — *Hast du irgendwelche anderen Vorschläge?*

Man benutzt
- *some*, *somebody* usw. vor allem in **bejahten Aussagesätzen**,
- *any*, *anybody* usw. vor allem in **verneinten Sätzen** und in **Fragen**.

in bejahten Aussagesätzen		in verneinten Sätzen		in Fragen	
some	*einige, ein paar; etwas*	**not ... any**	*keine; kein*	**any?**	*irgendwelche?*
somebody	*jemand*	**not ... anybody**	*niemand*	**anybody?**	*(irgend) jemand?*
something	*etwas*	**not ... anything**	*nichts*	**anything?**	*(irgend) etwas?*
somewhere	*irgendwo(hin)*	**not ... anywhere**	*nirgendwo(hin)*	**anywhere?**	*irgendwo(hin)?*

Oft kannst du *not ... any, not ... anybody* usw. durch *no, nobody, nothing, nowhere* ersetzen:

There are**n't any** shops / are **no** shops in our street. — *Es gibt keine Geschäfte in unserer Straße.*

They could**n't** see **anybody** / could see **nobody** in the office. — *Sie konnten niemanden im Büro sehen.*

We do**n't** know **anything** / know **nothing** about Robin Hood. — *Wir wissen nichts über Robin Hood.*

Beachte, daß *some* und *any* (in Fragen) oft keine Entsprechung im Deutschen haben:

Do you need **any** bread/biscuits? — *Brauchst du Brot/Kekse?*
– No, but I need **some** milk/eggs. — *– Nein, aber ich brauche Milch/Eier.*

Unit 3

1 Das *present perfect* (The present perfect)

→ Focus on Grammar, p.38

a

We **have been** to the headteacher.	*Wir sind bei der Schulleiterin gewesen.*
Mrs Price **has not informed** everybody.	*Mrs Price hat nicht alle informiert.*
Have you **written** to the German parents**?**	*Haben Sie an die deutschen Eltern geschrieben?*
– Yes, I **have**./No, I **haven't**.	*– Ja (, habe ich)./Nein (, habe ich nicht).*

Du kannst mit dem *present perfect* ausdrücken, **daß** jemand etwas getan hat oder **daß** etwas geschehen ist. Für die Sprecherin/den Sprecher ist es nicht wichtig (vielleicht ist es sogar nicht bekannt), wann es geschah. Deshalb wird ein genauer Zeitpunkt nicht genannt.

Vergleiche *present perfect* und *simple past*:

I**'ve read** your book. You can have it back now.	I **read** your book last night. You can have it back now.
Have you **bought** a new car**?**	When **did** you **buy** your new car**?**
Present perfect: Für die Sprecherin/den Sprecher ist es wichtig, **daß** etwas geschah, nicht wann es geschah.	***Simple past:*** Die Sprecherin/der Sprecher möchte auch mitteilen, **wann** etwas geschah *(last night)*. Deshalb muß das *simple past* verwendet werden.

Du benutzt das *simple past* auch, um über ein im *present perfect* eingeführtes Geschehen weiterzureden:
Look, I**'ve bought** a new computer. I **bought** it at *City Comp* (last Friday). It **wasn't** even expensive.

b Das *present perfect* wird mit *have/has* + Partizip Perfekt *(past participle)* gebildet. → Focus on Grammar, p.38

Kurzformen:

I**'ve**/you**'ve**/we**'ve**/they**'ve**	+ *past participle*
he**'s**/she**'s**/it**'s**	
I **haven't**/you **haven't**/we **haven't**/they **haven't**	
he **hasn't**/she **hasn't**/it **hasn't**	

⚠ She **has** helped me. Sie **hat** mir geholfen. — She **has** arrived. Sie **ist** angekommen.

Das *present perfect* wird immer mit *have/has* gebildet. Im Deutschen verwenden wir *haben* oder *sein*.

Das *past participle* der regelmäßigen Verben

(to) **inform** – **informed**, (to) **call** – **called** [-d]
(to) **help** – **helped**, (to) **look** – **looked** [-t]
(to) **wait** – **waited**, (to) **need** – **needed** [-ɪd]

Man bildet regelmäßige *past participles*, indem man *-ed* an den Infinitiv hängt. Es gibt für alle Personen nur eine Form.

⚠ Für die Schreibung und Aussprache der regelmäßigen *past participles* gelten dieselben Regeln wie für die *-ed*-Form des *simple past* (vgl. S. 145, 2 a), also *arrive* → *arrived*, *stop* → *stopped*, *try* → *tried*.

Das *past participle* der unregelmäßigen Verben

(to) **be** – **been**, (to) **do** – **done**, (to) **have** – **had**
(to) **come** – **come**, (to) **write** – **written**

Unregelmäßige *past participles* mußt du auswendig lernen. Es gibt für alle Personen nur eine Form.

Liste der unregelmäßigen Verben: p.230-231

c Das *present perfect* mit unbestimmten Zeitangaben

→ Focus on Grammar, p.38

(The present perfect with adverbs of indefinite time)

I've never been to London. **Have** you **ever been** there? – Yes, I have. **I've just come** back.

Marion **has spent** a month in England **before**.
I **haven't done** my homework **yet**.

Have you **done** your homework **yet?** – No, **so far** **I've been** too busy/**I've been** too busy **so far**.

In *present perfect*-Sätzen findest du oft Adverbien der unbestimmten Zeit, d.h. Adverbien, die keinen genauen Zeitpunkt angeben, z.B.

always	(schon) immer	*before*	schon einmal
never	nie, noch nie	*often*	oft
so far	bis jetzt	*not … yet*	noch nicht
ever?	je? jemals?	*yet?*	schon?

- *already, always, ever, just, often, never* stehen direkt vor dem *past participle*.
- *before* und *yet* stehen am Satzende.
- *so far* kann am Satzanfang oder am Satzende stehen.

d *since* und *for* mit dem *present perfect* (*since* and *for* with the present perfect)

→ Focus on Gram., p.41

The children **have been** at the club **since six o'clock**/**for three hours**.
Die Kinder sind seit sechs Uhr/seit drei Stunden im Klub.

Du verwendest *since* oder *for* mit dem *present perfect*, um auszudrücken, daß etwas in der Vergangenheit begonnen hat und jetzt noch andauert:

- *since* wird mit dem **Zeitpunkt** verbunden, zu dem etwas begann *(since seven o'clock, since Sunday, since July 3rd, since my birthday, …)*
- *for* wird mit dem **Zeitraum** verbunden, der angibt, wie lange etwas schon andauert *(for ten minutes, for two days, for a few weeks, for a long time, …)*.

⚠ **We've had** this car for many years/since 1984.
Wir **haben** dieses Auto (schon) seit vielen Jahren/ seit 1984.

Im Deutschen verwenden wir *seit* meist mit dem Präsens, wenn wir sagen wollen, wie lange etwas schon andauert.

e Die Verlaufsform des *present perfect* (The present perfect progressive)

→ Focus on Grammar, p.41

Das *present perfect progressive* wird mit *have/has* + *been* + *-ing form* gebildet.

Mr Buxton's pupils **have been working** for 20 minutes. Martin **hasn't been working**. He **has been talking** to his neighbour all the time.
Sorry I'm late. **Have** you **been waiting** long?

Mr Buxtons Schülerinnen und Schüler arbeiten seit 20 Minuten. Martin hat nicht gearbeitet. Er redet schon die ganze Zeit mit seinem Nachbarn.
… Wartest du schon lange?

Du verwendest das *present perfect progressive*, um auszudrücken, daß **Tätigkeiten** *(work, talk, …)* schon eine Zeitlang andauern. Du benutzt *since* oder *for* + Zeitangabe, wenn du sagen willst, wie lange die Tätigkeiten schon andauern. Beachte, daß die Tätigkeit nicht ununterbrochen im Gange gewesen sein muß:
Susan **has been playing** the piano since her 5th birthday. *Susan spielt seit ihrem 5. Geburtstag Klavier.*

⚠ Verben, die **Zustände** beschreiben *(be, have, know, like, cost, …)*, können nicht im *present perfect progressive* verwendet werden: **I've known** Jamie for more than ten years/since 1981.

G

2 Possessivpronomen (Possessive adjectives and possessive pronouns)

This isn't **my** pencil. **Mine** is green.	*Das ist nicht mein Bleistift. Meiner ist grün.*
Their car is new, **ours** is old.	*Ihr Auto ist neu, unseres ist alt.*

personal pronouns	I	you	he	she	it	we	you	they
possessive adjectives	**my** mein/e	**your** dein/e; Ihr/e	**his** sein/e	**her** ihr/e	**its** sein/e	**our** unser/e	**your** euer/eure; Ihr/e	**their** ihr/e
possessive pronouns	**mine** meine(r, s)	**yours** deine(r, s)	**his** seine(r, s)	**hers** ihre(r, s)	**its** seine(r, s)	**ours** unsere(r, s)	**yours** eure(r, s)	**theirs** ihre(r, s)

my, your, his, her usw. stehen immer vor einem Nomen, wie Adjektive. (Daher heißen sie *possessive **adjectives***.)

mine, yours, his, hers usw. kannst du verwenden, wenn du ein Nomen nicht wiederholen willst.
mine, yours, his, hers usw. stehen allein, **für** ein bereits genanntes Nomen. (Daher heißen sie *possessive **pro**nouns*.)

Unit 4

Möglichkeiten, über Zukünftiges zu sprechen (Ways to talk about the future)

Im Deutschen verwenden wir meist das Präsens, um über Zukünftiges zu sprechen. Im Englischen mußt du in der Regel eine Futurform benutzen, um über Zukünftiges zu sprechen.

1 Pläne für die Zukunft: Das Futur mit *going to* (Plans for the future: The *going to*-future)

→ Focus on Grammar, p.54

Wenn du ausdrücken möchtest, daß jemand geplant hat, etwas zu tun, verwendest du das *going to-future*. Das *going to-future* wird mit *am/are/is going to* + Infinitiv gebildet.

Bina and Latif **are going to spend** a weekend in a *Groundwork* camp.	*Bina und Latif haben vor, ein Wochenende in einem Groundwork-Camp zu verbringen.*
A girl from their class **is going to work** with them.	*Ein Mädchen aus ihrer Klasse plant, mit ihnen zu arbeiten.*
Some children **are not going to help** them.	*Einige Kinder werden ihnen nicht helfen.*
What kind of trees **are** they **going to plant?**	*Was für Bäume wollen sie pflanzen?*

Du kannst das *going to-future* auch verwenden, um auszudrücken, daß bald etwas mit großer Sicherheit geschehen wird:

Careful! You**'re going to drop** a glass.	*Vorsicht! Du läßt gleich ein Glas fallen.*

2 Vorhersagen/Vermutungen über Zukünftiges: Das Futur mit *will*
(Predictions about the future: The *will*-future)

→ Focus on Grammar, p.54-55

Wenn du Vorhersagen und Vermutungen über Zukünftiges äußern möchtest, verwendest du das *will-future*. In Vorhersagen und Vermutungen findest du oft Ausdrücke wie *I'm sure, I suppose, I hope, I think, perhaps* und *probably*.
Das *will-future* wird mit *will* + Infinitiv (ohne *to*) gebildet. Kurzformen: **will** = **'ll**, **will not** = **won't** [wəʊnt]
(Statt *I/we will* bzw. *won't* werden in formellem Englisch auch *I/we shall* [ʃæl, ʃəl] bzw. *shan't* [ʃɑːnt] verwendet.)

I'm sure the new forests **will bring** huge areas back to life. — *Ich bin sicher, daß die neuen Wälder große Gebiete wieder lebendig werden lassen.*

All this **won't happen** overnight. It **will take** years. — *All dies geschieht nicht über Nacht. Es wird Jahre dauern.*

What **will** the north **look** like in twenty years**?** **Will** it **look** better**?** — *Wie sieht der Norden wohl in zwanzig Jahren aus? Wird er besser aussehen?*

⚠ In Nebensätzen der Zeit verwendest du das *simple present*, nicht das *will-future*, um über Zukünftiges zu sprechen. Vergleiche:
When *Groundwork* **finishes** its work, I **will be** eighty.
Groundwork **will finish** its work in 2050. I **will be** eighty in 2050.

Du mußt das *will-future* auch verwenden, wenn du spontan auf etwas reagierst:

These bags are too heavy for me. – OK, we **'ll carry** them for you. ... – *Wir tragen sie für dich.*
What would you like to drink? – I **'ll have** tea, please. ... – *Ich nehme Tee./Tee, bitte.*

3 Die Hauptunterschiede zwischen *going to-future* und *will-future*

(The main differences between *going to-future* and *will-future*)

I **'m going to have** a big party on my birthday.
Look at the clouds. It **'s going to rain**.

going to-future:
- für Absichten/Pläne
- für zukünftige Ereignisse, die mit großer Sicherheit eintreten werden

People **will live** on the moon one day.
I suppose we **'ll get** some snow pretty soon.
There isn't any milk left. – Oh. OK, I **'ll get** some.

will-future:
- für Vorhersagen über Zukünftiges
- für Vermutungen über Zukünftiges
- für spontane Entschlüsse

4 Weitere Möglichkeiten, über Zukünftiges zu sprechen (Other ways to talk about the future)

→ Focus on Grammar, p.55

a Für etwas, das fest geplant oder verabredet ist, kannst du auch das *present progressive* verwenden. Durch eine Zeitbestimmung oder aus dem Zusammenhang muß deutlich sein, daß es um Zukünftiges geht.

My parents **are driving** me to the *Groundwork* camp tomorrow. **Are** you **coming**, too**?**

b Für zukünftiges Geschehen, das durch Programme, Fahrpläne usw. festgelegt ist, kannst du das *simple present* benutzen *("timetable future")*. Verben wie *arrive, open, close, start, stop* werden oft so verwendet.

The camp **opens** on May 1st. Our bus **arrives** at the camp at 11.00. Lunch **is** at 12.00. Work **starts** at 1.00, and we **stop** for dinner at 6.00.

[5] Die Verlaufsform des Futurs (The future progressive)

Wenn du ausdrücken möchtest, daß zu einem bestimmten Zeitpunkt oder während eines bestimmten Zeitraums in der Zukunft etwas im Gange (englisch: *in progress*) sein wird, verwendest du das *future progressive*. Es wird mit *will + be + -ing form* gebildet.

This time tomorrow I **won't be sitting** at my computer, I **'ll be lying** in the sun. What **will** you **be doing** this time tomorrow**?** — *Morgen um diese Zeit sitze ich nicht an meinem Computer, da liege ich in der Sonne. Was machst du morgen um diese Zeit?*

[6] Das *future perfect* (The future perfect)

Das *future perfect* gleicht dem *present perfect*. Du verwendest das *present perfect*, um auszudrücken, daß etwas vor der Gegenwart geschehen ist. Das *future perfect* verwendest du, um auszudrücken, daß etwas vor einem bestimmten Zeitpunkt in der Zukunft geschehen sein wird. Oft findest du Zeitbestimmungen wie *by Monday/by then/...* (bis ...), *next week/year/...* oder *in ten minutes/three days/...* in Sätzen mit dem *future perfect*.
Das *future perfect* wird mit *will* + *have* + *past participle* gebildet.

Groundwork will finish its work in 2050. Many things **will have changed** by then.	*Groundwork beendet seine Arbeit im Jahr 2050. Vieles wird sich bis dahin verändert haben.*
Next year everybody **will have heard** about *Groundwork*.	*Nächstes Jahr wird jeder von Groundwork gehört haben.*
Will you **have finished** your homework when I come back**?**	*Wirst du deine Hausaufgaben fertig haben, wenn ich zurückkomme?*
I'm sorry, but I **won't have repaired** your bike by Monday.	*Es tut mir leid, aber ich werde dein Fahrrad nicht bis Montag repariert haben.*

Unit 5

1 Adverbien der Art und Weise (Adverbs of manner)

→ Focus on Grammar, p.67

a Die folgenden Beispiele zeigen dir, was ...

– Adjektive näher bestimmen: **Gerald** is **quiet**. He likes **quiet** **music**.

– Adverbien der Art und Weise näher bestimmen: He **speaks** **quietly**.

It was a **terribly** **cold** night.

Jane solved the problem **unbelievably** **quickly**.

Die meisten Adverbien der Art und Weise sind aus Adjektiven abgeleitet. Sie werden gebildet, indem man *-ly* an das Adjektiv anhängt: *quiet* (Adjektiv) – *quietly* (Adverb).

Adverbien der Art und Weise, die das Verb näher bestimmen, haben im Englischen meist *end-position*:
Gerald closed the door **quietly**. — *Gerald schloß* ***leise*** *die Tür.*

b Die Schreibung der Adverbien der Art und Weise (The spelling of adverbs of manner)

→ Focus on Grammar, p.67

Beachte:

- *strange* → *strangely, polite* → *politely* — Das stumme End-*e* fällt bei der Bildung des Adverbs **nicht** weg (Ausnahme: *true* → *truly*).
- *easy* → *easily, noisy* → *noisily* — *-y* wird zu *-i-* (Ausnahme: *shy* → *shyly*).
- *terrible* → *terribly* — *-le* fällt bei der Bildung des Adverbs weg.

c Unregelmäßige Adverbien der Art und Weise (Irregular adverbs of manner)

→ Focus on Grammar, p.67

Gerald's English is **good**, and he speaks French quite **well**, too.
It's **hard** work to understand his German. I have to work very **hard**.
We're lucky that he isn't a **fast** talker. When people speak **fast** we can't understand them.

Adjektiv			Adverb
	good	– **well**	
	hard	– **hard**	
	fast	– **fast**	

d Adverb oder Adjektiv nach bestimmten Verben (Adverb or adjective after certain verbs)

→ Focus on Grammar, p.67

Wie du weißt, werden nach Verben gewöhnlich Adverbien der Art und Weise verwendet, um auszudrücken, wie jemand etwas tut: I learned English **easily**.
Es gibt aber Verben, die nicht Tätigkeiten, sondern **Eigenschaften** oder **Zustände** beschreiben. (Daher kannst du sie durch *be* ersetzen.) Nach diesen Verben stehen **Adjektive**:

For many people English **seems easy**. I don't think it is easy.	*Für viele Leute scheint Englisch leicht zu sein. …*
Does my accent **sound strange** to you? Some people say it is strange.	*Klingt mein Akzent komisch für dich? …*

Die wichtigsten Verben, nach denen Adjektive stehen, sind:
become werden ***seem*** (zu sein) scheinen ***sound*** klingen

⚠ Die Verben ***feel***, ***look***, ***smell***, ***taste*** können sowohl eine Tätigkeit als auch eine Eigenschaft beschreiben:

Mrs Price **looked angrily** at her class. Mrs Price sah ihre Klasse wütend an.	Mrs Price **looked angry**. Mrs Price sah wütend aus.
Susan **tasted/smelled** the soup **carefully**. Susan probierte vorsichtig die Suppe/roch vorsichtig an der Suppe.	The soup **tasted/smelled good**. Die Suppe schmeckte/roch gut.

2 Die Steigerung der Adverbien der Art und Weise (The comparison of adverbs of manner)

→ Focus on Grammar, p.71

	comparative	*superlative*
Gerald speaks **quietly**.	Patricia speaks **more quietly**.	David speaks **most quietly**.
Tina can run **fast**.	Ken can run **faster**.	Liz can run **fastest**.
Sue works **hard**.	Bob works **harder**.	Eve works **hardest**.

Adverbien der Art und Weise auf *-ly* werden durch Voranstellen von *more/most* gesteigert, einsilbige Adverbien durch Anhängen von *-er/-est*.

⚠ Unregelmäßige Steigerungsformen: ***well – better – best*** ***badly – worse – worst***

3 Frageanhängsel (Question tags)

In Gesprächen verwendet man häufig Frageanhängsel (im Deutschen z. B. *nicht wahr?, nicht?, ne?, gell?*), wenn man vom Gesprächspartner Zustimmung zur eigenen Aussage erwartet. Im Englischen bildet man diese Frageanhängsel immer mit einem Hilfsverb + Personalpronomen. Wenn im Aussagesatz kein Hilfsverb steht, bildet man das Frageanhängsel mit einer Form von *do*.

England **is** great, **isn't it?**
The boys **have** got a problem, **haven't they?**
Cindy **can** speak French, **can't she?**
Sue's parents **live** in Scotland, **don't they?**
Tony **likes** pop music, **doesn't he?**
You **saw** Alice yesterday, **didn't you?**

Your father **isn't** working, **is he?**
You **can't** cook very well, **can you?**
This shop **doesn't** sell cassettes, **does it?**
The boys **didn't** help you, **did they?**

Aussagesatz bejaht →	***question tag* verneint**
is/have/can usw. →	*isn't/haven't/can't* usw. + Personalpronomen
(Vollverb, bejaht) →	*don't/doesn't/didn't* + Personalpronomen
Aussagesatz verneint →	***question tag* bejaht**
isn't/haven't/can't usw. →	*is/have/can* usw. + Personalpronomen
don't/doesn't/didn't →	*do/does/did* + Personal-pronomen

Bei diesen *question tags* geht die Stimme am Ende des Satzes nach unten (wie bei einer Aussage): ↘

Grammar 5/6

4 Verben mit zwei Objekten (Verbs with two objects)

a Wie im Deutschen gibt es im Englischen Verben, nach denen zwei Objekte stehen können:
– ein **indirektes Objekt** (meist eine Person – daher auch **Personenobjekt**) und
– ein **direktes Objekt** (meist eine Sache – daher auch **Sachobjekt**).
Die normale Wortstellung ist **indirektes Objekt – direktes Objekt**. (Merkhilfe: ***p*** vor ***s*** – ***P***ersonenobjekt vor ***S***achobjekt)

Mrs Connor gave	**the children**	**some ice-cream**.	*Mrs Connor hat den Kindern Eis gegeben.*
Ken bought	**her**	**some flowers**.	*Ken hat ihr Blumen gekauft.*

b Das **Sachobjekt** steht vor dem **Personenobjekt**, …

		Sachobjekt	*"to" oder "for" + Personenobjekt*
• wenn das Personenobjekt – sehr lang ist:	She gave	**some ice-cream**	**to all the children in the garden**.
– besonders betont werden soll:	Ken bought	**some flowers**	**for his mother** (not for his sister).
• wenn beide Objekte Pronomen sind:	She gave	**it**	**to them**.
	Ken bought	**them**	**for her**.

⚠ Wenn das Personenobjekt nach dem Sachobjekt steht, wird es immer mit *to* oder – bei den Verben *buy, fetch, get, make* – mit *for* verbunden.
In Fragen nach dem Personenobjekt steht immer *to* bzw. *for* (hinter dem Sachobjekt):
Who did she give some ice-cream **to**? *(Wem …?)*
Who did he buy some flowers **for**? *(Wem …?/Für wen …?)*

Unit 6

1 Der *to*-Infinitiv nach Fragewörtern (The *to*-infinitive after question words)

Gaius didn't know	**what he should do.** **what to do.**		*…, was er tun sollte.*
Can anybody tell him	**how he can get** **how to get**	to the station?	*…, wie er zum Bahnhof kommen kann.*
He didn't know	**who he could ask** **who to ask**	for advice.	*…, wen er um Rat fragen könnte.*

Nach Fragewörtern (*how, what, when, where, which, who*) kannst du statt eines Nebensatzes mit *should, can, could, might* oder *must* auch den *to*-Infinitiv verwenden. Im Deutschen ist nur ein Nebensatz möglich.

G

2 Das Passiv (The passive)

→ Focus on Grammar, p.82

a Du bildest das Passiv mit einer Form von *be* + *past participle*. (Im Deutschen: *werden* + Partizip Perfekt)

	subject	*form of 'be'/ modal aux. + 'be'*	*past participle*	
passive infinitive		**(to) be**	**discussed**	*diskutiert werden*
simple present		**are**		*werden diskutiert*
present progressive		**are being**		*werden (gerade) diskutiert*
simple past		**were**		*sind diskutiert worden/ wurden diskutiert*
past progressive		**were being**		*wurden (gerade) diskutiert*
present perfect	Problems	**have been**	**discussed**.	*sind diskutiert worden/ wurden diskutiert*
will-future		**will be**		*werden diskutiert (werden)*
modal auxiliaries		**can be**		*können diskutiert werden*
		should be		*sollten diskutiert werden*
		must be		*müssen diskutiert werden*

Das Passiv kann von allen transitiven Verben (= Verben, die ein **direktes Objekt** nach sich haben) gebildet werden.
Beachte, daß im Englischen einige Verben transitiv sind, die im Deutschen intransitiv sind, z.B. ***answer sb.*** (jm. antworten), ***believe sb.*** (jm. glauben), ***follow sb.*** (jm. folgen), ***help sb.*** (jm. helfen).
Das direkte Objekt dieser englischen Verben kann ebenfalls zum Subjekt eines Passivsatzes werden.
Vergleiche:

	subject		*direct object*	
active:	Mrs Bailey	**helped**	them.	*Mrs Bailey half ihnen.*
	subject			
passive:	They	**were helped**.		*Ihnen* (= Dativobjekt) *wurde geholfen.*

b Der Gebrauch des Passivs (The use of the passive)

→ Focus on Grammar, p.82

Wie im Deutschen verwendest du das Passiv normalerweise, wenn der/die Handelnde *(the "doer")* nicht wichtig oder sogar nicht bekannt ist. Vergleiche:

(1) Some old coins **were found** near the cathedral last week.
(2) Dominic **found** a coin this morning. He thinks it is Roman.

In Satz 1 (Passivsatz) geht es um Münzen: Der Finder *(the "doer")* ist unwichtig, vielleicht auch gar nicht bekannt. Wichtig ist nur die Tatsache, daß wertvolle Münzen gefunden wurden.
In Satz 2 (Aktivsatz) geht es um Dominic: Für die Sprecherin/den Sprecher ist es wichtig zu sagen, wer der Finder *(the "doer")* war und daß Dominic glaubt, es sei eine römische Münze.

(3) These coins **were found by** Tessa Wheeler in 1938. *(Schild an Ausstellungsstücken)*

In Satz 3 (Passivsatz) geht es um die Münzen und um die Finderin *(the "doer")*. Ohne die Angabe der „Verursacherin" gäbe der Satz keinen wirklichen Sinn. Hinzu kommt, daß Tessa Wheeler für die Geschichte des Museums eine große Rolle spielte. Deshalb wird sie als Finderin erwähnt.
Wenn in einem Passivsatz der/die Handelnde genannt werden soll, verwendest du die Präposition *by*.

G

c Das Passiv von Verben mit zwei Objekten (The passive of verbs with two objects)

→ Focus on Grammar, p.83

	subject		indir. obj.	dir. obj.
active:	A guide	**gave**	them	a brochure.
	subject			*dir. obj.*
passive:	They	**were given**		a brochure.
	subject			*indir. obj.*
passive:	A brochure	**was given**		to them.

Vergleiche:
Ihnen wurde eine Broschüre gegeben./Man gab ihnen eine Broschüre.

Bei Verben mit zwei Objekten *(give sb. sth., show sb. sth., pay sb. sth., promise sb. sth.)* wird meist das indirekte Objekt (Personenobjekt) zum Subjekt des Passivsatzes (**„persönliches Passiv"**): *They were given … .*

Es kann aber auch das direkte Objekt (Sachobjekt) zum Subjekt werden: *A brochure was given … .*

Im Deutschen kann nur das Sachobjekt zum Subjekt des Passivsatzes werden, oder es steht ein Aktivsatz mit *man* oder *jemand.*

d Das Passiv von mehrteiligen Verben (Verbs + adverb/preposition in the passive)

→ Focus on Grammar, p.83

Auch von mehrteiligen Verben kann ein Passiv gebildet werden. Vergleiche:

	subject		object	
active:	They	**looked up**	new words.	*Sie schlugen neue Wörter nach.*
passive:	New words	**were looked up**.		*Neue Wörter wurden nachgeschlagen.*

Weitere Beispiele: *write sth. down, put sth. up, take sth. down, put sth. on, throw sth. away, give sth. up, … .*

Eine Reihe von mehrteiligen Verben kann deutschen Schülerinnen und Schülern Probleme bereiten, wenn vom Deutschen ins Englische bzw. vom Englischen ins Deutsche übersetzt wird. Vergleiche:

In unser Haus ist eingebrochen worden. → Our house was broken into.
All the tasks were spoken about. → *Über alle Aufgaben wurde gesprochen.*

Weitere Beispiele: *agree on* (sich einigen auf/über), *talk about* (sprechen über), *look after* (sich kümmern um), *laugh at* (lachen über), … .

Unit 7

1 Modale Hilfsverben (Modal auxiliaries)

Modale Hilfsverben *(can, may, must, mustn't, needn't, …)*

- werden im Englischen – im Gegensatz zum Deutschen – immer mit einem Infinitiv (ohne *to*) verbunden:
  We must **go** to school at 7.30. — *Wir müssen um 7.30 in die Schule (gehen).*
  You may **go** home at 2 o'clock today. — *Ihr dürft heute um 2 Uhr nach Hause (gehen).*
- sind unveränderlich:
  I can **help** in the kitchen. — *Ich kann in der Küche helfen.*
  John can **help** in the kitchen. — *John kann in der Küche helfen.*
- bilden Frage und Verneinung wie zusammengesetzte Zeiten (ohne *do*):
  May I **borrow** your bike? — *Darf/Kann ich dein Fahrrad ausleihen?*
  I can't **drive** a car, I'm only sixteen. — *Ich kann nicht autofahren, ich bin erst sechzehn.*
- können nicht alle Zeiten *(tenses)* bilden.

G

2 Deutsch „müssen“ (German “müssen”)

→ Focus on Grammar, p.99

Dem deutschen modalen Hilfsverb „müssen“ entsprechen im Englischen *must* (im Präsens) und sein Ersatzverb *(to) have to* (für alle Zeiten).
„Nicht müssen/brauchen“ wird durch *needn't* (im Präsens) oder verneintes *(to) have to* wiedergegeben.

simple present:	I **must** work./I **have to** work.	I **needn't** work./I **don't have to** work.
simple past:	I **had to** work.	I **didn't have to** work.
present perfect:	I**'ve had to** work.	I **haven't had to** work.
will-future:	I**'ll have to** work.	I **won't** (= will not) **have to** work.

⚠ Mit *mustn't* (Langform: *must not*) = *nicht dürfen* drückst du ein Verbot aus. Vergleiche:
You **mustn't** leave. (Du **darfst nicht** gehen.) You **needn't** leave. (Du **brauchst nicht** zu gehen.)

3 Deutsch „können/dürfen“ (German “können/dürfen”)

→ Focus on Grammar, p.102

Den deutschen modalen Hilfsverben „können/dürfen“ entsprechen im Englischen *can* und die beiden Ersatzverben *(to) be allowed to* (**Erlaubnis**) und *(to) be able to* (**Fähigkeit**).

can/mustn't **– Erlaubnis/Verbot:**

simple present:	We **can** go./We**'re allowed to** go.	We **mustn't** go./We **aren't allowed to** go.
simple past:	We **were allowed to** go.	We **weren't allowed to** go.
present perfect:	We**'ve been allowed to** go.	We **haven't been allowed to** go.
will-future:	We**'ll be allowed to** go.	We **won't be allowed to** go.

can/can't **– Fähigkeit:**

simple present:	She **can** swim./She**'s able to** swim.	She **can't** swim./She **isn't able to** swim.
simple past:	She **was able to** swim.	She **wasn't able to** swim.
present perfect:	She **has been able to** swim.	She **hasn't been able to** swim.
will-future:	She**'ll be able to** swim.	She **won't be able to** swim.

Mit *can* kann auch …
– eine Bitte ausgesprochen werden: **Can** you give me those books, please?
– die Bereitschaft, etwas zu tun, ausgedrückt werden: You don't have to walk, I **can** take you in my car.

Im *simple past* wird statt der Ersatzverben *(to) be allowed to* und *(to) be able to* auch *could* verwendet:
We **were allowed to** go./We **could** go. She **wasn't able to** swim./She **couldn't** swim.

Why does a mother kangaroo hate rain?
– Because the children can't play outside.

G

4 Die Pronomen auf *-self/-selves* … (The *-self/-selves* pronouns …)

	singular			*plural*		
(I)	**myself**	mir/mich (selbst)	(we)	**ourselves**		uns (selbst)
(you)	**yourself**	dir/dich (selbst)	(you)	**yourselves**	[-ˈselvz]	euch (selbst)
(he)	**himself** [-ˈself]	sich (selbst)	(they)	**themselves**		sich (selbst)
(she)	**herself**	sich (selbst)				
(it)	**itself**	sich (selbst)				

a … als Reflexivpronomen (… as reflexive pronouns)

Janet is teaching **herself** to play the guitar. — *Janet bringt sich das Gitarrespielen bei.*

Tommy hurt **himself** in the basketball game. — *Tommy hat sich beim Basketballspiel verletzt.*

In diesen Sätzen sind Subjekt *(Janet; Tommy)* und Objekt *(herself; himself)* dieselbe Person, das **Reflexivpronomen** ist rückbezüglich (= reflexiv).

⚠ Vielen im Deutschen reflexiven Verben entsprechen englische Verben ohne Reflexivpronomen, z.B.:

(to) ***change***	*sich (ver)ändern*	*(to)* ***look after***	*sich kümmern um*	*(to)* ***relax***	*sich entspannen*
(to) ***complain***	*sich beschweren*	*(to)* ***meet***	*sich treffen*	*(to)* ***remember***	*sich erinnern*
(to) ***decide***	*sich entscheiden*	*(to)* ***move***	*sich bewegen*	*(to)* ***show***	*sich zeigen*
(to) ***feel***	*sich fühlen*	*(to)* ***open***	*sich öffnen*	*(to)* ***wonder***	*sich fragen*
(to) ***imagine***	*sich vorstellen*	*(to)* ***refer to***	*sich beziehen auf*	*(to)* ***worry***	*sich Sorgen machen*

b … als verstärkende Pronomen (… as emphasizing pronouns)

I can't help you. **I**'m a stranger here **myself**. — *Ich kann Ihnen nicht helfen. Ich bin hier* ***selbst*** *fremd.*
Did **you** see the accident **yourself**? — *Hast du den Unfall* ***selbst*** *gesehen?*
We saw **the president himself**. — *Wir haben den Präsidenten* ***selbst*** *gesehen.*
My aunt drove the car **herself**./ — *Meine Tante hat das Auto* ***selbst*** *gefahren./*
My aunt herself drove the car. — *Meine Tante* ***selbst*** *hat das Auto gefahren.*

In diesen Sätzen stehen *myself, yourself* usw. als **verstärkende Pronomen**. Sie heben ein Nomen *(president; aunt)* oder Pronomen *(I; you)* besonders hervor und werden im Deutschen mit *selbst/selber* wiedergegeben.
Das verstärkende Pronomen steht in der Regel hinter dem Wort, das hervorgehoben werden soll. Wenn du das Subjekt des Satzes hervorheben willst, kann das verstärkende Pronomen auch ans Satzende treten.
Im Gegensatz zu den Reflexivpronomen werden verstärkende Pronomen immer betont.

Unit 8

1 *if* und *when* (*if* and *when*)

→ Focus on Grammar, p.114

***if …* – Nebensatz der Bedingung:**

Perhaps I'll see Nick tonight. **If** I see him, I'll tell him to phone you. *Wenn (= falls) ich ihn sehe, …*

Es ist nicht sicher, ob der Sprecher/die Sprecherin Nick trifft. Die Aussage im Hauptsatz *(I'll tell him to phone you)* kann nur eintreten, wenn die Bedingung im Nebensatz *(if I see him)* erfüllt wird.

***when …* – Nebensatz der Zeit:**

I see Nick quite often. **When** I see him, I'll tell him to phone you. *Wenn (= sobald) ich ihn sehe, …*

Der Sprecher/Die Sprecherin weiß, daß er/sie Nick trifft. Es ist nur eine Frage der Zeit, wann er/sie Nick informieren kann.

2 Bedingungssätze I (Conditional sentences I)

→ Focus on Grammar, p.114

a

If you **visit** California, you**'ll find** it very interesting.	*Wenn du Kalifornien besuchst, wirst du es sehr interessant finden.*
You **can stay** with us if you **come** to California next month.	*Du kannst bei uns wohnen, wenn du nächsten Monat nach Kalifornien kommst.*
If you **have** time now, we **can visit** Hollywood.	*Wenn du jetzt Zeit hast, können wir nach Hollywood fahren.*
If you really **want** to come, please **let** us know soon.	*Wenn du wirklich kommen möchtest, laß es uns bitte bald wissen.*

Wie die Beispiele zeigen, kommen in Bedingungssätzen (Typ I) hauptsächlich folgende Verbformen vor:

if-clause	*main clause*
simple present	**– *will*-future** **– *can/might/should/…* + Infinitiv** **– Imperativ**

Mit Bedingungssätzen vom Typ I kannst du ausdrücken, daß du es für wahrscheinlich/gut möglich hältst, daß die Bedingung erfüllt wird, oder daß die Bedingung bereits erfüllt ist.

Die *if-clauses*, die du hier siehst, beziehen sich auf die Gegenwart oder die Zukunft. Als Verbform wird immer das *simple present* verwendet, nie eine Futurform.

⚠ Zeichensetzung: Wenn der Hauptsatz **vor** dem *if*-Satz steht, verwendet man kein Komma.

b Andere Verbformen in Bedingungssätzen I (Different verb forms in conditional sentences I)

Die folgenden Beispielsätze zeigen dir, daß es weitere Möglichkeiten gibt, Bedingungssätze I zu bilden:

If it **rains** at night in winter, the roads **are** often icy in the morning. *(allgemeingültige Aussage)*	*Wenn es im Winter nachts regnet, sind die Straßen morgens oft vereist.*
If it**'s raining**, **take** the bus.	*Wenn es regnet, nimm den Bus.*
If you**'re visiting** San Francisco next month, you **must meet** my aunt.	*Wenn du nächsten Monat nach San Francisco fährst, mußt du meine Tante treffen.*
If you **can't speak** English, you **should learn** it.	*Wenn du kein Englisch sprichst, solltest du es lernen.*
If you**'ve been** there before, you **will** certainly **know**/you certainly **know** how beautiful it is.	*Wenn du schon mal dort warst, wirst du sicherlich wissen/weißt du sicherlich, wie schön es ist.*
If you **stayed** in a hotel and **didn't pay** a lot of money, you **were** lucky.	*Wenn du in einem Hotel übernachtet hast, ohne eine Menge Geld zu bezahlen, hast du Glück gehabt.*

G

<3> Bedingungssätze II (Conditional sentences II)

→ Focus on Grammar, p.117

a If Mr Vargas **won** $200,000, he**'d go** (= he **would go**) back to Mexico.

Wenn Herr Vargas 200.000 Dollar gewönne/gewinnen würde, ginge er zurück nach Mexiko/würde er zurück nach Mexiko gehen.

If he **was** in Mexico, he **might feel** happier.
Wenn er in Mexiko wäre, wäre er vielleicht glücklicher.

If he **had** enough money, he **could buy** a house.
Wenn er genug Geld hätte, könnte er ein Haus kaufen.

Wie die Beispiele zeigen, kommen folgende Verbformen in Bedingungssätzen (Typ II) vor:

if-clause	*main clause*
simple past	***would/might/could/should*** **+ Infinitiv**

Statt *was* wird in *if*-Sätzen (Typ II) manchmal *were* gebraucht: If dad **was/were** 20 years younger, … .
Wenn Vater 20 Jahre jünger wäre, … .

Für Ratschläge verwendet man die Wendung If I **were** you, I would … .
Wenn ich du wäre, würde ich … .

Auch mit Bedingungssätzen wie diesen kannst du dich über die Zukunft oder die Gegenwart äußern. Wenn ein Sprecher/eine Sprecherin diese Verbformen verwendet, hält er/sie es allerdings für unwahrscheinlich oder sogar unmöglich, daß die Bedingung im *if*-Satz erfüllt wird. Das heißt: Die Aussage ist lediglich eine Spekulation.

⚠ Um auszudrücken, daß man eine Bedingung für kaum oder nicht erfüllbar hält, verwendet man im Englischen in solchen *if*-Sätzen das *simple past* (nicht *would*). Im Deutschen verwendet man den Konjunktiv.

b Bedingungssätze I und II im Vergleich (Conditional sentences I and II in contrast)

conditional sentences I:

The salary in my new job is very good. If I **save** enough money, **I'll be able to fly** to California.
… Wenn ich genug Geld spare, kann ich nach Kalifornien fliegen.

Es ist möglich/wahrscheinlich, daß der Sprecher/die Sprecherin genug spart.

conditional sentences II:

My salary is just not good enough to go on holiday to California. But if I **earned** enough money, I **would fly** there.
… Wenn ich genug Geld verdiente/verdienen würde, flöge ich hin/würde ich hinfliegen.

Der Sprecher/Die Sprecherin hält es für wenig wahrscheinlich, vielleicht sogar unmöglich, daß er/sie genug Geld verdienen könnte. Deshalb ist diese Aussage lediglich eine Spekulation.

4 Das Stützwort *one/ones* (The prop-word *one/ones*)

That's my **car** – the **one** with the red doors.
Here are several **T-shirts**. Which **ones** do you like?
– The red **ones** are best. I think I'll take this **one**.

… – das mit den roten Türen.
… Welche magst du?
– Die roten sind die besten. Ich glaube, ich nehme dieses (hier).

Wenn man ein schon genanntes (zählbares) Nomen *(car; T-shirt)* nicht wiederholen will, muß man in bestimmten Fällen – z.B. nach Adjektiven und nach *the* – das Stützwort *one* (Singular) bzw. *ones* (Plural) verwenden. Es hat im Deutschen keine Entsprechung.

Unit 9

[1] Das Plusquamperfekt (The past perfect)

→ Focus on Grammar, p.130

a After we **had loaded** the car, we left.
By six o'clock the rangers **had finished** their work in the camp.
Had you **heard** of Yosemite before you read about it in your English book**?**

Nachdem wir das Auto beladen hatten, fuhren wir ab.
Um sechs Uhr hatten die Ranger ihre Arbeit im Camp beendet.
Hattest du von Yosemite gehört, bevor du etwas in deinem Englischbuch darüber gelesen hast?

Wenn du sagen willst, daß noch **vor** einem Zeitpunkt in der Vergangenheit etwas getan wurde oder etwas geschehen ist, verwendest du das *past perfect*.

I **had read** about Yosemite many times | and finally **went** there last month.

before last month *(past perfect)* | last month *(simple past)* | NOW

b Das *past perfect* wird mit *had* + Partizip Perfekt *(past participle)* gebildet.

Bildung des *past participle*: p.150

Kurzformen: I'**d**/You'**d**/He'**d**/She'**d**/We'**d**/They'**d**
I/You/He/She/It/We/They **hadn't** | + *past participle*

[2] Die Verlaufsform des *past perfect* (The past perfect progressive)

→ Focus on Grammar, p.130

a Yesterday we were very busy at summer camp. We got up at 7.30 and had breakfast. After we had had breakfast some of us went to the lake. It was 8.30.
We **had been sailing** for some time when we noticed that it was 12.30 – time for lunch.
We went back to meet the others. They **had been playing** tennis since breakfast. …

Gestern waren wir im Sommerlager sehr beschäftigt. Wir sind um 7 Uhr 30 aufgestanden und haben gefrühstückt. Nachdem wir gefrühstückt hatten, gingen einige von uns zum See. Es war 8 Uhr 30.
Wir hatten einige Zeit gesegelt, als wir feststellten, daß es 12 Uhr 30 war – Zeit zum Mittagessen.
Wir gingen zurück, um die anderen zu treffen. Sie hatten seit dem Frühstück Tennis gespielt. …

Das *past perfect progressive* drückt aus, daß eine Tätigkeit vor einem Zeitpunkt in der Vergangenheit begonnen hatte und zu diesem Zeitpunkt noch andauerte.

They **had been sailing** for some time when they noticed that it was 12.30.

8.30 *(past perfect progressive)* | 12.30 | NOW

Vergleiche dazu das *present perfect progressive*:

They **have been sailing** for twenty minutes now.

10.40 *(present perfect progressive)* | NOW (11.00)

⚠ Verben, die **Zustände** beschreiben *(be, have, know, like, cost, …)*, können nicht in der *progressive form* verwendet werden.

b Das *past perfect progressive* wird mit *had* + *been* + *-ing*-Form gebildet.

Kurzformen: I'**d**/You'**d**/He'**d**/She'**d**/We'**d**/They'**d**
I/You/He/She/It/We/They **hadn't** | + *been* + *-ing form*

G

Die indirekte Rede … (Reported speech …)

3 … nach einleitenden Verben im *simple present* (… after reporting verbs in the simple present)

Wenn du wiedergeben möchtest, was jemand sagt, schreibt oder denkt, benutzt du die indirekte Rede.

Aussagen in der indirekten Rede (Reported statements)

Indirekte Rede *(reported speech)*:
Mary **says** (that) she likes American ice-cream.

Direkte Rede *(direct speech)*:
Mary: I like American ice-cream. It's great.

Hier berichtet jemand, was Mary sagt. Das einleitende Verb *(reporting verb)* steht im *simple present ('says')*. Andere einleitende Verben sind z.B. *(to) tell sb., (to) write, (to) think, (to) believe.*

Weitere Beispiele: Mary **says** that she has always loved ice-cream.
She **says** she once tried Italian ice-cream.
She **believes** she'll always love American ice-cream.
She **thinks** she is going to eat lots of ice-cream when she is in the States.

Fragen in der indirekten Rede (Reported questions)

reported speech:	*direct speech:*
Mary **wants to know** <u>why</u> the train is late again.	*Mary:* Why is this train late again?
Mary **asks** <u>if/whether</u> she can use our computer.	*Mary:* Can I use your computer, please?

Bei indirekten Fragen ohne Fragewort verwendest du *if* oder auch *whether* (= ob).

⚠ Beachte, daß die Wortstellung in indirekten Fragen ***subject – verb – object*** ist:
They want to know where <u>they</u> <u>can get</u> <u>a permit</u>. *…, wo sie eine Genehmigung erhalten können.*
They want to know if <u>many people</u> <u>visit</u> <u>Yosemite</u>. *…, ob viele Leute Yosemite besuchen.*

- Im Englischen steht kein Komma nach dem *reporting verb.*
- *that* wird oft weggelassen (vor allem nach *say* und *tell sb.*).
- Im Englischen gibt es keinen Konjunktiv in *reported speech (She says she **is** ill. – Sie sagt, sie **sei** krank).*
- Wie im Deutschen werden die Pronomen aus der Sicht des/der Berichtenden gewählt:
  Tom: Mary asks if **she** can use **our** computer. *Mary:* Can **I** use **your** computer, please?

[4] … nach einleitenden Verben im *simple past* (… after reporting verbs in the simple past)

→ Focus on Grammar, p.132

a Aussagen in der indirekten Rede (Reported statements)

Direkte Rede *(direct speech)*:	Indirekte Rede *(reported speech)*:
Mary on Sunday, June 12th, 3 pm:	*A visitor, a few days later:* On Sunday …
Bobby **saved** three people last year.	Mary **told me** that Bobby **had saved** three people last year.
The weather **has been** terrible.	She **said** that the weather **had been** terrible.
Few people **are camping** up here.	She **added** that few people **were camping** up here.
It'**s going to get** warmer.	She **thought** that it **was going to get** warmer.
I'**ll show** you a place for your tent.	She **said** that she **would show** me a place for my tent.
We often **work** ten hours a day.	She **told me** they often **worked** ten hours a day.

Hier berichtet jemand, was Mary zu einem bestimmten Zeitpunkt **in der Vergangenheit** (hier: *Sunday, June 12th, 3 pm)* gesagt hat. Die einleitenden Verben stehen im *simple past.*

Pronomenwahl und Zeichensetzung in indirekten Aussagen: p.164, Abschnitt 3

Die Beispiele zeigen, daß du keine neuen Regeln für die Wahl der *verb forms* zu lernen brauchst. Die *verb forms* hängen wie sonst auch von der Situation ab, über die du berichtest.

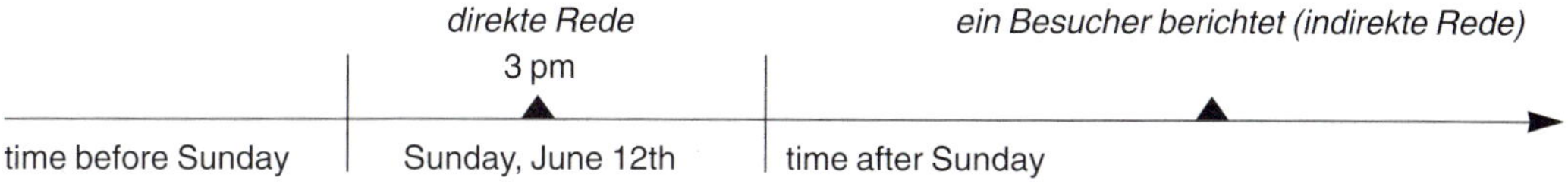

indirekte Rede			
had saved	→	before Sunday	*vor dem Zeitpunkt der ursprünglichen Äußerung*
had been	→	before Sunday	*vor dem Zeitpunkt der ursprünglichen Äußerung*
were camping	→	in progress on Sunday	*im Verlauf zum Zeitpunkt der ursprünglichen Äußerung*
was going to get	→	after Sunday	*nach dem Zeitpunkt der ursprünglichen Äußerung*
would show	→	after 3 pm on Sunday	*nach dem Zeitpunkt der ursprünglichen Äußerung*
worked	→	often	*immer/oft/gewöhnlich/...*

⚠ **1.** *Ruth:* Ice **melts** in the sun. — *Susan:* Ruth said that ice **melts** in the sun.

2. *Ruth:* My brother still **can't swim**. — *Susan:* Ruth told us that her brother still **can't swim**.

Bei allgemeingültigen Aussagen (Satz 1) und bei Aussagen, die zum Zeitpunkt ihrer Wiedergabe noch zutreffen (Satz 2), können die Verbformen in direkter und indirekter Rede identisch sein.

b Fragen in der indirekten Rede (Reported questions)

→ Focus on Grammar, p.133

Campers:	*Rangers, a few days later:*
Do many people **visit** Yosemite?	The campers **asked** if/whether many people **visited** Yosemite.
Why **were** there so many fires?	They **wondered** why there **had been** so many fires.
How long **will** it take to climb El Capitan?	Some of them **wanted to know** how long it **would** take to climb El Capitan.

Wortstellung, Pronomenwahl und Zeichensetzung in indirekten Fragen: p.164, Abschnitt 3

c Aufforderungen, Bitten usw. in der indirekten Rede (Reported orders, requests, etc.)

→ Focus on Grammar, p.133

A ranger:	*Visitors, a few days later:*
Please **park** in one of the car parks.	He **asked us to park** in one of the car parks.
Don't make fires in the forest.	The ranger **told us/warned us not to make** fires in the forest.
You **should take** warm clothes.	He **advised us to take** warm clothes.

Aufforderungen, Bitten, Verbote, Ratschläge usw. werden in der indirekten Rede meist durch eine Infinitivkonstruktion wiedergegeben. Du kannst *(to) tell/warn/ask/advise sb.* + *to*-Infinitiv verwenden. Die verneinte Form wird mit *not to* gebildet.

d Änderungen von Zeit- und Ortsangaben (Changes in adverbials of place and time)

Visitors on Monday:	*A ranger, a few weeks later:*
We're going to camp **here tomorrow**.	When I met them in the High Country a few weeks ago they said they were going to camp **there the next/following day**.
Yesterday we saw some bears.	... they told me they had seen some bears **the day before**.
Today we are going to hunt.	... they said they were going to hunt **that day**.
We're going home **next week**.	... they told me they were going home **the following week**.

Wie im Deutschen müssen in der indirekten Rede mit einleitendem Verb im *simple past* Zeit- und Ortsangaben aus der Perspektive des Berichtenden gewählt werden.

Vocabulary

Das folgende Wörterverzeichnis *(Vocabulary)* enthält die neuen Wörter des Buches in der Reihenfolge ihres Vorkommens.
Eingerückte Wörter sollen mit dem vorausgehenden Wort mitgelernt werden, obwohl sie nicht an der betreffenden Stelle der *Unit* vorkommen.
Fett gedruckte Wörter (z. B. „**air**") gehören zum „produktiven" Wortschatz – du sollst sie beim eigenen Sprechen und Schreiben verwenden können. **Normal gedruckte Wörter** (z. B. „court") gehören zum „rezeptiven" Wortschatz – du sollst sie verstehen, wenn du sie hörst oder liest.
Mit einem ° versehene Wörter (z. B. „°charter flight") gehören zum sogenannten „Situationswortschatz". Es sind Wörter, die zum Thema einer bestimmten *Unit* gehören, aber in nachfolgenden *Units* nicht als bekannt vorausgesetzt werden.
Eigennamen und **grammatische Fachausdrücke** werden nicht im *Vocabulary* aufgeführt. Sie stehen gesammelt auf den Seiten 228 und 229.
Nicht aufgeführt sind englische Wörter wie *clown, computer, filmstar, quizmaster, restaurant*, die du ohne weiteres verstehst. Alle diese Wörter findest du aber mit Angabe ihrer Aussprache in der alphabetischen Wortliste (S. 210 ff.).

~ – Die **Tilde** (~) in der dritten Spalte steht anstelle des Eintrags in der ersten Spalte. Pro Tilde muß ein Wort eingesetzt werden. (Beispiel: (to) **teach** – Mrs Green is a teacher. She *~es* music and history.)

▸◂ – Dieses Symbol in der dritten Spalte weist dich auf ein bekanntes Wort mit **gegensätzlicher Bedeutung** hin. (Beispiel: **poor** – arm – ▸◂ **rich**)

Betonungszeichen:	' = Hauptbetonung, ˌ = Nebenbetonung (Beispiel: **toilet article** ['tɔɪlət‿ˌɑːtɪkl] – Hauptbetonung: ['tɔɪlət], Nebenbetonung: [ˌɑːtɪkl])
Abkürzungen:	p. = page Ex = Exercise sb. = somebody sth. = something jd. = jemand jm. = jemandem jn. = jemanden *sing. = singular pl. = plural* *adj. = adjective adv. = adverb conj. = conjunction n. = noun prep. = preposition v. = verb* infml. = informal (umgangssprachlich, informell) AE = American English BE = British English

Topic 1: Arriving in Britain – by air and by sea

p. 6	**air** [eə]	Luft	The plane flies 3000 metres in the ~.
	title ['taɪtl]	Titel	What is the ~ of Sting's new song?
	airport ['eəpɔːt]	Flughafen	The plane arrived at the ~ an hour late.
	channel ['tʃænl]	Kanal	The English *C~* is the sea between England and France.
	(inter)national [(ˌɪntə)'næʃnəl]	(inter)national	*international* news = news from all over the world *national* news = news from one country
	central ['sentrəl]	Zentral-, Mittel-	Buckingham Palace is in ~ London (= in the centre of London).
	underground ['ʌndəgraʊnd]	U-Bahn	The ~ is a very popular, quick form of transport in London.
	°charter flight ['tʃɑːtə flaɪt]	Charterflug	
	trip (to) [trɪp]	Reise, Ausflug (nach)	Would you like to go on a ~ *to* London next week?

Some more irregular past participles

(to) beat	beat	**beaten** ['biːtn]	schlagen	(to) get	got	**got** [gɒt]	bekommen
(to) become	became	**become** [bɪ'kʌm]	werden	(to) keep	kept	**kept** [kept]	behalten
(to) drive	drove	**driven** ['drɪvn]	fahren	(to) know	knew	**known** [nəʊn]	wissen; kennen
(to) fall	fell	**fallen** ['fɔːlən]	(hin)fallen	(to) ring	rang	**rung** [rʌŋ]	klingeln, läuten
(to) fly	flew	**flown** [fləʊn]	fliegen	(to) write	wrote	**written** ['rɪtn]	schreiben

	assistant [ə'sɪstənt]	Assistent/in	Bill is Anne's ~. He helps her with her work.
	possible ['pɒsəbl]	möglich	Is it ~ to fly from London to New York in six hours?
	impossible [ɪm'pɒsəbl]	unmöglich	not possible
p. 7	(to) **cross** [krɒs]	überqueren; kreuzen	You mustn't ~ the road when the light is red.
	°hovercraft, *pl.* hovercraft ['hɒvəkrɑːft]	Luftkissenboot	
	(to) **build** [bɪld] – **built** [bɪlt] – **built** [bɪlt]	bauen	Jessica's parents want to ~ a swimming-pool behind their house.
	no longer	nicht mehr, nicht länger	Michelle ~ ~ works here. She found another job.
	island ['aɪlənd]	Insel	land with water on all sides

(p. 7)	**main** [meɪn]	Haupt-	the ~ question = the most important question
	(to) **carry** ['kærɪ]	befördern	Our car can ~ five people.
	lorry ['lɒrɪ]	Lastwagen, LKW	Special trains can carry cars and even *lorries*.
	high [haɪ]	hoch	The speed limit here is 50 km/h. That's too ~.
	project ['prɒdʒekt]	Projekt; Aufgabe	Our class is doing a ~ on the history of Wales.
	which? [wɪtʃ]	welche(r, s)?	*W~* is your favourite pop group?
	port [pɔːt]	Hafen(stadt)	Hamburg is on the Elbe. It is Germany's busiest ~.

Unit 1: Activity holidays for young people

p. 8	instructor [ɪn'strʌktə]	Ausbilder/in, Lehrer/in	a kind of teacher
	(to) **teach** [tiːtʃ] – **taught** [tɔːt] – **taught** [tɔːt]	lehren, unterrichten	Mrs Green is a teacher. She *~es* at Park School in Hatfield. She *~es* music and history.
	foreign ['fɒrən]	ausländisch, fremd	~ people = people from other countries I can't understand her. She's speaking a ~ language.
	student ['stjuːdənt]	Student/in; Schüler/in	a person at a university [ˌjuːnɪ'vɜːsətɪ] or a language school; also an AE word for BE "pupil"
	°barbecue ['bɑːbɪkjuː]	Grillparty	
	(to) **offer** ['ɒfə]	(an)bieten	The language school *~s* a new French course. He *~ed* me £200 for my guitar, so I sold it.
	court [kɔːt]	Spielfeld, Platz	You play tennis on a tennis ~.
	lake [leɪk]	(Binnen-)See	Wayne crossed the ~ in a boat.
	field [fiːəld]	Feld, Wiese; (Sport-)Platz	Lucy rode round the ~ on her bike. You play football on a football ~.
p. 9	(to) **decide** [dɪ'saɪd]	(sich) entscheiden, beschließen	Do you want the red or the black shirt? – I don't know. I can't ~.
	beginning [bɪ'gɪnɪŋ]	Anfang, Beginn	▸◂ end At the ~ of our English lesson we sang a song today.
	°specialist activity ['speʃlɪst]	*hier:* Hauptaktivität	
	(to) **make sure** [meɪk 'ʃʊə]	sicherstellen, sichergehen; dafür sorgen *(, daß)*	Please ~ ~ that the door is closed when you leave the house.
	shy [ʃaɪ]	schüchtern, zurückhaltend, scheu	Mike is ~. He doesn't like to talk in a group.

Activities at St David's

°abseiling ['æbseɪlɪŋ]	Abseilen	°grass-skiing ['grɑːsˌskiːɪŋ]	Grasski(laufen)
°archery ['ɑːtʃərɪ]	Bogenschießen	gymnastics [dʒɪm'næstɪks]	Gymnastik, Turnen
°arts and crafts [ˌɑːts‿ən 'krɑːfts]	Kunsthandwerk	°orienteering [ˌɔːrɪən'tɪərɪŋ]	Orientierungslauf, Orientierungswandern
canoeing [kə'nuːɪŋ]	Kanufahren	°pony-trekking ['pəʊnɪˌtrekɪŋ]	Ponyreiten
cookery ['kʊkərɪ]	Kochen	pottery ['pɒtərɪ]	Töpfern
creative writing [krɪˌeɪtɪv 'raɪtɪŋ]	schöpferisches Schreiben	sailing ['seɪlɪŋ]	Segeln
desk-top publishing (DTP) [ˌdesktɒp 'pʌblɪʃɪŋ, ˌdiːtiː'piː]	DTP *(Erstellung und Gestaltung von Druckschriften mittels Computer)*	°sub-aqua [ˌsʌb'ækwə]	Tauchsport, Tauchen
drama ['drɑːmə]	Drama, Schauspiel(kunst)	°trampolining ['træmpəliːnɪŋ]	Trampolinspringen

You can **do** abseiling / archery / arts and crafts / canoeing / cookery / creative writing / … at St David's.
Let's **go** abseiling / canoeing / dancing / grass-skiing / rock-climbing / sailing / swimming / trampolining / windsurfing.

should [ʃʊd, ʃəd]	sollte(n)	You *should* try to buy environment-friendly things.
shouldn't ['ʃʊdnt] **(= should not)**	sollte(n) nicht	You *shouldn't* buy plastic cups, they are bad for the environment.

V

Unit 1

(p. 9)	(to) **pack** [pæk]	(ein)packen	I *packed* my clothes in the bag. They should be OK when I *unpack* them later.
	(to) **unpack** [ʌn'pæk]	auspacken	
	following ['fɒləʊɪŋ]	folgend	Do you know the ~ books: *My Mate Shofiq*, *The Legend of King Arthur* or *Tom Sawyer*?
	(to) **follow** ['fɒləʊ]	folgen; verfolgen	I don't know where we are. – Don't worry. Just ~ me.
	illustration [ˌɪlə'streɪʃn]	Bild, Abbildung, Illustration	a picture to make a text clearer
	toilet article ['tɔɪlət‿ˌɑ:tɪkl]	Toilettenartikel	soap, shampoo, toothbrush, comb, etc.
	could [kʊd]	könnte(n)	*Could* you give me the salt, please?
	couldn't ['kʊdnt] **(= could not)**	könnte(n) nicht	I *couldn't* live in a city. I hate the cars and the pollution.
	(to) **imagine** [ɪ'mædʒɪn]	sich *(gedanklich)* vorstellen	*I~* you could spend £1,000,000. What would you like to buy?
	Focus on GRAMMAR		
p. 10	**point** [pɔɪnt]	Punkt	The red team has ten *~s*, the blue team has nine *~s*.
	°Olympics [ə'lɪmpɪks]	Olympische Spiele	
	as *(conj.; adv.)* [æz, əz]	wie	*As* you all know, Britain is an island. ⚠ *as* you know *(conj.)* = *wie* ihr wißt *as* in Germany *(adv.)* = *wie* in Deutschland *as* a teacher *(prep.)* = *als* Lehrer/in *like* a teacher *(prep.)* = *wie* ein/e Lehrer/in
	(to) **write** sth. **down** [ˌraɪt 'daʊn]	etwas aufschreiben	*W~ ~* the answers in your exercise-book.
	(to) **end (in)** [end]	enden (auf, mit); beenden	The word "write" *~s in* an "e". You should ~ a letter to a friend with "Yours, …".
	(to) **change (into)** [tʃeɪndʒ]	verändern, umwandeln (in); sich verändern	Water *~s (in)to* ice when it's very cold.
	(to) **enjoy** [ɪn'dʒɔɪ]	mögen, genießen, gern haben/tun	Did you like the film? – Yes, I really *~ed* it.
	column ['kɒləm]	Spalte *(auf Buchseite usw.)*	Newspapers write their articles in *~s*.
p. 11	**Scottish** ['skɒtɪʃ]	schottisch, Schottisch	Helen MacDonald isn't English, she's *Scottish*. So she speaks with a *Scottish accent*.
	accent ['æksənt]	Akzent	

Check your stress. (⚠ Die folgenden englischen Wörter werden auf der **ersten** Silbe betont.)

accent	Akzent	**de**tail	Detail	**mo**dern	modern	**pro**noun	Pronomen
alphabet	Alphabet	**di**alogue	Dialog	**ner**vous	nervös	**sub**ject	Subjekt
argument	Argument	**hos**pital	Hospital	**ob**ject	Objekt	**toi**let	Toilette
article	Artikel	**in**dustry	Industrie	**or**ganize	organisieren	**tran**sport	Transport
balcony	Balkon	**in**strument	Instrument	**pa**tient	Patient	**u**niform	Uniform
concert	Konzert	**in**teresting	interessant	**pro**gramme	Programm		

	table ['teɪbl]	Tabelle	list of facts, usually in columns
	(to) **translate** [træns'leɪt]	übersetzen	to change a text from one language into another language
	turbo-brain ['tɜ:bəʊbreɪn]	„Turbo-Gehirn"	
	brain [breɪn]	Gehirn	I don't know. – I'm sure you know it! Use your ~.
	similar (to sb./sth.**)** ['sɪmɪlə]	(jm./einer Sache) ähnlich	⧓ different (from) Joe's bike is ~ *to* my bike. It's the same size and colour.
p. 12	(to) **interview** ['ɪntəvju:]	befragen, interviewen	Mrs Smith *~ed* me for the job. She asked me a lot of difficult questions. …
	interview ['ɪntəvju:]	Interview	… The ~ took more than two hours.
	a bit [bɪt]	ein bißchen, etwas	a little Does it hurt? – Not too much. But it hurts *a ~*.
	time(s) [taɪm(z)]	Mal; -mal	The Kings visit London about four *~s* a year.

(p. 12)	**How do you like …?**	Wie gefällt dir …? Wie findest du …?	*How do you like* your meal? – It's OK. The beans are a bit cold.
	Focus on WORDS		
p. 13	(to) **share (with)** [ʃeə]	(sich) teilen (mit)	Our flat is very small, so I ~ a room *with* my sister.
	hair *(sing.)* [heə]	Haar, Haare	My ~ is too long. It falls in my eyes.
	wonderful ['wʌndəfəl]	wunderbar	great I've got a ~ present for Alan – an animal poster.
	stranger ['streɪndʒə]	Unbekannte(r), Fremde(r)	Nobody in the village knew him. He was a ~.
	Irish ['aɪrɪʃ]	irisch, Irisch	Pat isn't English, he's *Irish*. He speaks with an *Irish* accent.
	rich [rɪtʃ]	reich	A ~ person is a person with a lot of money.
	short [ʃɔːt]	klein *(von Gestalt)*; kurz	▸◂ tall ▸◂ long
	fat [fæt]	dick, fett	Adam is ~ because he eats too much.
	thin [θɪn]	dünn	Doris is ~ because she doesn't eat very much.
	quality ['kwɒlətɪ]	Eigenschaft; Qualität	A ~ of ice is that it is hard.
	tolerant (of) ['tɒlərənt]	tolerant (gegenüber)	Don't get angry. You should be ~ *of* people's faults.
	bored [bɔːd]	gelangweilt	I'm ~. There's nothing to do.
	adult ['ædʌlt]	Erwachsene(r)	Child tickets cost £1.50. *A~* tickets cost £2.00.
	relative ['relətɪv]	Verwandte(r)	The other members of your family are your *~s*.
	poor [pɔː, pʊə]	arm	▸◂ rich
	round [raʊnd]	rund	A ball is ~. A box isn't.
	well [wel]	gesund, wohlauf; gut	I was ill, but now I feel ~ again.
	lonely ['ləʊnlɪ]	einsam, verlassen	Kate hasn't got many friends. She's often very ~.
	annoyed [ə'nɔɪd]	verärgert	a bit angry
	alive [ə'laɪv]	lebendig, am Leben	▸◂ dead
	(to) **arrange** [ə'reɪndʒ]	(an)ordnen; vereinbaren, arrangieren	Let's try to ~ the new words in a network. We *~d* to meet at six o'clock in front of the school.
	nose [nəʊz]	Nase	You smell with your ~.
	use [juːs]	Gebrauch, Verwendung	noun from "(to) use" ⚠ Aussprache: *(the) use* [juːs] – *(to) use* [juːz]
1 Ex 2	(to) **practise** ['præktɪs]	üben, trainieren	Linda is very good at tennis. She *~s* every day.
5	**match** [mætʃ]	Spiel, Wettkampf	There's a good football ~ on TV today.
6	**me** [miː]	*hier:* ich	**Personalpronomen: Objektform in kurzen Antworten** Did you take my watch? – **Me**? Why **me**? Who took it? – It wasn't **me**, it was **her/him/them**.
	silly ['sɪlɪ]	albern, dumm	Are you going to work at the weekend? – Don't be ~. I'm going on holiday.
8	footstep ['fʊtstep]	Fußschritt	I knew somebody was coming. I heard ~s in the hall.
	second ['sekənd]	Sekunde	There are 60 *~s* in a minute.
	diagram ['daɪəgræm]	Diagramm, Schaubild	a picture or a plan to make something clearer
	outside *(prep.; adv.)* [aʊt'saɪd]	außerhalb (von); (nach) draußen	I heard people ~ my flat. I went ~ and asked them to be quiet.
	inside *(prep.; adv.)* [ɪn'saɪd]	innerhalb (von); (nach) drinnen	*I~* the classroom the students were working hard. I walked ~ and nobody even noticed me.
	°corridor ['kɒrɪdɔː]	Gang, Korridor, Flur	
	Words Words Words		
p. 17	care of the body [keə]	Körperpflege	
	trouble spot ['trʌbl spɒt]	„Achtung Falle!“	
	kilo ['kiːləʊ]	Kilo(gramm)	⚠ Plural in English – singular in German: *10 kilos, 2 pounds, 50 metres, 5 kilometres*

V

Unit 1

1 Text — I think this place is great!

p. 18

during ['djʊərɪŋ]	während	

> **German "während"**
> **While** I was on holiday I broke my leg. *(conj.)*
> **During** my holidays I broke my leg. *(prep.)*
> Vor Sätzen *while*, vor Nomen *during*.

cousin ['kʌzn]	Vetter, Kusine	Joan is my aunt's daughter. She's my ~.
(to) **be sick** [sɪk]	sich übergeben (müssen)	Adam ate four hamburgers and a lot of baked beans. He *was* ~ all night.

> **"ill" and "sick"**
>
> (to) **be ill:** Mrs Donovan is looking after her old mother – she **is ill**.
> **sick + noun:** Mrs Donovan is looking after her **sick** mother. (⚠ *not:* ~~ill mother~~)
> (to) **be/feel sick:** I **was sick** three times last night. I still **feel sick**. (= Mir ist immer noch schlecht/übel.)
> **travel-sick:** I'm always **travel-sick** when we travel by coach.

slowly *(adv.)* ['sləʊlɪ]	langsam	Please walk ~. I can't walk as fast as you.
°Indian ['ɪndɪən]	Indianer/in	
°finish line ['fɪnɪʃ laɪn]	Ziellinie	
°(to) go camping ['kæmpɪŋ]	zelten (gehen/fahren)	
mud [mʌd]	Schlamm, Matsch	The football field is full of ~ after all this rain.
everywhere ['evrɪweə]	überall	I can't find my bag. I've looked ~.
(to) **put** sth. **on** [ˌpʊt_'ɒn]	etwas anziehen	I feel cold. – Well, ~ a pullover *on*.
brilliant ['brɪljənt] (infml.)	toll, klasse	
weather ['weðə]	Wetter	The ~ is nice today. It is warm.

V

> **Pronunciation: Words with "-ea-"**
>
> 1. **-ea-** [e]: weather, healthy, bread, breakfast, meant
> 2. **-ea-** [iː]: mean, teach, read, meat, beat, bean, each
> 3. **-ea-** [eɪ]: break, great
> 4. **-ea(r)-** [ɪə]: real, idea, ear, hear, near
>
> ⚠ [eə]: wear – [ɜː]: early, learn, heard

p. 19

> **Great Britain – The United Kingdom (UK)** [juːˌnaɪtɪd 'kɪŋdəm]
>
> **Britain** (or **Great Britain**): **England, Scotland** and **Wales**
> **The United Kingdom:** **Britain** and **Northern Ireland** [ˌnɔːðən_'aɪələnd]
> (The **Republic of Ireland** [rɪˌpʌblɪk_əv_'aɪələnd] is not a part of the UK.)

country	*adjective*	**people** (= Volk)	**language(s)**
Britain:	British	the British	
– England	English	the English	English
– Scotland	Scottish	the Scots	English
– Wales	Welsh	the Welsh	English, Welsh
Northern Ireland	(Northern) Irish	the (Northern) Irish	English, Irish
the Republic of Ireland	Irish	the Irish	English, Irish

(to) **pull (out)** [ˌpʊl_'aʊt]	(heraus)ziehen	The young boy fell into the lake and I had to ~ him *out*. …
wet [wet]	naß; feucht	… His clothes were all ~.
°pirate ['paɪrət]	Pirat/in	
wheel [wiːl]	Rad	A bike has two *~s*.
(to) **explain** sth. **to** sb. [ɪk'spleɪn]	jm. etwas erklären, erläutern	I don't understand this exercise. Can you ~ it *to* me? ⚠ *not:* Can you ~~explain me~~ …?

(p. 19)	**could** [kʊd]	konnte(n)	⚠ *could* = **1.** konnte(n); **2.** könnte(n) My grandmother *could* play the piano very well. *Could* you bring your CDs to the party tomorrow?
	(to) **find the way back (to)**	zurückfinden (nach, zu)	Can you *find your way back* without me?
	across [ə'krɒs]	(quer) über, durch	It is difficult to walk ~ Main Street. There are always a lot of cars.
	fire ['faɪə]	Feuer, Brand	We cooked fish over a small camp ~.
	(to) **present (to)** [prɪ'zent]	darlegen, präsentieren	The youth club *~ed* a cheque for £100 to the hospital.
	the text says …	im Text steht …	
	conversation [ˌkɒnvə'seɪʃn]	Gespräch, Unterhaltung	Helen and I talked for over an hour. We had a nice ~.

Unit 2: London

p. 20	**as soon as** *(conj.)* [əz 'su:n‿əz]	sobald	*As ~ as* I came home Barry made dinner.
	any? ['enɪ]	irgendwelche? (⚠ *any?* bleibt oft unübersetzt)	Do you want ~ oranges? (= Wollen Sie Apfelsinen?)
	huge [hju:dʒ]	sehr groß, riesig	very large
	I enjoy living in …	Ich wohne gern in …	

Verbs + *-ing* form

I **enjoy/like/love living** in London.	Ich wohne gern/sehr gern in London.
I **hate going** by underground.	Ich hasse es, mit der U-Bahn zu fahren.
Can we **go swimming** tomorrow?	Können wir morgen schwimmen gehen?
We **stopped talking** when Mrs Price came in.	Wir hörten auf zu reden, als Mrs Price hereinkam.

	theatre ['θɪətə]	Theater	
	not … anything ['enɪθɪŋ]	nichts	nothing I'm hungry, but there's *not* ~ to eat in the house.
	°travelcard ['trævlkɑ:d]	*Londoner Dauerkarte für den Nahverkehr*	
	alone [ə'ləʊn]	allein	My parents went to the cinema last night, so I was ~ in the house. ⚠ *allein, einsam = lonely*
	(to) **get to know**	kennenlernen; erfahren	Come to our house and ~ *to* ~ my family. When I lived in York I *got to* ~ a lot about Britain.
	impression (of) [ɪm'preʃn]	Eindruck (von)	My first ~ *of* Alice was not very good, but now I like her very much.

Focus on WORDS

p. 21	terraced house ['terəst 'haʊs] (BE), **town house** ['taʊn haʊs] (AE)	Reihenhaus	
	detached house [dɪ'tætʃt]	freistehendes Haus	
	semi-detached house ['semɪdɪˌtætʃt 'haʊs]	Doppelhaushälfte	
	yard [jɑ:d] (AE)	*= BE garden*	
	roof [ru:f]	Dach	
	chimney ['tʃɪmnɪ]	Schornstein	

a terraced house *a detached house* *a semi-detached house*

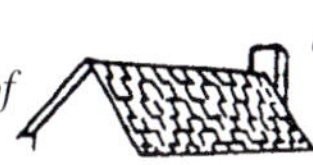

(p. 21)	**stairs** *(pl.)* [steəz]	Treppe(nstufen)	The Smiths live upstairs. Go up these ~ and turn right.

English plural – German singular

Be careful. These **stairs are** dangerous.	Sei vorsichtig. Diese **Treppe ist** gefährlich.
Clothes are quite expensive here.	**Kleidung ist** hier ziemlich teuer.
These **pyjamas/trousers are** too small for me.	Dieser **Schlafanzug**/Diese **Hose ist** zu klein für mich.
Your **glasses are** on the table.	Deine **Brille ist** auf dem Tisch.
The **police are** looking for you.	Die **Polizei sucht** dich.

	cellar ['selə]	Keller	the room(s) under a house
	furniture *(sing.)* ['fɜːnɪtʃə]	Möbel	Tables, chairs, beds, shelves, etc. are all pieces of ~.

English singular – German plural

Your new **furniture is** nice. **Was it** expensive?	Deine neuen **Möbel sind** schön. **Waren sie** teuer?
No **news is** good news.	Keine **Nachrichten sind** gute Nachrichten.
All this **information is** interesting.	All diese **Informationen sind** interessant.
That **is** too much **homework**.	Das **sind** zu viele **Hausaufgaben**.
Your **hair is** too long.	Deine **Haare sind** zu lang.

a cooker

a fridge

a washing machine

	cooker ['kʊkə] (BE)	Herd	
	fridge [frɪdʒ]	Kühlschrank	
	washing machine ['wɒʃɪŋ məˌʃiːn]	Waschmaschine	
	ceiling ['siːlɪŋ]	(Zimmer-)Decke	▸◂ floor
	front door [ˌfrʌnt 'dɔː]	Haustür	▸◂ back door
	lamp [læmp]	Lampe	This room is always dark. We should buy a ~.
	wardrobe ['wɔːdrəʊb]	Kleiderschrank	A ~ is a cupboard for clothes.
	after *(conj.)* ['ɑːftə]	nachdem	You can watch TV ~ you have done your homework. ▸◂ before
	so (that)	damit, so daß	Take an early bus ~ *(that)* you arrive on time.
	key word ['kiː wɜːd]	Schlüsselwort	
	key [kiː]	Schlüssel	I can't open the door. I can't find my ~*s*.
	(to) **keep** [kiːp] – **kept** [kept] – **kept** [kept]	aufbewahren	I'm thirsty. Where *do* you ~ your glasses?
	dream [driːm]	Traum	Do you remember your ~*s* in the morning?
	(to) **dream** [driːm] – **dreamt** [dremt]/ **dreamed** – **dreamt** [dremt]/**dreamed**	träumen	Last night I *dreamt/dreamed* I was flying.
	(to) **draw** [drɔː] – **drew** [druː] – **drawn** [drɔːn]	zeichnen	Take a pencil and a piece of paper and ~ a picture of your dream house.

p. 22	**bell** [bel]	Glocke, Klingel	Two kinds of ~*s*.
	palace ['pæləs]	Palast	Kings and queens live in ~*s*.
	parliament ['pɑːləmənt]	Parlament	
	bridge [brɪdʒ]	Brücke	You must walk over the ~ to get across the river.
	Christmas ['krɪsməs]	Weihnachten	
	Christmas Day [ˌkrɪsməs 'deɪ]	der erste Weihnachtsfeiertag (25.12.)	*C~* ~ is December 25th.
p. 23	**once** [wʌns]	einst, (früher) einmal; einmal	Sting, the pop singer, was ~ an English teacher. I've been to London only ~, and that was in 1987.
	royal ['rɔɪəl]	königlich	A ~ palace belongs to a queen or king.
	°execution [ˌeksɪ'kjuːʃn]	Hinrichtung	
	°Crown Jewels [ˌkraʊn 'dʒuːəlz]	Kronjuwelen	

(p. 23)	°Beefeaters ['bi:fˌi:təz]	*Wachpersonal am Tower of London*	
	ground [graʊnd]	(Erd-)Boden	We can't sit here, the ~ is too wet. ⚠ *Fußboden = floor*
	foot [fʊt], *pl.* **feet** [fi:t]	*Längenmaß (1 foot = 30,48 cm)*	Brian is six *feet* tall. (= 1,83 m)
	°architect ['ɑ:kɪtekt]	Architekt/in	
	°(to) design [dɪ'zaɪn]	entwerfen, gestalten, konstruieren	
	capital ['kæpɪtl]	Hauptstadt	The ~ of the USA is Washington, D.C.
	musician [mju:'zɪʃn]	Musiker/in	
	route [ru:t]	Route, Strecke	Which is the quickest ~ from London to Bristol?
	guide [gaɪd]	(Fremden-)Führer/in	The ~ showed us some interesting sights in London.
	Focus on GRAMMAR		
p. 24	clause [klɔ:z]	(Teil-, Glied-)Satz	⚠ *Satz, Satzgefüge = sentence*
	who [hu:]	der, die, das *(Relativpronomen)*	The man/woman/child ~ has a question is sitting over there.
	which [wɪtʃ]	der, die, das *(Relativpronomen)*	The only restaurant ~ is open all night is *Pizza Palace.*
	prime minister [ˌpraɪm 'mɪnɪstə]	Premierminister/in, Ministerpräsident/in	
	that [ðæt, ðət]	der, die, das *(Relativpronomen)*	The people ~ work here are nice. And the food ~ they have is wonderful.
	term [tɜ:m]	(Fach-)Begriff, Ausdruck	You can find a list of grammatical *~s* at the back of the book.
	defining [dɪ'faɪnɪŋ]	definierend, bestimmend	
	(to) **define** [dɪ'faɪn]	definieren, festlegen	
	(to) **be called** [kɔ:ld]	heißen	This is our new neighbour. She*'s* ~ Sandra Taylor. ⚠ *Wie heißt dies auf Englisch? = What's this called in English?*
	necessary ['nesəsərɪ]	notwendig, nötig	People must eat and drink. Food and water are ~.
	(to) **fill** sth. **in** [ˌfɪl_'ɪn]	etwas einsetzen; etwas ausfüllen	*F~ in* the right words to complete the text.
p. 25	°business ['bɪznɪs]	Geschäft(e); Geschäfts-	
	crowded ['kraʊdɪd]	überfüllt	There were many people on the bus. It was quite ~.
	(to) **be/get fed up (with** sth.**)** [ˌfed_'ʌp] (infml.)	die Nase voll haben (von etwas), etwas satt haben	I*'m* ~ ~ *with* my work. I must find a new job.
	(to) **move** [mu:v]	(um)ziehen; (sich) bewegen	Our flat was too small, so we *~d* to a house. I think I broke my finger. I can't ~ it.
	salary ['sælərɪ]	Gehalt	money that your firm pays you for your work
	independent (of) [ˌɪndɪ'pendənt]	unabhängig (von)	Cathy wanted to be ~ *of* her parents, so she decided to move to her own flat.
	unlike [ˌʌn'laɪk]	anders als, im Gegensatz zu	Simon loves cricket. *U~* Tom – he hates cricket. ⧓ like
	century ['sentʃərɪ]	Jahrhundert	We're living in the 20th ~.
	by sb. [baɪ]	von jm.	That was a song ~ Tina Turner. ⚠ German "von": *a song* ***by*** *her – a photo* ***of*** *her – a letter* ***from*** *her*
	area ['eərɪə]	Gebiet, Gegend	I really don't need a car. I live in an ~ where there are lots of buses.
	poverty ['pɒvətɪ]	Armut	India is a poor country. There's much ~ in India.
	°docks [dɒks]	Docks, Hafenanlagen	
	°site [saɪt]	Stätte, Stelle	
	°redevelopment [ˌri:dɪ'veləpmənt]	Wiederaufbau, Sanierung	

Unit 2

(p. 25)	(to) **develop** [dɪ'veləp]	(sich) entwickeln; aufbauen	Let's see how the story *~s.* Our firm *has ~ed* a new kind of computer.
	development [dɪ'veləpmənt]	Entwicklung; Auf-, Ausbau	The ~ of our new computer took three years.
	program ['prəʊgræm] (AE)	Programm; (Radio-, Fernseh-)Sendung	⚠ *AE program* { *BE program (Computerprogr.)* / *BE programme (Programm; Sendung)*
	°tower block ['taʊə blɒk]	Hochhaus	
	risk [rɪsk]	Risiko	It's dangerous to swim over there. Those people don't know the ~ they are taking.
	disaster [dɪ'zɑːstə]	Katastrophe, Desaster	We lost 6:0. The game was a ~.
	center ['sentə] (AE)	= *BE centre*	

Focus on GRAMMAR

p. 26	bracket ['brækɪt]	Klammer	(These words are in *~s.*)
	precise [prɪ'saɪs]	präzise, genau	Do you have the time? – Yes, it's about quarter to 5. Do you have the ~ time? – Yes, it's 4.47 pm.
2 Ex 1	(to) puzzle sth. out [ˌpʌzl_'aʊt]	etwas ausknobeln, austüfteln	
	tree [triː]	Baum	Behind our house is a forest with a lot of *~s.*
	elephant ['elɪfənt]	Elefant	
2	homeless ['həʊmləs]	obdachlos	A person without a home is a ~ person.
4	**little** ['lɪtl]	klein	What a nice ~ dog. And so small, too. (= Was für ein niedliches Hündchen! Und so klein!)
5	**whose** [huːz]	deren, dessen	Janice is the girl ~ mother is an accountant.

Relative pronouns

1. **who** [huː]:	the woman **who** lives in Hatfield	die Frau, **die** in Hatfield wohnt
2. **which** [wɪtʃ]:	a house **which** is old	ein Haus, **das** alt ist
3. **that** [ðæt, ðət]:	the woman **that** lives in Hatfield	die Frau, **die** in Hatfield wohnt
	a house **that** is old	ein Haus, **das** alt ist
4. **whose** [huːz]:	a boy **whose** mother drives a taxi	ein Junge, **dessen** Mutter Taxi fährt
	a country **whose** people speak English	ein Land, **dessen** Bewohner Englisch sprechen

6	mixed [mɪkst]	gemischt	The weather was very ~ last week: hot, cold, and then wet.
7	**crazy** ['kreɪzɪ]	verrückt	Joe is ~. He wants to go out in this terrible weather.
	(to) **make** sth. **up** [ˌmeɪk_'ʌp]	sich ausdenken; *hier:* bilden	Tell the class a story. It can be a story that you *have made ~.*
	°chalk [tʃɔːk]	Kreide	
	disk [dɪsk]	Diskette	I must go to the computer shop. I need some new *~s.*
8	**production** [prə'dʌkʃn]	Produktion, Herstellung	Car ~ is an important industry in Germany.

Words Words Words

p. 30	(to) **guess** [ges]	(er)raten	I don't really know how old she is. I can only ~.
	My watch is wrong.	Meine Uhr geht falsch.	
	corner ['kɔːnə]	Ecke	We saw Sandra when she came round the ~.

2 Text Song: Streets of London

p. 31	°closed down [ˌkləʊzd 'daʊn]	geschlossen, außer Betrieb
	°(to) kick [kɪk]	treten
	°worn-out [ˌwɔːn'aʊt]	verschlissen, kaputt
	°pride [praɪd]	Stolz
	°hands held loosely … ['luːslɪ]	die Hände lose baumelnd …
	°telling ['telɪŋ]	erzählend
	°chorus ['kɔːrəs]	Refrain
	°sun [sʌn]	Sonne
	°(to) shine [ʃaɪn] – shone [ʃɒn] – shone	scheinen
	°(to) lead [liːd] – led [led] – led	führen
	°I'll show you …	ich werde dir … zeigen
	°to make you change your mind	damit du deine Meinung änderst

What happened to Mrs Middleton?

p. 31	**heavy** ['hevɪ]	schwer	I can't carry that bag. It's too ~.
	(Yes,) please. [pli:z]	Danke, gern.	◂▸ No, thank you.
	husband ['hʌzbənd]	(Ehe-)Mann	John Lennon was Yoko Ono's ~. She was his wife.
p. 32	(to) **promise (to do** sth.) ['prɒmɪs]	versprechen (, etwas zu tun)	You must give me your cassette-recorder. You *~d*.
	although [ɔ:l'ðəʊ]	obwohl	*A~* I'm tired I can't sleep. (= Though I'm tired ...)

Be careful. These words sound similar:

obwohl	**Although** [-'-] I'm tired I can't sleep.	I'm tired, and I'm **also** ['ɔ:lsəʊ] hungry.	*auch*
kosten	How much does it **cost** [kɒst] ...	... to go to the **coast** [kəʊst]?	*Küste*
fühlte	Tim **felt** a hand on his arm, ...	... then he **fell** to the ground.	*fiel*
Essen	Do you like French **food** [fu:d]?	I've broken my left **foot** [fʊt].	*Fuß*
interessiert	I'm **interested** in old maps.	I find old maps **interesting**.	*interessant*
jetzt	Can we go **now** [naʊ]?	I don't **know** [nəʊ].	*wissen*
ganz	Sue is **quite** [kwaɪt] nice, ...	... but she's very **quiet** ['kwaɪət].	*ruhig*
sparen	I want to **save** [seɪv] some money.	I keep my money in a **safe** [seɪf] place.	*sicher*
dann	First think, **then** [ðen] write.	Lucy can run faster **than** [ðən] Tim.	*als*
wo(hin)	**Where** [weə] can she be?	Your parents **were** [wɜ:, wə] here.	*waren*

several ['sevrəl]	einige, mehrere	some, but fewer than many
(to) **suppose** [sə'pəʊz]	vermuten, annehmen, glauben	Anne isn't at school today. I ~ she's ill.
accident ['æksɪdənt]	Unfall	I'm always careful when I ride my bike. I don't want to have an ~.
(to) **fall over** [ˌfɔ:l_'əʊvə] – **fell** [fel] – **fallen** ['fɔ:lən]	hin-, umfallen	Tim *fell* ~ at school and hurt his leg.
(to) **lie** [laɪ] – **lay** [leɪ] – **lain** [leɪn]	liegen	I don't feel well. – You should *lie* on the sofa. ⚠ -ing form: *lying* – She*'s lying* on the sofa.
(to) **lift** [lɪft]	(hoch)heben	This bag is too heavy. I can't ~ it.
weak [wi:k]	schwach	◂▸ strong
(to) **think of** sth.	sich etwas ausdenken	Can you ~ *of* a good birthday present for Larry?

Hector the raven

p. 33	°raven ['reɪvn]	Rabe	
	°beak [bi:k]	Schnabel	
	°living ['lɪvɪŋ]	lebend	
	°colony ['kɒlənɪ]	Kolonie	
	tape [teɪp]	(Ton-)Band	I need some new *~s* for my cassette-recorder.
	human ['hju:mən]	menschlich	It is ~ to make mistakes.
	soul [səʊl]	Seele	Many people believe that the ~ goes on living when the body is dead.
	°front page [ˌfrʌnt 'peɪdʒ]	Titelseite	
	°sensational newspaper [sen'seɪʃnəl]	Boulevardzeitung	
	°typewriter ['taɪpraɪtə]	Schreibmaschine	
	°a pair of scissors ['sɪzəz]	eine Schere	
	°glue [glu:]	Klebstoff	
	°headline ['hedlaɪn]	Schlagzeile	

Topic 2: Travelling in London ... and in Britain

p. 34	tube [tju:b]	*die Londoner U-Bahn* (*eigentlich:* Rohr, Röhre)	the London underground
	(to) **change** [tʃeɪndʒ]	umsteigen	to go from one train, bus, etc. to another
	(to) **get off (a train/...)** [ˌget_'ɒf]	aussteigen (aus einem Zug/...)	⚠ You *get on* and *off* a bus, train, plane or bike, but you *get in(to)* and *out of* a car or taxi.

V

p. 35	**meeting** ['mi:tɪŋ]	Besprechung; Treffen, Versammlung	The photo club *~s* are in Room 10 on Mondays.
	return journey [rɪ'tɜ:n]	Rückfahrt, Rückreise	
	(to) **return** [rɪ'tɜ:n]	zurückkehren	I left for Canada on May 1st and *~ed* on May 23rd.
	departure (dep.) [dɪ'pɑ:tʃə]	Abfahrt, Abreise	The time of ~ is 11.10 from Heathrow airport.
	(to) **depart (from)** [dɪ'pɑ:t]	abfahren, abreisen (von, aus)	▸◂ (to) arrive (at)
	arrival (arr.) [ə'raɪvl]	Ankunft	The train to London leaves at 10.05. The time of ~ in London is 12.10.
	altogether [,ɔ:ltə'geðə]	insgesamt	The pencil is 14p, the biro is 25p. That's 39p ~.
	°continent ['kɒntɪnənt]	Kontinent, Erdteil	
	rest [rest]	Rest	Eat as much as you want and give the ~ to me.
	advantage [əd'vɑ:ntɪdʒ]	Vorteil	Tim can run fast. That's an ~ when he does sports.
	disadvantage [,dɪsəd'vɑ:ntɪdʒ]	Nachteil	▸◂ advantage
	direct [dɪ'rekt, daɪ'rekt]	direkt, unmittelbar	On a ~ flight you don't change planes on your journey.
	connection [kə'nekʃn]	Verbindung	Is there a direct ~ to Hatfield by train?
	°convenient [kən'vi:nɪənt]	zweckmäßig, günstig	
	fare [feə]	Fahrgeld, Fahrpreis	the money you pay to use a train, bus, etc.

Unit 3: A visit to a British school

Focus on WORDS

p. 36	**strict (with** sb.) [strɪkt]	streng (mit/zu jm.)	Peter mustn't watch TV after 7 o'clock. His parents are very ~ *with* him.
	headteacher [,hed'ti:tʃə]	Schuldirektor/in	the "boss" of a school
	grade [greɪd]	(Zeugnis-)Note, Zensur	In German schools pupils get *~s* from "1" to "6".
	physics *(sing.)* ['fɪzɪks]	Physik	Some school subjects: *physics, biology,* maths, geography, history, foreign languages (French, Latin, German), art, music, games
	biology [baɪ'ɒlədʒɪ]	Biologie	
	(to) **pay attention (to)** [,peɪ‿ə'tenʃn] – **paid** [peɪd] – **paid** [peɪd]	aufmerksam sein, aufpassen (auf)	To get good grades you must *pay ~ to* your teacher.
	(to) **catch** [kætʃ] – **caught** [kɔ:t] – **caught** [kɔ:t]	erwischen	Lucy's parents *caught* her while she was buying cigarettes [,sɪgə'rets]. ⚠ *(to) catch* = **1.** fangen; **2.** erwischen
	(to) **copy** ['kɒpɪ]	abschreiben; kopieren	Walter didn't know the answers in the maths test, so he *copied* from his neighbour.
	classmate ['klɑ:smeɪt]	Klassenkamerad/in, Mitschüler/in	Tina and Sandra are in the same class at school. They're *~s*.
	(to) **fail (an exam)** [feɪl]	(eine Prüfung) nicht bestehen, durchfallen	How was your exam? – Terrible. I *~ed*.
	(to) **pass** [pɑ:s]	*(eine Prüfung)* bestehen	▸◂ (to) fail
	GCSE [,dʒi: si:‿es‿'i:] (= General Certificate of Secondary Education)	*etwa:* Mittlere Reife mit eingeschlossenem Hauptschulabschluß	Martha is 15. Next year she wants to get her ~ and find a job.
	trouble ['trʌbl]	Schwierigkeit(en)	John is in ~ with the police. He took some money.
	note [nəʊt]	Entschuldigungsschreiben	My mother wrote the teacher a ~ because I was sick and couldn't go to school.
	(to) be absent ['æbsənt]	fehlen, abwesend sein	Ellen wasn't at school today. She *was* ~.
	straight *(adv.; adj.)* [streɪt]	direkt, geradewegs; gerade	After lessons I don't stay at school, I go ~ home. Oxford Street in London is long and ~.

(p. 36)	**(im)patient** [(ɪm)'peɪʃnt]	(un)geduldig	You must be *patient* to catch fish. Don't be so *impatient*. The bus should come soon.
p. 37	**system** ['sɪstəm]	System	The British school ~ is very different from the German school ~.
	age [eɪdʒ]	Alter	Pat and Liz are both 13 years old. They're the same ~. ⚠ *im Alter von = at the age of*
	primary school ['praɪmərɪ sku:l]	Grundschule	In Britain, pupils start ~ ~ at the age of five.
	secondary school ['sekəndrɪ sku:l]	Oberschule	After primary school, pupils go to ~ ~.
	A-level (exam) ['eɪˌlevl]	*etwa:* Abitur	Lori wants to be a teacher. After her *A-levels* she wants to leave school …
	university [ˌju:nɪ'vɜ:sətɪ]	Universität	… and go to *university*.
	college ['kɒlɪdʒ]	Fach-, Hochschule	After secondary school Anne went straight to ~.
	(to) **repeat** [rɪ'pi:t]	wiederholen	When you fail a class in Germany you must ~ it.
	set [set]	Kursgruppe, Leistungsgruppe	Monica is very good at maths. She's in the highest *set*. …
	low [ləʊ]	niedrig	… Her brother is quite lazy. He's in a very *low* set.
	(to) **check** [tʃek]	(über)prüfen, kontrollieren	Can you ~ my homework, please? I'm not sure if everything's OK.

Some more irregular past participles

(to) drink	drank	**drunk** [drʌŋk]	trinken	(to) pay	paid	**paid** [peɪd]	bezahlen
(to) feel	felt	**felt** [felt]	fühlen	(to) sleep	slept	**slept** [slept]	schlafen
(to) forget	forgot	**forgotten** [fə'gɒtn]	vergessen	(to) speak	spoke	**spoken** ['spəʊkn]	sprechen
(to) mean	meant	**meant** [ment]	bedeuten; meinen	(to) understand	understood	**understood** [ˌʌndə'stʊd]	verstehen
(to) meet	met	**met** [met]	treffen				

Focus on GRAMMAR

p. 38	**preparation** [ˌprepə'reɪʃn]	Vorbereitung	Can I help you with the ~*s* for the party, Jenny?
	exchange [ɪks'tʃeɪndʒ]	Austausch	Our teacher organized an ~ between our class and a class in Germany.
	(to) **invite** [ɪn'vaɪt]	*(Gäste)* einladen	Jenny ~*d* Ralph and Sandra to her party.
	result [rɪ'zʌlt]	Ergebnis	The plane arrived late as a ~ of the bad weather.
	(to) **form** [fɔ:m]	(sich) bilden, formen	You ~ the simple past of regular verbs with "-ed".
	bold print [bəʊld 'prɪnt]	fette Schrift, Fettdruck	**In this sentence** the first three words are in ~ ~.
	ever ['evə]	je, jemals, schon mal	Have you ~ played cricket? – No, never.
	so far [səʊ 'fɑ:]	bis jetzt, bisher	Is the film good? – *So far* it's OK, …
	not … yet [nɒt 'jet]	noch nicht	… but it's *not* over *yet*.
	… yet?	… schon …?	Has Linda arrived *yet?*– No, not yet.
	west [west]	westlich; Westen; nach Westen	Wales is ~ of England.
p. 39	°packed lunch	Lunchpaket	
p. 40	**opinion** [ə'pɪnjən]	Meinung	I agree with Sue. What's your ~? Do you agree, too?
	ours ['aʊəz]	unsere(r, s)	This car belongs to us – it's ~.
	part [pɑ:t]	Rolle	Music has always played a big ~ in Dave's life.
	competition [ˌkɒmpə'tɪʃn]	Wettkampf, Wettbewerb	A ~ is when one person or team plays against another person or team.
	theirs [ðeəz]	ihre(r, s) *(Plural)*	That car belongs to them – it's ~.
	assembly [ə'semblɪ]	Schulversammlung mit Andacht	In British schools students usually go to a morning ~ before their first lesson.
	English pupils might go out … [maɪt]	Englische Schüler/innen gehen vielleicht manchmal aus …	

V

Unit 3

(p. 40)	**might** [maɪt]	könnte(n) vielleicht	I ~ go to the cinema today. I don't know yet.

How you can say that something is possible or probable[1]: — [1] ['prɒbəbl] wahrscheinlich

My parents	**may**	be at home now.	Meine Eltern	sind jetzt **vielleicht** zu Hause.
	might			**könnten** jetzt **vielleicht** zu Hause sein.
	could			**könnten** jetzt zu Hause sein.
	should			**sollten/müßten eigentlich** jetzt zu Hause sein.
	must			**müssen** jetzt zu Hause sein.

	(to) **deliver** [dɪ'lɪvə]	*(Zeitungen)* austragen, zustellen; liefern	Many British pupils ~ newspapers before school. I bought a new fridge. The store *~ed* it yesterday.
	°leisure centre ['leʒə ˌsentə]	Freizeitzentrum	
	alcohol ['ælkəhɒl]	Alkohol	Wine is a drink with ~ in it.
	(to) **complain** [kəm'pleɪn]	sich beschweren, sich beklagen	Tony didn't like the meal. He *~ed* about it all evening.

Focus on GRAMMAR

p. 41	**since** 1282 [sɪns]	seit 1282	Helmut has lived (⚠ *not:* ~~lives~~) in Sydney ~ 1987.
	for 500 years	seit 500 Jahren	He has lived in Sydney ~ over six years. ⚠ *for* one year = **1.** seit einem Jahr; **2.** ein Jahr lang
	expression [ɪk'spreʃn]	Ausdruck	"Have a nice day" is an ~ you often hear in the USA.
	(to) **express** [ɪk'spres]	ausdrücken, äußern	Ingrid's English is very good. She can ~ all her ideas well.
	span of time [spæn]	Zeitspanne	
	(to) **lead (to)** [li:d] – **led** [led] – **led** [led]	führen, leiten (zu/nach)	In maths, the smallest mistake *~s to* a wrong answer.
3 Ex 1	(to) **inform** [ɪn'fɔ:m]	informieren, benachrichtigen	Please ~ your parents about the meeting on Thursday.
2	prompt [prɒmpt]	Stichwort, Anregung	Tell the story again with the help of the *~s*.
3	**power** ['paʊə]	Macht	In Britain parliament has the ~, not the Queen.
7	**invention** [ɪn'venʃn]	Erfindung	The telephone was Alexander Graham Bell's most important ~.
	overhead projector (OHP) [ˌəʊvəhed prə'dʒektə, ˌəʊ_eɪtʃ 'pi:]	Tageslichtprojektor	
8	introductory [ˌɪntrə'dʌktərɪ]	einleitend, Einführungs-	~ comments = comments you make at the beginning
	feeling ['fi:lɪŋ]	Gefühl	I feel funny. I've got a funny ~ in my head.
	proud (of) [praʊd]	stolz (auf)	The Martins are ~ *of* their new baby.

Words Words Words

p. 45	(to) **mix** sth. **up** [ˌmɪks_'ʌp]	etwas verwechseln, durcheinanderbringen	*Don't ~ up* the word "fault" with the word "mistake".

3 Text Unwelcome guests

p. 46	(to) **react (to)** [rɪ'ækt]	reagieren (auf)	How *did* Alison ~ when you told her the news?
	reaction (to) [rɪ'ækʃn]	Reaktion (auf)	noun from "(to) react"

Verbs with a preposition

How did they **react to** your suggestion?	Wie haben sie **auf** deinen Vorschlag **reagiert**?
Some of the children **laughed at** Pete's glasses.	Einige Kinder **lachten über** Petes Brille.
Don't **laugh at** her because she can't swim.	**Lach** sie nicht **aus**, weil sie nicht schwimmen kann.
Mrs Price was so angry that she **shouted at** us.	Mrs Price war so verärgert, daß sie uns **anschrie**.
Sue is very ill. We must **send for** a doctor.	… Wir müssen einen Arzt **holen/kommen lassen**.
I always have to **wait for** you.	Immer muß ich **auf** dich **warten**!
Do you **believe in** ghosts?	**Glaubst** du **an** Gespenster?

(p. 46)	There were five of them.	Sie waren zu fünft.	
	towards [tə'wɔ:dz]	auf … zu, in Richtung auf	▸◂ away from The child ran ~ its mother.
	youth [ju:θ]	Jugendlicher; Jugend	a young man; the time when you are young
	(to) **shut** [ʃʌt], **-tt-, – shut – shut**	schließen	▸◂ (to) open Can I ~ the window? I'm cold.
	(to) get worked up [ˌwɜ:kt_'ʌp]	sich aufregen	to get angry or excited
	(to) **calm down** [ˌkɑ:m 'daʊn]	(sich) beruhigen	▸◂ (to) get excited
	(to) provoke [prə'vəʊk]	provozieren	Tim *~d* the dog, so it bit him.
	tonight [tə'naɪt]	heute abend, heute nacht	this evening/this night Let's see a film ~.
p. 47	**change** [tʃeɪndʒ]	Wechselgeld	Excuse me, can you give me ~ for a pound?
	°karate [kə'rɑ:tɪ]	Karate	
	Never mind. [ˌnevə 'maɪnd]	Macht nichts. Egal.	Did you say something? – *Never ~*, it's not important.
	(to) **blame** sb. (**for** sth.) [bleɪm]	jm. Vorwürfe machen (wegen etwas); jm. die Schuld geben (an etwas)	Mrs Smith *~d* Simon *for* the broken window, but it wasn't Simon – the others did it.
	°lousy ['laʊzɪ] (infml.)	lausig, saumäßig	
	(to) **be afraid (of)** [ə'freɪd]	Angst haben (vor)	Gary *is ~ of* dark rooms. He sleeps with the light on. ⚠ *I'm afraid* I don't know. = Ich weiß es *leider* nicht.
	(to) **solve** [sɒlv]	*(Aufgabe, Problem)* lösen	to find the answer (to a problem)
	close [kləʊs]	genau, gründlich	⚠ *Aussprache:* close *(adj.)* [kləʊs] – (to) close *(v.)* [kləʊz]
	look [lʊk]	Blick	Stand next to the map so that you can have a *close look* at it.
	hero, *pl.* **heroes** ['hɪərəʊ]	Held/in	Superman is a famous comic ~.
	ending ['endɪŋ]	Ende, (Ab-)Schluß; Endung	▸◂ beginning I hate it when somebody tells me the ~ of a film.
	beyond [bɪ'jɒnd]	über … hinaus, jenseits von	The road goes ~ the village and into the hills.
	difference ['dɪfrəns]	Unterschied	noun from "different"
p. 48	**context** ['kɒntekst]	Kontext, Zusammenhang	What does "change" mean? – It has many meanings. Show me the word in ~.
	order ['ɔ:də]	Reihenfolge; (An-)Ordnung	The following words are in the wrong ~. Put them in the right ~: Can – me – help – you?

A radio broadcast on private and state schools in Britain

p. 48	°broadcast ['brɔ:dkɑ:st]	Sendung	°(to) give a talk	einen Vortrag halten
	°state [steɪt]	Staat	°indirectly *(adv.)* [ˌɪndɪ'rektlɪ]	indirekt
	°weekly ['wi:klɪ]	wöchentlich	°reason ['ri:zn]	Grund, Begründung
	°education [ˌedjʊ'keɪʃn]	Erziehung, (Schul-) Bildung	°tradition [trə'dɪʃn]	Tradition
	°twice [twaɪs]	zweimal	°from 1975 on	ab 1975, von 1975 an

Some more irregular past participles

(to) bite	bit	**bitten** ['bɪtn]	beißen	(to) sing	sang	**sung** [sʌŋ]	singen
(to) cost	cost	**cost** [kɒst]	kosten	(to) sit	sat	**sat** [sæt]	sitzen
(to) fight	fought	**fought** [fɔ:t]	kämpfen	(to) stand	stood	**stood** [stʊd]	stehen
(to) hurt	hurt	**hurt** [hɜ:t]	verletzen	(to) swim	swam	**swum** [swʌm]	schwimmen
(to) ride	rode	**ridden** ['rɪdn]	reiten; fahren	(to) throw	threw	**thrown** [θrəʊn]	werfen
(to) shake	shook	**shaken** ['ʃeɪkən]	schütteln	(to) wear	wore	**worn** [wɔ:n]	tragen, anhaben

V

Unit 3

Topic 3: Great Britain and the sea

p. 49	unknown [ˌʌn'nəʊn]	unbekannt	Nobody knows who wrote the story. The writer is ~.
	ship [ʃɪp]	Schiff	Did you go to the USA by plane? – No, we went by ~. It took six days.
	°navy ['neɪvɪ]	Marine	
	(to) rule [ru:l]	regieren, herrschen über	Charles I *~d* England for eleven years.
	°explorer [ɪk'splɔ:rə]	Forscher/in	
	(to) **discover** [dɪ'skʌvə]	entdecken	Columbus *~ed* America in 1492.
	°(to) trade [treɪd]	Handel treiben	
	(to) attack [ə'tæk]	angreifen	A gang *~ed* the old man and beat him.
	°colony ['kɒlənɪ]	Kolonie	
	Englishman/-woman ['ɪŋglɪʃmən, 'ɪŋglɪʃwʊmən]	Engländer/in	A man from England is an *Englishman*. A woman from England is an *Englishwoman*.
	°(to) explore [ɪk'splɔ:]	erforschen	
	as far as *(prep.)* [əz 'fɑ:r_əz]	bis (nach/zu)	We walked *as ~ as* the river and then went back.
	(to) invade [ɪn'veɪd]	einmarschieren in, einfallen in	Germany *~d* Poland in 1939.
	(to) defeat [dɪ'fi:t]	besiegen	Australia *~ed* England 3:2 in the football match.
	Spanish ['spænɪʃ]	Spanisch; spanisch	Garcia is from Spain. He's ~, so he speaks ~.
	successful [sək'sesfəl]	erfolgreich	Jane's plan was ~. (= the plan worked)
	success [sək'ses]	Erfolg	The race was a ~ for the Irish horse. (= the Irish horse won)

Spelling: ll *or* l?

ful**l** – *but:* successfu**l**, wonderfu**l**, beautifu**l**, carefu**l**
we**ll** – *but:* we**l**come
a**ll** – *but:* a**l**most, a**l**ready, a**l**so, a**l**though, a**l**together, a**l**ways

	(to) **introduce** [ˌɪntrə'dju:s]	einführen; vorstellen, bekanntmachen	Mrs Bailey wants to ~ computers into our school. I met Kim last week. Sue *~d* me to her at a party.
	°tobacco [tə'bækəʊ]	Tabak	
	east [i:st]	östlich; Osten; nach Osten	Germany is ~ of France.
	°captain ['kæptən]	Kapitän	
	°sailor ['seɪlə]	Matrose	
p. 50	county ['kaʊntɪ]	Grafschaft, Verwaltungsbezirk	
	°smuggler ['smʌglə]	Schmuggler/in	
	°cruel [kru:əl]	grausam	
	storm [stɔ:m]	Sturm; Gewitter	There was a lot of rain during the *storm* last night, and the *wind* was very strong.
	wind [wɪnd]	Wind	
	°shipwreck ['ʃɪprek]	Wrack	
	°cargo ship ['kɑ:gəʊ ʃɪp]	Frachtschiff	
	°coastguards ['kəʊstgɑ:dz]	Küstenwache	
	°(to) hit the rocks [hɪt], -tt-, – hit – hit	auf/gegen die Felsen laufen	
	helicopter ['helɪkɒptə]	Hubschrauber	Have you ever flown in a plane? – No, but I have flown in a ~.
	°(to) rescue ['reskju:]	retten	
	°link [lɪŋk]	Verbindung	
	oil [ɔɪl]	Öl	*Oil* and water don't mix.
	wide [waɪd]	breit	The river is 500 kilometres long and 30 metres ~. ⚠ "False friends": *wide = breit*; *bright = hell, leuchtend*
	traffic ['træfɪk]	Verkehr	I don't drive to work because the ~ is terrible. I go by bike.

Unit 4: The North of England

p. 51	surgery ['sɜːdʒərɪ]	(Arzt-)Praxis	place where a doctor sees his or her patients
	for a long time	lange (Zeit)	We had to wait *for a* ~ ~ before the train arrived.

for + present perfect – _for_ + simple past

1. Elizabeth II **has been** queen **for** about 40 years.
   *Elizabeth II **ist seit** etwa 40 Jahren Königin.*
   (1953 - today)
2. Elizabeth I **was** queen **for** about 40 years.
   *Elizabeth I **war** etwa 40 Jahre **(lang)** Königin.*
   (1558 - 1603)

for + present perfect: Etwas hat in der Vergangenheit begonnen und dauert noch an. (Deutsch: *seit* + Präsens)
for + simple past: Etwas dauerte einen bestimmten Zeitraum in der Vergangenheit an, ist aber beendet. (Deutsch: Präteritum)

	outskirts *(pl.)* ['aʊtskɜːts]	Außenbezirke, Stadtrand	Heathrow airport is on the ~ of London. ⚠ *am Stadtrand = on the outskirts*
	the **only** … [ðɪ‿'əʊnlɪ]	der/die/das einzige …	The 183 is *the* ~ bus that goes to Hatfield.
	°Urdu	*in Pakistan und Indien verwendete Sprache*	
	difficulty ['dɪfɪkəltɪ]	Schwierigkeit	noun from "difficult"
	immigrant ['ɪmɪgrənt]	Einwanderer/Einwanderin	person who has moved from one country to another
	government ['gʌvnmənt]	Regierung	The Prime Minister is the leader of the British ~.
	°National Health Service [ˌnæʃnəl 'helθ ˌsɜːvɪs], NHS	*britisches staatliches Gesundheitswesen*	
	°the promised land [ˌprɒmɪst 'lænd]	das Gelobte Land, Paradies	
p. 52	**region** ['riːdʒən]	Gebiet, Region	area
	contrast ['kɒntrɑːst]	Kontrast, Gegensatz	difference
	poem ['pəʊɪm]	Gedicht	"Erlkönig" is a famous ~ by Goethe.
	industrial [ɪn'dʌstrɪəl]	industriell; Industrie-	adjective from "industry" ⚠ *Aussprache*: industry ['ɪndəstrɪ] industrial [ɪn'dʌstrɪəl]
	population [ˌpɒpjʊ'leɪʃn]	Bevölkerung, Einwohner(zahl)	the number of people who live in a city, country, etc.
	(to) **produce** [prə'djuːs]	produzieren, herstellen, erzeugen	American car companies *~d* more cars this year than last year.
	coal [kəʊl]	Kohle	In the Ruhr there is a lot of ~.
	iron ['aɪən]	Eisen	You need coal and *iron* …
	steel [stiːl]	Stahl	… to make *steel.*
	°cloth [klɒθ]	Stoff, Tuch	
	°workshop ['wɜːkʃɒp]	Werkstatt	
	(to) **grow** [grəʊ] – **grew** [gruː] – **grown** [grəʊn]	wachsen	Brenda *has grown* six centimetres since last year.
	ruin ['ruːɪn]	Ruine	The Colosseum is a famous Roman ~.
p. 53	**especially** [ɪ'speʃlɪ]	besonders, insbesondere	Liz is good at school, ~ at English.
	rich (in) [rɪtʃ]	reich (an)	The Ruhr is a region that is ~ *in* coal. ◀▶ poor (in)
	mine [maɪn]	Bergwerk	Workers get coal and iron out of *~s.*
	smoke [sməʊk]	Rauch	Cigarette ~ hurts my eyes.
	(to) **smoke** [sməʊk]	rauchen	Doris *~s* fifteen cigarettes a day.
	(to) **pollute** [pə'luːt]	*(die Umwelt)* verschmutzen	To ~ the water or air means to make them dirty.
	countryside ['kʌntrɪsaɪd]	Landschaft, (ländliche) Gegend	the area outside a town or city
	law [lɔː]	Gesetz	In Britain, the parliament makes the country's *~s.*
	(to) **protect** [prə'tekt]	(be)schützen	You need warm clothes to ~ you against the cold.
	wages *(pl.)* ['weɪdʒɪz]	Lohn, Löhne	Kevin's ~ are very low. He only gets £100 a week. ⚠ *wages* = Lohn – *salary* = Gehalt
	(to) **earn** [ɜːn]	*(Geld)* verdienen	to get money for work

V

(p. 53)	**however** [haʊ'evə]	jedoch, aber	My room is quite small. It's very comfortable, ~. Dennis said no. Later, ~ , he changed his mind. ⚠ comma before and after "however"
	land [lænd]	Land, Grund und Boden	The city bought the farmer's ~ to build new flats. ⚠ ein Land/Staat = a country
	quickly *(adv.)* ['kwɪklɪ]	schnell	⧓ slowly

Focus on GRAMMAR

p. 54	derelict ['derəlɪkt]	verlassen und verfallen, heruntergekommen	Who lives in that terrible house? – Nobody, it's a ~ house.
	forest ['fɒrɪst]	Wald, Forst	area of land where there are many trees
	(to) **plant** [plɑ:nt]	(ein)pflanzen	Ms Lawrence *~ed* some flowers in her garden.
	clue [klu:]	Hinweis, Anhaltspunkt	The police looked for *~s* in the dead man's house.
	European Community (EC) [ˌjʊərəˌpi:ən kə'mju:nətɪ]	Europäische Gemeinschaft (EG)	There are 12 countries in the *European* ~.
	°(to) redevelop [ˌri:dɪ'veləp]	sanieren	
	(to) **create** [krɪ'eɪt]	schaffen	The firm was so successful that it *~d* fifty new jobs.
	(to) recreate [ˌri:krɪ'eɪt]	wiederbeleben, neu erschaffen	to create again
	(to) cut down [ˌkʌt 'daʊn] – cut – cut	*(Bäume)* fällen	Where's the tree that was here? – We ~ it *down*.
	atmosphere ['ætməsfɪə]	Atmosphäre	The ~ at dinner was warm and friendly.
	°(to) bring back to life	wieder lebendig werden lassen	
	up to	bis (zu)	*Up to* 20 % of British teenagers smoke cigarettes.
	overnight [ˌəʊvə'naɪt]	über Nacht	Poverty is a problem that won't go away ~.
p. 55	**bottom** ['bɒtəm]	unteres Ende	⧓ top
	probably *(adv.)* ['prɒbəblɪ]	wahrscheinlich	Are you going to Lucy's party? – *Probably*, but I'm not 100% sure.
	(to) **be/feel cold**	frieren	May I close the window? I'*m* ~.
	tablet ['tæblət]	Tablette	I feel ill. I think I'll take a ~.
	just [dʒʌst, dʒəst]	einfach	I've looked everywhere, but I ~ can't find my keys.

V

The simple present in sub-clauses with *when, while, before, till, as soon as*

main clause: *will*-future	sub-clause: simple present	
I'll phone you	**when** I **get** home.	Ich rufe dich an, wenn ich nach Hause komme.
We**'ll repair** your car	**while** you **wait**.	Wir reparieren Ihr Auto, während Sie warten.
It**'ll be** a long time	**before** we **meet** again.	Es wird lange dauern, bevor wir uns wiedersehen.
You**'ll have** to wait	**till** the bank **opens**.	Du mußt warten, bis die Bank aufmacht.
I'll tell mother	**as soon as** she **comes**.	Ich sage es Mutter, sobald sie kommt.

Focus on WORDS

p. 56	seaside resort ['si:saɪd rɪˌzɔ:t]	(beliebter) Urlaubsort am Meer, Seebad	a place that many people visit for their holidays because they like the sea
	district ['dɪstrɪkt]	Gebiet, Bezirk	Kreuzberg is a ~ of Berlin.
	ferry ['ferɪ]	Fähre	We took the six o'clock ~ from Calais to Dover.
	sandy ['sændɪ]	sandig	I don't like the beach because I hate wet and ~ shoes.
	lovely ['lʌvlɪ]	schön, herrlich, hübsch	pleasant
	fresh [freʃ]	frisch	Please open the window. I need some ~ air.
	wood(s) [wʊd(z)]	Wald	a small forest
	wood	Holz	Guitars are made of ~.
	continent ['kɒntɪnənt]	Kontinent	Asia ['eɪʃə, 'eɪʒə] is the largest ~.
4 Ex 2	°fortune-teller ['fɔ:tʃənˌtelə]	Wahrsager/in	
	(to) **be right** [raɪt]	recht haben	We'll miss the bus. – You'*re* ~. Let's take a taxi.
	°crystal ball ['krɪstl]	Kristallkugel	

(4 Ex 2)	(to) **take an exam/ your Abitur**	eine Prüfung/sein Abitur machen	Meike will ~ *her Abitur* next spring. In autumn she will go to university.

German "machen"

eine Prüfung **machen**	(to) **take** an exam	ein Picknick **machen**	(to) **have** a picnic
eine Pause **machen**	(to) **take** a break	einen Spaziergang **machen**	(to) **go for** a walk
Fotos **machen**	(to) **take** photos	eine Radtour **machen**	(to) **go on** a bike tour
ein Spiel **machen**	(to) **play** a game	Urlaub **machen**	(to) **be/go** on holiday
Das/Es **macht nichts.**	It **doesn't matter.**		

	(to) **fall in love with** sb.	sich in jn. verlieben	Ann *fell in ~ with* Ken. A year later they got married.
4	°one-upmanship [wʌn'ʌpmənʃɪp]	Angeberei, Profilierungsgehabe	
5	**less** [les]	weniger	⧓ more

***little/a little/less* + singular noun – *few/a few/fewer* + plural noun**

These flowers need very **little water** (= not much water).	wenig Wasser
But don't forget to give them **a little water** (= some water) every day.	ein bißchen, etwas Wasser
They need **less water** than you think.	weniger Wasser
Sarah isn't very popular. She has **few friends** (= not many friends).	wenige Freunde/-innen
Can I bring **a few friends** (= some friends) with me to the party?	ein paar, einige Freunde/-innen
Sarah has **fewer friends** (*infml. also:* less friends) than I thought.	weniger Freunde/-innen

6	(to) **cover** ['kʌvə]	bedecken, zudecken	Flowers ~ most of Monica's garden.
	third [θɜ:d]	Drittel	$1/3$ = a/one *third*; $2/3$ = two *thirds*
	(to) **suggest** [sə'dʒest]	vorschlagen, anregen	The doctor *~ed* that I should stop smoking.
7	muddled ['mʌdld]	durcheinander(gebracht)	mixed up
	developing country [dɪ'veləpɪŋ ˌkʌntrɪ]	Entwicklungsland	A ~ ~ is a poor country that is trying to build up its industry.
	in the end	schließlich, am Ende, zum Schluß	⚠ *in the end* = at last: I waited a long time, but the bus didn't come. *In the end* I walked to school. *at the end (of sth.)* = when sth. stops: *At the end of* our English lesson we sometimes sing a song.
[8]	(to) hold sth. up [ˌhəʊld‿'ʌp] – held [held] – held [held]	etwas hochhalten	I can't see the picture. Can you ~ it *up* please?
	advertisement [əd'vɜ:tɪsmənt]	Anzeige, Reklame	To sell your sofa you should put an ~ in the newspaper.
	(to) celebrate ['seləbreɪt]	feiern	I'm going to ~ my birthday next week. Would you like to come?
	moon [mu:n]	Mond	There's a full ~ tonight.
	earth [ɜ:θ]	Erde	Many years ago people didn't know the ~ was round.
	space [speɪs]	Weltraum	Astronauts travel through ~.
	serious ['sɪərɪəs]	ernst(haft)	Pollution is a ~ problem.
[9]	by the year 2025	bis (zum Jahr) 2025	*By the year* 2010 I will have finished school.
	(to) have sth. in common ['kɒmən]	etwas miteinander gemein haben	Mary and Jeff are interested in the same things. They *have* a lot *in* ~.

Words Words Words

p. 60	**aloud** *(adv.)* [ə'laʊd]	laut *(= hörbar)*	⚠ *aloud* = laut (für alle hörbar): Read the poem *aloud* so that we can all hear it. *loud* = laut (mit einer gewissen Lautstärke): You needn't speak so *loud*, we can all hear you.
	snow [snəʊ]	Schnee	We had a lot of ~ last winter.
	sun [sʌn]	Sonne	It's raining. There's no ~ today.
	fog [fɒg]	Nebel	When there is ~ you can't see very far.
	e.g. [ˌi:'dʒi:] *(from Latin "exempli gratia")*	z.B. (= zum Beispiel)	

V

Unit 4

4 Text A difficult daughter

p. 61	(to) **prepare** [prɪ'peə]	vorbereiten, zubereiten	to get sth. ready
	°shalwar kameez [ˌʃʌlwʌr kʌ'mi:z]	*pakistanische Frauenkleidung (Hose und passendes Oberteil)*	
	(to) **kiss** [kɪs]	küssen	Tonia *~ed* David on the mouth.
	next door [ˌnekst 'dɔ:]	nebenan	in the next room or house
	(to) sigh (with) [saɪ]	seufzen (vor)	He *~ed* after the good meal.
	You can say that again.	Das kannst du laut sagen.	It's really hot today. – *You can say that again.* ⚠ The main stress in this phrase is on "that".
	(to) **get changed**	sich umziehen	I have to *get* ~ for work. Where is my uniform?
	(to) **take** sth. **off** [ˌteɪk_'ɒf]	etwas ausziehen	Because it was so hot, I *took* my pullover *off*. ▸◂ (to) put sth. on
	record ['rekɔ:d]	Schallplatte	Do you prefer CDs, cassettes, or *~s*?
	shoulder ['ʃəʊldə]	Schulter	Laurie carried the heavy bag over her ~.
p. 62	(to) **wave** (**at** sb.) [weɪv]	(jm. zu)winken	Lisa *~d at* her family from the train.
	chance [tʃɑ:ns]	Gelegenheit, Chance	When Sarah met Alan at the disco, she saw her ~ to get to know him better.
	traffic lights *(pl.)* ['træfɪk laɪts]	(Verkehrs-)Ampel	the red, yellow and green lights that tell car drivers to stop or go
	(to) **turn** (green, red, …) [tɜ:n]	(grün, rot, …) werden	Cars can go when the traffic lights ~ green.

German "werden"

(to) **become/get**	**angry, tired, wet, rich, old, …** **cold, windy, dark, …** **boring, funny, more interesting, …**	For German "werden" you usually use the verbs *(to)* ***get*** and, a little more formal, *(to)* ***become***.

⚠ With nouns you only use *(to)* ***become***: **She became a doctor/a member of the chess club/…**
But: Was willst du später einmal werden? = What do you want to **be** when you grow up?

(to) **go/turn** red, brown, white, …	You can use *(to)* ***go*** and *(to)* ***turn*** to talk about changes in colour; *(to)* ***turn*** is a little more formal.
(to) **go** | **hard** (bread), **bad** (fish, eggs), … **crazy, blind** [blaɪnd], …	You can also use *(to)* ***go*** to describe negative changes.

	forward(s) ['fɔ:wəd(z)]	vorwärts, nach vorne	▸◂ backward(s)
	(to) turn away [ˌtɜ:n_ə'weɪ]	sich abwenden	to stop looking at or towards sb./sth.
	as *(conj.)* [æz, əz]	als, während	Bill's bus arrived just ~ Lynn's bus was leaving.
	at once [ət 'wʌns]	sofort, (so)gleich	Ms King, I need your help now. Please come *at* ~.
	(to) **scream** [skri:m]	schreien, kreischen	Tommy *~ed* that there was a fire.
	°mosque [mɒsk]	Moschee	
	(to) **greet** [gri:t]	(be)grüßen	In English you ~ people with "Hallo", "Hi", etc. ⚠ Grüß Nancy von mir. = Say hallo to Nancy.
	culture ['kʌltʃə]	Kultur	We should learn about the different *~s* in the world.
	(to) **realize** ['rɪəlaɪz]	erkennen, merken	I was already on the train when I *~d* I had no ticket.
	not (…) any more	nicht mehr, kein(e, n) … mehr	Are you hungry? – *Not any ~*, I've just eaten. I do*n't* have a car *any ~*. I sold it last month.
	(to) **support** [sə'pɔ:t]	unterstützen	My parents *~ed* me while I was at university. They paid for my flat, my food, etc.
p. 63	pre-question ['pri:ˌkwestʃn]	vorgeschaltete, vorangestellte Frage	
	(to) take sth. into consideration [kənˌsɪdə'reɪʃn]	etwas bedenken, etwas berücksichtigen	When I buy a car I always *take* colour and size *into consideration*.
	behaviour (towards) [bɪ'heɪvjə]	Verhalten, Benehmen (gegenüber)	noun from "(to) behave"
	responsible (for) [rɪ'spɒnsəbl]	verantwortlich (für)	Parents are ~ *for* their children.

V

(p. 63)	**exactly** *(adv.)* [ɪg'zæktlɪ]	genau	Are you taller than Sue? – No, we're ~ the same size.
	(to) take sides with sb. [ˌteɪk 'saɪdz]	für jn. Partei ergreifen	I agree with Grace. – You always *take ~ with* her when we have an argument.
	truth [tru:θ]	Wahrheit	Where did you go last night? Tell me the ~.

The miner's story

p. 63	°particular [pə'tɪkjʊlə]	bestimmte(r, s), besondere(r, s)	
	°event [ɪ'vent]	Ereignis	
	°(to) take place [ˌteɪk 'pleɪs]	stattfinden	
	°effect [ɪ'fekt]	(Aus-)Wirkung	
	°finally ['faɪnəlɪ]	schließlich, endlich	

Topic 4: At the doctor's

p. 64	°GP [ˌdʒi:'pi:] (General Practitioner) [ˌdʒenrəl præk'tɪʃnə]	praktische(r) Arzt/Ärztin	
	(to) treat [tri:t]	behandeln	Anne is very ill. Dr Brown *is ~ing* her.
	reason ['ri:zn]	Grund, Begründung	We're tired. For this ~ (= aus diesem Grund, deshalb) we should take a break now.
	pain [peɪn]	Schmerz(en)	I have a terrible ~ in my leg. It really hurts.
	chest [tʃest]	Brust(korb)	Doctor, my ~ hurts. – Do you smoke a lot?
	headache ['hedeɪk]	Kopfschmerz(en)	My head hurts. I've got a ~.
	(to) **ache** [eɪk]	schmerzen, weh tun	My feet ~. (= My feet hurt.)
	stomach ['stʌmək]	Bauch, Magen	If you eat too much your ~ hurts.
	sore [sɔ:]	wund, rauh, entzündet	
	throat [θrəʊt]	Hals, Kehle	I have a *sore throat*. It hurts when I talk.
	knee [ni:]	Knie	⚠ Stummes *k*: knee, knife, know
	cold [kəʊld]	Erkältung; Kälte	
	flu [flu:]	Grippe	
	temperature ['temprətʃə]	Fieber; Temperatur	

„Grippe"

Ich habe eine/die Grippe.	I've got **the** flu.
Ich bin erkältet.	I've got **a** cold.
Ich habe Kopfschmerzen.	I've got **a** headache.
Ich habe Halsschmerzen.	I've got **a** sore throat.
Ich habe Fieber.	I've got **a** temperature.

Fieber messen = (to) take your temperature

	There's something wrong with …	Etwas stimmt mit … nicht.	What's the matter, Jean? – *There's something wrong with* my eye, Doctor.
	(to) **examine** [ɪg'zæmɪn]	untersuchen	A doctor *~s* her or his patients.
p. 65	appointment [ə'pɔɪntmənt]	Termin	I have an ~ at the doctor's at 4 pm.
	upset stomach [ˌʌpset 'stʌmək]	Magenverstimmung	Sausages often give me an ~ *stomach.*
	normal ['nɔ:ml]	normal	*Normal* body temperature is 36.8°C.
	°virus ['vaɪrəs]	Virus	
	°prescription [prɪ'skrɪpʃn]	Rezept *(für Medikamente)*	
	medicine ['medsn]	Medizin, Arznei	Sick people have to take ~ to get well again.
	a couple of ['kʌpl] (infml.)	ein paar	We waited *a ~ of* hours before we left. (= a few hours)
	°X-ray ['eksreɪ]	Röntgenaufnahme; Röntgenstrahl	
	specialist ['speʃlɪst]	Facharzt/Fachärztin; Spezialist/in	person who is an expert in a special area
	cough [kɒf]	Husten	Smokers often have a bad ~.

Unit 5: Scotland

p. 66	**invitation** [ˌɪnvɪ'teɪʃn]	Einladung	noun from "(to) invite"
	proper ['prɒpə]	richtig, passend, geeignet	Don't put your clothes on the chair. The ~ place for them is in the wardrobe.
	°Gaelic ['geɪlɪk]	Gälisch, gälisch	
	in fact [ɪn 'fækt]	eigentlich, genau gesagt; in Wirklichkeit	I think she'll be at home; ~ ~ I know she will. Ken said Mel was in York, but ~ ~ she was in Leeds.
	mostly ['məʊstlɪ]	meistens, größtenteils, hauptsächlich	adverb from "most" I ~ wear jeans, but not always.
	°oil rig ['ɔɪl rɪg]	Ölbohrinsel, -turm	
	(to) get divorced [dɪ'vɔːst]	sich scheiden lassen	Jenny lives with her mother now. Her parents *got ~* last year. ⧓ (to) get married

***since* + noun – *since* + past tense clause**

We haven't seen Mr Smith	**since** this morning. *(preposition)* **since** he left. *(conjunction)*
Helen and her mother have shared the housework	**since** her parents' divorce. *(preposition)* **since** her parents got divorced. *(conjunction)*

	(to) be covered with/in sth. ['kʌvəd]	mit etwas bedeckt sein	After the football match Jill's shoes *were ~ with/in* mud.
	(to) **discuss** sth. [dɪ'skʌs]	etwas besprechen, über etwas diskutieren	to talk about sth. We *~ed* the problems of the poor. (⚠ *not: ~ed* ~~*about*~~)
	discussion [dɪ'skʌʃn]	Diskussion, Besprechung	noun from "(to) discuss"
	(to) **look forward to doing** sth. [ˌlʊk 'fɔːwəd]	sich darauf freuen, etwas zu tun	I'*m* really *looking ~ to* go*ing* to Hawaii this year. My last holiday was three years ago. I'*m* really *looking ~ to* the beach.

V

Focus on GRAMMAR

p. 67	(to) **pronounce** [prə'naʊns]	aussprechen	Americans ~ "dog" [dɑːg], the British ~ it [dɒg].
	(to) **refer to** [rɪ'fɜː], **-rr-**	sich beziehen auf	When I said that some people are lazy, I *wasn't referring to* you.
	formation [fɔː'meɪʃn]	Bildung, Formung	noun from "(to) form"
	position [pə'zɪʃn]	Position, Lage, Stellung	the place where a person, thing, etc is or stands
	°tricky ['trɪkɪ]	heikel, schwierig	
	dialect ['daɪəlekt]	Dialekt, Mundart	I like Bavarian German. The Bavarian ~ is nice.
	spelling ['spelɪŋ]	Schreibweise	noun from "(to) spell"
	true [truː]	wahr	⧓ false
	truly *(adv.)* ['truːlɪ]	wirklich, wahrhaftig	adverb from "true"
p. 68	wall display ['wɔːl dɪˌspleɪ]	Wandzeitung, -bild	Pupils sometimes put their work on the classroom wall as a *wall ~*.
	°wallpaper ['wɔːlpeɪpə]	Tapete	
	(to) glue [gluː]	kleben	Mel broke the plate. I *~d* the pieces together again.
	°cardboard ['kɑːdbɔːd]	Pappe, Pappkarton	
	empire ['empaɪə]	Reich	a group of countries under one government
	emperor ['empərə]	Kaiser	Augustus was the first Roman ~.
	(to) conquer ['kɒŋkə]	erobern; besiegen	The Normans *~ed* England in 1066.
	northern ['nɔːðən]	Nord-, nördlich	adjective from "north"
	frontier ['frʌntɪə]	Grenze	The Rio Grande is the ~ between Mexico and the US.
	(to) unite [juː'naɪt]	(sich) vereinigen, (sich) zusammenschließen	to come together; to bring together
	untouched [ˌʌn'tʌtʃt]	unberührt	An ~ area is land people haven't developed yet.
	deep [diːp]	tief	Our swimming-pool is 30 feet long and 8 feet ~.
	°diver ['daɪvə]	Taucher/in	
p. 69	**complete** [kəm'pliːt]	vollkommen; vollständig	A hamburger isn't ~ without ketchup and mustard.

(p. 69)	°prince [prɪns]	Prinz	
	army ['ɑ:mɪ]	Armee, Heer	The English *army* fought the Normans …
	battle ['bætl]	Schlacht, Kampf	… at the *battle* of Hastings in 1066.
	(to) **escape (from)** [ɪ'skeɪp]	entkommen, fliehen (aus)	Three men *~d from* prison. The police don't know where they are.
	independence (from) [ˌɪndɪ'pendəns]	Unabhängigkeit (von)	In 1776 the American colonies wanted *~ from* Britain.

Focus on WORDS

p. 70	historical [hɪ'stɒrɪkl]	historisch	adjective from "history"
	attractive [ə'træktɪv]	attraktiv, reizvoll	This is a good guitar, and £200 is an ~ price for it.
	(to) **attract** [ə'trækt]	anziehen, anlocken	New York *~s* many tourists each year. (= Many tourists visit New York each year.)
	public ['pʌblɪk]	öffentlich	A ~ park is a park for everybody. ▸◂ private
	harbour ['hɑ:bə]	Hafen	⚠ *harbour* = Hafen – *port* = **1.** Hafen; **2.** Hafenstadt
	supply ship [sə'plaɪ]	Versorgungsschiff	The ~ ~ brought food and medicine to the island.
	heliport ['helɪpɔ:t]	Hubschrauberlandeplatz, Heliport	airport for helicopters
	baker ['beɪkə]	Bäcker/in	A ~ makes and sells bread.
	town hall [ˌtaʊn 'hɔ:l]	Rathaus	The local government is in the ~ ~.
	stadium ['steɪdɪəm]	Stadion	place where you can watch football matches etc.
	guest house	Pension	a house where you can stay overnight
	well-known [ˌwel'nəʊn]	bekannt	Many people know Tracy Chapman. She's a *well-~* pop singer. ▸◂ unknown

Nouns and verbs with the same form

(to) **attack**	angreifen	(to) **kiss**	küssen	(to) **shout**	schreien, rufen
attack	Angriff	**kiss**	Kuß	**shout**	Schrei, Ruf
(to) **copy**	kopieren; abschreiben	(to) **promise**	versprechen	(to) **show**	zeigen
copy	Kopie, Abschrift	**promise**	Versprechen	**show**	Schau, Show
(to) **dance**	tanzen	(to) **report**	berichten	(to) **stay**	bleiben; übernachten
dance	Tanz; Ball	**report**	Bericht	**stay**	Aufenthalt
(to) **flower**	blühen	(to) **ride**	reiten; (rad)fahren	(to) **stress**	betonen
flower	Blume; Blüte	**ride**	Ritt; Fahrt	**stress**	Betonung

Focus on GRAMMAR

p. 71	°bloom [blu:m]	Blüte	
	advertisement [əd'vɜ:tɪsmənt], **advert, ad** ['ædvɜ:t, æd] (infml.)	Anzeige, Annonce, Reklame	To sell your sofa quickly you should put an ~ in the newspaper.
	apostrophe [ə'pɒstrəfɪ]	Apostroph	

Punctuation marks [ˌpʌŋktʃʊ'eɪʃn mɑ:ks] (Satzzeichen)

.	full stop (BE) / period (AE) ['pɪərɪəd]	,	comma ['kɒmə]	;	semi-colon [ˌsemɪ'kəʊlən]	:	colon ['kəʊlən]
!	exclamation mark [ˌeksklə'meɪʃn mɑ:k]	?	question mark ['kwestʃn mɑ:k]	-	hyphen[1] ['haɪfn]	–	dash[2] [dæʃ]
( )	parentheses, BE *also:* brackets [pə'renθəsi:z, 'brækɪts]	" "	quotation marks [kwəʊ'teɪʃn mɑ:ks]	'	apostrophe [ə'pɒstrəfɪ]		[1] Bindestrich [2] Gedankenstrich

p. 71	**discovery** [dɪ'skʌvərɪ]	Entdeckung	noun from "(to) discover"
	°sunrise technology [ˌsʌnraɪz tek'nɒlədʒɪ]	Zukunftstechnologie (*wörtl.:* „Sonnenaufgangstechnologie")	
	among [ə'mʌŋ]	(mitten) unter, zwischen *(mehreren Personen o. Dingen)*	Can you see Fiona? She's standing ~ all those boys.

V

Unit 5

(p. 71)	electronics *(sing.)* [ˌɪlek'trɒnɪks]	Elektronik	Tina's mother repairs radios, TVs and even computers. She's an expert in ~.
	effect (on) [ɪ'fekt]	(Aus-)Wirkung (auf)	Jenny has changed a lot since her parents got divorced. It has had a great ~ *on* her.
	economy [ɪ'kɒnəmɪ]	(Volks-)Wirtschaft	The price of oil has a strong effect on the world ~.
5 Ex 2	**calm** [kɑ:m]	ruhig, ausgeglichen	▸◂ nervous, excited *(people)*; stormy *(weather, sea)*
	certain ['sɜ:tn]	bestimmte(r, s); sicher, gewiß	*Certain* German cars are very popular in the USA. Are you ~ that your dogs can swim? – Yes, they *certainly* can. ▸◂ uncertain
	(police) officer ['ɒfɪsə]	(Polizei-)Beamte(r)/in, Polizist/in	
	°fit as a fiddle [ˌfɪt‿əz‿ə 'fɪdl] (infml.)	kerngesund	
5	trail [treɪl]	Pfad; Wanderweg	path, usually through undeveloped countryside
	°gathering ['gæðərɪŋ]	Zusammenkunft	
6	Celtic ['keltɪk]	Keltisch, keltisch	
	choir ['kwaɪə]	Chor	group of singers
	off [ɒf]	(von ...) herunter	The car went ~ the road and into the field. ▸◂ on(to)
7	**religious** [rɪ'lɪdʒəs]	religiös	I go to church every Sunday. I'm very ~.
	religion [rɪ'lɪdʒən]	Religion	What do you know about the Jewish ~?
	party ['pɑ:tɪ]	Partei	⚠ *party* = **1.** Party, Feier; **2.** Partei
	(to) **steal** [sti:l] – **stole** [stəʊl] – **stolen** ['stəʊlən]	stehlen	Oh no! Call the police. Somebody *has stolen* my bicycle.
8	brochure ['brəʊʃə]	Broschüre, Prospekt	A holiday ~ gives you tourist information.

Words Words Words

p. 75	**such (a)** [sʌtʃ]	solch, so (ein/e); solche	Have you read "Dracula"? – No, I don't like ~ books.

such a/an (+ adjective) + **noun**		**so + adjective**	
Helen is **such a** nice **person**.	(= **so** ein netter Mensch)	Helen is **so nice**.	(= **so** nett)
It was **such a** good **book** that I read it twice.	(= **so** ein gutes Buch)	The book was **so good** that I read it twice.	(= **so** gut)

The indefinite article after *such, quite, half* and *what*

such a cold night	**eine so/so eine** kalte Nacht	**half a** kilo of apples	**ein halbes** Kilo Äpfel
quite a good book	**ein recht** gutes Buch	**What a** big dog!	**Was für ein** großer Hund!

5 Text The price of oil

p. 76	**cloud** [klaʊd]	Wolke	The weather is great today. There aren't any *clouds* in the *sky*.
	sky [skaɪ]	Himmel	⚠ *am Himmel = in the sky*
	(to) **be on/off**	an, eingeschaltet sein/aus(geschaltet) sein	Why *is* the cooker *on*? – Because I'm making biscuits.
	(to) **miss** [mɪs]	vermissen	When I was in France, I *~ed* my friends from school.
	°gas turbine ['tɜ:baɪn]	Gasturbine	
	°cabin ['kæbɪn]	Kabine	
	wave [weɪv]	Welle	On the coast after a storm, the *~s* are quite large.
	(to) **train** [treɪn]	trainieren, üben	I'*ve ~ed* my dog to fetch the newspaper.
	°lifeboat ['laɪfbəʊt]	Rettungsboot	
	°survival suit [sə'vaɪvl su:t]	Rettungsanzug	
	as *(conj.)* [æz, əz]	weil, da	⚠ *as (conj.):* **1.** *as* you know – *wie* ihr wißt; **2.** *as/when* she left – *als* sie ging; **3.** *as/because* it's hot – *weil* es heiß ist
	Australian *(adj.; n.)* [ɒ'streɪlɪən]	australisch; Australier/in	
	°recreation room [ˌrekrɪ'eɪʃn ru:m]	Aufenthaltsraum, Freizeitraum	

(p. 76)	°pool [pu:l]	Pool(billard)	
	siren ['saɪrən]	Sirene	A ~ makes a loud noise to warn people.
	Get out (of here).	Raus (hier)!	
	°(to) be filled with fear ['fɪld wɪð 'fɪə]	voller Furcht sein	
	fear (of) [fɪə]	Angst, Furcht (vor)	Jim's ~ *of* dogs has got worse because he was bitten again last week. ⚠ *Angst haben (vor) = (to) be afraid (of)*
	flame [fleɪm]	Flamme	The Turners came home and found their house in ~*s*. They don't know what caused the fire.
	(to) **burn** [bɜ:n] – **burnt** [bɜ:nt]/ **burned – burnt/burned**	(ver)brennen	The wood *is ~ing* well. But the fire *burnt* my arm. I *burnt* my arm.
	heat [hi:t]	Hitze	noun from "hot"
	(to) **sink** [sɪŋk] – **sank** [sæŋk] – **sunk** [sʌŋk]	sinken, untergehen; versenken	A rock will ~ in water. Wood, however, will not ~. The storm *sank* the small boat.
	(to) **save** [seɪv]	retten	The doctor couldn't ~ the woman's life. She was dead when he arrived.
p. 77	(to) **hang** [hæŋ] – **hung** [hʌŋ] – **hung**	(auf)hängen	Where shall we ~ the poster? Marcia *hung* from the roof and waited for help.
	choice (of) [tʃɔɪs]	(Aus-)Wahl (an)	noun from "(to) choose"
	(to) hit (the water), -tt-, – hit – hit [hɪt]	(aufs Wasser auf)schlagen, treffen	The car went off the road and ~ a tree.
	(to) **hold** [həʊld] – **held** [held] – **held**	(fest)halten; *hier:* sich festhalten an	I *held* Barry's bag while he went to the toilet.
	They couldn't possibly help.	Sie konnten unmöglich helfen.	
	possibly ['pɒsəblɪ]	vielleicht, möglicherweise	adverb from "possible" Will you visit Florida? – *Possibly*. I don't know yet.
	°sealed [si:əld]	versiegelt, verschlossen	
	cool [ku:l]	kühl	▸◂ warm
	(to) **shine** [ʃaɪn] – **shone** [ʃɒn] – **shone**	scheinen, leuchten	The way the sun ~*s* on the water is beautiful.
	°inflatable [ɪn'fleɪtəbl]	aufblasbar	
	(to) **die (of)** [daɪ]	sterben (an)	Many people *have ~d of* Aids. ⚠ -ing form: *dying* – Our forests *are* slowly *dying*.

of

(to) **die of**	sterben an	the **Isle of** Skye	die Insel Skye
(to) **think of**	denken an; halten von; sich ausdenken	the **city of** Leeds	die Stadt Leeds
		the **town of** Hatfield	die Stadt Hatfield
(to) be **afraid of**	Angst haben vor	the **village of** Slapton	das Dorf Slapton
a **tour of** York	eine Tour durch York	a **piece of** cake	ein Stück Kuchen
a **member of** our football team	ein Mitglied (in) unserer Fußballmannschaft	a **glass of** milk	ein Glas Milch
		a **cup of** coffee	eine Tasse Kaffee
a **postcard of** Jena	eine Postkarte von Jena	two **pairs of** shoes	zwei Paar Schuhe
a **kind of** puzzle	eine Art Puzzle	a **pound/kilo of** apples	ein Pfund/Kilo Äpfel
north of London	nördlich von London	a **group of** fans	eine Gruppe (von) Fans
full of water	voll mit/voller Wasser	a **number of** fans	mehrere Fans
nice/typical of you	nett von dir/typisch für dich	**one of** our fans	einer unserer Fans

	both … and …	sowohl … als auch …	*Both* Paul *and* Ann were late for school today.
	(to) be worth doing sth. [wɜ:θ]	wert sein, getan zu werden	It*'s* ~ buy*ing* more expensive shoes. You can wear them longer.
p. 78	**impolite** [ˌɪmpə'laɪt]	unhöflich	▸◂ polite
	(to) **continue (with)** [kən'tɪnju:]	fortfahren (mit), fortsetzen	She *~d with* her work after lunch. ▸◂ (to) stop

The legend of Dunvegan Castle

p. 78	°(to) celebrate ['seləbreɪt]	feiern	°flag [flæg]	Fahne, Flagge

V

Unit 5/6

Topic 5: Clothes

p. 79	(to) **try** sth. **on** [ˌtraɪ‿'ɒn]	etwas anprobieren	I *tried on* the jacket …
	(to) fit [fɪt], -tt-	passen	… but it *didn't fit*. It was too big.
	(to) suit sb. [su:t]	jm. stehen	You look good in that skirt. It really ~*s* you.
	(to) match [mætʃ]	passen zu; zusammenpassen	The shoes ~ the skirt. The colours go together well. The shoes and the skirt ~. They go together well.
	somebody/something/ somewhere **else** [els]	jemand anderes/etwas anderes/woanders	

else

Somebody else will have to do the shopping.	**Jemand anders** muß einkaufen.
After the break we will do **something else**.	Nach der Pause machen wir **etwas anderes**.
Let's go **somewhere else** after school today.	Laß uns heute nach der Schule **woanders** hingehen.
Did you see **anybody else** in the café?	Hast du **sonst noch jemanden** im Café gesehen?
Do you need **anything else** from the baker's?	Brauchst du **sonst noch etwas** vom Bäcker?
So you went to a pub. Did you go **anywhere else**?	… Seid ihr **sonst noch irgendwo** hingegangen?
Who/What/Where/Why/… **else**?	Wer/Was/Wo/Warum/… **sonst (noch)**?

p. 80	**hole** [həʊl]	Loch	My feet are wet. There are ~*s* in my shoes.
	You're welcome.	Bitte (sehr). Nichts zu danken.	Thank you for your help. – Oh, *you're* ~.
	(to) **change your mind**	seine Meinung ändern	You're going to Spain? I thought you were going to France. – We*'ve ~d our minds*. Spain is cheaper.
	style [staɪl]	Stil	I like the ~ of that hat.
	(to) **leave** sb. **alone**	jn. in Ruhe lassen	Mia is very angry. You should probably *leave* her ~.
	excuse [ɪk'skju:s]	Entschuldigung; Ausrede	Sorry I'm late. I missed the bus. – That's no ~. You should get up earlier. ⚠ *Aussprache:* excuse *(n.)* [ɪk'skju:s] – (to) excuse [ɪk'skju:z]
	Shall I …? [ʃæl, ʃəl]	Soll ich …?	I'm cold. – *Shall I* close the window?
	fashion ['fæʃn]	Mode	the newest style (of clothes, hair, etc.)
	suitcase ['su:tkeɪs]	Koffer	When you go on holiday, you put your clothes in a ~.

Unit 6: Roman Britain

p.81	site [saɪt]	Stätte; Stelle, Platz	place where an event has taken/will take place

[-d]:	**side**	Seite	**ride**	reiten	**heard**	hörte(n)	**played**	spielte(n)	**build**	bauen
[-t]:	**site**	Stätte; Stelle	**write**	schreiben	**hurt**	verletzen	**plate**	Teller	**built**	baute(n)

remains *(pl.)* [rɪ'meɪnz]	Reste, Relikte	the rest; ruins
narrow ['nærəʊ]	eng, schmal	The road was too ~ for the big lorry. ⧓ wide
gate [geɪt]	Tor, Pforte	Close the ~ so the dog can't get out of the garden.
soldier ['səʊldʒə]	Soldat/in	somebody who fights in an army
long ago/not long ago [ə'gəʊ]	vor langer Zeit/vor kurzem	*Long* ~ the Romans came to Britain. When did she leave? – *Not* ~ ~. An hour ago, in fact.
worksheet ['wɜ:kʃi:t]	Arbeitsblatt	a piece of paper with questions and/or exercises
(to) **divide (into)** [dɪ'vaɪd]	(auf)teilen (in)	Our teacher ~*d* the class *into* six groups.

(p. 81)

Useful adverbials of time

long ago	vor langer Zeit	**from then on**	von da an
then/at that time	damals/zu jener Zeit	**from now on**	von jetzt an/ab jetzt
in those years/days	damals/in jenen Jahren/ Tagen	**these days**	heutzutage
		all (the) year	das ganze Jahr über
over the years	im Lauf der Jahre	**in fifty years (from now)**	in fünfzig Jahren
in the past few years	in den vergangenen/ letzten Jahren	**one day**	eines Tages
		sooner or later	früher oder später

Focus on GRAMMAR

p. 82	**careful** ['keəfəl]	sorgfältig	Be more ~ with your homework next time. ⚠ *careful* = **1.** vorsichtig; **2.** sorgfältig
	(to) **hand** sb. sth. [hænd]	jm. etwas (über)geben	to give sb. sth. When I left the party, Liz *~ed* me my coat.
p. 83	**aspect** ['æspekt]	Aspekt, Gesichtspunkt	The discussion about pollution on TV last night showed many *~s* of the problem.
	Christian *(n.; adj.)* ['krɪstʃən]	Christ/in; christlich	somebody who believes in Jesus ['dʒi:zəs] The ~ religion is almost 2,000 years old.
	Christianity [ˌkrɪstɪ'ænətɪ]	das Christentum, die Christenheit	the religion of the Christians
	Christ [kraɪst]	Christus	⚠ Christus = *Christ* – ein/e Christ/in = *a Christian*
	(to) **execute** ['eksɪkju:t]	hinrichten	In Rome many people *were ~d* because they were Christians.
	execution [ˌeksɪ'kju:ʃn]	Hinrichtung	noun from "(to) execute"

Pronunciation: words that begin with "ex-"

betontes „ex-"		unbetontes „ex-" vor Konsonanten		unbetontes „ex-" vor Vokalen	
(to) **execute**	['eksɪkju:t]	**exciting**	[ɪk'saɪtɪŋ]	**exactly**	[ɪg'zæktlɪ]
exercise	['eksəsaɪz]	(to) **expect**	[ɪk'spekt]	**exam**	[ɪg'zæm]
expert	['ekspɜ:t]	(to) **explain**	[ɪk'spleɪn]	(to) **examine**	[ɪg'zæmɪn]
		expensive	[ɪk'spensɪv]	**example**	[ɪg'zɑ:mpl]

	°braintwister ['breɪntwɪstə]	„Harte Nuß" (*wörtlich:* Gehirnverdreher)	
p. 84	tribe [traɪb]	(Volks-)Stamm	When the Romans invaded Britain, many different *~s* lived there.
	(to) capture ['kæptʃə]	erobern, einnehmen; gefangennehmen	Hannibal couldn't ~ Rome. Police *~d* the man and sent him to prison.
	°(to) claim [kleɪm]	Anspruch erheben auf	
	province ['prɒvɪns]	Provinz	Ireland has four *~s*: Connaught ['kɒnɔ:t], Leinster ['lenstə], Munster ['mʌnstə], Ulster ['ʌlstə].
	settlement ['setlmənt]	Siedlung; Besiedlung	The first English ~ in America was Jamestown.
	°conquest ['kɒŋkwest]	Eroberung	
	°(to) plunder ['plʌndə]	(aus)plündern	
	kingdom ['kɪŋdəm]	Königreich	the area that is ruled by a king or queen
	death [deθ]	Tod	noun from "(to) die"
	(to) **kill** [kɪl]	töten	to end sb.'s life
	(to) **destroy** [dɪ'strɔɪ]	zerstören, vernichten	The fire completely *~ed* their house.
	colony ['kɒlənɪ]	Kolonie	India was a British ~ till 1947.
	final ['faɪnl]	letzte(r, s); endgültige(r, s)	Today is the ~ day of our concert tour. (= last day) I won't give you more pocket-money, and that's ~.
p. 85	°barbarian [bɑ:'beərɪən]	Barbar/in	
	administration [ədˌmɪnɪ'streɪʃn]	Verwaltung	Because headteachers have got a lot to do with ~, they teach less than other teachers.
	heating ['hi:tɪŋ]	Heizung	It's cold in here. Isn't the ~ on?

Unit 6

Focus on WORDS

p. 86	(to) **transport** [træns'pɔːt]	befördern, transportieren	to carry sb./sth. from one place to another
	goods *(pl.)* [gʊdz]	Güter, Waren	articles for sale; things that a train or lorry transports
	(to) **land** [lænd]	landen, anlegen	The ferry *~ed* in Dover at 8.00. (= It arrived at 8.00.)
	spaceship ['speɪsʃɪp]	Raumschiff	Dr Spock's ~ travelled to another planet.
	engine ['endʒɪn]	Motor, Maschine	A lorry has a bigger ~ than a car.
	vehicle ['viːɪkl]	Fahrzeug	Cars, buses and lorries, for example, are *~s*.
	motorbike ['məʊtəbaɪk]	Motorrad	A ~ is like a moped but its engine is bigger.
	ambulance ['æmbjələns]	Krankenwagen	vehicle that is used to take people to hospital
	crossroads *(sing.)* ['krɒsrəʊdz]	(Straßen-)Kreuzung	A ~ is where two roads cross.
	traffic jam ['træfɪk dʒæm]	(Verkehrs-)Stau	A ~ ~ is when the streets are so crowded with cars that nobody can move.
	pedestrian crossing [pəˌdestrɪən 'krɒsɪŋ]	Fußgängerüberweg	It's safest to cross a road at a ~ ~.
	pedestrian [pəˌdestrɪən]	Fußgänger/in	a person who walks and doesn't use a vehicle
	pavement ['peɪvmənt]	Gehweg	It's much safer to walk on the ~ than on the road.
	petrol station ['petrəl ˌsteɪʃn]	Tankstelle	a place where you can buy petrol
	petrol ['petrəl]	Benzin	Let's take the car. – OK, but we must get some ~ first.
6 Ex 1	mixed bag	„bunte Mischung"	
	horse [hɔːs]	Pferd	Before there were cars, *~s* were used to carry people.
2	lost *(adj.)* [lɒst]	verloren	adjective from "(to) lose"
	(to) **have a bath** [bɑːθ]	baden, ein Bad nehmen	You're dirty. – But I *had a ~* this morning.
	bath [bɑːθ]	Bad	where you sit to have a bath *baths (pl.)* = a public swimming-pool
4	°Olympic Games [əˌlɪmpɪk 'geɪmz]	Olympische Spiele	
	(to) hold [həʊld]	*(eine Veranstaltung)* abhalten	The meeting/festival **will be held** next week. Can you **hold** my bag for a moment? The club leader **held out** her hand to her guests. I can't see the map. Can you **hold** it **up**, please? ⚠ *ein Versprechen **halten** = (to) **keep** a promise*
	°Gaelic ['geɪlɪk]	Gälisch, gälisch	
5	°orienteering [ˌɔːrɪən'tɪərɪŋ]	Orientierungslauf	
6	immigration [ˌɪmɪ'greɪʃn]	Einwanderung, Immigration	When immigrants arrive in America, they have to go to an ~ centre.
	non- [nɒn]	nicht-; Nicht-	People who don't smoke are ~-smokers.
	citizen ['sɪtɪzən]	(Staats-)Bürger/in, Staatsangehörige(r)	A person who was born in a country is usually a ~ of that country.
8	(to) be based on ['beɪst‿ɒn]	basieren auf	Often films *are ~ on* popular books.
	AD [ˌeɪ'diː] *(from Latin "anno Domini")*	n. Chr.	500 *AD* = 500 years after Christ
	BC [ˌbiː'siː] *(before Christ)*	v. Chr.	500 *BC* = 500 years before Christ
9	sheep, *pl.* sheep [ʃiːp]	Schaf	Farmer Brown has cows, pigs, horses and ~.

Words Words Words

p. 90	**prefix** ['priːfɪks]	Vorsilbe, Präfix	*un-, dis-* and *inter-*, for example, are *~es*.
	suffix ['sʌfɪks]	Nachsilbe, Suffix	*-able, -ful* and *-ly*, for example, are *~es*.
	stem [stem]	(Wort-)Stamm	The ~ of the word "friendliness" is "friend".
	nationality [ˌnæʃə'nælətɪ]	Staatsangehörigkeit, Nationalität	Horst comes from Germany. His ~ is German.
	such as ['sʌtʃ‿əz]	(wie) zum Beispiel	Pop stars ~ ~ Sting or Madonna earn a lot of money.
	that's why	deshalb, darum	Andrew is ill. *That's ~* he can't come to your party.
	syllable ['sɪləbl]	Silbe	"Hamburger" is a word with three *~s*: ham-bur-ger.

6 Text The story of St Alban

p. 91	**neither … nor …** ['naɪðə/'niːðə … nɔː]	weder … noch …	Tina doesn't smoke or drink. She ~ smokes ~ drinks.
	°(to) worship ['wɜːʃɪp], -pp-	verehren, anbeten	
	god, God [gɒd]	Gott	Do you practise a religion? Do you believe in ~?
	(to) **accept** [ək'sept]	akzeptieren, annehmen	Sue is going to the party. She *has ~ed* the invitation.
	(to) persecute ['pɜːsɪkjuːt]	verfolgen *(aus politischen oder religiösen Gründen)*	All over their Empire the Romans *~d* Christians.
	not only … but (also)	nicht nur … sondern (auch)	Yesterday it was *not only* cold *but also* wet. ▸◂ neither … nor
	(to) **order** sb. **to do** sth. ['ɔːdə]	jm. befehlen/jn. auffordern, etwas zu tun	The doctor *~ed* me *to* stay in bed for a week.
	priest [priːst]	Priester/in	Our church will get a new ~ soon.
	(to) **hide (from)** [haɪd] – **hid** [hɪd] – **hidden** ['hɪdn]	(sich) verstecken (vor)	Sarah *was hiding* behind the sofa. I couldn't see her.
	kind [kaɪnd]	freundlich, gütig, nett	It was ~ of you to help me yesterday. (= nice of you)
	danger ['deɪndʒə]	Gefahr	There's a lot of ~ in rock-climbing.
	(to) **pray** [preɪ]	beten	The priest *~ed* for the dying woman.
	finally ['faɪnəlɪ]	schließlich, endlich	in the end, at last
	°cloak [kləʊk]	Umhang	
	(to) run **after** sb.	hinter jm. herrennen	Our dog often *~s after* cars. One day she'll be killed.
	until [ən'tɪl, ʌn'tɪl]	bis	Sometimes I have to work ~ five o'clock, …
	not … until	nicht vor/erst um; nicht … bevor	… so I do*n't* get home ~ six o'clock. We should*n't* leave ~ the rain stops.
	judge [dʒʌdʒ]	Richter/in	The ~ gave the killer 25 years in prison.
	punishment ['pʌnɪʃmənt]	Strafe, Bestrafung	Sally didn't do her homework, so she was given some extra work as a ~. …
	(to) **punish** ['pʌnɪʃ]	(be)strafen	… Her teacher gave her extra work to ~ her.
	(to) **refuse** [rɪ'fjuːz]	sich weigern; verweigern, ablehnen	He *~d* to help us although we had a lot of problems. She asked him to marry her, but he *~d.* ▸◂ (to) accept
	(to) **give** sth. **up** [ˌgɪv_'ʌp]	etwas aufgeben	Mrs Roberts *has ~n up* smoking. She feels much better now.
	°(to) offer ['ɒfə]	opfern	
p. 92	**custom** ['kʌstəm]	Brauch, Sitte	It's a British ~ to drink tea in the afternoon.
	dry [draɪ]	trocken	▸◂ wet
	°executioner [ˌeksɪ'kjuːʃnə]	Henker/in, Scharfrichter/in	
	(to) **be frightened (of)** ['fraɪtnd]	Angst haben (vor)	to be afraid (of)
	sword [sɔːd]	Schwert	Do you remember King Arthur's ~ 'Excalibur'?
	instead of [ɪn'sted_əv]	(an)statt, an Stelle von	May I have chips ~ *of* potatoes, please?
	(to) **pick** sth. **up** [ˌpɪk_'ʌp]	etwas *(vom Boden)* aufheben	I *~ed up* the books which were lying on the floor.
	fountain ['faʊntɪn]	Springbrunnen	Throw a penny in a ~ and you'll have good luck.
	°martyr ['mɑːtə]	Märtyrer/in	
	wooden ['wʊdn]	hölzern	adjective from "wood"
	°(to) fall into ruin	verfallen	
	(to) retell [ˌriː'tel]	nacherzählen	to tell sth. again (in a different way)

just

What about other stories, not **just** cowboy stories?	…, nicht **nur** Cowboygeschichten?
(In a shop) I'm **just** looking.	Ich sehe mich **nur** mal um.
That's good coffee. It's **just like** German coffee.	… **genau wie** deutscher Kaffee.
I'm **just as** tired **as** you are.	… **genauso** müde **wie** du.
Just a moment!	Einen Moment **mal**!
They're **just** leaving./They've **just** left.	Sie gehen **gerade**./Sie sind **gerade** gegangen.
Just before lunch/**Just** then the phone rang.	**Kurz** vor dem Essen/**Genau** in dem Moment …
I **just** couldn't understand him.	Ich konnte ihn **einfach** nicht verstehen.
I live **just** round the corner.	Ich wohne **gleich** um die Ecke.

Unit 6

p. 93	**event** [ɪ'vent]	Ereignis	The first day at school is a big ~ in a child's life.

Giving reasons

We came here **to** play football.	…, **um** … **zu** spielen.
But we can't play **because** it's raining.	…, **weil** es regnet.
But we can't play **because of** the rain.	… **wegen** des Regens.
It's too wet. **That's why** / **So** we can't play.	… . **Deshalb/Daher** …
The reason (why we can't play) **is that** it's too wet.	**Der Grund** (dafür, daß …) **ist, daß** …
It's **so** wet **that** we can't possibly play.	… **so** naß, **daß** …
Let's go inside **so (that)** we don't get cold.	…, **damit** …

Aquae Sulis

p. 93	°mysterious [mɪ'stɪərɪəs]	geheimnisvoll, rätselhaft	

Topic 6: Some British holidays and customs

p. 94	**holiday** ['hɒlədeɪ]	Feiertag	Easter Monday is a ~. All the shops are closed.
	rhyme [raɪm]	Reim	a short poem, often funny
	fool [fu:l]	Narr/Närrin, Dummkopf	a very silly person
	(to) play a trick on sb.	jm. einen Streich spielen	Let's *play a ~ on* Nancy. Let's hide her coat.
	serious ['sɪərɪəs]	ernst, ernsthaft	Pollution is a ~ problem. You must be joking. You can't be ~.
	°spider ['spaɪdə]	Spinne	
	°witch [wɪtʃ]	Hexe	
	(to) go back to	zurückgehen auf, zurückreichen bis	Some Christmas customs ~ ~ *to* the 17th century. Our family is very old. It *goes ~ to* the year 1375.
	(to) **celebrate** ['seləbreɪt]	feiern	I'm going to ~ my birthday next week. Would you like to come?
	°trick or treat [ˌtrɪk‿ɔ: 'tri:t]	*Sitte an Halloween (etwa:* „Streich oder Belohnung"*)*	
p. 95	guy [gaɪ] (infml.)	Typ, Kerl	informal word for "man"
	°bonfire ['bɒnfaɪə]	*etwa:* Freudenfeuer	
	figure ['fɪgə]	Figur, Gestalt	The *~s* at Madam Tussaud's look like real people.
	°(to) blow sth. up [ˌbləʊ‿'ʌp] – blew [blu:] – blown [bləʊn]	etwas sprengen, etwas in die Luft jagen	
	fireworks *(pl.)* ['faɪəwɜ:ks]	Feuerwerk(skörper)	

Merry Christmas … [ˌmerɪ 'krɪsməs] Fröhliche Weihnachten …

… **and a Happy New Year!**	… und ein gutes neues Jahr!	the **Christmas holidays** [ˌkrɪsməs 'hɒlədeɪz]	die Weihnachtsfeiertage; (BE *auch:*) -ferien
Christmas time ['krɪsməs taɪm]	die Weihnachtszeit	**Father Christmas/Santa Claus** [ˌfɑ:ðə 'krɪsməs/'sæntə klɔ:z]	der Weihnachtsmann
Christmas Eve [ˌkrɪsməs‿'i:v]	Heiligabend		
Christmas Day [ˌkrɪsməs 'deɪ]	der 1. Weihnachtsfeiertag	**New Year's Eve** [ˌnju: jɪəz‿'i:v]	Silvester
Boxing Day ['bɒksɪŋ deɪ]	der 2. Weihnachtsfeiertag	**New Year's Day** [ˌnju: jɪəz 'deɪ]	Neujahr(stag)

turkey ['tɜ:kɪ]	Truthahn, Pute	
midnight ['mɪdnaɪt]	Mitternacht	Twelve o'clock at night is also called ~. ⚠ *um Mitternacht = at midnight*

V

The United States of America

p. 96	**way of life** [ˌweɪ_əv ˈlaɪf]	Lebensstil, Lebensweise	The American ~ *of* ~ is different from the German ~ *of* ~.
	flag [flæg]	Fahne, Flagge	The American ~ …
	the Stars and Stripes [ˌstɑːz_n ˈstraɪps]	*US-Flagge („Sterne und Streifen")*	… is called *the* ~ *and* ~.
p. 97	variety [vəˈraɪətɪ]	Sorte, Art	They sell 30 different *varieties* of ice-cream here.
	(to) **spell** [spel]	buchstabieren, schreiben	How *do* you ~ your name? – A-R-N-O-L-D.

American English and British English spelling

AE: '-or'	BE: '-our'	AE:	BE:
color	colour	catalog, dialog	catalogue, dialogue
neighbor	neighbour	traveled, traveler	travelled, traveller
favorite	favourite	pajamas	pyjamas

AE: '-er'	BE: '-re'
center	centre
kilometer	kilometre
theater	theatre

Remember:
In AE **Mr.**, **Mrs.**, **Ms.**, and **Dr.** are written with a full stop.

In AE the date **10.3.92** means **'3 October 1992'**, in BE it means **'10 March 1992'**.

confusing [kənˈfjuːzɪŋ]	verwirrend	difficult to understand
authentic [ɔːˈθentɪk]	authentisch, echt	real

American English and British English

AE	BE	
apartment [əˈpɑːtmənt]	**flat**	Wohnung
apartment house	**block of flats**	Mietshaus, Wohnblock
bill [bɪl]	**note**	(Geld-)Schein
car, auto(mobile) [ˈɔːtəməʊbiːl, ˈɔːtəʊ]	**car**	Auto, Wagen
fall, autumn [fɔːl]	**autumn**	Herbst
French fries [ˌfrentʃ ˈfraɪz]	**chips**	Pommes frites
gas [gæs]	**petrol**	Benzin
gas station	**petrol station**	Tankstelle
grade [greɪd]	**class**	Klasse(nstufe)
highway	**motorway**	Autobahn
intersection [ˌɪntəˈsekʃn]	**crossroads**	(Straßen-)Kreuzung
math	**maths**	Mathe
mom [BE: mɒm; AE: mɑːm]	**mum**	Mama, Mutti

AE	BE	
movie [ˈmuːvɪ], **film**	**film**	Film
movie theater/ movies	**cinema**	Kino
parking lot	**car park**	(großer) Parkplatz
(ball-point) pen	**biro**	Kugelschreiber
period [ˈpɪərɪəd]	**full stop**	Punkt
railroad	**railway**	Eisenbahn
sidewalk [ˈsaɪdwɔːk]	**pavement**	Gehweg
student	**pupil**	Schüler/in
(*But:* student	student	Student/in)
subway [ˈsʌbweɪ]	**underground**	U-Bahn
trailer [ˈtreɪlə]	**caravan**	Wohnwagen
truck [trʌk]	**lorry, truck**	LKW
vacation [BE: vəˈkeɪʃn; AE: veɪˈkeɪʃn]	**holiday(s)**	Ferien, Urlaub

Unit 7: Golden Kansas

p. 98	statistics *(pl.)* [stəˈtɪstɪks]	Statistik(en)	information given in numbers *S*~ show that 25% of all English teenagers smoke.
	wheat [wiːt]	Weizen	*W*~ is used to make bread.
	state [steɪt]	Staat, (Bundes-)Land	⚠ der *Staat* Frankreich = the *state* ***of*** France
	°breadbasket [ˈbredbɑːskɪt]	*etwa:* „Kornkammer" (*wörtl.:* „Brotkorb")	

Unit 7

(p. 98)	**flat** [flæt]	flach, eben	The countryside is very ~. There are no mountains. ⚠ *flat* = **1.** Wohnung; **2.** flach, eben
	corn [kɔːn]	Getreide, Korn; AE *auch:* Mais	
	man-made [ˌmæn'meɪd]	künstlich	Plastic, for example, is ~-~.
	Indian *(n.; adj.)* ['ɪndɪən]	Indianer/in; indianisch	⚠ *Indian* = **1.** Inder/in; indisch; **2.** Indianer/in; indianisch
	°buffalo, *pl.* buffalo/ buffalo(e)s ['bʌfələʊ]	Büffel	
	(to) hunt [hʌnt]	jagen	to kill wild animals for food or sport
	settler ['setlə]	Siedler/in	In the early 1600s English ~*s* …
	(to) settle ['setl]	sich niederlassen; *(Land)* besiedeln	… ~*d* along the North American coast. Do you think the planet Mars will *be* ~*d* some day?
	wagon, BE *auch:* waggon ['wægn]	(Plan-)Wagen	Before the American railway was built, people travelled west in ~*s* pulled by horses.
	cattle *(pl.)* ['kætl]	Rindvieh, Rinder	
	cow [kaʊ]	Kuh	Milk comes from ~*s*.
	c (= circa) ['sɜːkə]	ca. (= circa)	The Romans began to leave Britain ~ (= about) 410.
	sq (= square) [skweə]	Quadrat-	Many farms in the US cover 30 *sq* km or more.

Focus on GRAMMAR

p. 99	(to) **grow** sth. [grəʊ] – **grew** [gruː] – **grown** [grəʊn]	*(Weizen, Mais usw.)* anbauen, anpflanzen	My parents are farmers. They ~ corn. ⚠ *(to) grow* = **1.** wachsen; **2.** anbauen, anpflanzen
	further ['fɜːðə]	weiter; weitere(r, s), noch	The US is ~ (= farther) from Italy than from Britain. For ~ information write to our information centre.
	high school ['haɪ skuːl] (AE)	Oberschule *(entspricht etwa einer Gesamtschule)*	⚠ *Hochschule = university, college*
	around [ə'raʊnd]	um … (herum); in … umher, durch	The countryside ~ Dresden is very beautiful. We walked ~ Paris for hours and saw all the sights.
	(to) **pick** sb. **up** [ˌpɪk‿'ʌp]	jn. abholen, mitnehmen *(mit dem Auto)*	On the way to the game we ~*ed up* Tom and drove to the stadium together.
	kid [kɪd] (infml.)	Kind; Jugendliche(r)	an informal word for "child" or "youth"
	(to) feed [fiːd] – fed [fed] – fed	füttern	to give food (to an animal or baby)
	twice [twaɪs]	zweimal	She works ~ as hard as her brother.
	part-time [ˌpɑː't'taɪm]	Teilzeit-, halbtags	I have a ~-~ job. I work 4 hours a day. ◂▸ full-time
p. 100	**average** *(n.; adj.)* ['ævərɪdʒ]	Durchschnitt; durchschnittlich, Durchschnitts-	My grades were ~, but Ron's were higher than ~. On ~ we sell more than 100 CDs a day. *(= Im Durchschnitt …)*
	neighbourhood ['neɪbəhʊd]	Nachbarschaft	We don't know many people in our new ~. We've just moved here.
	ice-cream parlor ['aɪs-kriːm ˌpɑːlə] (AE)	Eisdiele	After school we often meet at the ~-~ ~ on Elm Street. They have the best ice-cream in town.
	°cheerleader ['tʃɪəliːdə] (AE)	*Mädchen, die die Zuschauer/innen (etwa eines Basketballspiels) zum Beifall anfeuern*	
	practice ['præktɪs]	Übung, Training	noun from "(to) practise" ⚠ *Schreibung:* (to) practise – practi**c**e
	class [klɑːs] (AE)	Unterricht(sstunde)	⚠ AE *class* = BE *lesson* – (Unterrichts-)Stunde AE *grade* = BE *class* – Klasse(nstufe)
	driver's license (AE)/ **driving licence** (BE) ['laɪsəns]	Führerschein	You have to pass a driving test to get a ~ ~. In the US you can usually get a ~ ~ when you are 16.
p. 101	(American) football [əˌmerɪkən 'fʊtbɔːl]	*rugbyähnliches Mannschaftsspiel*	*American* ~ is quite different from what we call "Fußball". The football is not even round.
	(to) **appear** [ə'pɪə]	erscheinen, auftauchen; scheinen	Judy *didn't* ~ at the party until ten o'clock. She ~*ed* (to be) sick. Her face felt very hot.

(p. 101)	(to) **enjoy yourself** [ɪn'dʒɔɪ jɔːˌself]	viel Spaß haben, sich amüsieren	*Did* you ~ *yourself* at Mark's party? – Yes, it was great.
	themselves [ðəm'selvz]	sich (selbst) *(3. Pers. pl.)*	At our music club we all play the guitar. Some of us had lessons, the others taught ~ to play the guitar.
	I myself am … [maɪ'self]	Ich selbst bin …	Nobody helped me with the puzzle. *I* did it ~.
	crowd [kraʊd]	(Menschen-)Menge	a large group of people
	(to) cheer [tʃɪə]	jubeln, Beifall spenden	When the team appeared the crowd *~ed* loudly. …
	cheering ['tʃɪərɪŋ]	Jubel, Beifall	… You could hear the ~ all over the town.
	°national anthem [ˌnæʃnəl‿'ænθəm]	Nationalhymne	
	that is (i.e.) *(from Latin "id est")*	das heißt (d.h.)	We had guests from all parts of the UK, *i.e.* from England, Wales, Scotland and Northern Ireland.
	(to) go for a ride	herumfahren, eine Spazierfahrt machen	We picked Barry and Nancy up and *went* ~ ~ ~ along the coast.
	°(to) go cruising ['kruːzɪŋ]	(langsam) in der Stadt herumfahren	
	(to) **combine (with)** [kəm'baɪn]	kombinieren, verbinden (mit)	On our trip we *~d* work *with* fun. This exercise *~s* all the verb forms you have learned.
	(to) change places (with)	die Plätze tauschen (mit) *(auch im übertragenen Sinn)*	I can't see the board. Can we ~ ~? Fanny's family is very poor. I wouldn't want to ~ ~ *with* her.

Nouns and verbs with the same form

(to) **comment** (on)	kommentieren, sich äußern (zu)	(to) **order**	befehlen
comment (on)	Kommentar (zu, über)	**order**	Befehl
(to) **contrast** ⚠ [kən'trɑːst]	kontrastieren, gegenüberstellen	(to) **question**	befragen, vernehmen
contrast ⚠ ['kɒntrɑːst]	Kontrast, Gegensatz	**question**	Frage
(to) **joke**	scherzen, witzeln	(to) **surprise**	überraschen
joke	Scherz, Witz	**surprise**	Überraschung
(to) **offer**	(an)bieten	(to) **transport** ⚠ [træns'pɔːt]	befördern, transportieren
offer	Angebot	**transport** ⚠ ['trænspɔːt]	Transport(mittel)

Focus on GRAMMAR

p. 102	**properly** ['prɒpəlɪ]	richtig, ordentlich, sachgemäß	adverb from "proper"
	(to) **be allowed to** do sth. [ə'laʊd]	etwas tun dürfen	Many pupils *are not* ~ *to* be out after midnight.
	(to) **allow** [ə'laʊ]	erlauben	*Do* your teachers ~ you to use dictionaries in tests?
	(to) **be able to** do sth. ['eɪbl]	etwas tun können; fähig sein, etwas zu tun	Kevin won't *be* ~ *to* come to the party on Saturday because he's ill.
	°(to) babysit ['beɪbɪsɪt], -tt-, – babysat – babysat	babysitten	
7 Ex 1	(to) **dry** [draɪ]	(ab)trocknen	I'll wash the dishes and you can ~ them. OK?
	°(to) be hard on sb. (infml.)	streng mit jm. sein	
2	Who is to blame?	Wer hat schuld?	*Who is to* ~ for the broken window? – Not me.
	action ['ækʃn]	Handlung, Tat	*A~s* speak louder than words. *(Sprichwort)*
	(to) **cut (**sth. **off)** [kʌt], **-tt-, – cut – cut**	(etwas ab)schneiden	He ~ his birthday cake and gave everybody a piece. After the storm the town *was* ~ *off* from the world.
3	°VCR (= video cassette recorder) [ˌviːsiː'ɑː]	Videorecorder	
8	**Italian** *(n.; adj.)* [ɪ'tæljən]	Italiener/in; Italienisch, italienisch	Umberto is from Italy. He's ~. Pizza is my favourite ~ food.
	slave [sleɪv]	Sklave/Sklavin	Many blacks were brought to America as *~s* in the 1700s.

V

Unit 7

Words Words Words

p. 106	**bitter** ['bɪtə]	bitter, verbittert	Sugar is sweet, coffee is ~.

7 Text The star player

p. 107	(to) **admire** [əd'maɪə]	bewundern	I really ~ Hannah's energy: She goes to school, is on the volleyball team, and has a part-time job.
	(to) **dislike** [dɪs'laɪk]	nicht gern haben, nicht mögen	I like my job, but I ~ getting up so early. ⧓ (to) like
	(to) **succeed** [sək'si:d]	Erfolg haben; gelingen	Work hard and you'll ~ in school. Our plan *~ed* – we won the game.
	gym [dʒɪm] (infml.)	Sport-/Turnhalle	room or building that is used for sports
	Come on! [ˌkʌm_'ɒn]	Los! Komm schon!	*C~ ~*, Karin! Run or we'll miss the train.
	one more	noch ein(e)	You only need ~ ~ point to pass the test.
	some more	noch einige/etwas	Can I have ~ ~ biscuits and ~ ~ milk?
	basket ['bɑ:skɪt]	Korb	When you go shopping, don't forget to take your ~.
	score [skɔ:]	Spielstand, (Spiel-) Ergebnis	The English team lost the match. The ~ was Italy 3, England 1.
	(to) **score**	*(einen Punkt/Treffer)* erzielen, *(ein Tor)* schießen	The Tigers *~d* two more baskets at the end of the game and won.
	(to) **shoot** [ʃu:t] – **shot** [ʃɒt] – **shot**	schießen, *(Ball)* werfen	Yesterday a man *was shot* in the leg in our street. The star player *shot* the ball and scored.
	(to) pass the ball	den Ball abspielen	to give the ball to another player
	instead *(adv.)* [ɪn'sted]	statt dessen	Sue couldn't find her jeans so she wore a skirt ~. ⚠ *instead (adv.)* = statt dessen *instead of (prep.)* = (an)statt, an Stelle von
	coach [kəʊtʃ]	Trainer/in	⚠ *coach* = **1.** (Reise-)Bus; **2.** Trainer/in
	°(to) draw sb. away from sb./sth.	jn. von jm./etwas weglocken	
	(to) **draw** [drɔ:] – **drew** [dru:] – **drawn** [drɔ:n]	ziehen	*D~* your chair closer to the table so you can reach your plate better. ⚠ *(to) draw* = **1.** zeichnen; **2.** ziehen
	(to) **control** [kən'trəʊl], **-ll-**	unter Kontrolle halten, beherrschen; kontrollieren, steuern	I couldn't ~ myself and hit him. This factory *is ~led* by computers. ⚠ *(to) control* = kontrollieren, steuern *(to) check* = kontrollieren, überprüfen
	rival ['raɪvl]	Konkurrent/in, Rivale/ Rivalin	*R~* companies are companies which produce the same thing.

German *groß* – English *great, big, large, tall, huge*

great: **1.** I think St David's is **great**. We had a **great** time there. *(infml.)* — **1.** großartig, toll
Great! No homework today. *(infml.)*

2. Many buildings were destroyed by the **Great** Fire of London in 1666. — **2.** groß, beträchtlich
London's docks were once an area of **great** poverty.
The children were in **great** danger.

3. Steve was Tommy's **greatest** rival. — **3.** bedeutend, berühmt
Do you know the LP "New Youth – **Greatest** Hits"?

big – large: When we talk about size, we use ***big*** or ***large***. ***large*** is more formal, and it is usually used to refer to things. ***big*** can refer to both people and things.
Examples: They own a **big/large** house on the outskirts of London.
Napoleon was not a very **big** man.
⚠ ***great*** is not used to talk about size. Compare:
Napoleon was not a **big** man, but he was a **great** man.

a tall man — a big man

tall: ***tall*** *(groß, hoch)* is used to talk about the height[1] of people and things.
Examples: Is Janet **taller** than Karen?
How **tall** is the World Trade Center?

huge: ***huge*** is used to stress the fact that something is unusually large.
Example: Have you seen their new house? It's **huge**!

[1] height [haɪt] Höhe, Größe

(p. 107)	(to) **take a chance**	ein Risiko eingehen; es darauf ankommen lassen	This may be the wrong road. We'll just have to ~ *a* ~.
	(to) **quit** [kwɪt], **-tt-, – quit – quit**	aufhören (mit); *(eine Stelle)* aufgeben	Karen ~ volleyball because she didn't like the coach. I ~ my job because it was too boring.
p. 108	I can't wait.	Ich kann es kaum erwarten.	My birthday party is on December 15th. *I can't wait.*
	(to) **turn round** [ˌtɜːn ˈraʊnd]	sich umdrehen	*T*~ ~ so I can see your back.
	°(to) walk all over sb. (infml.)	jn. mit Leichtigkeit besiegen, fertigmachen	
	captain [ˈkæptɪn]	Kapitän/in; Mannschaftsführer/in	the most important person on a ship; the leader of a sports team
	maybe [ˈmeɪbɪ]	vielleicht	perhaps, possibly Are you going to the party? – *M*~, I don't know yet. ⚠ In BE *maybe* is more informal than *perhaps* and *possibly*. *maybe* usually begins the sentence.
	whole [həʊl]	gesamte(r, s), ganze(r, s)	I spent the ~ morning in bed today. (= all morning)
	confident [ˈkɒnfɪdənt]	selbstbewußt, zuversichtlich	Sally is a very ~ player. She's ~ that she can beat Martina.

Topic 7: At the post office / Making a phone call

p. 110	°scales *(pl.)* [skeɪlz]	Waage	
	gram [græm]	Gramm	To make this cake I need 100 ~*s* of sugar.
	airmail [ˈeəmeɪl]	Luftpost	Letters that are sent by plane are called ~.
	mail [meɪl] *(meist* AE)/ **post** [pəʊst] (BE)	Post(sendungen)	

Nouns and verbs with the same form

(to) **control**	beherrschen; kontrollieren, steuern	(to) **mail** (*meist* AE)	*(Brief)* abschicken, einwerfen; *(Paket)* aufgeben
control	(Selbst-)Beherrschung; Kontrolle	**mail** (*meist* AE)	Post(sendungen)
(to) **cut**	schneiden	(to) **name**	(be-, er-)nennen
cut	Schnitt, Schnittwunde	**name**	Name
(to) **dislike**	nicht mögen, nicht gern haben	(to) **post** (BE)	*(Brief)* abschicken, einwerfen; *(Paket)* aufgeben
dislike (of, for)	Abneigung (gegen)	**post** (BE)	Post(sendungen)
(to) **function**	funktionieren, fungieren	(to) **respect**	respektieren, achten
function	Funktion	**respect**	Respekt, Achtung

p. 111	**sign** [saɪn]	Schild, Zeichen	The ~ said "DO NOT WALK ON THE GRASS".
	operator [ˈɒpəreɪtə]	Vermittlung; Telefonist/in	The ~ helps you to make a phone call.

***need* als Hilfs- und Vollverb**

Hilfsverb	Vollverb
You **needn't go** now. **Need** we **go** now?	You **don't need to go** now. **Do** we **need to go** now?
⚠ **keine** *do*-Umschreibung; Infinitiv-Anschluß **ohne** *to*	⚠ *do*-Umschreibung; Infinitiv-Anschluß **mit** *to*
Als **Hilfsverb** wird *need* nur im Präsens verwendet und steht hauptsächlich in verneinten Aussagesätzen, seltener auch in Fragesätzen.	Als **Vollverb** steht *need* auch in bejahten Aussagesätzen und wird auch in anderen Zeiten verwendet: I think you **need to go** now. I **needed to go** to the toilet. You **will need to learn** Spanish if you want to live in Spain.

Unit 7/8

(p. 111)	°itemized phone bill ['aɪtəmaɪzd 'fəʊn bɪl]	*Telefonrechnung mit einzeln aufgeführten Gesprächen*	
	bill [bɪl] (BE)/ **check** [tʃek] (AE)	Rechnung	Before you leave a restaurant you have to pay the ~. ⚠ BE *bill* = AE *check* – Rechnung BE *note* = AE *bill* – (Geld-)Schein, Banknote
	°dialing code, BE: dialling code ['daɪəlɪŋ kəʊd]	Vorwahl(nummer)	
	(to) dial, BE: -ll- ['daɪəl]	wählen *(beim Telefonieren)*	Hello, is Bill there? – Sorry, you*'ve ~led* the wrong number.
	(to) drop [drɒp], -pp-	weglassen, auslassen	⚠ *(to) drop* = **1.** fallen lassen; **2.** weg-, auslassen; **3.** abwählen, abgeben *(Schulfach)*
	zero ['zɪərəʊ]	Null	Five, four, three, two, one, ~.

Unit 8: San Francisco, CA

p. 112	climate ['klaɪmət]	Klima	The ~ in Africa ['æfrɪkə] is often hot and dry.
	one **in** ten	jede(r, s) zehnte, eine(r, s) von zehn	About *one ~ four* people born in New York City is black.
	(to) symbolize ['sɪmbəlaɪz]	symbolisieren	Red roses ~ love.
	earthquake ['ɜːθkweɪk]	Erdbeben	An ~ is when the ground moves and shakes.
	earth [ɜːθ]	Erde	⚠ *No article:* the tallest tree *on earth* (= in the world) ⚠ auf der *Erde (= Erdboden)* sitzen = (to) sit on the *ground*
	scientist ['saɪəntɪst]	(Natur-)Wissenschaftler/in	person who works in the field of science
	in such a way	so, dergestalt	Cars should be built *in ~ ~ ~* that they use less petrol.
	(to) **survive** [sə'vaɪv]	überleben	Eight people were in the accident. Three died and five *~d*.
p. 113	°gold rush ['gəʊld rʌʃ]	Goldrausch	
	°workman ['wɜːkmən]	Arbeiter	
	European *(n.; adj.)* [ˌjʊərə'piːən]	Europäer/in; europäisch	Latif is from Pakistan. He's Asian. Karen is from Germany. She's ~.
	chain [tʃeɪn]	Kette	The lorry pulled the car to the garage with a ~.
	mission ['mɪʃn]	Mission(sstation)	
	(to) educate ['edjʊkeɪt]	(aus)bilden, schulen; erziehen	The task of every school is to ~ its pupils. ⚠ Parents *bring up* (*not:* ~~educate~~) their children.
	education [ˌedjʊ'keɪʃn]	(Schul-, Aus-)Bildung; Erziehung	noun from "(to) educate"
	°(to) convert sb. (to) [kən'vɜːt]	jn. bekehren (zu)	
	popularly ['pɒpjʊləlɪ]	allgemein, landläufig	adverb from "popular"
	majority [mə'dʒɒrətɪ]	Mehrheit	In my class 5 pupils smoke and 15 pupils don't smoke. The ~ of pupils do not smoke. ⚠ In BE *majority* is often used with a plural verb.
	Hispanic *(n.; adj.)* [hɪ'spænɪk]	Hispano-Amerikaner/-in *(Einwanderer aus Lateinamerika und deren Nachkommen)*; hispanisch	person in the US from a Spanish-speaking country

Focus on GRAMMAR

p. 114	**if** [ɪf]	wenn, falls	*If* I get home before eight, I'll phone you. ⚠ *if* = wenn, falls – *when* = wenn, sobald

(p. 114)	**decision** [dɪ'sɪʒn]	Entscheidung, Entschluß	noun from "(to) decide"
	recently ['ri:sntlɪ]	vor kurzem, neulich	Jean is very brown because she's been on holiday ~.

Comma in German – *no* comma in English …

… before an *if*-clause	We can visit Hollywood **if you have time now**.
… (usually) before other short adverbial clauses	It all happened **because it was raining**. Let's wait **until it stops raining**.
… before an infinitive clause	We're planning **to visit *Disney World* in May**. Tommy didn't know **what to do**.
… before a *that*-clause	Janet realized **that it was too late**.
… before and after a defining relative clause	The man **who designed St Paul's** was Wren.
… in decimals ['desɪməlz]	4.3 m (= four **point** three metres) (*German:* 4,3 m) (⚠ *But:* 2.000 Bäume = 2,000 (two thousand) trees)

p. 115	(to) **sum** sth. **up** [ˌsʌm_'ʌp], **-mm-**	etwas zusammenfassen	to say in a few words what happened in a film or a book, for example
	architect ['ɑ:kɪtekt]	Architekt/in	person who makes plans for new buildings
	export ['ekspɔ:t]	Ausfuhr, Export	For Europe the ~ of cars to the USA is important.
	Catholic *(n.; adj.)* ['kæθlɪk]	Katholik/in; katholisch	*C~s* are part of the Christian church. In South America most Christians are ~.
	°nun [nʌn]	Nonne	
	(to) keep an eye on sb./sth.	auf jn./etwas aufpassen	Can you ~ *an* ~ *on* my bag while I go to the toilet?
	(to) keep sb. off sth.	jn. von etwas fernhalten	*K~* that dirty dog *off* the sofa!

(to) keep

Here's your pen. – Oh, you can **keep** it.	… Du kannst ihn **behalten**.
Butter is best **kept** in the fridge.	Butter **bewahrt** man am besten im Kühlschrank **auf**.
We **keep** a few chickens in our garden.	Wir **halten (uns)** ein paar Hühner im Garten.
We need a fence round the garden …	Wir brauchen einen Zaun um den Garten, …
… to **keep** the dogs **off** the grass.	… um die Hunde **vom** Gras **fernzuhalten**.
… to **keep** the dogs **out**.	… um die Hunde **draußen** zu **halten**.
The Vargases want to **keep** their Mexican traditions **alive**.	Die Vargases wollen ihre mexikanischen Traditionen **am Leben erhalten**.
Can you **keep an eye on** the children while I buy the tickets?	Kannst du **auf** die Kinder **aufpassen**, während ich die Fahrkarten kaufe?
That's not fair. You must **keep your promise**.	… Du mußt **dein Versprechen halten**.

°barrio ['bærɪəʊ] (AE)	*überwiegend spanischsprachiges Stadtviertel in amerikanischen Städten*	
gotten ['gɒtn] (AE)	*Partizip Perfekt von „to get"* (= BE „got")	AE: The weather has *gotten* colder. BE: The weather has *got* colder.
°a rough neighbourhood [rʌf]	*hier:* ein hartes Pflaster, eine harte Gegend	
°Mexican *(n.; adj.)* ['meksɪkən]	Mexikaner/in; mexikanisch	
°Cuban *(n.; adj.)* ['kju:bən]	Kubaner/in; kubanisch	
°Filipino [ˌfɪlɪ'pi:nəʊ]	Filipino/Filipina	
°Mass [mæs]	Messe *(kathol. Gottesdienst)*	

Unit 8

(p. 115)	ethnic ['eθnɪk]	ethnisch; Volks-	People from the whole world live in New York. The Hispanics are one of the largest ~ groups there.
	by the year 2010	bis zum Jahr 2010, im Jahr 2010	Can you finish the work ~ *tomorrow*? The world might look completely different ~ *the year 2010.*

English *by*

The work should be finished **by** 3 o'clock.	Die Arbeit sollte **bis (spätestens)** 3 Uhr fertig sein.
St Paul's was designed **by** Christopher Wren.	St Pauls wurde **von** Christopher Wren entworfen.
London was destroyed **by** a fire in 1666.	London wurde 1666 **durch** ein Feuer zerstört.
The best way to get there is **by** train.	Am besten kommt man dorthin **mit** dem Zug.
We camped **by** the river.	Wir haben **am** Fluß gezeltet.

German *bei*

Ich war gestern **bei** meiner Tante.	I was **at** my aunt's (house) yesterday.
Du kannst ein paar Tage **bei** uns bleiben/wohnen.	You can stay **with** us for a few days.
Ms Green ist sehr beliebt **bei** ihrer Klasse.	Ms Green is very popular **with** her class.
Meine Schwester arbeitet **bei** einer Computerfirma, mein Bruder ist Buchhalter **bei** einer Exportfirma.	My sister works **for** a computer firm, my brother is an accountant **with** an export company.
Bei diesem Wetter können wir nicht Tennis spielen.	We can't play tennis **in** this weather.

Focus on WORDS

V

p. 116	the Mexican **ones**	die mexikanischen	I've got three mountain bikes – two blue *ones* and a red *one*. Which *one* (= *Welches)* do you like best?
	(to) grill [grɪl]	grillen	Let's have a barbecue and ~ some steaks.
	fast-food restaurant ['fɑːstˌfuːd 'restərɒnt]	Schnellrestaurant, Schnellimbiß	At most ~-~ *restaurants* in the US you can get hamburgers and French fries.
	(to) **serve** [sɜːv]	(be)dienen, servieren	Nancy ~*s* customers at a fast-food restaurant. Most fast-food restaurants ~ hamburgers.
	drive-in restaurant ['draɪvɪn 'restərɒnt] (*meist* AE)	*Schnellimbiß, wo Kunden im Auto bedient werden*	At a ~-~ *restaurant* you eat in your car.
	light [laɪt]	leicht	You can carry the bag. It's very ~. ▸◂ heavy *L*~ beer is beer that is not very strong. ▸◂ strong ⚠ *light* = **1.** Licht, Lampe; **2.** leicht
	diner ['daɪnə] (AE)	(kleines, billiges) Restaurant	a small, cheap restaurant, often without tables
	type (of) [taɪp]	Art, Sorte, Typ	Beer, wine, and whisky are different ~*s of* alcohol.
	(bread) roll [rəʊl]	Brötchen	For breakfast I often eat a *(bread)* ~ with butter.
	bowl [bəʊl]	Schüssel, Schale	You eat cornflakes or soup, for example, from a ~.
	tin [tɪn] (*meist* BE)/ can [kæn] (*meist* AE)	Dose, Büchse	Have you got anything to open this ~ of fruit?
	mug [mʌg]	Becher, Krug	You often drink coffee or hot chocolate from a ~.
	saucer ['sɔːsə]	Untertasse	small plate under your cup
	menu ['menjuː]	Speisekarte	Let's ask for the ~ and see what they serve here.
	waiter ['weɪtə]/ **waitress** ['weɪtrəs]	Kellner/in	person who serves in a restaurant
	(to) **book** [bʊk]	buchen, reservieren	I ~*ed* a table for four at Fred's Fish House.
	(to) **order** ['ɔːdə]	bestellen	The waiter asked, "What would you like to ~?"
	(to) **pass** sth. [pɑːs]	etwas (herüber)reichen	Could you ~ the salt, please? I can't reach it. ⚠ *(to) pass* = **1.** *(Prüfung)* bestehen; **2.** *(Ball)* abspielen; **3.** *(jm. etwas)* reichen

Focus on GRAMMAR

<p. 117>	speculation [ˌspekjʊ'leɪʃn]	Vermutung, Spekulation	Although there was a lot of ~ about the accident, nobody really knew what happened.
	(to) be unlikely to come true [ʌn'laɪklɪ]	wahrscheinlich nicht wahr werden, wahrscheinlich nicht in Erfüllung gehen	Madame Zora said that I'll be rich before I'm twenty, but I think it*'s* ~ *to come* ~.

(<p.117>)	economic [ˌiːkəˈnɒmɪk]	ökonomisch, wirtschaftlich	adjective from "economy" ⚠ *Aussprache:* economic [ˌiːkəˈnɒmɪk] – economy [ɪˈkɒnəmɪ]
	ink [ɪŋk]	Tinte	Grandad gave me an old pen. I need some ~ for it.
	at least [ət ˈliːst]	mindestens, wenigstens	My computer is slow, but ~ ~ it still works.
	comparison [kəmˈpærɪsn]	Vergleich	noun from "(to) compare" ⚠ *comparison* = **1.** Vergleich; **2.** Steigerung *(von Adjektiven, Adverbien)*
	reality [rɪˈælətɪ]	Wirklichkeit, Realität	noun from "real" Many people think a world without poverty will never become ~.
8 Ex 1	(to) **study** [ˈstʌdɪ]	studieren; lernen	My brother *is ~ing* to be a teacher. There's a test tomorrow and I *haven't studied* yet.
2	°cable car [ˈkeɪbl kɑː]	*(mit Kabel gezogene)* Straßenbahn	
	attraction [əˈtrækʃn]	Attraktion	noun from "(to) attract"
3	**politician** [ˌpɒləˈtɪʃn]	Politiker/in	person who is part of the government, for example
<4>	stop [stɒp]	Aufenthalt, Halt	noun from "(to) stop" There will be two *~s* for coffee on the way.
7	**(il)legal** [(ɪ)ˈliːgl]	(un)gesetzlich, (il)legal	In many states in the US it is *il~* to drink alcohol if you are under 21.
	°coyote [BE: kɔɪˈəʊtɪ; AE: kaɪˈəʊtiː]	Kojote	
	border [ˈbɔːdə]	Grenze	The US shares a ~ with Canada and with Mexico.
	$ = dollar [ˈdɒlə]	Dollar *(US-Währung)*	Germans use marks, Americans use *~s*.

US money

There are 100 **cents** (¢) in a **dollar** ($).
$2.96 – *you say:* two (dollars) ninety-six (cents)

some coins			**some bills** (AE)/**notes** (BE)		
1¢	one cent	– a **penny**	$ 1	one dollar	– a dollar **bill**
5¢	five cents	– a **nickel** [ˈnɪkl]	$ 5	five dollars	– a five-dollar **bill**
10¢	ten cents	– a **dime** [daɪm]	$ 10	ten dollars	– a ten-dollar **bill**
25¢	twenty-five cents	– a **quarter**	$ 20	twenty dollars	– a twenty-dollar **bill**

Words Words Words

p. 121	clearly [ˈklɪəlɪ]	eindeutig, klar	adverb from "clear"
	male *(adj.; n.)* [meɪl]	männlich; männliche Person	We thought our hamster was ~ so we called him Henry. But then …
	female *(adj.; n.)* [ˈfiːmeɪl]	weiblich; weibliche Person	… "he" had six babies and we realized "he" was a ~. So we named her Henrietta.
	nurse [nɜːs]	Krankenpfleger/in, -schwester	Doctors and *~s* work in hospitals.

8 Text The big brother

p. 122	instinct [ˈɪnstɪŋkt]	Instinkt	Birds learn to fly by ~.
	°That's the way it was today.	Das war heute der Fall. So war es heute.	
	(to) **walk/drive/… on**	weitergehen/weiterfahren/weiter…	If you see an accident you should stop, not *drive ~*.
	athletic [æθˈletɪk]	athletisch	Sue is very ~. She's good at a lot of different sports.
	(to) **rob** [rɒb], **-bb-**	be-, ausrauben	"Put the money in the bag," the man said as he *~bed* the bank.
	(to) nod [nɒd], -dd-	nicken	When you ~ your head you mean "yes".
	°This is it. (infml.)	Nun ist es soweit. Jetzt bin ich dran.	
	I'm going your way.	Ich fahre/gehe in deine Richtung.	Mary *was going* Lucy's ~, so she took her into town.
	(to) work on sb. (infml.)	jn. bearbeiten	My mum won't let me go. – Well, *~ on her* some more. Perhaps she'll change her mind.

V

Unit 8

p. 123	(to) **turn to** sb. [tɜːn]	sich an jn. wenden, sich jm. zuwenden	I can always ~ ~ my parents when I need help. ▸◂ (to) turn away from sb.

(to) turn

Sheila **turned to** her brother.	Sheila **wandte sich** ihrem Bruder **zu/wandte sich an** ihren Bruder.
Her brother **turned away** (from her).	Ihr Bruder **wandte sich** (von ihr) **ab**.
Tommy **turned round** and looked at Steve.	Tommy **drehte sich um** und sah Steve an.
The station? Well, **turn right** at the next traffic lights. Then **turn left into** James Street.	… Also, **biegen Sie** an der nächsten Ampel **rechts ab**. **Biegen Sie** dann **links ab in** die James Street.
Wait till the traffic lights **turn green**.	Warte, bis die Ampel **grün wird**.
Today **it's your turn** to do the dishes.	Heute **bist du dran/an der Reihe** …

	°How are you keeping? (infml.)	Wie geht's?	
	°soda ['səʊdə] (AE)	*Oberbegriff für süße kohlensäurehaltige Getränke wie Cola u.ä.;* Soda(wasser)	
	(to) **rest (from)** [rest]	sich ausruhen (von)	I'm tired. Can't we stop and ~ for a minute?
	obvious ['ɒbvɪəs]	offensichtlich	You failed the test. It's ~ you didn't study.
	ought to ['ɔːtə]	sollte(n) eigentlich	should

ought to – should

It's cold outside. You **ought to/should** put on a coat.	solltest
Your friend **oughtn't to/shouldn't** stay any longer. She'll miss the bus.	sollte nicht
I've worked hard. I **ought to/should** do well in the next test.	müßte eigentlich
It's not far from here. It **oughtn't to/shouldn't** take long to get there.	dürfte eigentlich nicht

	heart [hɑːt]	Herz	You die when your ~ stops beating.
	one [wʌn]	man	*One* should brush *one's* teeth twice a day.

German *man*

One should wash **oneself/one's** hair regularly. **You** should wash **yourself/your** hair regularly.	**Man** sollte **sich/seine** Haare regelmäßig waschen.
They/People say that the weather will change soon.	**Man** sagt, daß das Wetter sich bald ändern wird.
This colour **isn't worn** any more. *(passive)*	Diese Farbe trägt **man** nicht mehr.

In formal English ***one*** is often used instead of ***you***. In informal speech you can also use ***they***.

The good life

p. 124	°attitude (to, towards) ['ætɪtjuːd]	Haltung, Einstellung (gegenüber, zu)	
	°experiment [ɪk'sperɪmənt]	Experiment	
	°(to) advertise ['ædvətaɪz]	werben, Reklame machen für	

Topic 8: Holidays in the USA

p. 125	civil rights *(pl.)* [ˌsɪvl 'raɪts]	Bürgerrechte	In the 1960s, Martin Luther King and Malcolm X fought for ~ ~ for all black Americans.
	°gunman ['gʌnmən]	*(mit einer Schußwaffe)* Bewaffneter	
	president ['prezɪdənt]	Präsident/in	the head of a company or government, for example
	war [wɔː]	Krieg	*W~* is when one country fights against another one.

(p. 125)	memorial [mɪ'mɔ:rɪəl]	Denkmal, Gedenkstätte	The *Völkerschlachtdenkmal* in Leipzig is a war ~.
	civil war [ˌsɪvl 'wɔ:]	Bürgerkrieg	a war between people in one country
	grave [greɪv]	Grab	a hole in the ground where dead people are put
	monument ['mɒnjʊmənt]	Denkmal	The Statue of Liberty is one of America's most well-known *~s*.
	federal holiday [ˌfedərəl 'hɒlədeɪ] (AE)	Feiertag *(, an dem alle Bundesbehörden geschlossen sind)*	
	federal ['fedərəl]	Bundes-	die Bundesrepublik Deutschland = the *F~* Republic of Germany
	(to) **take place**	stattfinden	Our next school trip *will ~ place* in two months.
p. 126	**declaration** [ˌdeklə'reɪʃn]	Erklärung	With the *D~* of Independence on July 4th, 1776, …
	(to) break away (from) [ˌbreɪk‿ə'weɪ]	sich lösen, trennen (von); sich losreißen (von)	… the thirteen American colonies *broke ~ from* Britain.
	celebration [ˌselə'breɪʃn]	(Gedenk-)Feier	noun from "(to) celebrate"
	parade [pə'reɪd]	Parade, Umzug	
	°Thanksgiving (Day) [θæŋks'gɪvɪŋ]	*(amerikanisches)* Erntedankfest	
	Native American [ˌneɪtɪv‿ə'merɪkən]	amerikanische(r) Ureinwohner/in („Indianer/in")	Many ~ *~s* don't like to be called "Indians".
	°harvest ['hɑ:vɪst]	Ernte	
	not … either ['aɪðə, 'i:ðə]	auch nicht; auch kein	I'm not going to Larry's party. – I'm *not* going ~. Can you give me some money for the bus? – Sorry, I have*n't* got any money ~.

German *auch*

auch	auch nicht
Liz is nice. – I think so **too**. I've been to England. – Me **too**. I can speak English. – Me **too**. I can swim, and I **also** play volleyball.	I don't think Peter is nice. – I do**n't** (think so) **either**. I haven't been to the USA. – I have**n't** (been there) **either**. I can't speak Spanish. – I ca**n't** (speak Spanish) **either**. I can't sing, and I do**n't** play an instrument **either**.
sowohl … als auch …	**nicht nur …, sondern auch …**
Yesterday it was **both** cold **and** wet.	Yesterday it was **not only** cold **but also** wet.

Unit 9: The National Park Service

p. 127	(to) **misunderstand** [ˌmɪsʌndə'stænd] – **-stood** [-'stʊd] – **-stood**	mißverstehen	▸◂ (to) understand (correctly) I thought she said the meeting would begin at 11, but it began at 10. I probably *misunderstood* her.
	spectacular [spek'tækjʊlə]	spektakulär, sensationell	The film was a ~ success. In less than two weeks it earned more than twenty million dollars.
	scenery *(sing.)* ['si:nərɪ]	(malerische) Landschaft(en)	During our week in Yosemite National Park we saw some of the most spectacular ~ I've ever seen.
	°spring [sprɪŋ]	(Wasser-)Quelle	
	waterfall ['wɔ:təfɔ:l]	Wasserfall	A ~ is where a river suddenly falls many metres.
	°wildlife *(sing.)* ['waɪldlaɪf]	Tierwelt, *seltener auch:* Pflanzenwelt	
	°bison, *pl.* bison ['baɪsn]	Bison	
	natural wonder [ˌnætʃrəl 'wʌndə]	Naturwunder	In the American west you can see many ~ *~s*, for example the Grand Canyon.

V

Unit 9

(p. 127)	**natural** ['nætʃrəl]	natürlich, Natur-	It's ~ to feel nervous when you go to a new school.
	nature ['neɪtʃə]	Natur	⚠ *Aussprache:* nature ['neɪtʃə] – natural ['nætʃrəl]
	°erosion [ɪ'rəʊʒn]	Erosion	
	(to) preserve [prɪ'zɜːv]	erhalten, bewahren	to keep something as it is
	colonial [kə'ləʊnɪəl]	kolonial, Kolonial-	adjective from "colony ['kɒlənɪ]"

Nouns and verbs with the same form

(to) **camp**	zelten, campen	(to) **order**	**1.** befehlen; **2.** bestellen
camp	(Zelt-)Lager	**order**	**1.** Befehl; **2.** Bestellung, Auftrag
(to) **export** ⚠ [ɪk'spɔːt]	exportieren	(to) **rest**	sich ausruhen
export ⚠ ['ekspɔːt]	Ausfuhr, Export	**rest**	Ruhepause

p. 128	**each other** [ˌiːtʃ‿'ʌðə]	einander, sich (gegenseitig)	Paul and Linda helped ~ ~. Paul helped Linda and Linda helped Paul.
	(to) **cycle** ['saɪkl]	radfahren	to ride a bike
	°barbecue ['bɑːbɪkjuː]	Grillparty	
	campground ['kæmpgraʊnd] (AE)/ campsite ['kæmpsaɪt] (BE)	Zeltplatz, Campingplatz	You can camp on a ~.
	entrance fee ['entrəns fiː]	Eintritt(sgeld)	the money you pay to get into a concert, for example
	entrance (to)	Eingang (zu)	At the ~ *to* the disco there was a long queue.
	grizzly bear ['grɪzlɪ beə]	Grizzly(bär)	You shouldn't leave any food outside when you camp. It attracts *grizzly ~s.*
	beauty ['bjuːtɪ]	Schönheit	noun from "beautiful"
	giant *(n.; adj.)* ['dʒaɪənt]	Riese; riesig, Riesen-	a really huge and strong person, often in legends; huge, very large
p. 129	**valley** ['vælɪ]	Tal	the land between two mountains or hills
	storey, *pl.* **storeys** (BE)/ **story,** *pl.* **stories** (AE) ['stɔːrɪ]	Stock(werk)	The tallest building in the world has 110 *~s.*
	°the experienced *(pl.)* [ɪk'spɪərɪənst]	die Erfahrenen, Erfahrene	
	(to) be experienced (in doing sth.)	erfahren sein (in etwas); Erfahrung haben (mit etwas)	Jo has been working at a garage for five years. She*'s* very ~ *in* repair*ing* cars.
	experience [ɪk'spɪərɪəns]	Erfahrung, Erlebnis	I didn't get the job because I don't have enough ~. How was Africa? – Great! It was such an ~.
	°wilderness ['wɪldənəs]	Wildnis	
	°unspoiled [ˌʌn'spɔɪld]	unverdorben	
	permit ['pɜːmɪt]	Genehmigung(sschein), Erlaubnis	document ['dɒkjʊmənt] that gives you permission to do something
	°ranger ['reɪndʒə] (AE)	Parkwächter/in, Aufseher/in *(in einem Nationalpark)*	

Focus on GRAMMAR

[p. 130]	(to) run into a traffic jam	in einen Verkehrsstau geraten	On weekdays before and after work I usually ~ *into traffic ~s.*

Focus on WORDS

p. 131	(to) **include** [ɪn'kluːd]	beinhalten, (mit) einschließen, enthalten	*Does* the trip ~ a tour of London?
	as well as	und auch, ebenso wie	Mr Greenjeans grows flowers ~ *well* ~ vegetables.
	desert ['dezət]	Wüste	a very hot and dry area
	(to) conserve [kən'sɜːv]	erhalten, bewahren	to keep something as it is We must try to ~ the rain forests.
	plant [plɑːnt]	Pflanze	Nature includes animals and *~s.*
	panther ['pænθə]	Panther	a kind of wild cat that is usually black
	timber *(sing.)* ['tɪmbə]	(Bau-)Holz	wood that is used for houses or furniture

V

(p. 131)	memory ['memərɪ]	Gedächtnis	My ~ is terrible. I always forget your phone number.
	landscape ['lændskeɪp]	Landschaft, Landschaftsbild	everything you can see when you look at an area of land; a picture which shows a *landscape*
	sunshine ['sʌnʃaɪn]	Sonnenschein	I like to lie on the beach and enjoy the warm ~.
	(to) **melt** [melt]	schmelzen	Ice ~*s* and becomes water when it's warm.
	monkey ['mʌŋkɪ]	Affe	Tarzan's best friend was a ~.
	bush [bʊʃ]	Busch	plant which is like a very small tree
	ripe [raɪp]	reif	This apple is not ~ yet. It's still green. ⧓ green
	sour ['saʊə]	sauer	– It'll probably be quite ~ then. ⧓ sweet

Focus on GRAMMAR

[p. 132]	(to) get injured ['ɪndʒəd]	sich verletzen, verletzt werden	to get hurt Ralph had an accident. – I hope he *didn't get* ~.
	(to) lose one's way	sich verirren, sich verlaufen	to get lost Bill hasn't arrived yet. I hope he *hasn't lost his* ~.
	careless ['keələs]	unvorsichtig, nachlässig, unaufmerksam	⧓ careful
	bubble ['bʌbl]	(Sprech-)Blase	
	in progress ['prəʊgres]	im Gange	Dave was late for the race. It was already *in* ~.
[p. 133]	actually ['æktʃʊəlɪ]	tatsächlich	really
	punctuation [ˌpʌŋktʃʊ'eɪʃn]	Zeichensetzung, Interpunktion	In reported speech English ~ is different from German ~: There is no comma after "said".
	(to) tell sb. to do sth. [tel]	jn. auffordern, etwas zu tun	a phrase similar to "(to) order sb. to do sth.", but not as strong
9 Ex 1	purse [pɜːs]	Geldbörse, Geldbeutel; AE *auch:* Handtasche	where you keep your money; in AE also: a woman's handbag
	comparison [kəm'pærɪsn]	Vergleich	noun from "(to) compare" ⚠ *comparison* = **1.** Vergleich; **2.** Steigerung

German *sich*

The girls are smiling at **themselves**.
Die Mädchen lächeln sich (= sich selbst) an.

⚠ **-self/-selves** = sich selbst

The girls are smiling at **each other**.
Die Mädchen lächeln sich (= sich gegenseitig) an.

⚠ **each other** = sich gegenseitig, einander

⚠ Vielen im Deutschen reflexiven Verben entsprechen englische Verben ohne Reflexivpronomen, z.B.:

(to) ***behave***	*sich benehmen, verhalten*	*(to)* ***refer to***	*sich beziehen auf*
(to) ***change***	*sich (ver)ändern*	*(to)* ***relax***	*sich entspannen*
(to) ***complain***	*sich beschweren*	*(to)* ***remember***	*sich erinnern*
(to) ***decide***	*sich entscheiden*	*(to)* ***rest***	*sich ausruhen*
(to) ***feel***	*sich fühlen*	*(to)* ***settle***	*sich niederlassen*
(to) ***hide***	*sich verstecken*	*(to)* ***show***	*sich zeigen*
(to) ***imagine***	*sich vorstellen*	*(to)* ***sit down***	*sich hinsetzen*
(to) ***look after***	*sich kümmern um*	*(to)* ***turn round***	*sich (um)drehen*
(to) ***look forward to***	*sich freuen auf*	*(to)* ***turn to***	*sich wenden an*
(to) ***meet***	*sich treffen*	*(to)* ***wonder***	*sich fragen*
(to) ***move***	*sich bewegen*	*(to)* ***worry***	*sich Sorgen machen*
(to) ***open***	*sich öffnen*		

	(to) take a decision	eine Entscheidung treffen, fällen	to decide
	wherever [weər'evə]	wo (auch) immer, wohin (auch) immer; überall wo	Everywhere in the world you'll meet friendly and helpful people. = *W*~ you go you'll meet friendly and helpful people.

(Ex 1)

wherever, whenever, whatever, …

Wherever you go, I'll come with you.	**Wo auch immer** du hingehst, … .
Visit me **whenever** you like.	…, **wann immer** du willst.
Whatever problems you have, you can always ask me for help. I'll help you **whatever** happens.	**Was** für Probleme **auch immer** du hast, … . Ich helfe dir, **was immer auch** geschieht.
You'll be welcome, **whichever** day you come.	…, **welchen** Tag **auch immer** du kommst.
I'm not going to open the door, **whoever** you are.	…, **wer immer** du **auch** bist.
Whoever you marry, make sure he can cook.	**Wen immer** du heiratest, … .
Whoever told you that was wrong.	**Wer immer** dir das **auch** erzählt hat, hatte unrecht.
However you travel, it'll take you at least two days.	**Wie** du **auch** reist, … .
It'll take you two hours, **however** fast you drive.	…, **wie** schnell du **auch** fährst.
(⚠ I've got a big car. It was very cheap, **however**.	… Es war **jedoch** sehr billig.)

[2]

society [sə'saɪətɪ]	Gesellschaft	People who live together in a community form a ~.
handicapped ['hændɪkæpt]	*(körperlich, geistig)* behindert	People who can't walk or see, for example, are ~.
minority [maɪ'nɒrətɪ]	Minderheit	⧓ majority
(to) achieve [ə'tʃi:v]	*(ein Ziel)* erreichen	To ~ success you must work very hard.
generally ['dʒenrəlɪ]	im allgemeinen, im großen und ganzen	I ~ drink coffee instead of tea. But today I'm having tea.
access ['ækses]	Zugang	way in, entrance "*Access* for doctors only" *(sign in hospital)*
restroom ['restrʊm] (AE)	öffentliche Toilette	toilet
particular [pə'tɪkjʊlə]	bestimmte(r, s), spezielle(r, s)	special Is there a ~ colour you want? – Yes, blue, please.
the other way round	andersherum, umgekehrt	This key doesn't fit. – Turn it *the other* ~ ~ and it'll fit.
original *(n.; adj.)* [ə'rɪdʒnəl]	Original; ursprünglich, Original-	This is a translation. The ~ is in French. I liked your ~ idea better than this one.

Adjectives and participles used as nouns

The handicapped have to fight for their rights.
***Behinderte** müssen für ihre Rechte kämpfen.*

Referring to people: In English you can only use adjectives or participles as nouns if you are talking about **a whole group of people in general**:
the handicapped = Behinderte schlechthin, alle Behinderten dieses Landes/dieser Stadt.
⚠ Definite article obligatory[1]. No plural *-s*, but plural verb: *The handicapped have …*

Many **handicapped people** protested in town.
*Viele **Behinderte** protestierten in der Innenstadt.*

If you are talking about **particular people**, you have to add *man, woman, people* etc.:
eine Behinderte, mehrere Behinderte = a handicapped woman, several handicapped people.

In many films **the good** wins over **the bad**.
*In vielen Filmen siegt **das Gute** über **das Böse**.*

Referring to things or ideas: Adjectives can only be used as nouns to talk about things or ideas **in general**.
⚠ Definite article obligatory[1]. Singular verb: *The good wins …*

The good thing about this film is that it is so short.
***Das Gute** an diesem Film ist, daß er so kurz ist.*

If you have **a particular aspect** in mind, you have to add *thing.*

[1] obligatory [ə'blɪgətərɪ] *obligatorisch*

[4]

(to) replace (with) [rɪ'pleɪs]	ersetzen (durch), austauschen (gegen)	Our physics teacher, Mr Kline, was ill. So our headteacher had to ~ him *with* Ms Flood.
(to) admit, -tt- [əd'mɪt]	zugeben	The man *~ted* that he had stolen the watch.
(to) deny [dɪ'naɪ]	leugnen, bestreiten	The newspaper said the Tigers' coach was quitting, but he *denied* it the next day. ⧓ (to) admit
(to) remind sb. (of sth). [rɪ'maɪnd]	jn. (an etwas) erinnern	Please ~ me to call Bob. I'm sure I won't remember. ⚠ ***sich** an etwas erinnern = (to) remember sth.*
(to) reply [rɪ'plaɪ]	erwidern, antworten	to answer

9 Text A prophet in the wilderness

p. 137	°prophet ['prɒfɪt]	Prophet/in	
	°he had come/had read/had found …	er war gekommen/hatte gelesen/hatte gefunden …	
	(to) make sth. sth.	etwas zu etwas machen	Emperor Claudius *made* Britain a Roman province.
	fence [fens]	Zaun	Farmers use *~s* to keep their animals in the fields.
	(to) be fascinated ['fæsəneɪtɪd]	fasziniert, begeistert sein	to be highly interested The children *were* ~ by the toys in the window.
	°silver *(n.; adj.)* ['sɪlvə]	Silber; silbern	
	(to) **pass** [pɑːs]	vergehen, vorübergehen *(Zeit)*	As the years *~ed* his hair turned grey.
	(to) be horrified (at, by) ['hɒrɪfaɪd]	entsetzt sein (über)	We *were* ~ *by* the number of car accidents on German motorways last year.
	original *(n.; adj.)* [ə'rɪdʒnəl]	Original; ursprünglich, Original-	This is a translation. The ~ is in French. I liked your ~ idea better than this one.
	state [steɪt]	Zustand	The economy is in a bad ~. Many have lost their jobs. ⚠ *state* = **1.** Staat; **2.** Zustand
	°conservationist [ˌkɒnsə'veɪʃnɪst]	Naturschützer/in, Umweltschützer/in	
	conservation [ˌkɒnsə'veɪʃn]	Naturschutz, Umweltschutz	noun from "(to) conserve"
	influence ['ɪnfluəns]	Einfluß	The Beatles had a strong ~ on modern music.
	°(to) establish [ɪ'stæblɪʃ]	gründen	
	(to) **point (at, to)** [pɔɪnt]	zeigen, deuten (auf)	She *~ed to* the building and said, "That's where I work."
	°acre ['eɪkə]	*Flächenmaß (ca. 0,4 Hektar)*	
p. 138	°anything ['enɪθɪŋ]	*hier:* alles	
	°dam [dæm]	Staudamm, Talsperre	
	sad [sæd]	traurig	⧓ happy
	(to) turn sth. into sth.	etwas in etwas verwandeln; etwas zu etwas machen	The warm sun *~ed* the ice *into* water.
	°reservoir ['rezəvwɑː]	Reservoir, Stausee	
	(to) **supply** [sə'plaɪ]	(be)liefern; versorgen	The lake *supplies* the city with water.
	electricity [ɪˌlek'trɪsətɪ]	Strom, Elektrizität	Lights, computers, TVs, radios, etc. need ~ to work.
	°(to) flood [flʌd]	überschwemmen, überfluten	
	°(to) bury ['berɪ]	begraben	
	the worst fight ever	der härteste Kampf, den es je/bis jetzt gegeben hat	This was *the worst* storm ~. I have never seen such a storm.
	they don't care [keə]	das/es ist ihnen egal; sie kümmern sich nicht darum	Many children watch TV all the time, and their parents *don't* ~.
	universal [ˌjuːnɪ'vɜːsl]	universal, allgemein	English has become the ~ language of science.
	°anybody ['enɪbɒdɪ]	*hier:* (irgend) jemand	
	just as well	genausogut	You'll miss the last tube. You might ~ *as* ~ stay here.
	°commercially [kə'mɜːʃəlɪ]	kommerziell	
	°(to) dam, -mm- [dæm]	eindämmen, aufstauen	
	crime [kraɪm]	Verbrechen	A ~ is when somebody does something illegal.
	(to) come true [ˌkʌm 'truː]	Wirklichkeit werden, wahr werden	Madame Zora said that I'll be famous before I'm twenty, but I don't think it will *come* ~.
p. 139	**biography** [baɪ'ɒgrəfɪ]	Biographie	a book about somebody's life I'm reading a ~ of John Lennon at the moment.
	(to) **record** [rɪ'kɔːd]	aufnehmen, aufzeichnen *(auf Band)*	The band *is ~ing* a new record. ⚠ *Aussprache:* record *(n.)* ['rekɔːd] (Schallplatte) – (to) record *(v.)* [rɪ'kɔːd]

Das *Dictionary* enthält den Wortschatz der Bände C1 und C2. Mit einem ° versehene Wörter stammen aus Abschnitten, die je nach Bundesland fakultativ sind. Diese Wörter werden bei erneutem Vorkommen nicht als bekannt vorausgesetzt.

A

a [ə] ein(e); **five lessons a week** fünf Stunden pro Woche
A-level (exam) ['eɪˌlevl] (BE) *etwa:* Abitur
ability [ə'bɪlətɪ] Fähigkeit
able ['eɪbl]**: be able to** können, fähig sein
about [ə'baʊt] **1.** ungefähr, etwa; **2.** wegen, bezüglich; um; über; **What about ...?** ['wɒt‿əˌbaʊt] Wie wäre es mit ...? Was ist mit ...? **The book is about ...** Das Buch handelt von ...; **write about** schreiben über
absent ['æbsənt]**: be absent** fehlen, abwesend sein
accent ['æksənt] Akzent
accept [ək'sept] akzeptieren, annehmen
°**access** ['ækses] Zugang
accident ['æksɪdənt] Unfall
accountant [ə'kaʊntənt] Buchhalter/in
ache [eɪk] schmerzen, weh tun; **earache** ['ɪəreɪk] Ohrenschmerzen; **headache** ['hedeɪk] Kopfschmerzen, Kopfweh; **stomach ache** ['stʌmək‿eɪk] Bauchschmerzen, Magenschmerzen
°**achieve** [ə'tʃi:v] *(ein Ziel)* erreichen
across [ə'krɒs] (quer) über, durch
act [ækt] spielen, aufführen
action ['ækʃn] Handlung, Tat
active ['æktɪv] aktiv, rege
activity [æk'tɪvətɪ] Betätigung, Aktivität, Tätigkeit
°**actually** ['æktʃʊəlɪ] tatsächlich
AD [ˌeɪ'di:] *(from Latin "anno Domini")* n. Chr.
add (to) [æd] hinzufügen (zu)
address [ə'dres] Adresse, Anschrift
administration [ədˌmɪnɪ'streɪʃn] Verwaltung
admire [əd'maɪə] bewundern
°**admit** [əd'mɪt] zugeben
adult ['ædʌlt] Erwachsene(r)
advantage [əd'vɑ:ntɪdʒ] Vorteil
advertisement [əd'vɜ:tɪzmənt]**,** (infml.:) **advert** ['ædvɜ:t] (BE)**, ad** [æd] Anzeige, Annonce, Reklame
advice [əd'vaɪs] Rat, Ratschlag; Ratschläge; **Take my advice.** Hör(t) auf meinen Rat.
aerobics [eə'rəʊbɪks] Aerobic
afraid [ə'freɪd]**: be afraid (of)** Angst haben (vor); **I'm afraid** leider, ich fürchte
after ['ɑ:ftə] **1.** nach *(zeitlich)*; **after lunch** nach dem Mittagessen; **2.** nachdem; **3.** hinter ... her; **look after** sich kümmern um
afternoon [ˌɑ:ftə'nu:n] Nachmittag; **Good afternoon.** Guten Tag. *(nachmittags)*; **in the afternoon(s)** am Nachmittag, nachmittags; **this afternoon** heute nachmittag
again [ə'gen] wieder, noch einmal
against [ə'genst] gegen
age [eɪdʒ] Alter; **at the age of** im Alter von
ago [ə'gəʊ]**: a year ago** vor einem Jahr; **long ago** [ˌlɒŋ‿ə'gəʊ] vor langer Zeit; **not long ago** vor kurzem
agree [ə'gri:] **1.** übereinstimmen, zustimmen; **2.** sich einigen, sich einig werden/sein; **agree on** vereinbaren
air [eə] Luft; **airmail** ['eəmeɪl] Luftpost; **airport** ['eəpɔ:t] Flughafen
alarm [ə'lɑ:m] Alarm; Alarmanlage
alcohol ['ælkəhɒl] Alkohol
alive [ə'laɪv] lebendig, am Leben; **keep alive** am Leben (er)halten
all [ɔ:l] alle; **all day** den ganzen Tag; **all over the bungalow** im ganzen Bungalow verteilt, überall im Bungalow; **all (the) year** das ganze Jahr über; **Are you all right?** Geht es dir/Ihnen (noch) gut? **That's all right.** Schon gut. Nichts zu danken.
allow [ə'laʊ] erlauben; **be allowed to** [ə'laʊd] dürfen
almost ['ɔ:lməʊst] fast, beinahe
alone [ə'ləʊn] allein; **leave sb. alone** jn. in Ruhe lassen
along [ə'lɒŋ] entlang, *(eine Straße)* hinunter
aloud *(adv.)* [ə'laʊd] laut *(= hörbar)*
alphabet ['ælfəbet] Alphabet
already [ɔ:l'redɪ] schon, bereits
also ['ɔ:lsəʊ] auch
although [ɔ:l'ðəʊ] obwohl
altogether [ˌɔ:ltə'geðə] insgesamt
always ['ɔ:lweɪz] immer
am [æm]**: I am** ich bin
... am [ˌeɪ‿'em] *(from Latin "ante meridiem")* ... Uhr morgens *(zwischen 0 und 12 h)*
ambulance ['æmbjələns] Krankenwagen
American [ə'merɪkən] **1.** amerikanisch; **2.** Amerikaner/in
among [ə'mʌŋ] (mitten) unter, zwischen *(mehreren Personen oder Dingen)*
an [ən] ein(e)
and [ænd, ənd, ən] und; **both ... and ...** sowohl ... als auch ...
Anglo-Saxon [ˌæŋgləʊ'sæksn] **1.** angelsächsisch; **2.** Angelsachse/Angelsächsin
angry (with) ['æŋgrɪ] wütend, böse (auf)
animal ['ænɪməl] Tier
annoyed [ə'nɔɪd] verärgert
anorak ['ænəræk] Anorak
another [ə'nʌðə] ein(e) andere(r, s); noch ein(e)
answer ['ɑ:nsə] **1.** antworten, beantworten; **answer the phone** ans Telefon gehen; **2. answer (to)** Antwort (auf)
any? ['enɪ] irgendwelche? **not ... any** kein(e); **not (...) any more** nicht mehr, kein(e, n) ... mehr
anybody? ['enɪbɒdɪ] (irgend) jemand? **not ... anybody** niemand
anything? ['enɪθɪŋ] (irgend) etwas? **not ... anything** nichts
anywhere? ['enɪweə] irgendwo?; irgendwohin? **not ... anywhere** nirgendwo; nirgendwohin
apartment [ə'pɑ:tmənt] *(meist* AE) Wohnung; **apartment house** (AE) Mietshaus, Wohnblock
apostrophe [ə'pɒstrəfɪ] Apostroph
appear [ə'pɪə] **1.** erscheinen, auftauchen; **2.** scheinen
appetite (for) ['æpɪtaɪt] Appetit (auf)
apple ['æpl] Apfel
appointment [ə'pɔɪntmənt] Termin
April ['eɪprəl] April
architect ['ɑ:kɪtekt] Architekt/in
are [ɑ:]**: you are** du bist/ihr seid/Sie sind; **they are** sie sind
area ['eərɪə] Gebiet, Gegend
argument ['ɑ:gjʊmənt] **1.** Streit, Auseinandersetzung; **2.** Argument
arm [ɑ:m] Arm
army ['ɑ:mɪ] Armee, Heer
around [ə'raʊnd] um ... (herum); in ... umher, durch
arrange [ə'reɪndʒ] **1.** (an)ordnen; **2.** vereinbaren, arrangieren; **arrangement** [ə'reɪndʒmənt] Vereinbarung, Abmachung
arrival [ə'raɪvl] Ankunft; **arrive** [ə'raɪv] ankommen, eintreffen
art [ɑ:t] (bildende) Kunst
article ['ɑ:tɪkl] Artikel
as [æz, əz] **1.** als, während; **2.** weil, da; **3.** wie; **as big as** so groß wie; **as far as** bis (nach/zu); **as if** als ob; **as soon as** sobald; **as well as** und auch, ebenso wie; **just as tired** genauso müde
Asian ['eɪʃn, 'eɪʒn] **1.** asiatisch; **2.** Asiate/Asiatin
ask [ɑ:sk] fragen; **ask a question** eine Frage stellen; **ask for** bitten um; **ask sb. to do sth.** jn. bitten, etwas zu tun; **ask the way** nach dem Weg fragen
aspect ['æspekt] Aspekt, Gesichtspunkt
assembly [ə'semblɪ] Schulversammlung mit Andacht

assistant [ə'sɪstənt] Assistent/in; **shop assistant** Verkäufer/in
at [æt, ət] bei, an; **at a holiday park** in einem Ferienpark; **at Easter** zu/an Ostern; **at first** zuerst, am Anfang; **at home** zu Hause, daheim; **at last** schließlich, endlich; °**at least** mindestens, wenigstens; **at lunchtime** mittags, in der Mittagspause; **at midnight** um Mitternacht; **at night** nachts, in der Nacht, am (späten) Abend; **at number 5** im Haus Nr. 5; **at once** sofort, (so)gleich; **at platform 1** am Bahnsteig 1, auf Gleis 1; **at school** in der Schule; **at 7 o'clock** um 7 Uhr/19 Uhr; **at that time** damals, zu jener Zeit; **at the end of** am Ende von; **at the house** am/beim Haus; **at the moment** im Augenblick, gerade; **at the weekend** am Wochenende; **good at** gut in, geschickt in
athletic [æθ'letɪk] athletisch
atmosphere ['ætməsfɪə] Atmosphäre
attack [ə'tæk] **1.** Angriff; **2.** angreifen
attention [ə'tenʃn]**: pay attention (to)** aufmerksam sein, aufpassen (auf)
attract [ə'trækt] anziehen, anlocken; **attraction** [ə'trækʃn] Attraktion; **attractive** [ə'træktɪv] attraktiv, reizvoll
August ['ɔ:gəst] August
aunt [ɑ:nt] Tante
Australian [ɒ'streɪlɪən] **1.** australisch; **2.** Australier/in
authentic [ɔ:'θentɪk] authentisch, echt
auto(mobile) ['ɔ:təʊ, 'ɔ:təməʊbi:l] (AE) Auto(mobil)
autumn ['ɔ:təm] Herbst
average ['ævərɪdʒ] **1.** Durchschnitt; **2.** durchschnittlich, Durchschnitts-
avoid [ə'vɔɪd] vermeiden
awake [ə'weɪk]**: be awake** wach sein
away [ə'weɪ] weg, fort; **break away (from)** [ˌbreɪk‿ə'weɪ] sich lösen, trennen (von); sich losreißen (von)

B

baby ['beɪbɪ] Baby, Säugling
back [bæk] **1.** hinterer Teil, Rückseite; Rücken; **back door** Hintertür; **2.** zurück; **go back to** zurückgehen auf, zurückreichen bis; **backwards** ['bækwədz] rückwärts; nach hinten
bad [bæd] schlecht, schlimm; unartig; **bad at** schlecht/ungeschickt in
badminton ['bædmɪntən] Badminton, Federball
bag [bæg] Tasche, Beutel, Tüte
baked beans [ˌbeɪkt 'bi:nz] gebackene Bohnen (in Tomatensoße)
baker ['beɪkə] Bäcker/in
balcony ['bælkənɪ] Balkon
ball [bɔ:l] Ball; **ball-point pen** (AE) Kugelschreiber
banana [bə'nɑ:nə] Banane
band [bænd] Band, (Musik-)Gruppe
bank [bæŋk] Bank, Sparkasse; **bottle bank** Altglascontainer
bar [bɑ:] *(Schokoladen-, Müsli-)* Riegel
bark [bɑ:k] bellen
based: be based on ['beɪst‿ɒn] basieren auf
basket ['bɑ:skɪt] Korb; **basketball** ['bɑ:skɪtbɔ:l] Basketball
bath [bɑ:θ] Bad; **baths** (Schwimm-)Bad; **have a bath** baden, ein Bad nehmen; **bathroom** Bad(ezimmer)
battle ['bætl] Schlacht, Kampf
BC [ˌbi:'si:] **(before Christ)** v. Chr.
be [bi:] sein; **Be careful.** [ˌbi: 'keəfəl] Sei/Seid/Seien Sie vorsichtig!
beach [bi:tʃ] Strand
bean [bi:n] Bohne
bear [beə] Bär
beat [bi:t] schlagen
beautiful ['bju:təfəl] (wunder)schön; **beauty** ['bju:tɪ] Schönheit
because [bɪ'kɒz] weil; **because of** wegen
become [bɪ'kʌm] werden
bed [bed] Bett; **in bed** im Bett; **bedroom** ['bedru:m] Schlafzimmer
beer [bɪə] Bier
before [bɪ'fɔ:] **1.** vor *(zeitlich, Reihenfolge)*; **2.** bevor, ehe; **3.** schon einmal, zuvor
begin [bɪ'gɪn] anfangen, beginnen; **beginner** Anfänger/in, Neuling; **beginning** Anfang, Beginn
behave [bɪ'heɪv] sich benehmen, sich verhalten; **behaviour (towards)** [bɪ'heɪvjə] Verhalten, Benehmen (gegenüber)
behind [bɪ'haɪnd] hinter
believe (in) [bɪ'li:v] glauben (an)
bell [bel] Glocke, Klingel
belong to [bɪ'lɒŋ] gehören (zu)
best [best]**: (the) best** (der/die/das) beste; am besten
better ['betə] besser
between [bɪ'twi:n] zwischen
beyond [bɪ'jɒnd] über … hinaus, jenseits von
big [bɪg] groß
bike [baɪk] (Fahr-)Rad; **ride a bike** radfahren; **bike path** Radweg
bill [bɪl] **1.** (BE) Rechnung; **2.** (AE) (Geld-)Schein
bingo ['bɪŋgəʊ] Bingo *(Glücksspiel mit Zahlen)*
biography [baɪ'ɒgrəfɪ] Biographie
biology [baɪ'ɒlədʒɪ] Biologie
bird [bɜ:d] Vogel; **birdseed** ['bɜ:dsi:d] Vogelfutter
biro ['baɪrəʊ] (BE) Kugelschreiber
birthday ['bɜ:θdeɪ] Geburtstag; **birthplace** ['bɜ:θpleɪs] Geburtsort
biscuit ['bɪskɪt] (BE) Keks, Plätzchen
bit [bɪt]**: a bit** ein bißchen, etwas
bite [baɪt] beißen
bitter ['bɪtə] bitter, verbittert; **bitterness** Bitterkeit
black [blæk] **1.** schwarz; **2.** Schwarze(r)
blame sb. (for sth.) [bleɪm] jm. Vorwürfe machen (wegen etwas); jm. die Schuld geben (an etwas); **Who is to blame?** Wer hat schuld?
blind [blaɪnd] blind
block of flats [ˌblɒk‿əv 'flæts] (BE) (Miets-)Haus, Wohnblock
blouse [blaʊz] Bluse
blue [blu:] blau
board [bɔ:d] (Wand-)Tafel; Brett
boat [bəʊt] Boot, Schiff
body ['bɒdɪ] Körper; **care of the body** Körperpflege; **part of the body** Körperteil
bold print [ˌbəʊld 'prɪnt] fette Schrift, Fettdruck
bone [bəʊn] Knochen
book [bʊk] **1.** buchen, reservieren; **2.** Buch; Heft; **bookshop** Buchhandlung
border ['bɔ:də] Grenze
bored [bɔ:d] gelangweilt; **boring** ['bɔ:rɪŋ] langweilig
born [bɔ:n]**: I was born …** Ich bin … geboren
borrow ['bɒrəʊ] (sich) borgen, (sich) ausleihen
boss [bɒs] Chef/in, Vorgesetzte(r)
both [bəʊθ] beide, beides; **both … and …** sowohl … als auch …
bottle ['bɒtl] Flasche; **bottle bank** (BE) Altglascontainer
bottom ['bɒtəm] unteres Ende
bowl [bəʊl] Schüssel, Schale
box [bɒks] Kiste, Karton; **letter box** Briefkasten
Boxing Day ['bɒksɪŋ deɪ] (BE) zweiter Weihnachtsfeiertag (26.12.)
boy [bɔɪ] Junge; **boyfriend** ['bɔɪfrend] (fester) Freund
boycott ['bɔɪkɒt] Boykott
bracket ['brækɪt] Klammer *(Satzzeichen)*
brain [breɪn] Gehirn
bread [bred] Brot; **bread roll** Brötchen
break [breɪk] **1.** Pause; **take a break** eine Pause machen; **2. break-in** ['breɪk‿ɪn] Einbruch; **3.** *(etwas)* zerbrechen; brechen; **break away (from)** [ˌbreɪk‿ə'weɪ] sich lösen, trennen (von); sich losreißen (von)
breakfast ['brekfəst] Frühstück; **have breakfast** frühstücken; **for breakfast** zum Frühstück
bridge [brɪdʒ] Brücke
bright [braɪt] hell, leuchtend
brilliant ['brɪljənt] toll, klasse
bring [brɪŋ] bringen; **bring up children** Kinder großziehen, Kinder erziehen
Britain, Great Britain ['brɪtn] Großbritannien; **British** ['brɪtɪʃ] **1.** britisch; **2.** Brite/Britin

D

brochure ['brəʊʃə] Broschüre, Prospekt
brother ['brʌðə] Bruder
brown [braʊn] braun
brush [brʌʃ] **1.** (Haar-)Bürste; **2. brush one's teeth** (sich) die Zähne putzen
°**bubble** ['bʌbl] (Sprech-)Blase
budgie ['bʌdʒɪ] Wellensittich
build [bɪld] bauen; **building** Gebäude
bully ['bʊlɪ] *jd., der Schwächere schikaniert*
bungalow ['bʌŋgələʊ] Bungalow, einstöckiges Haus
burn [bɜ:n] (ver)brennen
bus [bʌs] (Auto-)Bus; **on the bus** im Bus; **bus stop** Bushaltestelle
bush [bʊʃ] Busch
busy ['bɪzɪ] **1.** beschäftigt; **2.** belebt, verkehrsreich; hektisch
but [bʌt, bət] aber; **not only ... but (also) ...** nicht nur ... sondern (auch) ...
butcher ['bʊtʃə] Metzger/in, Fleischer/in; **butcher's** Metzgerei, Metzgerladen, Fleischerei
butter ['bʌtə] Butter
buy [baɪ] kaufen
by [baɪ] **1.** bis (zu); **2.** von, durch; **by air/sea** auf dem Luft-/Seeweg; **by bike/car/bus/...** mit dem Fahrrad/ Auto/Bus/...; **by the river** am Fluß; **by the year 2010** bis zum Jahr 2010, im Jahr 2010
Bye. [baɪ] Tschüs!

C

c (= circa) ['sɜ:kə] ca. (= circa)
café ['kæfeɪ] kleines Restaurant; Café; Imbißstube; **cafeteria** [ˌkæfə'tɪərɪə] Selbstbedienungsrestaurant, Cafeteria
cake [keɪk] Kuchen, Torte
call [kɔ:l] **1.** Anruf; **2.** rufen; nennen; **call sb. names** Schimpfwörter zu jm. sagen; **be called** heißen
calm [kɑ:m] ruhig, ausgeglichen; **calm down** (sich) beruhigen
camera ['kæmrə] Fotoapparat, Kamera
camp [kæmp] **1.** (Zelt-)Lager; **2.** zelten, campen; **campground** ['kæmpgraʊnd] (AE)**/campsite** ['kæmpsaɪt] (BE) Zeltplatz, Campingplatz
can [kæn, kən] können, dürfen; **can't** [kɑ:nt] **(= cannot** ['kænɒt]) nicht können, nicht dürfen
can [kæn] (*meist* AE) Dose, Büchse
canoeing [kə'nu:ɪŋ] Kanufahren
canyon ['kænjən] Cañon
capital ['kæpɪtl] **1.** Großbuchstabe; Groß-; **2.** Hauptstadt
captain ['kæptɪn] Kapitän/in; Mannschaftsführer/in
capture ['kæptʃə] erobern, einnehmen; gefangennehmen
car [kɑ:] Auto; **car park** (BE) (großer) Parkplatz, Parkhaus
caravan ['kærəvæn] (BE) Wohnwagen
card [kɑ:d] (Spiel-, Post-)Karte; **credit card** ['kredɪt kɑ:d] Kreditkarte
care [keə]**: they don't care** das ist ihnen egal; **careful** ['keəfəl] **1.** vorsichtig; **2.** sorgfältig; °**careless** ['keələs] unvorsichtig, nachlässig, unaufmerksam; **care of the body** Körperpflege
carpet ['kɑ:pɪt] Teppich
carrot ['kærət] Möhre, Karotte, Mohrrübe
carry ['kærɪ] tragen; befördern
cash [kæʃ] Bargeld; (infml. *auch:*) Geld
cassette [kə'set] Kassette; **cassette-recorder** Kassettenrecorder
castle ['kɑ:sl] Burg; Schloß
cat [kæt] Katze
catalogue ['kætəlɒg] Katalog
catch [kætʃ] fangen; erwischen
cathedral [kə'θi:drəl] Kathedrale, Dom
Catholic ['kæθlɪk] **1.** Katholik/in; **2.** katholisch
cattle *(pl.)* ['kætl] Rindvieh, Rinder
cause [kɔ:z] **1.** verursachen; **2. a good cause** ein guter Zweck
cave [keɪv] Höhle
CD [ˌsi:'di:]**, compact disc** [ˌkɒmpækt 'dɪsk] CD
ceiling ['si:lɪŋ] (Zimmer-)Decke
celebrate ['seləbreɪt] feiern; **celebration** [ˌselə'breɪʃn] (Gedenk-)Feier
cellar ['selə] Keller
Celtic ['keltɪk] Keltisch, keltisch
cent (¢) [sent] Cent *(US-Münze)*
centimetre ['sentɪmi:tə] Zentimeter
central ['sentrəl] Zentral-, Mittel-
centre ['sentə] Zentrum, Mitte
century ['sentʃərɪ] Jahrhundert
certain ['sɜ:tn] **1.** bestimmte(r, s); **2.** sicher, gewiß
chain [tʃeɪn] Kette
chair [tʃeə] Stuhl
chance [tʃɑ:ns] Gelegenheit, Chance; **take a chance** ein Risiko eingehen; es darauf ankommen lassen
change [tʃeɪndʒ] **1.** (sich) verändern; **change (into)** verändern, umwandeln (in); **change one's mind** seine Meinung ändern; **change places (with)** die Plätze tauschen (mit) *(auch im übertragenen Sinn)*; **2.** umsteigen; **3.** (Ver-)Änderung, Wechsel; **4.** Wechselgeld
channel ['tʃænl] Kanal
charity ['tʃærətɪ] wohltätige Einrichtung
cheap [tʃi:p] billig, preiswert
check [tʃek] **1.** (über)prüfen, kontrollieren; **2.** (AE) Rechnung
cheer [tʃɪə] jubeln, Beifall spenden; **cheering** ['tʃɪərɪŋ] Jubel, Beifall
chemical ['kemɪkl] Chemikalie; **chemist** ['kemɪst] (BE) Apotheker/in; Drogist/in; **chemist's** (BE) Apotheke; Drogerie
cheque (for) [tʃek] Scheck (über *eine Summe)*
chess [tʃes] Schach
chest [tʃest] Brust(korb)
chicken ['tʃɪkən] Huhn; (Brat-)Hähnchen
child [tʃaɪld], *pl.* **children** ['tʃɪldrən] Kind
chimney ['tʃɪmnɪ] Schornstein
Chinese [tʃaɪ'ni:z] **1.** Chinesisch, chinesisch; **2.** Chinese/Chinesin
chips *(pl.)* [tʃɪps] (BE) Pommes frites
chocolate ['tʃɒklət] Schokolade
choice (of) [tʃɔɪs] (Aus-)Wahl (an)
choir ['kwaɪə] Chor
choose [tʃu:z] (aus)wählen, aussuchen
Christ [kraɪst] Christus; **Christian** ['krɪstʃən] **1.** Christ/in; **2.** christlich; **Christianity** [ˌkrɪstɪ'ænətɪ] das Christentum, die Christenheit
Christmas ['krɪsməs] Weihnachten; **Christmas Day** [ˌkrɪsməs 'deɪ] der erste Weihnachtsfeiertag (25.12.); **Christmas Eve** [ˌkrɪsməs‿'i:v] Heiligabend (24.12.); **the Christmas holidays** die Weihnachtsfeiertage; (BE *auch:*) die Weihnachtsferien; **Father Christmas** der Weihnachtsmann
church [tʃɜ:tʃ] Kirche
cinema ['sɪnəmə] (*meist* BE) Kino
citizen ['sɪtɪzən] (Staats-)Bürger/in, Staatsangehörige(r)
city ['sɪtɪ] Stadt, Großstadt
civil: civil rights *(pl.)* [ˌsɪvl 'raɪts] Bürgerrechte; **civil war** [ˌsɪvl 'wɔ:] Bürgerkrieg
class [klɑ:s] **1.** (BE) Klasse(nstufe); **2.** (AE) (Unterrichts-)Stunde; **classmate** ['klɑ:smeɪt] Klassenkamerad/in, Mitschüler/in; **classroom** Klassenzimmer
classical ['klæsɪkl] klassisch
clause [klɔ:z] (Teil-, Glied-)Satz
clean [kli:n] **1.** sauber; **2.** saubermachen, reinigen
clear [klɪə] klar, deutlich; **clearly** eindeutig, klar
clever ['klevə] klug, schlau; **cleverness** Klugheit, Schlauheit
cliff [klɪf] Klippe, Fels
climate ['klaɪmət] Klima
climb [klaɪm] klettern, steigen; **climber** Bergsteiger/in
clock [klɒk] (Wand-, Stand-)Uhr
close [kləʊz] schließen, zumachen; **closed** [kləʊzd] geschlossen, zu
close [kləʊs] genau, gründlich
clothes *(pl.)* [kləʊðz, kləʊz] Kleidung(sstücke)
cloud [klaʊd] Wolke
clown [klaʊn] Clown
club [klʌb] Klub; Verein
clue [klu:] Hinweis, Anhaltspunkt

D

coach [kəʊtʃ] **1.** (Reise-)Bus; **2.** Trainer/in
coal [kəʊl] Kohle
coast [kəʊst] Küste; **on the coast** an der Küste
coat [kəʊt] Mantel
coffee ['kɒfɪ] Kaffee; **make coffee** Kaffee kochen
coin [kɔɪn] Münze
coke [kəʊk] Cola
cold [kəʊld] **1.** kalt; **be/feel cold** frieren; **2.** Kälte; **3.** Erkältung; **I've got a cold.** Ich bin erkältet.
collage [kɒ'lɑːʒ] Collage
collect [kə'lekt] **1.** sammeln; einsammeln; **2.** abholen
college ['kɒlɪdʒ] Fach-, Hochschule
collocation [ˌkɒlə'keɪʃn] Kollokation *(Wörter, die oft zusammen vorkommen)*
colon ['kəʊlən] Doppelpunkt; **semicolon** [ˌsemɪ'kəʊlən] Semikolon
colonial [kə'ləʊnɪəl] kolonial, Kolonial-; **colony** ['kɒlənɪ] Kolonie
colour ['kʌlə] Farbe
column ['kɒləm] Spalte *(auf Buchseite usw.)*
comb [kəʊm] **1.** Kamm; **2.** kämmen
combination [ˌkɒmbɪ'neɪʃn] Kombination, Zusammenstellung; **combine (with)** [kəm'baɪn] kombinieren, verbinden (mit)
come [kʌm] kommen; **come in** hereinkommen; **Come on!** Los! Komm schon! **come true** Wirklichkeit werden, wahr werden
comfortable ['kʌmftəbl] bequem, behaglich
comic ['kɒmɪk] Comic-Heft
comma ['kɒmə] Komma
comment (about/on) ['kɒment] **1.** Kommentar, Bemerkung (über/zu); **2. comment (on)** kommentieren, sich äußern (zu)
°**common** ['kɒmən]**: have sth. in common** etwas miteinander gemein haben
community [kə'mjuːnətɪ] Gemeinschaft
company ['kʌmpənɪ] Firma
compare [kəm'peə] vergleichen; **compared to** verglichen mit, im Vergleich zu; **comparison** [kəm'pærɪsn] **1.** Vergleich; **2.** Steigerung
competition [ˌkɒmpə'tɪʃn] Wettkampf, Wettbewerb
complain [kəm'pleɪn] sich beschweren, sich beklagen
complete [kəm'pliːt] **1.** vervollständigen, ergänzen; **2.** vollkommen; vollständig; **completely** völlig
comprehensive school [ˌkɒmprɪ'hensɪv] (BE) Gesamtschule
computer [kəm'pjuːtə] Computer, Rechner; **computer science** [kəmˌpjuːtə 'saɪəns] Informatik
concert ['kɒnsət] Konzert
confident ['kɒnfɪdənt] selbstbewußt, zuversichtlich
confusing [kən'fjuːzɪŋ] verwirrend
connection [kə'nekʃn] Verbindung
conquer ['kɒŋkə] erobern; besiegen
conservation [ˌkɒnsə'veɪʃn] Naturschutz, Umweltschutz; **conserve** [kən'sɜːv] erhalten, bewahren
consideration [kənˌsɪdə'reɪʃn]**: take sth. into consideration** etwas in Erwägung ziehen, etwas bedenken
context ['kɒntekst] Kontext, Zusammenhang
continent ['kɒntɪnənt] Kontinent
continue (with) [kən'tɪnjuː] fortfahren (mit), fortsetzen
contrast 1. ['kɒntrɑːst] Kontrast, Gegensatz; **2.** [kən'trɑːst] kontrastieren, gegenüberstellen
control [kən'trəʊl] **1.** Kontrolle; **2.** unter Kontrolle halten, beherrschen; kontrollieren
conversation [ˌkɒnvə'seɪʃn] Gespräch, Unterhaltung
cook [kʊk] **1.** kochen, zubereiten; **2.** Koch, Köchin; **cooker** (BE) Herd; **cookery** ['kʊkərɪ] Kochen
cool [kuːl] kühl
copy ['kɒpɪ] **1.** Kopie, Abschrift; **2.** kopieren; abschreiben
corn [kɔːn] Getreide, Korn; (AE *auch:*) Mais
corner ['kɔːnə] Ecke
cornflakes *(pl.)* ['kɔːnfleɪks] Cornflakes
Cornish ['kɔːnɪʃ] kornisch, aus/in Cornwall
correct [kə'rekt] **1.** richtig, korrekt; **2.** berichtigen, korrigieren
cost [kɒst] **1.** *(Geld)* kosten; **2.** *(sing.)* Kosten; Preis
cough [kɒf] Husten
could [kʊd] **1.** konnte(n); **2.** könnte(n)
count [kaʊnt] zählen
country ['kʌntrɪ] Land; **in the country** auf dem Land; **countryside** Landschaft, (ländliche) Gegend
county ['kaʊntɪ] Grafschaft, Verwaltungsbezirk
couple ['kʌpl]**: a couple of** (infml.) ein paar
course [kɔːs] Kurs, Lehrgang; **course work** *projektähnlicher Unterricht*; **of course** [əv 'kɔːs] natürlich, selbstverständlich
court [kɔːt] Spielfeld, Platz
cousin ['kʌzn] Vetter, Kusine
cover ['kʌvə] bedecken, zudecken; **be covered with/in** bedeckt sein mit
cow [kaʊ] Kuh; **cowboy** ['kaʊbɔɪ] Cowboy
crazy ['kreɪzɪ] verrückt
cream [kriːm] **1.** Sahne; **2.** Creme
create [krɪ'eɪt] schaffen; **creative** [krɪ'eɪtɪv] schöpferisch, kreativ; **creative writing** [krɪˌeɪtɪv 'raɪtɪŋ] schöpferisches Schreiben
credit card ['kredɪt kɑːd] Kreditkarte
cricket ['krɪkɪt] Kricket *(englisches Schlagballspiel)*
crime [kraɪm] Verbrechen
crisps [krɪsps] (BE) Kartoffelchips
cross [krɒs] überqueren; kreuzen; **pedestrian crossing** [pəˌdestrɪən 'krɒsɪŋ] (BE) Fußgängerüberweg; **crossroads** *(sing.)* ['krɒsrəʊdz] (BE) (Straßen-)Kreuzung
crowd [kraʊd] (Menschen-)Menge; **crowded** ['kraʊdɪd] überfüllt
cry [kraɪ] **1.** weinen; **2.** rufen, schreien; **3.** Schrei
culture ['kʌltʃə] Kultur
cup [kʌp] Tasse; **a cup of tea** eine Tasse Tee
cupboard ['kʌbəd] Schrank
curry ['kʌrɪ] *scharfes, mit Curry gewürztes Gericht*
curtain ['kɜːtn] Vorhang, Gardine
custom ['kʌstəm] Brauch, Sitte
customer ['kʌstəmə] Kunde/Kundin
cut [kʌt] **1.** Schnitt; Schnittwunde; **2. cut (off)** (etwas ab)schneiden; **cut down** *(Bäume)* fällen
cycle ['saɪkl] radfahren

D

Dad/dad [dæd] Vati, Papa
daily ['deɪlɪ] täglich
dance [dɑːns] **1.** tanzen; **2.** Tanz; Ball; **dancer** Tänzer/in
danger ['deɪndʒə] Gefahr; **dangerous** ['deɪndʒərəs] gefährlich
dark [dɑːk] dunkel; **darkness** ['dɑːknəs] Dunkelheit
darts [dɑːts] *britisches Pfeilwurfspiel*
dash [dæʃ] Gedankenstrich
date [deɪt] Datum
daughter ['dɔːtə] Tochter
day [deɪ] Tag; **all day** den ganzen Tag; **one day** eines Tages; **these days** heutzutage; **in those days** damals, in jenen Tagen
dead [ded] tot; **death** [deθ] Tod
Dear …, [dɪə] Liebe(r) …, **Dear Sir or Madam, …** Sehr geehrte Damen und Herren, …
death [deθ] Tod
December [dɪ'sembə] Dezember
decide [dɪ'saɪd] (sich) entscheiden, beschließen; **decision** [dɪ'sɪʒn] Entscheidung, Entschluß; **take a decision** eine Entscheidung treffen, fällen
declaration [ˌdeklə'reɪʃn] Erklärung
decorate ['dekəreɪt] renovieren *(tapezieren, streichen usw.)*
deep [diːp] tief
defeat [dɪ'fiːt] besiegen
define [dɪ'faɪn] definieren, festlegen; **defining** definierend, bestimmend
deliver [dɪ'lɪvə] **1.** liefern; **2.** *(Zeitungen)* austragen, zustellen
°**deny** [dɪ'naɪ] leugnen, bestreiten

D

depart (from) [dɪ'pɑ:t] abfahren, abreisen (von, aus); **departure** [dɪ'pɑ:tʃə] Abfahrt, Abreise

department store [dɪ'pɑ:tmənt stɔ:] Kaufhaus

departure [dɪ'pɑ:tʃə] Abfahrt, Abreise

derelict ['derəlɪkt] verlassen und verfallen, heruntergekommen

describe [dɪ'skraɪb] beschreiben

desert ['dezət] Wüste

desk [desk] Schreibtisch, Schülertisch; **desk-top publishing** [ˌdesktɒp 'pʌblɪʃɪŋ], **DTP** [ˌdi:ti:'pi:] DTP *(Erstellung und Gestaltung von Druckschriften mittels Computer)*

destroy [dɪ'strɔɪ] zerstören, vernichten

detached [dɪ'tætʃt]**: detached house** (BE) freistehendes Haus; **semi-detached house** ['semɪdɪˌtætʃt] (BE) Doppelhaushälfte

detail ['di:teɪl] Einzelheit, Detail

develop [dɪ'veləp] (sich) entwickeln; aufbauen; **developing country** [dɪ'veləpɪŋ ˌkʌntrɪ] Entwicklungsland; **development** [dɪ'veləpmənt] Entwicklung; Aufbau, Ausbau

diagram ['daɪəgræm] Diagramm, Schaubild

dial ['daɪəl] wählen *(beim Telefonieren)*

dialect ['daɪəlekt] Dialekt, Mundart

dialogue ['daɪəlɒg] Dialog

diary ['daɪərɪ] **1.** Tagebuch; **2.** Notizbuch, Taschenkalender

dictionary ['dɪkʃənrɪ] Wörterbuch

die (of) [daɪ] sterben (an)

diet ['daɪət] Ernährung, Eßgewohnheit; Diät; **be on a diet** eine Diät machen

difference ['dɪfrəns] Unterschied; **different (from)** ['dɪfrənt] verschieden, andere(r, s); anders (als)

difficult ['dɪfɪkəlt] schwierig; **difficulty** ['dɪfɪkəltɪ] Schwierigkeit

dime [daɪm] (AE) Zehncentmünze

diner ['daɪnə] (AE) (kleines, billiges) Restaurant

dining-room ['daɪnɪŋ ru:m] Eßzimmer

dinner ['dɪnə] Mittag-, Abendessen

direct [dɪ'rekt, daɪ'rekt] direkt, unmittelbar

dirt [dɜ:t] Schmutz, Dreck; **dirty** schmutzig, dreckig

disadvantage [ˌdɪsəd'vɑ:ntɪdʒ] Nachteil

disappointed [ˌdɪsə'pɔɪntɪd] enttäuscht

disaster [dɪ'zɑ:stə] Katastrophe, Desaster

disco ['dɪskəʊ] Disko(thek)

discover [dɪ'skʌvə] entdecken; **discovery** [dɪ'skʌvərɪ] Entdeckung

discuss [dɪ'skʌs] etwas besprechen, über etwas diskutieren; **discussion** [dɪ'skʌʃn] Diskussion, Besprechung

dishes ['dɪʃɪz]**: wash the dishes** (das Geschirr) spülen, abwaschen

disk [dɪsk] Diskette

dislike [dɪs'laɪk] **1.** nicht gern haben, nicht mögen; **2. dislike (of, for)** Abneigung (gegen)

display [dɪ'spleɪ]**: wall display** Wandzeitung, Wandbild

distance ['dɪstəns] Entfernung, Strecke

district ['dɪstrɪkt] Gebiet, Bezirk

divide (into) [dɪ'vaɪd] (auf)teilen (in)

divorced [dɪ'vɔ:st] geschieden; **get divorced** sich scheiden lassen

DIY [ˌdi:‿aɪ'waɪ] (BE)**, Do it yourself** Heimwerken

do [du:] tun, machen

doctor ['dɒktə] Arzt/Ärztin

dog [dɒg] Hund

dollar ($) ['dɒlə] Dollar

door [dɔ:] Tür; **front door** [ˌfrʌnt 'dɔ:] Haustür

double ['dʌbl] Doppel-; doppelt

doubt [daʊt] Zweifel

down [daʊn] hinunter, herunter; **down there** da unten; **upside down** [ˌʌpsaɪd 'daʊn] verkehrt herum, auf dem Kopf; **downstairs** [ˌdaʊn'steəz] unten (im Haus); nach unten, (die Treppe) hinunter

Dr = Doctor ['dɒktə] Dr. = Doktor

drama ['drɑ:mə] Drama, Schauspiel(kunst)

draw [drɔ:] **1.** zeichnen; **2.** ziehen

dream [dri:m] **1.** Traum; **2.** träumen; **dreamer** Träumer/in

dress [dres] Kleid

drink [drɪŋk] **1.** trinken; **2.** Getränk; **drinkable** trinkbar

drive [draɪv] *(ein Auto/einen Bus usw.)* fahren; **drive-in restaurant** ['draɪvɪn 'restərɒnt] *(meist* AE) *Schnellimbiß, wo Kunden im Auto bedient werden*; **driver** Fahrer/in; **driving licence** (BE)**/driver's license** (AE) ['laɪsəns] Führerschein

drop [drɒp] **1.** fallen lassen; **2.** *(Schulfach)* abwählen, abgeben; **3.** weglassen, auslassen

drummer ['drʌmə] Schlagzeuger/in

dry [draɪ] **1.** (ab)trocknen; **2.** trocken

during *(prep.)* ['djʊərɪŋ] während

E

each [i:tʃ] jede(r, s) einzelne; **each other** einander, sich (gegenseitig)

ear [ɪə] Ohr; **earache** ['ɪəreɪk] Ohrenschmerzen

early ['ɜ:lɪ] früh, zu früh

earn [ɜ:n] *(Geld)* verdienen

earth [ɜ:θ] Erde; **on earth** auf der Erde; **earthquake** ['ɜ:θkweɪk] Erdbeben

east [i:st] **1.** Osten; **2.** nach Osten; **3. east (of)** östlich (von); **eastern** ['i:stən] Ost-, östlich

Easter ['i:stə] Ostern; **at Easter** zu/an Ostern

easy ['i:zɪ] einfach, leicht

eat [i:t] essen

°**economic** [ˌi:kə'nɒmɪk] ökonomisch, wirtschaftlich; **economy** [ɪ'kɒnəmɪ] (Volks-)Wirtschaft

educate ['edjʊkeɪt] (aus)bilden, schulen; erziehen; **education** [ˌedjʊ'keɪʃn] (Schul-, Aus-)Bildung; Erziehung

effect [ɪ'fekt] (Aus-)Wirkung

e.g. [ˌi:'dʒi:] *(from Latin "exempli gratia")* z.B. (= zum Beispiel)

egg [eg] Ei

either ['aɪðə, 'i:ðə]**: not ... either** auch nicht; auch kein

electricity [ɪˌlek'trɪsətɪ] Strom, Elektrizität

electronics *(sing.)* [ɪˌlek'trɒnɪks] Elektronik

elephant ['elɪfənt] Elefant

else [els]**: anybody/anything/anywhere else?** sonst (noch) jemand/etwas/(irgend)wo? **somebody/something/somewhere else** jemand anderes/etwas anderes/woanders; **who/what/where/why/... else?** wer/was/wo/warum/... sonst (noch)?

embarrassing [ɪm'bærəsɪŋ] peinlich, beschämend

emperor ['empərə] Kaiser

empire ['empaɪə] Reich

empty ['emptɪ] leer

end [end] **1.** Ende; **at the end (of)** am Ende (von); **in the end** schließlich, am Ende, zum Schluß; **2. end (in)** enden (auf, mit); beenden; **ending** Ende, (Ab-)Schluß; Endung

energy ['enədʒɪ] Energie; Ausdauer

engine ['endʒɪn] Motor, Maschine

England ['ɪŋglənd] England; **English** ['ɪŋglɪʃ] **1.** Englisch; englisch; **2.** Engländer/in; **Englishman/Englishwoman** Engländer/in

enjoy [ɪn'dʒɔɪ] genießen; **enjoy doing sth.** etwas gern tun; **enjoy oneself** viel Spaß haben, sich amüsieren; **enjoyable** [ɪn'dʒɔɪəbl] unterhaltsam, nett

enough [ɪ'nʌf] genug

entrance (to) ['entrəns] Eingang (zu); **entrance fee** ['entrəns fi:] Eintritt(sgeld)

envelope ['envələʊp] Briefumschlag

environment [ɪn'vaɪrənmənt] Umwelt; **environment-friendly** umweltfreundlich

equipment [ɪ'kwɪpmənt] Ausrüstung

escape (from) [ɪ'skeɪp] entkommen, fliehen (aus)

especially [ɪ'speʃlɪ] besonders, insbesondere

etc. (= et cetera, etcetera) [et'setrə] usw.

ethnic ['eθnɪk] ethnisch; Volks-

European [ˌjʊərə'pi:ən] **1.** Europäer/in; **2.** europäisch; **European Community (EC)** [kə'mju:nətɪ] Europäische Gemeinschaft (EG)

even ['i:vn] sogar, selbst; **not even** nicht einmal; **even if** selbst wenn
evening ['i:vnɪŋ] Abend; **in the evening(s)** am Abend, abends; **on the first evening** am ersten Abend; **this evening** heute abend
event [ɪ'vent] Ereignis
ever ['evə] je, jemals, schon mal; **the worst fight ever** der härteste Kampf, den es je/bis jetzt gegeben hat
every ['evrɪ] jede(r, s); **for every 100 metres** pro 100 Meter
everybody ['evrɪbɒdɪ] jede(r), alle
everything ['evrɪθɪŋ] alles
everywhere ['evrɪweə] überall
exact [ɪg'zækt] genau; **exactly** genau
exam [ɪg'zæm] Prüfung, Examen; **do/ take an exam** eine Prüfung machen
examine [ɪg'zæmɪn] untersuchen
example [ɪg'zɑ:mpl] Beispiel; **for example (e.g.)** zum Beispiel (z.B.)
except [ɪk'sept] außer, bis auf
exchange [ɪks'tʃeɪndʒ] **1.** Austausch, Umtausch; **2.** (aus)tauschen; **exchange for** umtauschen, eintauschen gegen
excited (about) [ɪk'saɪtɪd] aufgeregt, freudig erregt (wegen); **exciting** aufregend, spannend
exclamation mark [ˌekskləˈmeɪʃn mɑ:k] Ausrufezeichen
excuse 1. [ɪk'skju:s] Entschuldigung; Ausrede; **2. Excuse me.** [ɪk'skju:z mi:] Entschuldigung. Darf ich Sie mal stören?
execute ['eksɪkju:t] hinrichten; **execution** [ˌeksɪ'kju:ʃn] Hinrichtung
exercise ['eksəsaɪz] Übung
expect [ɪk'spekt] erwarten; annehmen
expensive [ɪk'spensɪv] teuer
experience [ɪk'spɪərɪəns] Erfahrung, Erlebnis; **be experienced (in)** erfahren sein (in); Erfahrung haben (mit)
expert ['ekspɜ:t] Fachmann/Fachfrau, Experte/Expertin
explain [ɪk'spleɪn] erklären, erläutern
explosion [ɪk'spləʊʒn] Explosion, Knall
export 1. ['ekspɔ:t] Ausfuhr, Export; **2.** [ɪk'spɔ:t] ausführen, exportieren
express [ɪk'spres] ausdrücken, äußern; **expression** [ɪk'spreʃn] Ausdruck
eye [aɪ] Auge

F

face [feɪs] Gesicht
fact [fækt] Tatsache; **in fact** eigentlich, genau gesagt; in Wirklichkeit
factory ['fæktrɪ] Fabrik
fail (an exam) [feɪl] (eine Prüfung) nicht bestehen, durchfallen
fair [feə] gerecht, fair
faithfully ['feɪθfəlɪ]**: Yours faithfully, ...** Mit freundlichen Grüßen; Hochachtungsvoll
fall [fɔ:l] (hin)fallen; **fall in love with sb.** sich in jn. verlieben; **fall over** umfallen, hinfallen
fall [fɔ:l] (AE) Herbst
false [fɒls, fɔ:ls] falsch, unecht
family ['fæmlɪ] Familie
famous ['feɪməs] berühmt
fan [fæn] Fan, begeisterte(r) Anhänger/in
fantastic [fæn'tæstɪk] fantastisch
far [fɑ:] weit; **so far** bis jetzt, bisher
fare [feə] Fahrgeld, Fahrpreis
farm [fɑ:m] Bauernhof, Farm; **farmer** Bauer/Bäuerin; Farmer/in
farther ['fɑ:ðə] weiter (entfernt)
fascinated ['fæsəneɪtɪd] fasziniert, begeistert
fashion ['fæʃn] Mode
fast [fɑ:st] schnell; **fast-food restaurant** ['fɑ:stˌfu:d 'restərɒnt] Schnellrestaurant, Schnellimbiß
fat [fæt] **1.** Fett; **2.** dick, fett
father ['fɑ:ðə] Vater; **Father Christmas** [ˌfɑ:ðə 'krɪsməs] der Weihnachtsmann
fault [fɒlt, fɔ:lt] Schuld, Fehler
favourite ['feɪvrət] Lieblings-
fax [fæks] Telefax; Telefaxgerät
fear (of) [fɪə] Angst, Furcht (vor)
February ['febrʊərɪ] Februar
fed up [ˌfed‿'ʌp]**: be/get fed up (with)** die Nase voll haben (von), etwas satt haben
federal ['fedərəl] Bundes-; **federal holiday** [ˌfedərəl 'hɒlədeɪ] (AE) Feiertag *(, an dem alle Bundesbehörden geschlossen sind)*
fee [fi:] Gebühr, Beitrag; **entrance fee** ['entrəns fi:] Eintritt(sgeld)
feed [fi:d] füttern
feel [fi:l] fühlen, sich fühlen; empfinden, meinen; **I feel sick.** Mir ist schlecht/übel. **feeling** ['fi:lɪŋ] Gefühl
felt-tip ['felttɪp] Filzstift
female ['fi:meɪl] **1.** weibliche Person; **2.** weiblich
fence [fens] Zaun
ferry ['ferɪ] Fähre
festival ['festɪvl] Fest, Festival
fetch [fetʃ] holen
few [fju:] wenige; **a few** ein paar, einige; **in the past few years** in den vergangenen/letzten Jahren
field [fi:əld] Feld, Wiese; (Sport-)Platz
fight [faɪt] **1.** Kampf; **2.** (be)kämpfen; **fighter** Kämpfer/in
figure ['fɪgə] Figur, Gestalt
fill in [ˌfɪl‿'ɪn] **1.** einsetzen; **2.** ausfüllen *(Formular)*
film [fɪlm] Film; **filmstar** Filmstar
final ['faɪnl] letzte(r, s); endgültige(r, s); **finally** ['faɪnəlɪ] schließlich, endlich
find [faɪnd] finden; **Find out about ...** Erkundige dich über ...
fine [faɪn] gut, fein, schön; **She's fine.** Ihr geht's gut. Es geht ihr gut.
finger ['fɪŋgə] Finger
finish ['fɪnɪʃ] (be)enden; aufhören (mit)
fire ['faɪə] Feuer, Brand; **fireworks** *(pl.)* Feuerwerk(skörper)
firm [fɜ:m] Firma
first [fɜ:st] **1.** erste(r, s); **2.** zuerst, zunächst; **at first** zuerst, am Anfang; **firstly** erstens
fish, *pl.* **fish** [fɪʃ] Fisch; **go fishing** angeln gehen, fischen gehen
fit [fɪt] **1.** gesund, fit; **2.** passen; **fitness** ['fɪtnəs] Fitneß
fitter ['fɪtə] Maschinenschlosser/in, Mechaniker/in
flag [flæg] Fahne, Flagge
flame [fleɪm] Flamme
flat [flæt] **1.** flach, eben; **2.** (BE) (Miet-)Wohnung; **block of flats** (BE) (Miets-)Haus, Wohnblock
floor [flɔ:] (Fuß-)Boden
flour ['flaʊə] Mehl
flower ['flaʊə] **1.** Blume; Blüte; **2.** blühen
flu [flu:] **I've got the flu.** Ich habe die/eine Grippe.
fly [flaɪ] fliegen
fog [fɒg] Nebel; **foggy** neblig
follow ['fɒləʊ] folgen; verfolgen; **following** folgend
food [fu:d] Essen, Nahrung; Lebensmittel; Futter
fool [fu:l] Narr/Närrin, Dummkopf
foot [fʊt], *pl.* **feet** [fi:t] **1.** Fuß; **2.** *Längenmaß (= 30,48 cm)*; **football** ['fʊtbɔ:l] **1.** (BE) Fußball; **2.** (AE) amerikanischer Fußball; **footstep** ['fʊtstep] (Fuß-)Schritt
for [fɔ:, fə] für; **for a long time** lange (Zeit); **for an hour** eine Stunde (lang); seit einer Stunde; **for breakfast/ lunch/...** zum Frühstück/Mittagessen/...; **for example (e.g.)** zum Beispiel (z.B.)
foreign ['fɒrən] ausländisch, fremd
forest ['fɒrɪst] Wald, Forst
forget [fə'get] vergessen
fork [fɔ:k] Gabel
form [fɔ:m] **1.** Form; **form of transport** [ˌfɔ:m‿əv 'trænspɔ:t] Verkehrsmittel; **2.** (sich) bilden, formen; **formal** ['fɔ:ml] formell, förmlich; **formation** [fɔ:'meɪʃn] Bildung, Formung
forum ['fɔ:rəm] Forum
forward(s) ['fɔ:wəd(z)] vorwärts, nach vorn; **look forward to sth./doing sth.** sich auf etwas freuen/sich darauf freuen, etwas zu tun
fountain ['faʊntɪn] Springbrunnen
free [fri:] **1.** frei, Frei-; **2.** kostenlos
French [frentʃ] **1.** Französisch, französisch; **2.** Franzose/Französin; **French fries** [ˌfrentʃ 'fraɪz] *(meist* AE) Pommes frites
fresh [freʃ] frisch
Friday ['fraɪdɪ, 'fraɪdeɪ] Freitag
fridge [frɪdʒ] Kühlschrank
friend [frend] Freund/in; **make friends (with)** Freunde finden; sich anfreunden (mit); **friendliness** Freundlichkeit; **friendly** freundlich, nett
frightened ['fraɪtnd]**: be frightened (of)** Angst haben (vor)

D

from [frɒm, frəm] von, aus; **from now on** von jetzt an, ab jetzt; **from then on** von da an; **from … to** von … bis; **where … from** woher
front [frʌnt]: **front door** [ˌfrʌnt 'dɔː] Haustür; **in front of** vor
frontier ['frʌntɪə] Grenze
fruit [fruːt] Obst, Früchte; Frucht
full [fʊl] voll; **full stop** [ˌfʊl 'stɒp] (BE) Punkt *(Satzzeichen)*; **full time** [ˌfʊl'taɪm] Vollzeit-, ganztags
fun [fʌn] Spaß; **they're fun** sie sind lustig; es macht Spaß mit ihnen; **funny** ['fʌnɪ] lustig, komisch
function ['fʌŋkʃn] **1.** Funktion; **2.** funktionieren, fungieren
furniture *(sing.)* ['fɜːnɪtʃə] Möbel; **piece of furniture** Möbelstück
further ['fɜːðə] **1.** weiter; **2.** weitere(r, s), noch
future ['fjuːtʃə] Zukunft

G

game [geɪm] Spiel; **games** (BE) Mannschaftsspiele und Leichtathletik *(in der Regel im Freien)*
gang [gæŋ] Bande
garage ['gærɑːdʒ] Garage
garden ['gɑːdn] Garten
gas [gæs] (AE) Benzin; **gas station** (AE) Tankstelle
gate [geɪt] Tor, Pforte
GCSE [ˌdʒiːsiː_es_'iː] (BE) *etwa:* Mittlere Reife mit eingeschlossenem Hauptschulabschluß
°**generally** ['dʒenrəlɪ] im allgemeinen, im großen und ganzen
geography [dʒɪ'ɒgrəfɪ] Geographie
German ['dʒɜːmən] **1.** deutsch; Deutsch; **2.** Deutsche(r); **Germany** ['dʒɜːmənɪ] Deutschland
get [get] **1.** bekommen; **2.** besorgen, (ab)holen; **3. get angry/tired/cold/…** ärgerlich/müde/kalt/… werden; **4. get (to)** (hin)kommen, gelangen (zu/nach); **get an idea (of)** einen Eindruck/eine Vorstellung bekommen (von); sich einen Eindruck verschaffen (von); **get changed** sich umziehen; **get divorced** sich scheiden lassen; **get in(to) a car/get on a bus/train/plane** in ein Auto/einen Bus/Zug/ein Flugzeug (ein)steigen; **get married** heiraten; **get off a bus/train/plane/get out of a car** aus einem Bus/Zug/Flugzeug/Auto aussteigen; **Get out (of here).** Raus (hier)! **get to know** kennenlernen; erfahren; **get up** aufstehen
ghost [gəʊst] Geist, Gespenst
giant ['dʒaɪənt] **1.** Riese; **2.** riesig, Riesen-
girl [gɜːl] Mädchen; **girlfriend** ['gɜːlfrend] (feste) Freundin
give [gɪv] geben; schenken; **give (sth.) up** (etwas) aufgeben

glad [glæd] froh
gladiator ['glædɪeɪtə] Gladiator/in
glass [glɑːs] Glas
glasses *(pl.)* ['glɑːsɪz] (eine) Brille
glove [glʌv] Handschuh
glue [gluː] kleben
go [gəʊ] **1.** gehen, fahren; **2. go blind/red/hard/…** blind/rot/hart/… werden; **go fishing** angeln gehen, fischen gehen; **go for a ride** herumfahren, eine Spazierfahrt machen; **go for a walk** spazierengehen; **go on** weitermachen; **go to work** arbeiten gehen; **They are going to do it.** Sie werden es tun. Sie haben vor, es zu tun.
God, god [gɒd] Gott
gold [gəʊld] Gold; **golden** ['gəʊldn] golden; Gold-
golf [gɒlf] Golf
good [gʊd] gut; **good at** gut in, geschickt in; **Good afternoon.** Guten Tag. *(nachmittags)*; **Good morning.** Guten Morgen. Guten Tag. *(vormittags)*; **Goodbye.** [ˌgʊd'baɪ] Auf Wiedersehen. Tschüs.
goods *(pl.)* [gʊdz] Güter, Waren
got [gɒt]: **have got** haben, besitzen; **have got to** *(tun)* müssen
gotten ['gɒtn] (AE) *Partizip Perfekt von „to get"* (= BE „got")
government ['gʌvnmənt] Regierung
grade [greɪd] **1.** (Zeugnis-)Note, Zensur; **2.** (AE) Klasse(nstufe)
gram [græm] Gramm
grammar ['græmə] Grammatik
Gran [græn] (infml.) Oma
Grandad ['grændæd] (infml.) Opa
grand-: granddaughter ['grændɔːtə] Enkelin; **grandfather** ['grænfɑːðə] Großvater; **Grandma** ['grænmɑː] (infml.) Oma; **grandmother** ['grænmʌðə] Großmutter; **grandparents** ['grænpeərənts] Großeltern; **grandson** ['grænsʌn] Enkel
grass [grɑːs] Gras
grateful ['greɪtfəl]: **be grateful (to sb.)** (jm.) dankbar sein
grave [greɪv] Grab
great [greɪt] **1.** groß, beträchtlich; **2.** großartig, super, klasse; **3.** bedeutend, berühmt; **Great Britain** [ˌgreɪt 'brɪtn] Großbritannien
green [griːn] grün
greet [griːt] (be)grüßen
grey [greɪ] grau
grill [grɪl] grillen
grizzly bear ['grɪzlɪ ˌbeə] Grizzly(bär)
ground [graʊnd] (Erd-)Boden
group [gruːp] Gruppe
grow [grəʊ] **1.** wachsen; **2.** anbauen, anpflanzen
guard dog ['gɑːd dɒg] Wachhund
guess [ges] (er)raten
guest [gest] Gast; **guest house** ['gest haʊs] Pension
guide [gaɪd] (Fremden-)Führer/in; **guide-book** ['gaɪdbʊk] Reiseführer, Stadtführer

guitar [gɪ'tɑː] Gitarre
guy [gaɪ] (infml.) Typ, Kerl
gym [dʒɪm] Sport-, Turnhalle; **gymnastics** [dʒɪm'næstɪks] Gymnastik, Turnen

H

hair *(sing.)* [heə] Haar, Haare
half [hɑːf], *pl.* **halves** [hɑːvz] Hälfte; **one and a half** eineinhalb, anderthalb; **half a …** ein(e) halbe(r, s) …; **half past eight** [ˌhɑːf pɑːst_'eɪt] halb neun (8.30/20.30); **half the …** der/die/das halbe …
hall [hɔːl] Saal, Halle; Flur, Diele
Hallo. [hə'ləʊ] (Guten) Tag. Hallo. **Say hallo to … .** Grüß(t) … (von mir).
hamburger ['hæmbɜːgə] Hamburger
hamster ['hæmstə] Hamster
hand [hænd] **1.** Hand; **2. hand sb. sth.** jm. etwas (über)geben
°**handicapped** ['hændɪkæpt] *(körperlich, geistig)* behindert
hang [hæŋ] (auf)hängen
happen (to) ['hæpən] geschehen, passieren (mit)
happiness ['hæpɪnəs] Zufriedenheit, Glück; **happy** ['hæpɪ] glücklich, froh
harbour ['hɑːbə] Hafen
hard *(adj.; adv.)* [hɑːd] hart; schwer; **hardly** kaum
hat [hæt] Hut
hate [heɪt] hassen, gar nicht mögen; **hate doing sth.** etwas sehr ungern tun
have [hæv] haben; **have a bath** baden, ein Bad nehmen; **have a coke/a hamburger** eine Cola trinken/einen Hamburger essen; **have a party** eine Party feiern; **have a race** ein Rennen veranstalten; **have breakfast/tea/…** frühstücken/Abendbrot/… essen; **have got** haben, besitzen; **have got to** *(tun)* müssen; **have to** *(tun)* müssen
he [hiː] er
head [hed] Kopf; **headache** ['hedeɪk] Kopfschmerz(en); **headteacher** [ˌhed'tiːtʃə] (BE) Schuldirektor/in
healthy ['helθɪ] gesund
hear [hɪə] hören; **hear of** hören von
heart [hɑːt] Herz
heat [hiːt] Hitze; **heating** Heizung
heavy ['hevɪ] schwer
height [haɪt] Höhe, Größe
helicopter ['helɪkɒptə] Hubschrauber; **heliport** ['helɪpɔːt] Hubschrauberlandeplatz, Heliport
help (with) [help] **1.** Hilfe (bei); **2.** helfen (bei); **helper** Helfer/in
her [hɜː, hə] **1.** sie, ihr; **2.** *(poss. adj.)* ihr(e); **hers** *(poss. pron.)* ihre(r, s); **herself** [hɜː'self] sich (selbst)
here [hɪə] hier
hero, *pl.* **heroes** ['hɪərəʊ] Held/in
hide (from) [haɪd] (sich) verstecken (vor)

D

high [haɪ] hoch; **high school** (AE) Oberschule; **highly** ['haɪlɪ] höchst, sehr, hoch-; **highway** (AE) Autobahn
hill [hɪl] Hügel, Berg
him [hɪm] ihn, ihm; **himself** [hɪm'self] sich (selbst)
hire ['haɪə] (*meist* BE) *(Auto, Boot usw.)* mieten, leihen *(gegen Gebühr)*
his [hɪz] **1.** *(poss. adj.)* sein(e); **2.** *(poss. pron.)* seine(r, s)
Hispanic [hɪ'spænɪk] **1.** Hispano-Amerikaner/in; **2.** hispanisch
historical [hɪ'stɒrɪkl] historisch; **history** ['hɪstrɪ] Geschichte
hit [hɪt] **1.** Hit; **2.** schlagen, treffen; **hit the water** aufs Wasser aufschlagen
hobby ['hɒbɪ] Hobby, Freizeitbeschäftigung
hockey ['hɒkɪ] Hockey
hold [həʊld] **1.** (fest)halten; **2.** *(eine Veranstaltung)* abhalten; **hold out one's hand to sb.** jm. die Hand entgegenstrecken; **hold up** hochhalten
hole [həʊl] Loch
holiday ['hɒlədeɪ] **1.** Feiertag; **2.** (BE) Urlaub, Ferien; **on holiday** in Urlaub; **be/go on holiday** Urlaub machen; **holiday home** Ferienwohnung
home [həʊm] **1.** Heim, Zuhause; **2.** nach Hause, heim; **at home** zu Hause, daheim; **holiday home** Ferienwohnung; **home economics** [ˌhəʊm‿iːkə'nɒmɪks] Hauswirtschaft(slehre); **home-made** [ˌhəʊm'meɪd] selbstgemacht; **home town** Heimatstadt; **homeless** obdachlos; **homework** *(sing.)* ['həʊmwɜːk] Hausaufgaben
honest ['ɒnɪst] ehrlich
hope [həʊp] **1.** Hoffnung; **2. hope for** hoffen auf
horrified ['hɒrɪfaɪd] entsetzt
horse [hɔːs] Pferd
hospital ['hɒspɪtl] Krankenhaus; **in hospital** im Krankenhaus
hostel: youth hostel ['juːθ hɒstl] Jugendherberge
hot [hɒt] **1.** heiß; warm *(Mahlzeit, Wasser)*; **2.** scharf gewürzt
hotel [həʊ'tel] Hotel
hour ['aʊə] Stunde
house [haʊs] Haus; **housework** ['haʊswɜːk] Haus(halts)arbeit
how [haʊ] wie; **How are you?** Wie geht es dir? **How do you like …?** Wie gefällt dir …? Wie findest du …? **How many?** Wie viele? **How much?** Wieviel? **How much is/are …?** Was kostet/kosten …?
however [haʊ'evə] **1.** jedoch, aber; **2.** wie (auch) immer
huge [hjuːdʒ] sehr groß, riesig
human ['hjuːmən] menschlich
humour ['hjuːmə]**: a sense of humour** [ˌsens‿əv 'hjuːmə] (Sinn für) Humor
hunger ['hʌŋgə] Hunger; **hungry** ['hʌŋgrɪ] hungrig; **I'm hungry.** Ich habe Hunger.
hunt [hʌnt] jagen; **hunter** Jäger/in
hurt [hɜːt] verletzen, weh tun
husband ['hʌzbənd] (Ehe-)Mann
hyphen ['haɪfn] Bindestrich

I

I [aɪ] ich
ice [aɪs] Eis; **ice-cream** [ˌaɪs'kriːm] (Speise-)Eis; **ice-cream parlor** ['pɑːlə] (AE) Eisdiele; **icy** eisig, vereist
idea [aɪ'dɪə] Idee, Einfall; Vorstellung
i.e. [ˌaɪ‿'iː] *(from Latin "id est")* **(= that is)** d.h. (= das heißt)
if [ɪf] **1.** ob; **as if** als ob; **2.** wenn, falls; **even if** selbst wenn
ill [ɪl]**: be ill** krank sein; **illness** Krankheit
illegal [ɪ'liːgl] ungesetzlich, illegal
illustration [ˌɪlə'streɪʃn] Bild, Abbildung, Illustration
imagine [ɪ'mædʒɪn] sich *(gedanklich)* vorstellen
immigrant ['ɪmɪgrənt] Einwanderer/Einwanderin; **immigration** [ˌɪmɪ'greɪʃn] Einwanderung, Immigration
impatient [ɪm'peɪʃnt] ungeduldig
impolite [ˌɪmpə'laɪt] unhöflich; **impoliteness** Unhöflichkeit
important [ɪm'pɔːtnt] wichtig
impossible [ɪm'pɒsəbl] unmöglich
impression [ɪm'preʃn] Eindruck
impulse buyer ['ɪmpʌls ˌbaɪə] „Spontankäufer/in"
in [ɪn] in; **one in ten** jede(r, s) zehnte, eine(r, s) von zehn; **in English** auf englisch; **in fifty years (from now)** in fünfzig Jahren; **in front of** vor; **in such a way (that)** so, dergestalt (, daß); **in the country** auf dem Land; **in the morning(s)/afternoon(s)/evening(s)** am Morgen/Nachmittag/Abend; morgens/nachmittags/abends; **in the picture** auf dem Bild, auf dem Foto; **in the sky** am Himmel; **in the world** auf der (ganzen) Welt; **in this weather** bei diesem Wetter
include [ɪn'kluːd] beinhalten, (mit) einschließen, enthalten
independence (from) [ˌɪndɪ'pendəns] Unabhängigkeit (von); **independent (of)** [ˌɪndɪ'pendənt] unabhängig (von)
Indian ['ɪndɪən] **1.** Inder/in; indisch; **2.** Indianer/in; indianisch
industrial [ɪn'dʌstrɪəl] industriell; Industrie-; **industry** ['ɪndəstrɪ] Industrie, Industriezweig
influence ['ɪnflʊəns] Einfluß
inform [ɪn'fɔːm] informieren, benachrichtigen; **information** *(sing.)* [ˌɪnfə'meɪʃn] Information(en); Auskunft, Auskünfte
informal [ɪn'fɔːml] informell, nicht förmlich
°**injured** ['ɪndʒəd]**: get injured** sich verletzen, verletzt werden
°**ink** [ɪŋk] Tinte
inside [ˌɪn'saɪd] **1.** innerhalb (von); **2.** (nach) drinnen
instead [ɪn'sted] statt dessen; **instead of** (an)statt, an Stelle von
instinct ['ɪnstɪŋkt] Instinkt
instructor [ɪn'strʌktə] Ausbilder/in, Lehrer/in
instrument ['ɪnstrəmənt] Instrument
interested (in) ['ɪntrəstɪd] interessiert (an); **interesting** ['ɪntrəstɪŋ] interessant
international [ˌɪntə'næʃnəl] international
intersection [ˌɪntə'sekʃn] (*meist* AE) (Straßen-)Kreuzung
interview ['ɪntəvjuː] **1.** Interview; **2.** befragen, interviewen; **interviewer** ['ɪntəvjuːə] Interviewer/in
into ['ɪntuː, 'ɪntʊ, 'ɪntə] in (… hinein)
introduce [ˌɪntrə'djuːs] einführen; vorstellen, bekanntmachen; **introduction** [ˌɪntrə'dʌkʃn] Einführung, Einleitung; **introductory** [ˌɪntrə'dʌktərɪ] einleitend, Einführungs-
invade [ɪn'veɪd] einmarschieren in, einfallen in
invention [ɪn'venʃn] Erfindung
invitation [ˌɪnvɪ'teɪʃn] Einladung; **invite** [ɪn'vaɪt] *(Gäste)* einladen
Irish ['aɪrɪʃ] irisch, Irisch
iron ['aɪən] Eisen
irregular [ɪ'regjʊlə] unregelmäßig
island ['aɪlənd] Insel
it [ɪt] es; *(bei Sachen und Tieren auch:)* er, sie; **its 1.** *(poss. adj.)* sein(e), ihr(e); **2.** *(poss. pron.)* seine(r, s), ihre(r, s); **itself** [ɪt'self] sich (selbst)
Italian [ɪ'tæljən] **1.** Italienisch, italienisch; **2.** Italiener/in

J

jacket ['dʒækɪt] Jacke, Jacket, Sakko
jam: traffic jam ['træfɪk dʒæm] (Verkehrs-)Stau
January ['dʒænjʊərɪ] Januar
jazz [dʒæz] Jazz(musik)
jeans *(pl.)* [dʒiːnz] Jeans
job [dʒɒb] **1.** Arbeit(sstelle), Beruf; **2.** Aufgabe
joke [dʒəʊk] **1.** Witz, Scherz; **2.** scherzen, witzeln
journey ['dʒɜːnɪ] Reise, Fahrt
judge [dʒʌdʒ] Richter/in
judo ['dʒuːdəʊ] Judo
juice [dʒuːs] Saft; **juicy** saftig
July [dʒuː'laɪ] Juli
jump [dʒʌmp] springen
June [dʒuːn] Juni
juniors ['dʒuːnjəz] (BE) Junioren(mannschaft)
just [dʒʌst, dʒəst] **1.** bloß, nur; **2.** einfach; **3.** gerade (jetzt); **just as tired** genauso müde; **just as well** genausogut; **just like** genau wie; **just over a pound** knapp über ein Pfund; **just round the corner** gleich um die Ecke

K

keep [ki:p] **1.** behalten; **2.** halten *(Tiere)*; **3.** aufbewahren; **keep a diary** Tagebuch führen; **keep a promise** ein Versprechen halten; **keep alive** am Leben (er)halten; **keep an eye on sb./sth.** auf jn./etwas aufpassen; **keep sb. off sth.** jn. von etwas fernhalten; **keep sb. out** jn. draußen halten
ketchup ['ketʃəp] Ketchup
key [ki:] Schlüssel; **key word** Schlüsselwort
kid [kɪd] (infml.) Kind; Jugendliche(r)
kidney ['kɪdnɪ] Niere; **kidney machine** Dialyseapparat zur Blutwäsche, künstliche Niere
kill [kɪl] töten
kilo ['ki:ləʊ] Kilo(gramm)
kilometre (km) ['kɪləmi:tə] Kilometer (km)
kind [kaɪnd] **1.** freundlich, gütig, nett; **2. kind (of)** Art
king [kɪŋ] König; **kingdom** ['kɪŋdəm] Königreich
kiss [kɪs] **1.** Kuß; **2.** küssen
kitchen ['kɪtʃn] Küche
knee [ni:] Knie
knife [naɪf], *pl.* **knives** [naɪvz] Messer
know [nəʊ] wissen; kennen; **get to know** kennenlernen; erfahren; **you know** weißt du, nämlich; **known** bekannt

L

label ['leɪbl] Etikett
lake [leɪk] (Binnen-)See
lamp [læmp] Lampe
land [lænd] **1.** Land, Grund und Boden; **2.** landen, anlegen; **landowner** ['lændəʊnə] Grundbesitzer/in; **landscape** ['lændskeɪp] Landschaft, Landschaftsbild
language ['læŋgwɪdʒ] Sprache
large [lɑ:dʒ] groß, umfangreich
last [lɑ:st] **1.** (an-, fort)dauern; **2.** letzte(r, s); **3.** vorige(r, s); **last night** gestern abend; letzte Nacht; **at last** schließlich, endlich
late [leɪt] **1.** spät; **2. late (for)** zu spät, verspätet (für/zu); **lately** ['leɪtlɪ] in letzter Zeit; **latest** ['leɪtɪst] letzte(r, s), neueste(r, s); **sooner or later** früher oder später
Latin ['lætɪn] Latein, lateinisch
laugh (at) [lɑ:f] lachen (über); *(jn.)* auslachen
law [lɔ:] Gesetz
laziness ['leɪzɪnəs] Faulheit; **lazy** ['leɪzɪ] faul, träge; **lazybones** *(sing.)* ['leɪzɪbəʊnz] (infml.) Faulpelz
lead (to) [li:d] führen, leiten (zu/nach); **leader** ['li:də] Leiter/in
learn [lɜ:n] lernen; **learner** Lerner/in
leave [li:v] **1.** verlassen; **2.** weggehen, abfahren; **3.** (zurück)lassen, liegen/stehen lassen; **leave out** auslassen, nicht berücksichtigen; **leave sb. alone** jn. in Ruhe lassen; **leave school** (BE) von der Schule abgehen
left [left] linke(r, s), nach links; **on the left** links, auf der linken Seite
leg [leg] Bein
legal ['li:gl] gesetzlich, legal
legend ['ledʒənd] Legende, Sage
lemonade [ˌlemə'neɪd] Limonade
less [les] weniger
lesson ['lesn] *(meist* BE) (Unterrichts-)Stunde; **lessons** Unterricht
let [let]**: Let's … = Let us …** Laß(t) uns …/Lassen Sie uns …
letter ['letə] **1.** Buchstabe; **2.** Brief; **letter box** (BE) Briefkasten
library ['laɪbrərɪ] Bücherei, Bibliothek
licence (BE)**/license** (AE) ['laɪsəns]**: driving licence** (BE)**/driver's license** (AE) Führerschein
lie [laɪ] liegen
life [laɪf], *pl.* **lives** [laɪvz] (das) Leben
lift [lɪft] (hoch)heben
light [laɪt] **1.** leicht; **2.** Licht, Lampe; **traffic lights** *(pl.)* ['træfɪk laɪts] (Verkehrs-)Ampel
like [laɪk] **1.** (ähnlich) wie; **like this** so, auf diese Weise; folgendermaßen; **2.** (gern) mögen, gern haben; **like doing sth.** etwas gern tun; **How do you like …?** Wie gefällt dir …? Wie findest du …? **I'd like = I would like** ich möchte (gern), ich hätte gern
limit: speed limit ['spi:d ˌlɪmɪt] Geschwindigkeitsbeschränkung
line [laɪn] **1.** Zeile; **2.** Linie
liquid: washing liquid ['wɒʃɪŋ ˌlɪkwɪd] (BE) flüssiges Waschmittel
list [lɪst] Liste, Verzeichnis
listen (to sb./sth.) ['lɪsn] (jm.) zuhören; (sich etwas) anhören; horchen; **listener** Zuhörer/in
little ['lɪtl] klein; **(a) little** (ein) wenig
live [laɪv] live, direkt
live [lɪv] leben, wohnen; **living-room** ['lɪvɪŋ ru:m] Wohnzimmer
local ['ləʊkl] örtlich, Lokal-, am Ort
loneliness ['ləʊnlɪnəs] Einsamkeit; **lonely** ['ləʊnlɪ] einsam, verlassen
long [lɒŋ] lang; **no longer** nicht mehr, nicht länger
look [lʊk] **1.** aussehen; **look (at)** (an)sehen, (an)schauen; **look after** sich kümmern um; **look for** suchen; **look forward to** sich freuen auf; **look up** *(ein Wort)* nachschlagen; **2.** Blick
lorry ['lɒrɪ] (BE) Lastwagen, LKW
lose [lu:z] verlieren; °**lose one's way** sich verirren, sich verlaufen; **loser** Verlierer/in; **lost** [lɒst] verloren
lot [lɒt]**: a lot (of)/lots (of)** viele, viel
lot [lɒt]**: parking lot** (AE) (großer) Parkplatz
loud [laʊd] laut
lovable ['lʌvəbl] liebenswert
love [lʌv] **1.** lieben, sehr mögen, sehr gern haben; **love doing sth.** etwas sehr gern tun; **2.** Liebe; **fall in love with sb.** sich in jn. verlieben; **Love, …** Viele liebe Grüße von …; **love** mein Lieber/meine Liebe *(informelle Anrede)*; **lovable** liebenswert; **lovely** schön, herrlich, hübsch
low [ləʊ] niedrig
luck [lʌk] Glück; **Good luck.** Viel Glück! **be lucky** ['lʌkɪ] Glück haben; **lucky boy/girl/…** Glückspilz
luggage ['lʌgɪdʒ] Gepäck
lunch [lʌntʃ] Mittagessen; **for lunch** zum Mittagessen; **lunch hour** ['lʌntʃ‿ˌaʊə] Mittagspause; **lunchtime** Mittagspause; **at lunchtime** mittags, in der Mittagspause

M

machine [mə'ʃi:n] Maschine, Apparat, Gerät
Madam, madam ['mædəm] meine Dame *(höfliche Anrede)*
magazine [ˌmægə'zi:n] Zeitschrift
magician [mə'dʒɪʃn] Zauberer/Zauberin
mail [meɪl] *(meist* AE) **1.** *(Brief)* abschicken, einwerfen; *(Paket)* aufgeben; **2.** Post(sendungen); **airmail** ['eəmeɪl] Luftpost
main [meɪn] Haupt-
majority [mə'dʒɒrətɪ] Mehrheit
make [meɪk] machen, zubereiten; bilden; **make coffee/soup** Kaffee/Suppe kochen; **make friends (with)** Freunde finden; sich anfreunden (mit); **make sth. sth.** etwas zu etwas machen; **make sure** sicherstellen, sichergehen; dafür sorgen *(, daß)*; **make up** sich ausdenken
male [meɪl] **1.** männliche Person; **2.** männlich
man [mæn], *pl.* **men** [men] Mann; **man-made** [ˌmæn'meɪd] künstlich
manager ['mænɪdʒə] Geschäftsführer/in
many ['menɪ] viele; **How many?** Wie viele?
map [mæp] Stadtplan, Landkarte
March [mɑ:tʃ] März
mark [mɑ:k] Note, Zensur
market ['mɑ:kɪt] Markt
married ['mærɪd] verheiratet; **get married** heiraten
match [mætʃ] **1.** Spiel, Wettkampf; **2.** passen zu; zusammenpassen
mate [meɪt] (BE; infml.) Kumpel
math [mæθ] (AE)**/maths** [mæθs] (BE) Mathe(matik)
matter ['mætə]**: It doesn't matter.** Das macht nichts. **What's the matter?** Was ist los?
may [meɪ] dürfen; **it may be** es kann sein, es ist vielleicht

D

May [meɪ] Mai
maybe ['meɪbɪ] vielleicht
me [miː] mich, mir; **it wasn't me** ich war es nicht
meal [miːl] Mahlzeit, Essen
mean [miːn] **1.** bedeuten; **2.** meinen (= sagen wollen); **meaning** ['miːnɪŋ] Bedeutung
meat [miːt] Fleisch
medicine ['medsn] Medizin, Arznei
meet [miːt] sich treffen; *(jn.)* treffen; *(jn.)* kennenlernen; **meeting** ['miːtɪŋ] Besprechung; Treffen, Versammlung
melt [melt] schmelzen
member (of) ['membə] Mitglied (von, in)
memorial [mɪ'mɔːrɪəl] Denkmal, Gedenkstätte
memory ['memərɪ] Gedächtnis
menu ['menjuː] Speisekarte
merry: Merry Christmas! [ˌmerɪ 'krɪsməs] Fröhliche Weihnachten!
metre ['miːtə] Meter
middle ['mɪdl] Mitte
midnight ['mɪdnaɪt] Mitternacht; **at midnight** um Mitternacht
might [maɪt] könnte(n) vielleicht; **they might go out ...** sie gehen vielleicht (manchmal) aus ...
mile [maɪl] Meile *(= ca. 1,6 km)*; **miles per hour (mph)** [ˌmaɪlz pər_'aʊə] Meilen pro Stunde
milk [mɪlk] Milch
million ['mɪlɪən] Million, Millionen
mind [maɪnd] **1.** etwas einzuwenden haben gegen; **Never mind.** [ˌnevə 'maɪnd] Macht nichts. Egal. **2. change one's mind** seine Meinung ändern
mine [maɪn] *(poss. pron.)* meine(r, s)
mine [maɪn] Bergwerk; **miner** Bergarbeiter/in
minibus ['mɪnɪbʌs] Kleinbus
°**minority** [maɪ'nɒrətɪ] Minderheit
minute ['mɪnɪt] Minute; **a ten-minute walk** zehn Minuten zu Fuß; **in a minute** gleich, sofort; **Wait a minute!** Einen Augenblick! Moment mal!
Miss [mɪs] Fräulein/Frau ... *(unverheiratet)*
miss [mɪs] **1.** verpassen, verfehlen; **2.** vermissen; **missing** fehlend; **be missing** fehlen
mission ['mɪʃn] Mission(sstation)
mistake [mɪ'steɪk] Fehler, Irrtum
misunderstand [ˌmɪsʌndə'stænd] mißverstehen
mix up [ˌmɪks_'ʌp] verwechseln, durcheinanderbringen; **mixed** [mɪkst] gemischt; **mixed bag** [ˌmɪkst 'bæg] „bunte Mischung"
model ['mɒdl] Modell
modern ['mɒdn] modern
mom [BE: mɒm, AE: mɑːm] (AE) Mutti, Mama
moment ['məʊmənt]**: at the moment** im Augenblick, gerade, zur Zeit
Monday ['mʌndɪ, 'mʌndeɪ] Montag
money ['mʌnɪ] Geld
monkey ['mʌŋkɪ] Affe
monster ['mɒnstə] Monster, Ungeheuer
month [mʌnθ] Monat
monument ['mɒnjʊmənt] Denkmal
°**moon** [muːn] Mond
moped ['məʊped] Moped
more [mɔː] mehr; weitere; **more than** mehr als; **one more** noch ein(e); **some more** noch einige, noch etwas; **more interesting** interessanter
morning ['mɔːnɪŋ] Morgen, Vormittag; **Good morning.** Guten Morgen. Guten Tag. *(vormittags)*; **in the morning(s)** am Morgen, morgens; **on Monday morning** am Montag morgen; **this morning** heute morgen
most [məʊst] **1.** (der/die/das) meiste, die meisten; **2.** am meisten; **most of the time** die meiste Zeit; **(the) most famous** (der/die/das) berühmteste; am berühmtesten; **mostly** meist(ens), größtenteils
mother ['mʌðə] Mutter
motorbike ['məʊtəbaɪk] (BE) Motorrad; **motorway** ['məʊtəweɪ] (BE) Autobahn
mountain ['maʊntɪn] Berg
mouse [maʊs]**,** *pl.* **mice** [maɪs] Maus
mouth [maʊθ] Mund
move [muːv] **1.** (um)ziehen; **2.** (sich) bewegen
movie ['muːvɪ] (*meist* AE) Film; **movie theater/movies** (AE) Kino
Mr ['mɪstə] Herr ...
Mrs ['mɪsɪz] Frau ... *(verheiratet)*
Ms [məz] Frau ... *(verheiratet oder unverheiratet)*
much [mʌtʃ] viel; **How much?** Wieviel? **How much is/are ...?** Was kostet/kosten ...? **like/love/... very much** sehr mögen/lieben/...
mud [mʌd] Schlamm, Matsch
muddled ['mʌdld] durcheinander(gebracht)
muesli ['mjuːzlɪ] Müsli
mug [mʌg] Becher, Krug
Mum/mum [mʌm] (BE) Mutti, Mama
museum [mjuː'ziːəm] Museum
music ['mjuːzɪk] Musik; **musical** ['mjuːzɪkl] Musical; **musician** [mjuː'zɪʃn] Musiker/in
must [mʌst] müssen; **mustn't** nicht dürfen
mustard ['mʌstəd] Senf
my [maɪ] *(poss. adj.)* mein(e); **myself** [maɪ'self] mir, mich (selbst)

N

name [neɪm] **1.** Name; **What's your name?** Wie heißt du? Wie heißen Sie? **What's in a name?** Was bedeutet schon ein Name? Namen sind Schall und Rauch. **call sb. names** Schimpfwörter zu jm. sagen; **2.** (be-, er-)nennen
narrow ['nærəʊ] eng, schmal
nation ['neɪʃn] Nation, Volk; **national** ['næʃnəl] national; **nationality** [ˌnæʃə'nælətɪ] Staatsangehörigkeit, Nationalität
Native American [ˌneɪtɪv_ə'merɪkən] amerikanische(r) Ureinwohner/in
natural ['nætʃrəl] natürlich, Natur-; **nature** ['neɪtʃə] Natur
near [nɪə] **1.** in der Nähe, nahe; **2. near/near to** *(prep.)* in der Nähe (von), nahe (bei); **nearest** nächstgelegene(r, s); **nearly** fast, beinahe
necessary ['nesəsərɪ] notwendig, nötig
neck [nek] Hals
need [niːd] brauchen, benötigen; **needn't** nicht brauchen, nicht müssen
neighbour ['neɪbə] Nachbar/in; **neighbourhood** ['neɪbəhʊd] Nachbarschaft
neither ... nor ... ['naɪðə/'niːðə ... nɔː] weder ... noch ...
nervous ['nɜːvəs] nervös, aufgeregt, ängstlich; **nervousness** Nervosität
network ['netwɜːk] Netz(werk)
never ['nevə] nie, niemals; **Never mind.** [ˌnevə 'maɪnd] Macht nichts. Egal.
new [njuː] neu; **New Year's Day** [ˌnjuː jɪəz 'deɪ] Neujahr(stag); **New Year's Eve** [ˌnjuː jɪəz_'iːv] Silvester; **newcomer** ['njuːkʌmə] Neuling; **news** *(sing.)* [njuːz] Nachricht(en); **newsagent** ['njuːzeɪdʒənt] (BE) Zeitungshändler/in; **newsagent's** (BE) Zeitungsladen; **newspaper** Zeitung
next [nekst] **1.** nächste(r, s) *(zeitlich, Reihenfolge)*; **2.** *(adv.)* als nächstes; das nächste Mal; **3. next to** (direkt) neben; **next door** nebenan
nice [naɪs] schön, nett
nickel [nɪkl] (AE) Fünfcentmünze
night [naɪt] Nacht, (später) Abend; **at night** nachts, in der Nacht, am (späten) Abend
no [nəʊ] **1.** nein; **2.** kein, keine; **no longer** nicht mehr, nicht länger
nobody ['nəʊbədɪ] niemand
nod [nɒd] nicken
noise [nɔɪz] Lärm, Geräusch; **noisy** ['nɔɪzɪ] laut, lärmend
non- [nɒn] nicht-; Nicht-
nonsense ['nɒnsəns] Unsinn
nor: neither ... nor ... ['naɪðə/'niːðə ... nɔː] weder ... noch ...
normal ['nɔːml] normal; **normally** ['nɔːməlɪ] normalerweise
north [nɔːθ] **1.** Norden; **2.** nach Norden; **3. north (of)** nördlich (von); **northern** ['nɔːðən] Nord-, nördlich
nose [nəʊz] Nase
not [nɒt] nicht; **not ... either** auch nicht; auch kein; **not even** nicht einmal; **not ... until** nicht vor/erst um; nicht ... bevor; **not ... yet** noch nicht
note [nəʊt] **1.** (BE) (Geld-)Schein, Banknote; **2.** Notiz; Entschuldigungsschreiben; **notepaper** ['nəʊtpeɪpə] Briefpapier

D

nothing ['nʌθɪŋ] nichts
notice ['nəʊtɪs] (be)merken
November [nəʊ'vembə] November
now [naʊ] nun, jetzt; **from now on** von jetzt an, ab jetzt
nowhere ['nəʊweə] nirgendwo; nirgendwohin
nuisance ['nju:sns]**: it's a nuisance** es ist lästig, es ist ärgerlich
number ['nʌmbə] Zahl, Nummer; **a number of** mehrere
nurse [nɜ:s] Krankenpfleger/in, Krankenschwester

O

obvious ['ɒbvɪəs] offensichtlich
ocean ['əʊʃn] Ozean
o'clock [ə'klɒk]**: 7 o'clock** 7 Uhr/ 19 Uhr
October [ɒk'təʊbə] Oktober
odd one out [ˌɒd wʌn_'aʊt] „Fremdkörper" (= Welches Wort paßt hier nicht?)
of [ɒv, əv] von; **a cup of tea** eine Tasse Tee; **of course** [əv 'kɔ:s] natürlich, selbstverständlich; **out of …** ['aʊt_əv] aus … hinaus; **There were five of them.** Sie waren zu fünft.
off [ɒf] **1.** aus, ausgeschaltet; **2.** (von …) herunter
offer ['ɒfə] **1.** Angebot; **special offer** [ˌspeʃl_'ɒfə] Sonderangebot; **2.** (an)bieten
office ['ɒfɪs] Büro
officer ['ɒfɪsə]**: (police) officer** (Polizei-)Beamter/Beamtin, Polizist/in
often ['ɒfn] oft
oil [ɔɪl] Öl
OK. [əʊ'keɪ] Gut. In Ordnung.
old [əʊld] alt
on [ɒn] **1.** auf; **2.** an, eingeschaltet; **on holiday** in Urlaub; **on Monday (morning)** am Montag (morgen); **on Mondays** montags; **on the bus/ train/plane** im Bus/Zug/Flugzeug; **on the coast** an der Küste; **on the first evening** am ersten Abend; **on the radio/on TV** im Radio/im Fernsehen; **on the (tele)phone** am Telefon; **on the Thames** an der Themse; **on time** pünktlich; **go on** weitermachen; **walk/drive/… on** weitergehen/weiterfahren/…; **from now on** von jetzt an, ab jetzt; **from then on** von da an
once [wʌns] **1.** einst, (früher) einmal; **2.** einmal; **at once** sofort, (so)gleich
one [wʌn] man; **oneself** [wʌn'self] sich (selbst); **one day** eines Tages; **the Mexican ones** die mexikanischen; **which one** welche(r, s)
only ['əʊnlɪ] nur, bloß; erst; **not only … but (also)** nicht nur … sondern (auch); **the only …** der/die/das einzige …
onto ['ɒntʊ, 'ɒntə] auf (… hinauf)
open ['əʊpən] **1.** offen, geöffnet; **2.** öffnen, aufmachen; sich öffnen
operator ['ɒpəreɪtə] Vermittlung; Telefonist/in
opinion [ə'pɪnjən] Meinung; **in my opinion** meiner Meinung nach
opposite ['ɒpəzɪt] **1.** gegenüber (von); **2.** Gegenteil
or [ɔ:] oder
orange ['ɒrɪndʒ] **1.** orangefarben; **2.** Apfelsine, Orange
order ['ɔ:də] **1.** Reihenfolge; Ordnung, Anordnung; **2.** Bestellung, Auftrag, Order; **3.** Befehl; **4.** bestellen; **5. order sb. to do sth.** jm. befehlen/jn. auffordern, etwas zu tun
organization [ˌɔ:gənaɪ'zeɪʃn] Organisation; **organize** ['ɔ:gənaɪz] organisieren; aufbauen
original [ə'rɪdʒnəl] **1.** Original; **2.** ursprünglich, Original-
other ['ʌðə]**: (the) other** (der/die/das) andere; die anderen; **each other** [ˌi:tʃ_'ʌðə] einander, sich (gegenseitig)
ought to ['ɔ:tə] sollte(n), müßte(n) eigentlich
our ['aʊə, ɑ:] *(poss. adj.)* unser(e); **ours** ['aʊəz] *(poss. pron.)* unsere(r, s); **ourselves** [aʊə'selvz] uns (selbst)
out (of …) ['aʊt_əv] aus (… hinaus), aus (… heraus)
outing ['aʊtɪŋ] Ausflug
outside [ˌaʊt'saɪd] **1.** außerhalb (von); **2.** (nach) draußen
outskirts ['aʊtskɜ:ts] *(pl.)* Außenbezirke, Stadtrand; **on the outskirts** am Stadtrand
oven ['ʌvn] Backofen
over ['əʊvə] über; **all over the bungalow** im ganzen Bungalow verteilt, überall im Bungalow; **over the years** im Lauf der Jahre; **over there** da drüben, dort drüben; **fall over** hin-, umfallen; **overhead projector** [ˌəʊvəhed prə'dʒektə] **(OHP)** [ˌəʊ_eɪtʃ 'pi:] Tageslichtprojektor; **overnight** [ˌəʊvə'naɪt] über Nacht
own [əʊn]**: my/your/… own** mein(e)/ dein(e)/… eigene(r, s)
own [əʊn] besitzen; **owner** ['əʊnə] Besitzer/in

P

pack [pæk] (ein)packen
page [peɪdʒ] (Buch-/Heft-)Seite
pain [peɪn] Schmerz(en)
pair (of) [peə] Paar
pajamas *(pl.)* [pə'dʒɑ:məz] (AE) Schlafanzug
palace ['pæləs] Palast
panic ['pænɪk] Panik
panther ['pænθə] Panther
paper ['peɪpə] Papier
parade [pə'reɪd] Parade, Umzug
paragraph ['pærəgrɑ:f] Absatz, Abschnitt
Pardon? ['pɑ:dn] Wie bitte?
parentheses [pə'renθəsi:z] *(meist* AE) Klammern *(Satzzeichen)*
parents ['peərənts] Eltern
park [pɑ:k] **1.** Park; **2.** parken; **car park** (BE)**/parking lot** (AE) (großer) Parkplatz
parliament ['pɑ:ləmənt] Parlament
part [pɑ:t] **1.** Teil; **part of the body** Körperteil; **part of town** Stadtteil, Stadtviertel; **part-time** [ˌpɑ:t'taɪm] Teilzeit-, halbtags; **2.** Rolle *(in Theaterstück, Film usw.)*
°**particular** [pə'tɪkjʊlə] bestimmte(r, s), spezielle(r, s)
partner ['pɑ:tnə] Partner/in
party ['pɑ:tɪ] **1.** Party, Feier; **have a party** eine Party feiern; **2.** Partei
pass [pɑ:s] **1.** *(eine Prüfung)* bestehen; **2.** vergehen, vorübergehen *(Zeit)*; **3. pass sth.** etwas (herüber)reichen; **pass the ball** den Ball abspielen
passenger ['pæsɪndʒə] Passagier/in
past [pɑ:st] **1.** Vergangenheit; **2.** vergangen; **in the past few years** in den vergangenen/letzten Jahren; **3.** vorbei, vorüber (an); **quarter past eight** [ˌkwɔ:tə pɑ:st_'eɪt] Viertel nach acht (8.15/20.15)
pasta ['pæstə] Teigwaren, Nudeln
path [pɑ:θ], *pl.* **paths** [pɑ:ðz] Weg, Pfad; **bike path** Radweg
patient ['peɪʃnt] **1.** geduldig; **2.** Patient/in
pavement ['peɪvmənt] (BE) Gehweg
pay [peɪ] **1.** Bezahlung; Lohn, Löhne; **2. pay (for)** bezahlen; **pay attention (to)** aufmerksam sein, aufpassen (auf)
P.E. [ˌpi:_'i:] **(Physical Education)** [ˌfɪzɪkl_edjʊ'keɪʃn] Turnen, Sport(unterricht) *(in der Regel in der Halle)*
pea [pi:] Erbse
pedestrian [pə'destrɪən] Fußgänger/in; **pedestrian crossing** [pəˌdestrɪən 'krɒsɪŋ] (BE) Fußgängerüberweg
pen [pen] Füller; **ball-point pen** (AE) Kugelschreiber; **pen-friend** Brieffreund/in
pence [pens] Pence *(Mehrzahl von BE „penny")*
pencil ['pensl] Bleistift; **pencil-case** ['penslkeɪs] Federmappe, Federtasche
penny ['penɪ] **1.** (BE) *kleinste britische Münze*; **2.** (AE) Eincentmünze
people ['pi:pl] (die) Leute, (die) Menschen
per [pɜ:, pə] pro; **per cent (%)** [pə'sent] Prozent; **miles per hour (mph)** ['maɪlz pər_'aʊə] Meilen pro Stunde
perfect ['pɜ:fɪkt] vollkommen, perfekt
perhaps [pə'hæps] vielleicht
period ['pɪərɪəd] (AE) Punkt *(Satzzeichen)*
permission [pə'mɪʃn] Erlaubnis, Genehmigung
permit ['pɜ:mɪt] Genehmigung(sschein), *(schriftliche)* Erlaubnis

persecute ['pɜːsɪkjuːt] verfolgen *(aus politischen oder religiösen Gründen)*
person ['pɜːsn] Person
petrol ['petrəl] (BE) Benzin; **petrol station** (BE) Tankstelle
phone [fəʊn] **1.** anrufen; **2.** Telefon; **answer the phone** ans Telefon gehen; **on the phone** am Telefon
photo (of) ['fəʊtəʊ] Foto (von); **take photos** Fotos machen
phrase [freɪz] (Rede-)Wendung, Ausdruck; **phrasebook** ['freɪzbʊk] Sprachführer
Physical Education [ˌfɪzɪkl_ edjʊ'keɪʃn] **(P.E.)** Turnen, Sport(unterricht) *(in der Regel in der Halle)*
physics *(sing.)* ['fɪzɪks] Physik
piano [pɪ'ænəʊ] Klavier
pick up [ˌpɪk_'ʌp] **1.** abholen, mitnehmen *(mit dem Auto)*; **2.** *(vom Boden)* aufheben
picnic ['pɪknɪk] Picknick; **have a picnic** ein Picknick machen
picture (of) ['pɪktʃə] Bild, Foto (von); **in the picture** auf dem Bild/Foto
pie [paɪ] **1.** (Obst-)Kuchen; **2.** (Fleisch-)Pastete
piece (of) [piːs] Stück; **piece of furniture** Möbelstück
pink [pɪŋk] rosa, pink
pity ['pɪtɪ]**: What a pity!** Wie schade!
pizza ['piːtsə] Pizza
place [pleɪs] Ort, Platz, Stelle; **take place** stattfinden
plan [plæn] **1.** Plan; **2.** planen
plane [pleɪn] Flugzeug; **on the plane** im Flugzeug
plant [plɑːnt] **1.** Pflanze; **2.** (ein)pflanzen
plastic ['plæstɪk] Plastik, Kunststoff; Plastik-
plate [pleɪt] Teller
platform ['plætfɔːm] **1.** Bahnsteig, Gleis; **2.** Plattform
play [pleɪ] **1.** spielen; **play the piano** Klavier spielen; **player** Spieler/in; **2.** Schauspiel, (Theater-)Stück
pleasant ['pleznt] angenehm
please [pliːz] bitte *(in Fragen und Aufforderungen)*; **(Yes,) please.** Danke, gern.
plural ['plʊərəl] Plural, Mehrzahl
plus [plʌs] plus
... pm [ˌpiː_'em] *(from Latin "post meridiem")* ... Uhr nachmittags oder abends *(zwischen 12 und 24 h)*
pocket ['pɒkɪt] Tasche *(an einem Kleidungsstück)*; **pocket-money** Taschengeld
poem ['pəʊɪm] Gedicht
point [pɔɪnt] **1.** Punkt; **2. point (at, to)** zeigen, deuten (auf)
police [pə'liːs] Polizei; **police officer** [pə'liːs_ˌɒfɪsə] Polizeibeamter/Polizeibeamtin, Polizist/in; **police station** Polizeiwache, Polizeirevier
polite [pə'laɪt] höflich; **politeness** [pə'laɪtnəs] Höflichkeit
politician [ˌpɒlə'tɪʃn] Politiker/in
pollute [pə'luːt] *(die Umwelt)* verschmutzen; **pollution** [pə'luːʃn] (Umwelt-)Verschmutzung
poor [pɔː, pʊə] arm
pop music ['pɒp mjuːzɪk] Popmusik
popular (with) ['pɒpjʊlə] beliebt (bei); **popularly** ['pɒpjʊləlɪ] allgemein, landläufig
population [ˌpɒpjʊ'leɪʃn] Bevölkerung, Einwohner(zahl)
port [pɔːt] Hafen(stadt)
position [pə'zɪʃn] Position, Lage, Stellung
possible ['pɒsəbl] möglich; **possibly** ['pɒsəblɪ] vielleicht, möglicherweise; **They couldn't possibly help.** Sie konnten unmöglich helfen.
post [pəʊst] **1.** (BE) *(Brief)* abschicken, einwerfen; *(Paket)* aufgeben; **2.** (BE) Post(sendungen); **post office** Post(amt); **postcard (of)** Postkarte, Ansichtskarte (von *einer Gegend usw.*); **postcode** (BE) Postleitzahl
poster ['pəʊstə] Poster
pot [pɒt] Kanne; Topf
potato [pə'teɪtəʊ], *pl.* **potatoes** Kartoffel
pottery ['pɒtərɪ] Töpfern
pound [paʊnd] **1. (£)** Pfund *(britische Währung)*; **2.** Pfund *(454 g)*
poverty ['pɒvətɪ] Armut
power ['paʊə] Macht
practice ['præktɪs] Übung, Training; **practise** ['præktɪs] üben, trainieren
pray [preɪ] beten
precise [prɪ'saɪs] präzise, genau
prediction [prɪ'dɪkʃn] Voraussage, Vorhersage
prefer (to) [prɪ'fɜː] lieber haben (als), *(etwas einer anderen Sache)* vorziehen
prefix ['priːfɪks] Vorsilbe, Präfix
preparation [ˌprepə'reɪʃn] Vorbereitung; **prepare** [prɪ'peə] vorbereiten, zubereiten
pre-question ['priːˌkwestʃn] vorgeschaltete, vorangestellte Frage
present 1. ['preznt] Gegenwart; **2.** ['preznt] Geschenk; **3. present (to)** [prɪ'zent] darlegen, präsentieren
preserve [prɪ'zɜːv] erhalten, bewahren
president ['prezɪdənt] Präsident/in
price [praɪs] (Kauf-)Preis
priest [priːst] Priester/in
primary school ['praɪmərɪ skuːl] Grundschule
prime minister [ˌpraɪm 'mɪnɪstə] Premierminister/in, Ministerpräsident/in
print: bold print [bəʊld 'prɪnt] fette Schrift, Fettdruck; **printer** Drucker
prison ['prɪzn] Gefängnis
private ['praɪvət] privat; persönlich
probably ['prɒbəblɪ] wahrscheinlich
problem ['prɒbləm] Problem
produce [prə'djuːs] produzieren, herstellen, erzeugen; **production** [prə'dʌkʃn] Produktion, Herstellung
program ['prəʊgræm] **1.** (Computer-)Programm; **2.** (AE) Programm; (Radio-, Fernseh-)Sendung; **3.** programmieren *(Computer)*; **programmer** Programmierer/in
programme ['prəʊgræm] (BE) **1.** Programm; (Radio-, Fernseh-)Sendung; **2.** programmieren *(Videorecorder u.ä.)*
°**progress** ['prəʊgres]**: in progress** im Gange
project ['prɒdʒekt] Projekt; Aufgabe
promise ['prɒmɪs] **1.** versprechen; **2.** Versprechen; **keep a promise** ein Versprechen halten
prompt [prɒmpt] Stichwort, Anregung
pronounce [prə'naʊns] aussprechen; **pronunciation** [prəˌnʌnsɪ'eɪʃn] Aussprache
proper ['prɒpə] richtig, passend, geeignet; **properly** ['prɒpəlɪ] richtig, ordentlich, sachgemäß
protect [prə'tekt] (be)schützen
proud (of) [praʊd] stolz (auf)
province ['prɒvɪns] Provinz
provoke [prə'vəʊk] provozieren
P.S. [ˌpiː_'es] *(from Latin "post scriptum")* P.S. *(Nachtrag zu einem Brief)*
pub [pʌb] (*meist* BE) Kneipe, Lokal
public ['pʌblɪk] öffentlich
pudding ['pʊdɪŋ] (BE) Nachtisch, Süßspeise; **for pudding** zum Nachtisch
pull (out) [ˌpʊl_'aʊt] (heraus)ziehen
pullover ['pʊləʊvə] Pullover
°**punctuation** [ˌpʌŋktʃʊ'eɪʃn] Zeichensetzung, Interpunktion; **punctuation marks** [ˌpʌŋktʃʊ'eɪʃn mɑːks] Satzzeichen
puncture ['pʌŋktʃə] (BE) Reifenpanne
punish ['pʌnɪʃ] (be)strafen; **punishment** ['pʌnɪʃmənt] Strafe, Bestrafung
pupil ['pjuːpl] Schüler/in
purse [pɜːs] Geldbörse, Geldbeutel, AE *auch:* Handtasche
push [pʊʃ] schieben, stoßen, drücken
put [pʊt] stellen; legen; **put in** einsetzen; **put on** anziehen *(Kleidung)*; **put up** aufhängen, anbringen
puzzle out [ˌpʌzl_'aʊt] ausknobeln, austüfteln; **puzzled** ['pʌzld] verwirrt, verblüfft
pyjamas *(pl.)* [pə'dʒɑːməz] (BE) Schlafanzug

Q

quality ['kwɒlətɪ] Eigenschaft; Qualität
quarter ['kwɔːtə] **1.** Viertel; **quarter of an hour** eine Viertelstunde; **2.** (AE) 25-Centmünze
queen [kwiːn] Königin
question ['kwestʃn] **1.** Frage; **ask a question** eine Frage stellen; **question mark** ['kwestʃn mɑːk] Fragezeichen; **2.** befragen, vernehmen
queue [kjuː] (Warte-)Schlange
quiche [kiːʃ] Quiche
quick [kwɪk] schnell; **quickly** schnell

quiet ['kwaɪət] ruhig, leise, still
quit [kwɪt] aufhören (mit); *(eine Arbeitsstelle)* aufgeben
quite [kwaɪt] ziemlich; ganz
quiz [kwɪz] Quiz; **quizmaster** ['kwɪzmɑːstə] Quizmaster
quotation marks [kwəʊ'teɪʃn mɑːks] Anführungszeichen

R

rabbit ['ræbɪt] Kaninchen
race [reɪs] **1.** Rennen, Wettlauf; **have a race** ein Rennen veranstalten; **2.** rennen, rasen
racist ['reɪsɪst] **1.** Rassist/in; **2.** rassistisch
radio ['reɪdɪəʊ] Radio; Rundfunk; **on the radio** im Radio
railroad ['reɪlrəʊd] (AE)/**railway** ['reɪlweɪ] (*meist* BE) Eisenbahn
rain [reɪn] **1.** Regen; **2.** regnen; **rainy** regnerisch
rare [reə] selten; **rarely** ['reəlɪ] selten
razorbill ['reɪzəbɪl] Tordalk *(Seevogel)*
R.E. [ˌɑːr_'iː] (BE) **(Religious Education)** [rɪˌlɪdʒəs_edjʊ'keɪʃn] Religionsunterricht
reach [riːtʃ] erreichen
react (to) [rɪ'ækt] reagieren (auf); **reaction (to)** [rɪ'ækʃn] Reaktion (auf)
read [riːd] lesen, vorlesen; **readable** ['riːdəbl] lesbar; **reader** Leser/in
ready ['redɪ] fertig, bereit; **ready-made meal** [ˌredɪmeɪd 'miːl] Fertiggericht
real [rɪəl] echt, wirklich; **really** ['rɪəlɪ] wirklich, eigentlich; °**reality** [rɪ'ælətɪ] Wirklichkeit, Realität; **realize** ['rɪəlaɪz] erkennen, merken
reason ['riːzn] Grund, Begründung; **for this reason** aus diesem Grund, deshalb
receipt [rɪ'siːt] Beleg; Quittung, Kassenzettel
recently ['riːsntlɪ] vor kurzem; neulich
record 1. ['rekɔːd] Schallplatte; **2.** [rɪ'kɔːd] aufnehmen, aufzeichnen *(auf Band)*
recreate [ˌriːkrɪ'eɪt] wiederbeleben, neu erschaffen
recycled [ˌriː'saɪkld] Recycling-
red [red] rot
refer to [rɪ'fɜː] sich beziehen auf
refuse [rɪ'fjuːz] sich weigern; verweigern, ablehnen
region ['riːdʒən] Gebiet, Region
regular ['regjʊlə] regelmäßig; **regularly** ['regjʊləlɪ] regelmäßig
relative ['relətɪv] Verwandte(r)
relax [rɪ'læks] sich entspannen, sich ausruhen; **relaxed** entspannt, ruhig, locker
religion [rɪ'lɪdʒən] Religion; **religious** [rɪ'lɪdʒəs] religiös; **Religious Education** [rɪˌlɪdʒəs_edjʊ'keɪʃn] **(R.E.)** Religionsunterricht
remains *(pl.)* [rɪ'meɪnz] Reste, Relikte
remember [rɪ'membə] sich erinnern an; daran denken *(, etwas zu tun)*
°**remind (of)** [rɪ'maɪnd] *(jn.)* erinnern (an)
reopen [riː'əʊpən] wieder (er)öffnen
reorganize [riː'ɔːgənaɪz] neu organisieren, umorganisieren
repair [rɪ'peə] **1.** Reparatur; **2.** reparieren
repay [rɪ'peɪ] zurückzahlen
repeat [rɪ'piːt] wiederholen
°**replace (with)** [rɪ'pleɪs] ersetzen (durch), austauschen (gegen)
°**reply** [rɪ'plaɪ] erwidern, antworten
report [rɪ'pɔːt] **1.** Bericht; (BE *auch*:) Schulzeugnis; **2.** berichten; **reporter** Reporter/in
request [rɪ'kwest] Bitte; Wunsch
resort: seaside resort ['siːsaɪd rɪˌzɔːt] (beliebter) Urlaubsort am Meer, Seebad
respect [rɪ'spekt] **1.** Respekt, Achtung; **2.** respektieren, achten
responsible (for) [rɪ'spɒnsəbl] verantwortlich (für)
rest [rest] **1.** Rest; **2.** Ruhepause; **3. rest (from)** sich ausruhen (von); °**restroom** (AE) öffentliche Toilette
restaurant ['restərɒnt] Restaurant
result [rɪ'zʌlt] Ergebnis
retell [ˌriː'tel] nacherzählen
return [rɪ'tɜːn] zurückkehren; **return journey** Rückfahrt, Rückreise
reuse [ˌriː'juːz] wiederverwenden
rewrite [ˌriː'raɪt] neu schreiben, noch einmal schreiben
rhyme [raɪm] Reim
rice [raɪs] Reis
rich (in) [rɪtʃ] reich (an)
ride [raɪd] **1.** Fahrt; Ritt; **2.** reiten; **ride a bike** radfahren; **rider** Reiter/in; Radfahrer/in
right [raɪt] **1.** richtig; **be right** recht haben; **Are you all right?** Geht es dir (noch) gut? **2.** rechte(r, s), nach rechts; **on the right** rechts, auf der rechten Seite; **3. rights** Rechte; **civil rights** [ˌsɪvl 'raɪts] Bürgerrechte
ring [rɪŋ] **1.** Ring; **2.** klingeln, läuten
ripe [raɪp] reif
risk [rɪsk] Risiko; **take a risk** ein Risiko eingehen
rival ['raɪvl] Konkurrent/in, Rivale/Rivalin
river ['rɪvə] Fluß
road [rəʊd] Straße, Landstraße
roast [rəʊst] geröstet, gebraten *(im Backofen)*; **roast beef** [ˌrəʊst 'biːf] Rinderbraten, Roastbeef
rob [rɒb] berauben, ausrauben
rock [rɒk] Fels(en); **rock (music)** Rock(musik); **rocky** felsig, steinig
role-play ['rəʊlpleɪ] Rollenspiel
roll [rəʊl]**: (bread) roll** Brötchen
Roman ['rəʊmən] **1.** römisch; **2.** Römer/in
roof [ruːf] Dach
room [ruːm] Zimmer, Raum
rose [rəʊz] Rose
round [raʊnd] **1.** rund; **2.** (BE) um … (herum); in … umher, durch; **just round the corner** gleich um die Ecke; **turn round** sich umdrehen
route [ruːt] Route, Strecke
routine [ˌruː'tiːn] Routine
royal ['rɔɪəl] königlich
rubber ['rʌbə] (BE) Radiergummi
rubbish ['rʌbɪʃ] Abfall, Unrat
rucksack ['rʌksæk] Rucksack
ruin ['ruːɪn] Ruine
rule [ruːl] **1.** Regel, Vorschrift; **2.** regieren, herrschen über
ruler ['ruːlə] Lineal
run [rʌn] laufen, rennen; **run after sb.** hinter jm. herrennen; °**run into a traffic jam** in einen Verkehrsstau geraten; **We've run out of coffee.** Uns ist der Kaffee ausgegangen. Wir haben keinen Kaffee mehr. **runner** Läufer/in

S

sad [sæd] traurig
safe [seɪf] sicher, gefahrlos
sail [seɪl] **1.** Segel; **2.** segeln; **sailing** ['seɪlɪŋ] Segeln
salad ['sæləd] Salat *(als Gericht bzw. Beilage)*
salary ['sælərɪ] Gehalt
salt [sɒlt, sɔːlt] Salz; **salty** salzig
same [seɪm]**: the same** der-/die-/dasselbe, dieselben; der/die/das gleiche, die gleichen
sand [sænd] Sand; **sandy** sandig
sandwich ['sænwɪtʃ] *(zusammengeklapptes)* belegtes Brot
Santa Claus ['sæntə klɔːz, ˌsæntə 'klɔːz] der Weihnachtsmann
Saturday ['sætədɪ, 'sætədeɪ] Samstag/Sonnabend; **on Saturday** am Samstag; **on Saturdays** samstags
saucer ['sɔːsə] Untertasse
sausage ['sɒsɪdʒ] (Brat-, Bock-)Würstchen, Wurst
save [seɪv] sparen; retten
say [seɪ] sagen; **Say hallo to …** Grüß(t) … (von mir); **the text says …** im Text steht …; **You can say that again.** Das kannst du laut sagen.
scarf [skɑːf], *pl.* **scarves** [skɑːvz] Schal
scene [siːn] Szene; **scenery** *(sing.)* ['siːnərɪ] (malerische) Landschaft(en)
school [skuːl] Schule; **at school** in der Schule
science ['saɪəns] (Natur-)Wissenschaft; **scientist** ['saɪəntɪst] (Natur-)Wissenschaftler/in
score [skɔː] **1.** Spielstand, (Spiel-)Ergebnis; **2.** *(einen Punkt/Treffer)* erzielen, *(ein Tor)* schießen
Scot [skɒt] Schotte/Schottin; **the Scots** die Schotten; **Scottish** ['skɒtɪʃ] schottisch, Schottisch

D

scream [skri:m] schreien, kreischen
sea [si:] Meer, (die) See; **seaside resort** ['si:saɪd rɪˌzɔ:t] (beliebter) Urlaubsort am Meer, Seebad
season ['si:zn] Jahreszeit
seat [si:t] Sitz, Sitzplatz; **Take a seat.** Nimm Platz. Nehmen Sie Platz.
second ['sekənd] Sekunde
second: second-hand [ˌsekənd 'hænd] aus zweiter Hand; **secondly** zweitens
secondary school ['sekəndrɪ sku:l] Oberschule
secretary ['sekrətrɪ] Sekretär/in
see [si:] sehen; **See you later.** Bis dann. Bis später. **you see** weißt du, nämlich
seem [si:m] *(zu sein/tun)* scheinen
sell [sel] verkaufen
semi-colon [ˌsemɪ'kəʊlən] Semikolon
semi-detached house ['semɪdɪˌtætʃt 'haʊs] (BE) Doppelhaushälfte
send [send] senden, schicken; **send for** kommen lassen, holen
sense: a sense of humour [ˌsens‿əv 'hju:mə] (Sinn für) Humor
sentence ['sentəns] Satz
September [sep'tembə] September
serious ['sɪərɪəs] ernst, ernsthaft
serve [sɜ:v] (be)dienen, servieren; **service** ['sɜ:vɪs] *(Bus-, Zug-, Flug-)* Verbindung(en)
set [set] (BE) Kurs-, Leistungsgruppe
settle ['setl] sich niederlassen; *(Land)* besiedeln; **settlement** ['setlmənt] Siedlung; Besiedlung; **settler** ['setlə] Siedler/in
several ['sevrəl] einige, mehrere
shake [ʃeɪk] schütteln; **shake hands with sb.** jm. die Hand geben
shall [ʃæl, ʃəl]**: Shall I …?** Soll ich …? **I shall** … Ich werde …
shampoo [ʃæm'pu:] Haarwaschmittel, Shampoo
share (with) [ʃeə] teilen (mit); sich *(etwas)* teilen (mit)
she [ʃi:] sie *(Singular)*
shed [ʃed] Schuppen
sheep, *pl.* **sheep** [ʃi:p] Schaf
shelf [ʃelf], *pl.* **shelves** [ʃelvz] Regal(brett), Bord
shine (on) [ʃaɪn] scheinen, leuchten (auf)
ship [ʃɪp] Schiff
shirt [ʃɜ:t] (Ober-)Hemd
shock [ʃɒk] Schock
shoe [ʃu:] Schuh
shoot [ʃu:t] schießen; *(Ball)* werfen
shop [ʃɒp] Laden, Geschäft; **shopkeeper** ['ʃɒpki:pə] Ladenbesitzer/in; **shoplifter** ['ʃɒplɪftə] Ladendieb/in; **shopper** ['ʃɒpə] Käufer/in; **shopping** Einkaufen; Einkäufe; **do the shopping** einkaufen; **go shopping/go to the shops** einkaufen gehen; **window-shopping** ['wɪndəʊˌʃɒpɪŋ] Schaufensterbummeln
short [ʃɔ:t] kurz; klein *(von Gestalt)*; **shorts** *(pl.)* Shorts, kurze Hose
should [ʃʊd, ʃəd] sollte(n), müßte(n)
shoulder ['ʃəʊldə] Schulter
shout [ʃaʊt] **1.** Schrei, Ruf; **2. shout (at)** (an)schreien, laut rufen
show [ʃəʊ] **1.** Schau, Show; **2.** zeigen; sich zeigen, deutlich werden
shut [ʃʌt] schließen
shy [ʃaɪ] schüchtern, zurückhaltend, scheu
sick [sɪk]**: be sick** sich übergeben (müssen); **I feel sick.** Mir ist schlecht/übel. **sickness** ['sɪknəs] Krankheit
side [saɪd] Seite; **take sides with** Partei ergreifen für; **sidewalk** ['saɪdwɔ:k] (AE) Gehweg
sigh (with) [saɪ] seufzen (vor)
sights [saɪts] Sehenswürdigkeiten
sign [saɪn] **1.** Schild, Zeichen; **2.** unterschreiben
silliness ['sɪlɪnəs] Albernheit; **silly** ['sɪlɪ] albern, dumm
similar ['sɪmɪlə] ähnlich
since *(prep.; conj.)* [sɪns] seit
sincerely [sɪn'sɪəlɪ]**: Yours sincerely, …** (*meist* BE) Mit herzlichen/freundlichen Grüßen
sing [sɪŋ] singen; **singer** Sänger/in
sink [sɪŋk] **1.** sinken, untergehen; **2.** versenken
Sir, sir [sɜ:] mein Herr *(höfliche Anrede)*
siren ['saɪrən] Sirene
sister ['sɪstə] Schwester
sit [sɪt] sitzen; **sit (down)** sich setzen
site ['saɪt] Stätte; Stelle, Platz
situation [ˌsɪtʃʊ'eɪʃn] Situation
size [saɪz] Größe; **What size do you take?** Welche Größe haben Sie?
ski [ski:] Ski laufen, Ski fahren
skirt [skɜ:t] Rock
sky [skaɪ] Himmel; **in the sky** am Himmel
slave [sleɪv] Sklave/Sklavin
sleep [sli:p] **1.** Schlaf; **2.** schlafen; **sleeping-bag** ['sli:pɪŋ bæg] Schlafsack
slogan ['sləʊgən] Slogan, Wahlspruch
slow [sləʊ] langsam; **slowly** langsam
small [smɔ:l] klein
smell [smel] riechen
smile [smaɪl] **1.** Lächeln; **2. smile (at)** (an)lächeln
smoke [sməʊk] **1.** Rauch; **2.** rauchen
snack [snæk] Imbiß; **snack bar** ['snæk bɑ:] Imbißstube
snob [snɒb] Snob, eingebildeter Mensch
snooker ['snu:kə] Snooker *(billardähnliches Spiel)*
snow [snəʊ] Schnee; **snowy** verschneit
so [səʊ] **1.** so; **2.** also; deshalb, daher; **so (that)** damit, so daß; **so far** bis jetzt, bisher
soap [səʊp] Seife; **soap (opera)** ['səʊp‿ˌɒprə] „Seifenoper" *(sentimentale Hörspiel- oder Fernsehserie)*
°**society** [sə'saɪətɪ] Gesellschaft
sock [sɒk] Socke, Strumpf
sofa ['səʊfə] Sofa
soldier ['səʊldʒə] Soldat/in
solve [sɒlv] *(Aufgabe, Problem)* lösen
some [sʌm, səm] **1.** einige, ein paar; **2.** etwas
somebody ['sʌmbədɪ] jemand
something ['sʌmθɪŋ] etwas
sometimes ['sʌmtaɪmz] manchmal
somewhere ['sʌmweə] irgendwo; irgendwohin
son [sʌn] Sohn
song [sɒŋ] Lied
soon [su:n] bald; **sooner or later** früher oder später
sore [sɔ:] wund, rauh, entzündet; **a sore throat** [ˌsɔ: 'θrəʊt] Halsschmerzen
Sorry. ['sɒrɪ] **(= I'm sorry.)** Tut mir leid. **I'm sorry about …** Ich bedauere …, Ich bin traurig über …
sort [sɔ:t] sortieren, ordnen
soul [səʊl] Seele
sound [saʊnd] **1.** Geräusch, Ton, Laut; Klang; **2.** klingen, sich *(gut usw.)* anhören
soup [su:p] Suppe
sour ['saʊə] sauer
south [saʊθ] **1.** Süden; **2.** nach Süden; **3. south (of)** südlich (von); **southern** ['sʌðən] Süd-, südlich
souvenir [ˌsu:və'nɪə] Souvenir, Andenken
°**space** [speɪs] Weltraum; **spaceship** ['speɪsʃɪp] Raumschiff
span of time [spæn] Zeitspanne
Spanish ['spænɪʃ] Spanisch; spanisch
speak [spi:k] sprechen, reden; **speak out (against)** offen seine Meinung sagen (gegen); **speaker** Redner/in, Sprecher/in
special ['speʃl] Sonder-, besondere(r, s); **special offer** Sonderangebot; **specialist** ['speʃlɪst] Spezialist/in
spectacular [spek'tækjʊlə] spektakulär, sensationell
°**speculation** [ˌspekjʊ'leɪʃn] Vermutung, Spekulation
speed [spi:d] Geschwindigkeit; **speed limit** ['spi:d ˌlɪmɪt] Geschwindigkeitsbeschränkung
spell [spel] buchstabieren, schreiben; **spelling** ['spelɪŋ] Schreibweise
spend (on) [spend] **1.** *(Geld)* ausgeben (für); **2.** *(Zeit)* verbringen (mit)
sponge [spʌndʒ] Schwamm
sponsor ['spɒnsə] **1.** Sponsor/in, Spender/in; **2.** durch Geldspenden unterstützen
spoon [spu:n] Löffel
sport [spɔ:t] Sport
spring [sprɪŋ] Frühling, Frühjahr
sq (= square) [skweə] Quadrat; Quadrat-
squash [skwɒʃ] Squash
stadium ['steɪdɪəm] Stadion
stairs *(pl.)* [steəz] Treppe(nstufen)
stamp [stæmp] Briefmarke
stand [stænd] stehen; **I can't stand … .** Ich kann … nicht ausstehen.

D

star [stɑː] (Film-, Pop- usw.)Star; **the Stars and Stripes** [ˌstɑːz‿n 'straɪps] *US-Flagge („Sterne und Streifen")*
start [stɑːt] **1.** Anfang, Start; **2.** anfangen, beginnen (mit); **start school** eingeschult werden
state [steɪt] **1.** Staat, (Bundes-)Land; **2.** Zustand
statement ['steɪtmənt] Aussage, Feststellung
station ['steɪʃn] **1.** Bahnhof; **2.** (Rundfunk-/Fernseh-)Sender
statistics *(pl.)* [stə'tɪstɪks] Statistik(en)
stay [steɪ] **1.** Aufenthalt; **2.** bleiben; übernachten
steak [steɪk] Steak
steal [stiːl] stehlen
steel [stiːl] Stahl
stem [stem] (Wort-)Stamm
step [step] Stufe; Schritt
stick [stɪk] Stock
still [stɪl] (immer) noch
stomach ['stʌmək] Bauch, Magen; **stomach ache** ['stʌmək‿eɪk] Bauchschmerzen, Magenschmerzen
stone [stəʊn] Stein
stop [stɒp] **1.** aufhören; stoppen, anhalten; **stop doing sth.** aufhören, etwas zu tun; °**2.** Aufenthalt, Halt; **3. bus stop** Bushaltestelle
store [stɔː] großes Geschäft, Kaufhaus; **department store** [dɪ'pɑːtmənt stɔː] Kaufhaus
storey ['stɔːrɪ] (BE) Stock(werk)
storm [stɔːm] Sturm; Gewitter; **stormy** stürmisch
story ['stɔːrɪ] **1.** Geschichte, Erzählung; **storyteller** ['stɔːrɪtelə] Erzähler/in; **2.** (AE) Stockwerk
straight *(adv.; adj.)* [streɪt] direkt, geradewegs; gerade
strange [streɪndʒ] **1.** seltsam, sonderbar; **2.** fremd; **stranger** Unbekannte(r), Fremde(r)
street [striːt] Straße *(meist in einer Stadt)*
stress [stres] **1.** Betonung; **2.** betonen
strict [strɪkt] streng
strong [strɒŋ] stark
student ['stjuːdənt] Student/in; Schüler/in
studio ['stjuːdɪəʊ] Studio
study ['stʌdɪ] studieren; lernen
stupid ['stjuːpɪd] dämlich, dumm, blöd
style [staɪl] Stil
subject ['sʌbdʒɪkt] (Unterrichts-)Fach
suburb ['sʌbɜːb] Vorort, Vorstadt, Randbezirk
subway ['sʌbweɪ] (AE) U-Bahn
succeed [sək'siːd] Erfolg haben; gelingen; **success** [sək'ses] Erfolg; **successful** [sək'sesfəl] erfolgreich
such (a) [sʌtʃ] solch, so (ein/e); solche; **such as** (wie) zum Beispiel
suddenly ['sʌdnlɪ] plötzlich
suffix ['sʌfɪks] Nachsilbe, Suffix
sugar ['ʃʊgə] Zucker
suggest [sə'dʒest] vorschlagen, anregen; **suggestion** [sə'dʒestʃn] Vorschlag, Anregung
suit sb. [suːt] jm. stehen; **suitable** ['suːtəbl] passend, geeignet
suitcase ['suːtkeɪs] Koffer
sum up [ˌsʌm‿'ʌp] zusammenfassen
summer ['sʌmə] Sommer
sun [sʌn] Sonne; **sunny** sonnig; **sunshine** ['sʌnʃaɪn] Sonnenschein
Sunday ['sʌndɪ, 'sʌndeɪ] Sonntag
super ['suːpə] super, toll
supermarket ['suːpəmɑːkɪt] Supermarkt
supply [sə'plaɪ] (be)liefern; versorgen; **supply ship** [sə'plaɪ ʃɪp] Versorgungsschiff
support [sə'pɔːt] unterstützen; **supporter** [sə'pɔːtə] Unterstützer/in, Befürworter/in
suppose [sə'pəʊz] vermuten, annehmen, glauben
sure [ʃɔː, ʃʊə] sicher; **make sure** sicherstellen, sichergehen; dafür sorgen *(, daß)*
surgery ['sɜːdʒərɪ] (BE) (Arzt-)Praxis
surprise [sə'praɪz] **1.** Überraschung; **2.** überraschen; **surprised (at)** überrascht (über); **surprising** überraschend, erstaunlich; **surprisingly** überraschenderweise
survive [sə'vaɪv] überleben
sweatshirt ['swetʃɜːt] Sweatshirt
sweet [swiːt] süß; **sweets** *(pl.)* [swiːts] Süßigkeiten
swim [swɪm] schwimmen; **swimmer** Schwimmer/in; **swimming costume** ['swɪmɪŋ ˌkɒstjuːm] (BE) Badebekleidung, Badeanzug; **swimming-pool** ['swɪmɪŋ puːl] Schwimmbad
sword [sɔːd] Schwert
syllable ['sɪləbl] Silbe
symbolize ['sɪmbəlaɪz] symbolisieren
system ['sɪstəm] System

T

table ['teɪbl] **1.** Tisch; **2.** Tabelle; **table-tennis** ['teɪbltenɪs] Tischtennis
tablet ['tæblət] Tablette
take [teɪk] **1.** nehmen; mitnehmen, (hin)bringen; **take a chance** ein Risiko eingehen; es darauf ankommen lassen; **take a decision** eine Entscheidung treffen, fällen; **take an exam** eine Prüfung machen; **Take my advice.** Hör(t) auf meinen Rat. **take photos** Fotos machen, knipsen; **take place** stattfinden; **take sides with** Partei ergreifen für; **take sth. off** etwas ausziehen; **2. it takes** es dauert
talk (to) [tɔːk] reden, sprechen, sich unterhalten (mit)
tall [tɔːl] groß (gewachsen); hoch *(Bäume, Türme usw.)*
tape [teɪp] (Ton-)Band
task [tɑːsk] Aufgabe
taste [teɪst] schmecken
taxi ['tæksɪ] Taxi
tea [tiː] **1.** Tee; **2.** (BE) Abendbrot, Abendessen; **have tea** Abendbrot essen; **for tea** zum Abendbrot
teach [tiːtʃ] lehren, unterrichten; **teacher** ['tiːtʃə] Lehrer/in
team [tiːm] Mannschaft, Team, Gruppe
tear [tɪə] Träne
technology [tek'nɒlədʒɪ] Technologie, Technik
teenager ['tiːneɪdʒə] Teenager, Jugendliche(r)
telephone ['teləfəʊn] Telefon; **on the telephone** am Telefon
television ['telɪvɪʒn] **(TV)** Fernsehen
tell [tel] erzählen, berichten; sagen; **Can you tell me the way to …?** Können Sie mir sagen, wie ich zu/nach … komme? °**tell sb. to do sth.** jn. auffordern, etwas zu tun
temperature ['temprətʃə] **1.** Temperatur; **2.** Fieber; **I've got a temperature.** Ich habe Fieber. **take one's temperature** Fieber messen
tennis ['tenɪs] Tennis
tent [tent] Zelt
term [tɜːm] (Fach-)Begriff, Ausdruck
terraced house ['terəst] (BE) Reihenhaus
terrible ['terəbl] schrecklich, furchtbar
test [test] **1.** Test, (Klassen-)Arbeit; **2. test (on)** prüfen, testen (an)
text [tekst] Text
than [ðæn, ðən] als *(nach Komparativ)*
thank [θæŋk] danken; **Thank you.** Danke (schön). Vielen Dank. **Thanks.** (infml.) Danke.
that [ðæt, ðət] **1.** der, die, das (da), jene(r, s) (dort); **that is (i.e.)** das heißt (d.h.); **that's why** deshalb, darum; **2.** der, die, das; die *(Relativpronomen)*; **3.** daß
the [ðə, ðɪ] der, die, das; die
theatre ['θɪətə] Theater
their [ðeə] *(poss. adj.)* ihr(e); **theirs** [ðeəz] *(poss. pron.)* ihre(r, s)
them [ðem, ðəm] sie, ihnen; **themselves** [ðəm'selvz] sich (selbst)
then [ðen] dann; damals, zu jener Zeit; **from then on** von da an
there [ðeə] da, dort; dahin, dorthin; **up there** dort oben; **there is** da ist, es gibt, es ist (vorhanden)
these [ðiːz] diese, die (hier); **these days** heutzutage
they [ðeɪ] sie *(Plural)*
thin [θɪn] dünn
thing [θɪŋ] Ding, Sache
think [θɪŋk] denken; meinen; glauben; **think of 1.** denken an; **2.** halten von; **3.** sich ausdenken
third [θɜːd] Drittel
thirst [θɜːst] Durst; **thirsty** durstig
this [ðɪs] dies; der/die/das (hier), diese(r, s); **this morning/afternoon/evening** heute morgen/nachmittag/abend

those [ðəʊz] die (da), diese (da), jene (dort); **in those years/days** damals; in jenen Jahren/Tagen
though [ðəʊ] obwohl
throat [θrəʊt] Hals, Kehle; **a sore throat** [ˌsɔː ˈθrəʊt] Halsschmerzen
through [θruː] durch, hindurch
throw [θrəʊ] werfen
thumb [θʌm] Daumen
Thursday [ˈθɜːzdɪ, ˈθɜːzdeɪ] Donnerstag
ticket [ˈtɪkɪt] **1.** Fahrkarte; Eintrittskarte; **ticket office** [ˈtɪkɪt‿ˌɒfɪs] Fahrkartenschalter
tidiness [ˈtaɪdɪnəs] Ordentlichkeit; **tidy** [ˈtaɪdɪ] **1.** ordentlich, aufgeräumt; **2. tidy (up)** aufräumen
tiger [ˈtaɪgə] Tiger
till [tɪl] bis *(zeitlich)*
timber [ˈtɪmbə] (Bau-)Holz
time [taɪm] **1.** Uhrzeit; Zeit; **What time is it?** Wie spät ist es? **What time is the film?** Wann fängt der Film an? **at that time** damals, zu jener Zeit; **on time** pünktlich; **timetable** [ˈtaɪmteɪbl] Stundenplan; Fahrplan; **2. time** Mal; -mal
tin [tɪn] (*meist* BE) Dose, Büchse
tip [tɪp] Tip, Hinweis
tired [ˈtaɪəd] müde; **be tired of** genug haben von; **tiredness** [ˈtaɪədnəs] Müdigkeit
title [ˈtaɪtl] Titel
to [tʊ, tə] **1.** (um) zu; **2.** nach, zu, in; **from ... to ...** von ... bis ...; **quarter to nine** Viertel vor neun (8.45/20.45); **Welcome to ...** Willkommen in ...
toast [təʊst] Toast(brot)
today [təˈdeɪ] heute; **today's activities** die heutigen Aktivitäten, die Aktivitäten (von) heute
together [təˈgeðə] zusammen
toilet [ˈtɔɪlət] Toilette; **toilet article** [ˈtɔɪlət‿ˌɑːtɪkl] Toilettenartikel
tolerant (of) [ˈtɒlərənt] tolerant (gegenüber)
tomato [təˈmɑːtəʊ], *pl.* **tomatoes** Tomate
tomorrow [təˈmɒrəʊ] morgen
tonight [təˈnaɪt] heute abend, heute nacht
too [tuː] **1.** *(am Satzende)* auch, ebenfalls; **2. too good** zu gut
tooth [tuːθ], *pl.* **teeth** [tiːθ] Zahn; **toothbrush** [ˈtuːθbrʌʃ] Zahnbürste; **toothpaste** [ˈtuːθpeɪst] Zahnpasta, Zahncreme
top [tɒp] oberes Ende, Kopfende; **top group** oberste/stärkste/beste Gruppe; Leistungskurs
topic [ˈtɒpɪk] Thema
tour (of) [tʊə] Tour, (Rund-)Reise, (Rund-)Fahrt (durch); **tourist** [ˈtʊərɪst] Tourist/in
towards [təˈwɔːdz] auf ... zu, in Richtung auf
towel [ˈtaʊəl] Handtuch
tower [ˈtaʊə] Turm
town [taʊn] Stadt; **in town** in der (Innen-)Stadt; **town hall** [ˌtaʊn ˈhɔːl] Rathaus; **town house** [ˈtaʊn haʊs] (AE) Reihenhaus
toy [tɔɪ] Spielzeug
tradition [trəˈdɪʃn] Tradition, Brauch
traffic [ˈtræfɪk] Verkehr; **traffic jam** [ˈtræfɪk dʒæm] (Verkehrs-)Stau; **traffic lights** *(pl.)* (Verkehrs-)Ampel
trail [treɪl] Pfad; Wanderweg
trailer [ˈtreɪlə] (AE) Wohnwagen
train [treɪn] **1.** Zug; **on the train** im Zug;
2. trainieren, üben; **training** [ˈtreɪnɪŋ] Training
tram [træm] Straßenbahn, Trambahn
trampoline [ˌtræmpəˈliːn] Trampolin
translate [trænsˈleɪt] übersetzen; **translation** [trænsˈleɪʃn] Übersetzung
transport 1. [ˈtrænspɔːt] Transport(mittel); Verkehrsmittel;
2. [trænsˈpɔːt] befördern, transportieren
travel [ˈtrævl] **1.** reisen; **2.** (das) Reisen; **travel-sick** [ˈtrævlsɪk] reisekrank; **traveller** Reisende(r)
treat [triːt] behandeln
tree [triː] Baum
tribe [traɪb] (Volks-)Stamm
trick [trɪk] Trick, Streich, List; **play a trick on sb.** jm. einen Streich spielen
trip [trɪp] Reise, Ausflug
trolley [ˈtrɒlɪ] (BE) (Einkaufs-, Gepäck-)Wagen
trouble [ˈtrʌbl] Schwierigkeit(en); **get in(to) trouble** Ärger bekommen, in Schwierigkeiten geraten; **give sb. trouble** jm. Ärger machen, bereiten; **trouble spot** [ˈtrʌbl spɒt] „Achtung Falle!“
trousers *(pl.)* [ˈtraʊzəz] (lange) Hose
truck [trʌk] (*meist* AE) LKW
true [truː] wahr; **come true** Wirklichkeit werden, wahr werden; **truly** [ˈtruːlɪ] wirklich, wahrhaftig; **truth** [truːθ] Wahrheit
try [traɪ] versuchen, (aus)probieren; **try on** anprobieren *(Kleidung)*
T-shirt [ˈtiːʃɜːt] T-shirt
tube [tjuːb] **1.** Londoner U-Bahn; **2.** Rohr, Röhre
Tuesday [ˈtjuːzdɪ, ˈtjuːzdeɪ] Dienstag
tunnel [ˈtʌnl] Tunnel
turbo-brain [ˈtɜːbəʊbreɪn] „Turbo-Gehirn“
turkey [ˈtɜːkɪ] Truthahn, Pute
turn [tɜːn]**: 1. turn away** [ˌtɜːn‿əˈweɪ] sich abwenden; **turn left/right (into)** nach links/rechts abbiegen (in); **turn round** sich umdrehen; **turn to** sich wenden an, sich zuwenden;
2. turn sth. into sth. etwas in etwas verwandeln; etwas zu etwas machen;
3. turn green/red/... grün/rot/... werden;
4. It's my turn. Ich bin dran. Ich bin an der Reihe.
TV [ˌtiːˈviː]**, television** [ˈtelɪvɪʒn] Fernsehen; Fernsehgerät; **on TV** im Fernsehen; **watch TV** fernsehen
twice [twaɪs] zweimal
twin [twɪn] Zwilling
type (of) [taɪp] Art, Sorte, Typ; **typical (of)** [ˈtɪpɪkl] typisch (für)

U

unanswerable [ʌnˈɑːnsərəbl] nicht zu beantworten, unbeantwortbar
unavoidable [ˌʌnəˈvɔɪdəbl] unvermeidlich, unausweichlich
unbeatable [ʌnˈbiːtəbl] unschlagbar
unbelievable [ˌʌnbɪˈliːvəbl] unglaublich
unbreakable [ʌnˈbreɪkəbl] unzerbrechlich
uncertain [ˌʌnˈsɜːtn] ungewiß, unsicher
uncle [ˈʌŋkl] Onkel
uncomfortable [ʌnˈkʌmftəbl] unbequem, unbehaglich
under [ˈʌndə] unter
underground [ˈʌndəgraʊnd] (BE) U-Bahn
underlined [ˌʌndəˈlaɪnd] unterstrichen
understand [ˌʌndəˈstænd] verstehen, begreifen; **understandable** [ˌʌndəˈstændəbl] verständlich
underwater tunnel [ˌʌndəˈwɔːtə] Unterwassertunnel
undrinkable [ʌnˈdrɪŋkəbl] untrinkbar, ungenießbar
unfair [ˌʌnˈfeə] ungerecht, unfair; **unfairness** Ungerechtigkeit
unforgettable [ˌʌnfəˈgetəbl] unvergeßlich
unfriendliness [ʌnˈfrendlɪnəs] Unfreundlichkeit; **unfriendly** [ʌnˈfrendlɪ] unfreundlich
unhappy [ʌnˈhæpɪ] unglücklich
unhealthy [ʌnˈhelθɪ] ungesund
uniform [ˈjuːnɪfɔːm] Uniform
unimaginable [ˌʌnɪˈmædʒɪnəbl] unvorstellbar
unit [ˈjuːnɪt] Lektion, Einheit
unite [juːˈnaɪt] (sich) vereinigen, (sich) zusammenschließen
universal [ˌjuːnɪˈvɜːsl] universal, allgemein
university [ˌjuːnɪˈvɜːsətɪ] Universität
unknown [ˌʌnˈnəʊn] unbekannt
unlike [ˌʌnˈlaɪk] anders als, im Gegensatz zu
°**unlikely** [ʌnˈlaɪklɪ]**: be unlikely to come true** wahrscheinlich nicht wahr werden, wahrscheinlich nicht in Erfüllung gehen
unmarried [ˌʌnˈmærɪd] unverheiratet
unpack [ʌnˈpæk] auspacken
unpleasant [ʌnˈpleznt] unangenehm
unthinkable [ʌnˈθɪŋkəbl] undenkbar
untidy [ˌʌnˈtaɪdɪ] unordentlich, unaufgeräumt
until [ʌnˈtɪl, ənˈtɪl] bis; **not ... until** nicht vor/erst um; nicht ... bevor
untouched [ˌʌnˈtʌtʃt] unberührt

unusual [ˌʌn'juːʒʊəl] ungewöhnlich, außergewöhnlich
unwelcome [ʌn'welkəm] unwillkommen
up [ʌp] hinauf, herauf; **up there** dort oben; **up to** bis (zu)
upset [ˌʌp'set]**: be upset** aufgeregt, aufgebracht sein; betrübt sein; **upset stomach** Magenverstimmung
upside down [ˌʌpsaɪd 'daʊn] verkehrt herum, auf dem Kopf
upstairs [ˌʌp'steəz] oben (im Haus); nach oben, (die Treppe) hinauf
urgent ['ɜːdʒənt] dringend
us [ʌs] uns
use 1. [juːz] gebrauchen, verwenden; **2.** [juːs] Gebrauch, Verwendung; **useful** ['juːsfəl] nützlich
usual ['juːʒʊəl] üblich, gewöhnlich; **usually** ['juːʒʊəlɪ] gewöhnlich, meistens, normalerweise

V

vacation [BE: və'keɪʃn, AE: veɪ'keɪʃn] (*meist* AE) Ferien, Urlaub
valley ['vælɪ] Tal
van [væn] Lieferwagen; Möbelwagen
variety [və'raɪətɪ] Sorte, Art
vase [vɑːz] Vase
vegetable ['vedʒtəbl] (ein) Gemüse
vegetarian [ˌvedʒɪ'teərɪən], (infml:) **veggie** ['vedʒɪ] Vegetarier/in
vehicle ['viːɪkl] Fahrzeug
very ['verɪ] sehr; **like/love/... very much** sehr mögen/lieben/...
video ['vɪdɪəʊ] Video(film)
Viking ['vaɪkɪŋ] Wikinger/in
villa ['vɪlə] Villa
village ['vɪlɪdʒ] Dorf
vinegar ['vɪnɪgə] Essig
visit ['vɪzɪt] **1.** besuchen; besichtigen; **2. visit (to)** Besuch, Aufenthalt (in); **visitor** ['vɪzɪtə] Besucher/in, Gast
voice [vɔɪs] Stimme
volleyball ['vɒlɪbɔːl] Volleyball

W

wages *(pl.)* ['weɪdʒɪz] Lohn, Löhne
wagon, BE *auch:* **waggon** ['wægn] (Plan-)Wagen
wait (for) [weɪt] warten (auf); **I can't wait.** Ich kann es kaum erwarten.
waiter ['weɪtə] Kellner, Ober; **waitress** ['weɪtrəs] Kellnerin, Serviererin
walk [wɔːk] **1.** (zu Fuß) gehen, laufen; **2.** Spaziergang, Rundgang; **go for a walk** spazierengehen; **take the dog for a walk** mit dem Hund rausgehen; **walker** Spaziergänger/in; **walking shoes** Wanderschuhe; **walkman** Walkman
wall [wɔːl] Wand; Mauer
want [wɒnt] (haben) wollen; **want to do sth.** etwas tun wollen
war [wɔː] Krieg; **civil war** [ˌsɪvl 'wɔː] Bürgerkrieg
wardrobe ['wɔːdrəʊb] Kleiderschrank
warehouse ['weəhaʊs] Lagerhalle
warm [wɔːm] warm
warn [wɔːn] warnen; **warn sb. not to do sth.** jn. ermahnen, etwas nicht zu tun; jn. davor warnen, etwas zu tun
wash [wɒʃ] waschen; **wash the dishes** (das Geschirr) spülen, abwaschen; **washable** waschbar; **washing liquid** ['wɒʃɪŋ ˌlɪkwɪd] (BE) flüssiges Waschmittel; **washing machine** Waschmaschine
watch [wɒtʃ] **1.** (Armband-)Uhr; **watchmaker** Uhrmacher/in; **2.** sich *(etwas)* ansehen; *(jm.)* zuschauen, *(jn.)* beobachten; **watch TV** fernsehen
water ['wɔːtə] Wasser; **water-skiing** ['wɔːtəˌskiːɪŋ] Wasserski(laufen); **waterfall** ['wɔːtəfɔːl] Wasserfall
wave [weɪv] **1.** Welle; **2. wave (at)** (zu)winken
way [weɪ] **1.** Weg; **ask the way** nach dem Weg fragen; **Can you tell me the way to ...?** Können Sie mir sagen, wie ich zu/nach ... komme? **find the way back (to)** zurückfinden (nach, zu); °**lose one's way** sich verirren, sich verlaufen; **I'm going your way.** Ich fahre/gehe in deine/Ihre Richtung. **2.** Art und Weise; **this way** auf diese Art und Weise; **in different ways** auf verschiedene Weise(n); °**the other way round** andersherum, umgekehrt; **way of life** Lebensstil, Lebensweise
we [wiː, wɪ] wir
weak [wiːk] schwach; **weakness** ['wiːknəs] Schwäche
wear [weə] *(Kleidung, Brille)* tragen, anhaben
weather ['weðə] Wetter
Wednesday ['wenzdɪ, 'wenzdeɪ] Mittwoch
week [wiːk] Woche; **weekday** ['wiːkdeɪ] Werktag, Wochentag; **weekend** [ˌwiːk'end] Wochenende; **at the weekend** am Wochenende
welcome ['welkəm] willkommen heißen, begrüßen; **Welcome to ...** Willkommen in ...; **You're welcome.** Bitte (sehr). Nichts zu danken.
well [wel] gesund, wohlauf; gut; **well-known** (wohl)bekannt; **as well as** und auch, ebenso wie; **just as well** genausogut; **Well!** Na so was! Du meine Güte! Wirklich? **Well, ...** Nun, ...
Welsh [welʃ] **1.** walisisch, Walisisch; **2.** Waliser/in
west [west] **1.** Westen; **2.** nach Westen; **3. west (of)** westlich (von); **western** ['westən] West-, westlich
wet [wet] naß; feucht
what [wɒt] was; **What ...?** Was für ein(e) ...? Welche(r, s) ...? **What colour?** Welche Farbe? **What about ...?** Wie wäre es mit ...? Was ist mit ...? **What is ... like?** Wie ist ...? **What time is it?** Wie spät ist es? **What time is the film?** Wann fängt der Film an? **What's your name?** Wie heißt du?/Wie heißen Sie? **whatever** [wɒt'evə] was (auch) immer
wheat [wiːt] Weizen
wheel [wiːl] Rad
when [wen] **1.** wenn, sobald; **2.** als; **3.** wann; **whenever** [wen'evə] wann (auch) immer
where [weə] wo; wohin; **where from** woher; **wherever** [weər'evə] wo (auch) immer, wohin (auch) immer; überall wo
whether ['weðə] ob
which [wɪtʃ] **1.** der, die, das; die *(Relativpronomen)*; **2. which?** welche(r, s)? **which one** welche(r, s); **whichever** [wɪtʃ'evə] welche(r, s) (auch) immer
while *(conj.)* [waɪl] während
whisky ['wɪskɪ] Whisky
white [waɪt] weiß
who [huː] **1.** der, die, das; die *(Relativpronomen);* **2.** wer; wen, wem; **whoever** [huː'evə] wer (auch) immer
whole [həʊl] gesamte(r, s), ganze(r, s)
whose [huːz] **1.** wessen; **2.** deren, dessen *(Relativpronomen)*
why [waɪ] warum, weshalb; **that's why** deshalb, darum; **Why don't you ask ...?** Warum fragst du nicht ...? Frag doch ... .
wide [waɪd] breit
wife [waɪf], *pl.* **wives** [waɪvz] (Ehe-)Frau
wild [waɪld] wild
will [wɪl] werden *(Futur)*
win [wɪn] gewinnen, siegen; erringen, erwerben; **winner** Sieger/in, Gewinner/in
wind [wɪnd] Wind; **windsurfer** ['wɪndsɜːfə] Windsurfer/in; **windsurfing** Windsurfen; **windy** windig
window ['wɪndəʊ] Fenster; **window-shopping** ['wɪndəʊˌʃɒpɪŋ] Schaufensterbummeln
wine [waɪn] Wein
winter ['wɪntə] Winter
wish: Best wishes [ˌbest 'wɪʃɪz] Mit besten Wünschen; Viele Grüße
with [wɪð] mit; bei
without [wɪð'aʊt] ohne
woman ['wʊmən], *pl.* **women** ['wɪmɪn] Frau
wonder ['wʌndə] **1.** sich fragen, gern wissen wollen; **2. natural wonder** [ˌnætʃrəl 'wʌndə] Naturwunder; **wonderful** ['wʌndəfəl] wunderbar
won't [wəʊnt] **(= will not): I won't ...** Ich werde nicht ...
wood [wʊd] **1.** Holz; **wooden** hölzern; **2. wood(s)** [wʊd(z)] Wald

D

word [wɜːd] Wort
work [wɜːk] **1.** Arbeit; **at work** bei der Arbeit, am Arbeitsplatz; **go to work** arbeiten gehen;
2. arbeiten; funktionieren; **work on sb.** (infml.) jn. bearbeiten; **get worked up** sich aufregen; **worker** Arbeiter/in; **worksheet** ['wɜːkʃiːt] Arbeitsblatt
world [wɜːld] Welt; **in the world** auf der (ganzen) Welt; **world-famous** [ˌwɜːld'feɪməs] weltberühmt
worry ['wʌrɪ] sich Sorgen machen; **be worried (about)** sich Sorgen machen (um); beunruhigt sein (wegen)
worse [wɜːs] schlechter, schlimmer; **(the) worst** [wɜːst] (der/die/das) schlechteste; am schlechtesten
worth [wɜːθ] wert; **be worth doing** wert sein, getan zu werden
would [wʊd, wəd] würde(n); **I'd like ...** [aɪd 'laɪk] = **I would like ...** ich möchte (gern) ..., ich hätte ... gern; **What would you like?** Was möchtest du? Was hättest du gern?
write (to; about) [raɪt] schreiben (an; über); **write down** aufschreiben; **writer** Schreiber/in; Schriftsteller/in
wrong [rɒŋ] falsch; **be wrong** unrecht haben, im Unrecht sein; **go wrong** schiefgehen; **My watch is wrong.** Meine Uhr geht falsch. **There's something wrong with ...** Etwas stimmt mit ... nicht. **What's wrong?** Was ist los?

Y

yard [jɑːd] (AE) Garten
year [jɪə] Jahr; **all (the) year** das ganze Jahr über; **in fifty years (from now)** in fünfzig Jahren; **in the past few years** in den vergangenen/letzten Jahren; **in those years** damals, in jenen Jahren; **over the years** im Lauf der Jahre
yellow ['jeləʊ] gelb
yes [jes] ja
yesterday ['jestədɪ, 'jestədeɪ] gestern
... yet? [jet] ... schon ...? **not ... yet** noch nicht
yogurt, yoghurt ['jɒgət] Joghurt
Yorkshire pudding [ˌjɔːkʃə 'pʊdɪŋ] *gebackener Eierteig als Beilage zum Rinderbraten*
you [juː, jʊ, jə] **1.** du; ihr; Sie;
2. dich, dir; euch; Sie, Ihnen;
3. man
young [jʌŋ] jung
your [jɔː, jə] *(poss. adj.)* dein(e); euer/eure; Ihr(e); **yours** [jɔːz] *(poss. pron.)* deine(r, s); eure(r, s); Ihre(r, s); **Yours, ...** Dein(e) ...; Ihr(e) ...; Euer/Eure ... *(am Briefende)*; **Yours faithfully, ...** ['feɪθfəlɪ] Mit freundlichen Grüßen; Hochachtungsvoll; **Yours sincerely, ...** [sɪn'sɪəlɪ] (BE) Mit herzlichen/freundlichen Grüßen; **yourself** [jɔː'self] dich, dir (selbst); sich (selbst); **yourselves** [jɔː'selvz] euch (selbst); sich (selbst)
youth [juːθ] Jugendliche(r); Jugend; **youth club** ['juːθ klʌb] Jugendklub; **youth hostel** ['juːθ hɒstl] Jugendherberge

Z

zero ['zɪərəʊ] Null
zoo [zuː] Zoo, Tierpark

Bildquellen:
Aerofilm, London (S. 6); Anthony Verlag, Starnberg (S. 96 Monument Valley; S. 101 oben links); Archiv für Kunst und Geschichte, Berlin (S. 105 oben; S. 112 unten; S. 113 oben rechts; S. 140 unten; S. 144 links); Bavaria Bildagentur, Gauting (S. 96 Los Angeles, New York; S. 126 oben, unten); British Telecom, London (S.111 Mitte links, unten); J. Allan Cash, London (S. 7 oben links; S. 8 oben; S. 25 unten links; S. 52; S. 66 oben Mitte; S. 96 Flagge, Baseball, White House; S. 98 oben; S. 110 oben rechts; S. 112 Mitte links, Mitte rechts; S. 113 Mitte, unten; S. 129 links); Jim Cook, Basehor, Kansas (S. 120 oben rechts); David Dore, Guildford (S. 12 rechts; S. 37 Mitte links; S. 51 oben; S. 65 unten; S. 104; S. 114 rechts; S. 140 oben); Ted Fink, San Francisco (S. 6 unten rechts; S. 113 oben links, oben Mitte; S. 115; S. 120 oben links); Angelika Fischer; Berlin (S. 64; S. 65 oben); Werner Forman, London (S. 74); Foto-Wort-Steenmans, Korschenbroich (S. 96 Navajo; S. 127; S. 129 rechts); David Graham, London (S. 7 oben rechts; S. 12 links; S. 20; S. 21 Mitte; S. 22; S. 23; S. 24; S. 25 oben, Mitte; S. 26; S. 28; S. 31; S. 34; S. 37 oben, oben rechts, Mitte rechts; S. 39; S. 40; S. 51 Mitte, rechts; S. 66 oben rechts; S. 76; S. 81; S. 83; S. 91; S. 110 unten links; S. 111 oben links, unten rechts); Gruner + Jahr (Stradtmann: S. 116 oben, Mitte; Krüger: S. 116 unten); Michael Heath, London (S. 55); Udo J. Hennig, Neuwied (S. 21 oben); Highlands and Islands Development Board, Inverness (S. 71 unten); David Hissey, Oklahoma (S. 6 unten links; S. 29; S. 98 unten; S. 99; S. 100; S. 101 oben Mitte, oben rechts, unten; S. 102; S. 107); The Hulton Picture Library, London (S. 53 oben); Hyde House, Dorset (S. 8 unten; S. 9); JAT Photo, München (S. 96 Konzert); Gordon Jackson, Wigan (S. 54); Todd James, New York (S. 111 Mitte rechts); Birgit Kleber, Berlin (S. 110 oben links, unten rechts; S. 111 Mitte Mitte); Bernd Lenzner, Berlin (S. 33); Phil Monckton, Hayle, Cornwall (S. 50); Monkmeyer, New York (S. 126 Mitte); Ulf Müller-Moewes, Königswinter (S. 128 unten links, unten rechts); Henrik Pohl, Berlin (S. 84/85); QA Photos, Hythe, Kent (S. 7 Mitte); Private Eye (David Austin), London (S. 88); Lonnie Schlein, New York (S. 114 links); Hellmut Schwarz, Mannheim (S. 131); Syndication International, London (S. 58; S. 71 oben; S. 141; S. 142 rechts); Carl Taylor, Maidencombe (S. 128 oben rechts); Evin Thayer, Houston (S. 111 oben rechts); Ullstein Bilderdienst (S. 125 oben); USIS, Bonn (S. 105 unten; S. 125 Mitte); Verulamium Museum, St Albans (S.142 links); Virginia State Travel Service (S. 144 rechts); Wigan Heritage Service (S. 53 Mitte); Yosemite N.P. Collections (S. 137; S. 138); ZEFA, Düsseldorf (S. 125 unten)

Einband: David Graham, London

Textquellen:
Poem by W.H. Davies from *The complete poems of W.H. Davies* published by Jonathan Cape Ltd.
A prophet in the wilderness based on *John Muir in Yosemite* by Shirley Sargent © Flying Spur Press, California

Liedquellen:
Streets of London, (Text und Musik: Ralph McTell) © Westminster Music Ltd. Für Deutschland, Österreich und die Schweiz: Essex Musikvertrieb GmbH, Köln

List of names

Girls/Women

Alice ['ælɪs]
Amy ['eɪmɪ]
Bina ['bi:nə]
Cristina [krɪs'ti:nə]
Elaine [ɪ'leɪn]
Fiona [fɪ'əʊnə]
Janet ['dʒænɪt]
Jessica ['dʒesɪkə]
Joan [dʒəʊn]
Joanne [dʒəʊ'æn]
Jody ['dʒəʊdɪ]
Laura ['lɔ:rə]
Marcia ['mɑ:sɪə, 'mɑ:ʃə]
Maxine [mæ'ksi:n]
Miranda [mɪ'rændə]
Naomi [neɪ'əʊmɪ]
Nasneen [næz'ni:n]
Natalie ['nætəlɪ]
Ruth [ru:θ]
Susan ['su:zn]
Tahira [tə'hɪərə]
Tracy ['treɪsɪ]
Tricia ['trɪʃə]
Virginia [və'dʒɪnjə]
Zora ['zɔ:rə]

Boys/Men

Andrew ['ændru:]
Arthur ['ɑ:θə]
Carlos ['kɑ:lɒs]
Dino ['di:nəʊ]
Dominic ['dɒmɪnɪk]
Joey ['dʒəʊɪ]
Latif [lʌ'ti:f]
Manuel [ˌmænʊ'el]
Paul [pɔ:l]
Richard ['rɪtʃəd]
Ryan ['raɪən]
Simon ['saɪmən]
Stephen ['sti:vn]
Stuart ['stju:ət]

Family names

Awan [ʌ'wʌn]
Bailey ['beɪlɪ]
Benally [bə'nælɪ]
Bishop ['bɪʃəp]
Buxton ['bʌkstn]
Dillon ['dɪlən]
Duran [dʊ'rɑ:n]
Evans ['evnz]
Flour ['flaʊə]
Foster ['fɒstə]
Hitchcock ['hɪtʃkɒk]
Khan [kɑ:n]
Lawrence ['lɒrəns]
Leech [li:tʃ]
Louis ['lʊɪs]
Malik ['mælɪk]
Mattos ['mætɒs]
McLeod [mə'klaʊd]
Middleton ['mɪdltən]
Parnell [pɑ:'nel]
Ripley ['rɪplɪ]
Ryan ['raɪən]
Shelley ['ʃelɪ]
Thompson ['tɒmpsən]
Vargas ['vɑ:gəs]
Walden ['wɔ:ldən]
Wallace ['wɒlɪs]
Watson ['wɒtsən]
Welch [weltʃ, welʃ]

Place names

Abilene ['æbəli:n]
Aden ['eɪdən]
Alcatraz ['ælkətræz]
Arizona [ˌærɪ'zəʊnə]
Asia ['eɪʃə, 'eɪʒə] *Asien*
Athens ['æθɪnz] *Athen*
Australia [ɒ'streɪljə]
Banff and Buchan [ˌbænf_ən 'bʌkən]
Benjamin Franklin High School [ˌbendʒəmɪn ˌfræŋklɪn 'haɪ sku:l]
Blackpool ['blækpu:l]
Bournemouth ['bɔ:nməθ]
Brazil [brə'zɪl] *Brasilien*
Brighton ['braɪtn]
Broadgate ['brɔ:dgeɪt]
Brussels ['brʌslz] *Brüssel*
Buckingham Palace [ˌbʌkɪŋəm 'pæləs]
Calais ['kæleɪ]
California [ˌkælə'fɔ:nɪə]
Canada ['kænədə]
Chicago [ʃɪ'kɑ:gəʊ]
Colchester ['kəʊltʃɪstə]
Cologne [kə'ləʊn] *Köln*
Costa Rica [ˌkɒstə 'ri:kə]
Covent Garden [ˌkɒvənt 'gɑ:dn]
Cuba ['kju:bə] *Kuba*
Culloden [kə'lɒdn]
Dartmoor ['dɑ:tmɔ:]
Dartmouth ['dɑ:tməθ]
Dead Man's Cove [ˌded mænz 'kəʊv]
Derby ['dɑ:bɪ]
Docklands ['dɒkləndz]
Dodge City [ˌdɒdʒ 'sɪtɪ]
Dover ['dəʊvə]
Dunvegan Castle [dʌnˌvegən 'kɑ:sl]
Duthie Park [ˌdʌθɪ 'pɑ:k]
El Capitan [ˌel kʌpɪ'tæn]
El Salvador [ˌel 'sælvədɔ:]
Eldorado [ˌeldə'rɑ:dəʊ]
Europe ['jʊərəp]
Euston ['ju:stn]
Everglades ['evəgleɪdz]
Exeter ['eksətə]
Exhibition Road [ˌeksɪˌbɪʃn 'rəʊd]
Exmoor ['eksmɔ:]
Florida ['flɒrɪdə]
Glasgow ['glɑ:zgəʊ]
Golden Gate [ˌgəʊldən 'geɪt]
Grand Canyon [ˌgræn 'kænjən]
Great Plains [ˌgreɪt 'pleɪnz]
Great Russell Street [ˌgreɪt 'rʌsl stri:t]
Greece [gri:s] *Griechenland*
Halifax ['hælɪfæks]
Harwich ['hærɪtʃ]
Heathrow [ˌhi:θ'rəʊ]
Hell's Mouth [ˌhelz 'maʊθ] *„Höllenmund"*
Herne Hill [ˌhɜ:n 'hɪl]
Hetch Hetchy [ˌhetʃ 'hetʃɪ]
Iceland ['aɪslənd]
Ireland ['aɪələnd]
Japan [dʒə'pæn]
Kansas ['kænzəs]
Lake District ['leɪk ˌdɪstrɪkt]
Land's End [ˌlænz_'end]
Loch Ness [lɒx 'nes]
Longleat Safari Park [ˌlɒŋli:t sə'fɑ:rɪ ˌpɑ:k]
Los Angeles [lɒs_'ændʒəli:z]
Madame Tussaud's [ˌmædəm tə'sɔ:dz]
Mariposa Grove [ˌmærɪ'pəʊsə 'grəʊv]
Marylebone ['mærələbən]
Massachusetts [ˌmæsə'tʃu:sɪts]
Memphis ['memfɪs]
Mexico ['meksɪkəʊ]
Mission Dolores [ˌmɪʃn də'lɒrəs]
Mission San Francisco de Asis [ˌmɪʃn sæn frən'sɪskəʊ deɪ_ə'sɪ:s]
Munich ['mju:nɪk] *München*
New York [nju: 'jɔ:k]
New Zealand [nju: 'zi:lənd] *Neuseeland*
Newcastle ['nju:kɑ:sl]
Newport ['nju:pɔ:t]
Nicaragua [ˌnɪkə'rægjʊə]
Norwich ['nɒrɪtʃ]
Nottingham ['nɒtɪŋəm]
Pacific Ocean [pə'sɪfɪk_ˌəʊʃn]
Paris ['pærɪs]
Peru [pə'ru:]
Plymouth ['plɪməθ]
Portugal ['pɔ:tʃʊgl]
Rainbow Street ['reɪnbəʊ stri:t]
Reading ['redɪŋ]
Rhine [raɪn] *Rhein*
Rio Grande [ˌri:əʊ 'grænd]
Rome [rəʊm] *Rom*
San Andreas Fault [ˌsæn_ænˌdrɪəs 'fɔ:lt]
San Antonio [ˌsæn_æn'təʊnɪəʊ]
San Francisco [ˌsæn frən'sɪskəʊ]
Santa Fe [ˌsæntə 'feɪ]
Scone [sku:n]
Sheffield ['ʃefi:ld]
Sherwood Forest [ˌʃɜ:wʊd 'fɒrɪst]
Skye [skaɪ]
Slains Castle [ˌsleɪnz 'kɑ:sl]
Southampton [saʊθ'hæmptən]
St Albans [snt_'ɔ:lbənz]
St Ives [snt_'aɪvz]
St Pancras [snt 'pæŋkrəs]
Statue of Liberty [ˌstætʃu:_əv 'lɪbətɪ] *Freiheitsstatue*
Swansea ['swɒnsɪ]
Times Square [ˌtaɪmz 'skweə]
Tennessee [ˌtenə'si:]
Tonganoxie [ˌtɒŋgə'nɒksɪ]
Tottenham Court Road [ˌtɒtnəm ˌkɔ:t 'rəʊd]
Trafalgar Square [trə'fælgə 'skweə]
the United Kingdom [juˌnaɪtɪd 'kɪŋdəm] *das Vereinigte Königreich*
the United States [juˌnaɪtɪd 'steɪts] *die Vereinigten Staaten*
Ver [vɜ:]
Verulamium [ˌverʊ'leɪmɪəm]
Virginia [və'dʒɪnɪə]
Washington ['wɒʃɪŋtən]
Waterloo [ˌwɔ:tə'lu:]
Watling Street ['wɒtlɪŋ stri:t]
Westminster Abbey [ˌwestmɪnstər_'æbɪ]
Wichita ['wɪtʃɪtə]
Wigan ['wɪgən]
Wisconsin [wɪ'skɒnsɪn]
Wyoming [waɪ'əʊmɪŋ]
Yellowstone ['jeləʊstəʊn]
Yosemite [jəʊ'semɪtɪ]

Other names

Abraham Lincoln [ˌeɪbrəhæm 'lɪŋkən]
Alban ['ɔ:lbən]
Al Capone [ˌæl kə'pəʊn]
Amerigo Vespucci [ˌæmə'ri:gəʊ ves'pu:tʃi:]
Angles ['æŋglz] *(die) Angeln*
Armada [ɑ:'mɑ:də]
BBC [ˌbi:bi:'si:] (the British Broadcasting Corporation)
Bonnie Prince Charlie [ˌbɒnɪ prɪns 'tʃɑ:lɪ]
Bram Stoker [ˌbræm 'stəʊkə]
Britoil ['brɪtɔɪl]
Charles Edward Stuart [ˌtʃɑ:lz_edwəd 'stju:ət]
Chieftains ['tʃi:ftənz]
Christopher Columbus [ˌkrɪstəfə kə'lʌmbəs]
Constantine ['kɒnstəntaɪn]
Dracula ['drækjʊlə]
Flora MacDonald [ˌflɔ:rə mək'dɒnəld]
George Washington [ˌdʒɔ:dʒ 'wɒʃɪŋtən]
Grizzly Giant [ˌgrɪzlɪ 'dʒaɪənt]
Guy Fawkes [ˌgaɪ 'fɔ:ks]
Hadrian ['heɪdrɪən]
Halloween [ˌhæləʊ'i:n]
Hogmanay ['hɒgməneɪ]
Jack the Ripper [ˌdʒæk ðə 'rɪpə]
James Cook [ˌdʒeɪmz 'kʊk]
John Evelyn [ˌdʒɒn_'i:vlɪn]
John Muir [ˌdʒɒn 'mjʊə]
Kansa [ˌkænzə]
Kaw [kɔ:]
Marilyn Monroe [ˌmærəlɪn mən'rəʊ]
Mark Twain [ˌmɑ:k 'tweɪn]
Martin Luther King [ˌmɑ:tɪn ˌlu:θə 'kɪŋ]
National Park Service [ˌnæʃnəl 'pɑ:k ˌsɜ:vɪs]
Normans ['nɔ:mənz] *(die) Normannen*
Pilgrims ['pɪlgrɪmz]
Queen Boudicca [ˌkwi:n 'bu:dɪkə]
Queen Elizabeth [ˌkwi:n ɪ'lɪzəbəθ]
Robinson Crusoe [ˌrɒbɪnsn 'kru:səʊ]
Saxons ['sæksnz] *(die) Sachsen*
Secil Japan [ˌsesɪl dʒə'pæn]
Shirley Sargent [ˌʃɜ:lɪ 'sɑ:dʒənt]
Sir Christopher Wren [sə ˌkrɪstəfə 'ren]
Sir Francis Drake [sə ˌfrɑ:nsɪs 'dreɪk]
Sir Walter Raleigh [sə ˌwɔ:ltə 'rɔ:lɪ]
Tessa Wheeler [ˌtesə 'wi:lə]
Theodore Roosevelt [ˌθi:ədɔ: 'rəʊzəvelt]
W.H. Davies [ˌdʌbəlju:_eɪtʃ 'deɪvɪz]
William Howard Taft [ˌwɪljəm ˌhaʊəd 'tæft]
Woodrow Wilson [ˌwʊdrəʊ 'wɪlsən]

Grammatical terms*

abstract noun ['æbstrækt]	*abstraktes Nomen, Abstraktum*
active ['æktɪv]	*Aktiv*
active infinitive [ɪn'fɪnɪtɪv]	*Infinitiv Aktiv*
adjective ['ædʒɪktɪv]	*Adjektiv*
adverb ['ædvɜ:b]	*Adverb*
of frequency ['fri:kwənsɪ]	*der Häufigkeit*
of indefinite time [ɪn'defɪnɪt]	*der unbestimmten Zeit*
of manner ['mænə]	*der Art und Weise*
adverbial [əd'vɜ:bɪəl]	*adverbiale Bestimmung*
of place	*des Ortes*
of time	*der Zeit*
article ['ɑ:tɪkl]	*Artikel*
auxiliary (verb) [ɔ:g'zɪljərɪ]	*Hilfsverb*
clause [klɔ:z]	*Gliedsatz, Teilsatz*
comparative [kəm'pærətɪv]	*Komparativ, erste Steigerungsform*
comparison (of adjectives/ of adverbs) [kəm'pærɪsn]	*Steigerung (der Adjektive/ der Adverbien)*
compound (word) ['kɒmpaʊnd]	*Kompositum, zusammengesetztes Wort*
conditional sentence [kən'dɪʃnəl]	*Bedingungssatz*
conjunction [kən'dʒʌŋkʃn]	*Konjunktion*
consonant ['kɒnsənənt]	*Konsonant, Mitlaut*
contact clause ['kɒntækt]	*Relativsatz ohne Relativpronomen*
defining relative clause [dɪ'faɪnɪŋ]	*bestimmender Relativsatz*
definite article ['defɪnɪt]	*bestimmter Artikel*
direct object ['daɪrekt]	*direktes Objekt, „Sachobjekt“*
direct speech [spi:tʃ]	*direkte Rede*
emphasizing pronoun ['emfəsaɪzɪŋ]	*verstärkendes Pronomen*
future ['fju:tʃə]	*Futur, Zukunft*
[future perfect ['pɜ:fɪkt]	*vollendete Zukunft, Futur II („Futur des Perfekts“)*]
[future progressive [prə'gresɪv]	*Verlaufsform des Futurs*]
going to-future	*Futur mit* going to
if-clause	*Nebensatz mit* if, if-*Satz*
imperative [ɪm'perətɪv]	*Imperativ*
indefinite article [ɪn'defɪnɪt]	*unbestimmter Artikel*
indirect object ['ɪndɪrekt]	*indirektes Objekt, „Personenobjekt“*
infinitive [ɪn'fɪnɪtɪv]	*Infinitiv*
-ing form ['ɪŋ fɔ:m]	-ing-*Form*
intransitive verb [ɪn'trænsətɪv]	*intransitives Verb*
irregular verb [ɪ'regjʊlə]	*unregelmäßiges Verb*
long form ['lɒŋ fɔ:m]	*Langform*
main clause [meɪn]	*Hauptsatz*
main verb	*Vollverb*
modal (auxiliary) [ˌməʊdl‿ɔ:g'zɪljərɪ]	*modales Hilfsverb*
negative imperative [ˌnegətɪv‿ɪm'perətɪv]	*verneinter Imperativ*
negative statement [ˌnegətɪv 'steɪtmənt]	*verneinter Aussagesatz*
noun [naʊn]	*Nomen, Substantiv*
object ['ɒbdʒɪkt]	*Objekt*
object form	*Objektform (eines Personalpronomens)*
of-phrase [freɪz]	of-*Fügung*
participle ['pɑ:tɪsɪpl]	*Partizip*
passive ['pæsɪv]	*Passiv*
passive infinitive [ɪn'fɪnɪtɪv]	*Infinitiv Passiv*
past participle [ˌpɑ:st 'pɑ:tɪsɪpl]	*Partizip Perfekt*
[past perfect [ˌpɑ:st 'pɜ:fɪkt]	*Plusquamperfekt*]
[past perfect progressive [prə'gresɪv]	*Verlaufsform des* past perfect]
past progressive [ˌpɑ:st prə'gresɪv]	*Verlaufsform der Vergangenheit*
personal pronoun [ˌpɜ:sənl 'prəʊnaʊn]	*Personalpronomen*
plural ['plʊərəl]	*Plural*
positive ['pɒzɪtɪv]	*Positiv, Grundform (eines Adjektivs/Adverbs)*
positive statement [ˌpɒzɪtɪv 'steɪtmənt]	*bejahter Aussagesatz*
possessive adjective [pəˌzesɪv‿'ædʒɪktɪv]	*adjektivisch gebrauchtes Possessivpronomen*
possessive form [pə'zesɪv]	*„besitzanzeigende Form“, s-Genitiv*
possessive pronoun [pəˌzesɪv 'prəʊnaʊn]	*nominal gebrauchtes Possessivpronomen*
prefix ['pri:fɪks]	*Vorsilbe, Präfix*
preposition [ˌprepə'zɪʃn]	*Präposition*
present perfect [ˌpreznt 'pɜ:fɪkt]	present perfect *(Perfekt)*
present perfect progressive [prə'gresɪv]	*Verlaufsform des* present perfect
present progressive [ˌpreznt prə'gresɪv]	*Verlaufsform des Präsens*
pronoun ['prəʊnaʊn]	*Pronomen*
prop-word ['prɒpwɜ:d]	*Stützwort*
quantifier ['kwɒntɪfaɪə]	*Mengenbezeichnung*
question ['kwestʃən]	*Frage(satz)*
question tag ['kwestʃən tæg]	*Frageanhängsel*
question word	*Fragewort*
reflexive pronoun [rɪˌfleksɪv 'prəʊnaʊn]	*Reflexivpronomen*
reflexive verb	*reflexives Verb*
regular verb ['regjʊlə]	*regelmäßiges Verb*
relative clause ['relətɪv]	*Relativsatz*
relative pronoun	*Relativpronomen*
reported speech [spi:tʃ]	*indirekte Rede*
reporting verb	*die indirekte Rede einleitendes Verb, „berichtendes Verb“*
sentence ['sentəns]	*Satz, Satzgefüge*
short answer	*Kurzantwort*
short form	*Kurzform*
simple past [ˌsɪmpl 'pɑ:st]	*einfache Form der Vergangenheit*
simple present [ˌsɪmpl 'preznt]	*einfache Form des Präsens*
singular ['sɪŋgjʊlə]	*Singular*
stem [stem]	*(Wort-)Stamm*
sub-clause ['sʌbklɔ:z], subordinate clause [sə'bɔ:dnət]	*Nebensatz*
subject ['sʌbdʒɪkt]	*Subjekt*
suffix ['sʌfɪks]	*Nachsilbe, Suffix*
superlative [su:'pɜ:lətɪv]	*Superlativ, zweite Steigerungsform*
tense [tens]	*Tempus, Zeitform*
transitive verb ['trænsətɪv]	*transitives Verb*
verb [vɜ:b]	*1. Prädikat, Satzaussage; 2. Verb*
vowel ['vaʊəl]	*Vokal, Selbstlaut*
will-future	*Futur mit* will
word class ['wɜ:d klɑ:s]	*Wortart, Wortklasse*
word order ['wɜ:d‿ɔ:də]	*Wortstellung*
word stress ['wɜ:d stres]	*Wortbetonung*
yes/no-question	*Entscheidungsfrage*

* Begriffe in eckigen Klammern ([ ]) stammen aus Abschnitten, die nur in Bayern obligatorisch sind.

Irregular verbs

Infinitive	Simple past	Past participle	
(to) be	was, were	been	sein
(to) beat	beat	beaten	schlagen
(to) become	became	become	werden
(to) begin	began	begun	beginnen
(to) bite	bit	bitten	beißen
(to) break	broke	broken	brechen; zerbrechen
(to) bring	brought	brought	(mit-, her)bringen
(to) build	built	built	bauen
(to) burn	burnt/burned	burnt/burned	(ver)brennen
(to) buy	bought	bought	kaufen
(to) catch	caught	caught	fangen, erwischen
(to) choose [uː]	chose [əʊ]	chosen [əʊ]	(aus)wählen, aussuchen
(to) come	came	come	kommen
(to) cost	cost	cost	kosten
(to) cut	cut	cut	schneiden
(to) do	did	done [ʌ]	tun
(to) draw	drew	drawn	zeichnen; ziehen
(to) dream [iː]	dreamt [e]/ dreamed [iː]	dreamt [e]/ dreamed [iː]	träumen
(to) drink	drank	drunk	trinken
(to) drive [aɪ]	drove	driven [ɪ]	*(ein Auto)* fahren
(to) eat	ate [BE: e, eɪ; AE: eɪ]	eaten	essen
(to) fall	fell	fallen	(hin)fallen
(to) feed	fed	fed	füttern
(to) feel	felt	felt	(sich) fühlen; empfinden
(to) fight	fought	fought	kämpfen; bekämpfen
(to) find	found	found	finden
(to) fly	flew	flown	fliegen
(to) forget	forgot	forgotten	vergessen
(to) get	got	BE: got, AE: gotten	bekommen; (ab)holen, besorgen; (hin)kommen, gelangen; werden
(to) give	gave	given	geben
(to) go	went	gone [ɒ]	gehen; fahren
(to) grow	grew	grown	wachsen; anbauen, anpflanzen
(to) hang	hung	hung	(auf)hängen
(to) have (have got)	had	had	haben
(to) hear [ɪə]	heard [ɜː]	heard [ɜː]	hören
(to) hide	hid	hidden	(sich) verstecken
(to) hit	hit	hit	schlagen, treffen
(to) hold	held	held	(fest)halten
(to) hurt	hurt	hurt	verletzen, weh tun
(to) keep	kept	kept	behalten; aufbewahren
(to) know [əʊ]	knew [juː]	known [əʊ]	wissen; kennen
(to) lead	led	led	führen, leiten
(to) leave	left	left	(zurück)lassen; verlassen; weggehen, abfahren
(to) lie [aɪ]	lay [eɪ]	lain [eɪ]	liegen
(to) lose [uː]	lost [ɒ]	lost [ɒ]	verlieren

Infinitive	Simple past	Past participle	
(to) make	made	made	machen, zubereiten
(to) mean [iː]	meant [e]	meant [e]	bedeuten; meinen
(to) meet	met	met	(sich) treffen, kennenlernen
(to) misunderstand	misunderstood	misunderstood	mißverstehen
(to) pay	paid	paid	(be)zahlen
(to) put	put	put	stellen, legen
(to) quit	quit	quit	aufhören (mit); aufgeben
(to) read [iː]	read [e]	read [e]	lesen, vorlesen
(to) ride	rode	ridden	reiten; (rad)fahren
(to) ring	rang	rung	klingeln, läuten
(to) run	ran	run	laufen, rennen
(to) say [eɪ]	said [e]	said [e]	sagen
(to) see	saw	seen	sehen
(to) sell	sold	sold	verkaufen
(to) send	sent	sent	schicken, senden
(to) shake	shook	shaken	schütteln
(to) shine	shone [BE: ɒ; AE: əʊ]	shone [BE: ɒ; AE: əʊ]	scheinen, leuchten
(to) shoot	shot	shot	schießen, *(Ball)* werfen
(to) shut	shut	shut	schließen
(to) sing	sang	sung	singen
(to) sink	sank	sunk	sinken; versenken
(to) sit	sat	sat	sitzen; sich setzen
(to) sleep	slept	slept	schlafen
(to) speak	spoke	spoken	sprechen
(to) spend	spent	spent	*(Geld)* ausgeben; *(Zeit)* verbringen
(to) stand	stood	stood	stehen
(to) steal	stole	stolen	stehlen
(to) swim	swam	swum	schwimmen
(to) take	took	taken	(mit)nehmen; (weg)bringen
(to) teach	taught	taught	lehren, unterrichten
(to) tell	told	told	erzählen, berichten
(to) think	thought	thought	denken, meinen, glauben
(to) throw	threw	thrown	werfen
(to) understand	understood	understood	verstehen, begreifen
(to) wear	wore	worn	*(Kleidung, Brille)* tragen, anhaben
(to) win	won [ʌ]	won [ʌ]	gewinnen
(to) write	wrote	written	schreiben

Useful classroom phrases

What you can say …

… when you're late or have to leave earlier:

(I'm) Sorry I'm late.	Es tut mir leid, daß ich zu spät komme.
May I leave earlier today, please?	Darf ich heute bitte früher gehen?
I must go to the doctor's/dentist's[1].	Ich muß zum Arzt/Zahnarzt.
I'm not feeling well. I've got a headache/…	Ich fühle mich nicht wohl. Ich habe Kopfschmerzen/…

… when you're talking about homework and tests:

I haven't done my homework.	Ich habe meine Hausaufgaben nicht gemacht.
I couldn't do number 5.	Ich konnte Nummer 5 nicht machen.
I've got something different.	Ich habe etwas anderes.
I've written … . Is that right, too?	Ich habe … geschrieben. Ist das auch richtig?
What's for homework, please?	Was haben wir auf?
Will this be in the next test?	Wird das in der nächsten Arbeit vorkommen?

… when you don't understand something:

What does … mean?	Was bedeutet …?
What's … in English/German?	Was heißt … auf englisch/deutsch?
Can you spell …, please?	Können Sie bitte … buchstabieren?
How do you pronounce …, please?	Wie spricht man … aus, bitte?
Sorry?/Pardon? What did you say?	Wie bitte? Was haben Sie/hast du gesagt?
I don't understand this word/sentence.	Ich verstehe dieses Wort/diesen Satz nicht.
Could you explain/repeat it, please?	Könnten Sie es bitte erklären/wiederholen?
I can't read what's on the board.	Ich kann nicht lesen, was an der Tafel steht.
What page are we on?	Auf welcher Seite sind wir?

… when you're working with cassettes and transparencies[2]:

Can you turn the volume[3] up/down, please?	Können Sie den Ton bitte lauter/leiser stellen?
Can you play … again, please?	Können Sie … bitte noch mal vorspielen?
Can I set the (overhead) projector up?	Kann ich den (Tageslicht-)Projektor aufstellen?
Can I write the answers on the transparency?	Kann ich die Antworten auf die Folie schreiben?

… when you're talking about texts:

I think the story/text is funny/interesting/exciting/boring/stupid/terrible.	Ich finde diese Geschichte/den Text lustig/interessant/spannend/langweilig/blöd/schrecklich.
I found the part where … the best/funniest …	Ich fand den Teil, wo …, am besten/lustigsten …
I didn't quite understand why …	Ich habe nicht ganz verstanden, warum …
I prefer stories about …	Ich habe Geschichten über … lieber.
The ending was very unusual/…	Das Ende war sehr ungewöhnlich/…
There are several reasons why …	Es gibt mehrere Gründe, warum …
In line … on page … the text says …	In Zeile … auf Seite … steht …
The text says …, and I think that means …	Im Text steht …, und ich glaube, das bedeutet …
The text doesn't say it directly, but from lines … to … I got the impression that …	Es steht nicht direkt im Text, aber von Zeile … bis … hatte ich den Eindruck, daß …
When you take the following question into consideration …	Wenn man die folgende Frage berücksichtigt …
I think it's hard to say why/if …	Ich glaube, es ist schwer zu sagen, warum/ob …

[1] ['dentɪst] [2] [træns'pærənsɪ] [3] ['vɒlju:m]